Java EE 6 with GlassFish 3 Application Server

A practical guide to install and configure the GlassFish 3 Application Server and develop Java EE 6 applications to be deployed to this server

David Heffelfinger

BIRMINGHAM - MUMBAI

Java EE 6 with GlassFish 3 Application Server

First published: July 2010

Production Reference: 1160710

Published by Packt Publishing Ltd.
32 Lincoln Road
Olton
Birmingham, B27 6PA, UK.

ISBN 978-1-849510-36-3

`www.packtpub.com`

Cover Image by John M. Quick (`john.m.quick@gmail.com`)

Credits

Author
David Heffelfinger

Reviewers
Allan Bond
Arun Gupta

Development Editors
Dhiraj Chandiramani
Mehul Shetty

Technical Editor
Roger D'souza

Indexer
Hemangini Bari

Editorial Team Leader
Mithun Sehgal

Project Team Leader
Late Basantani

Project Coordinator
Shubhanjan Chatterjee

Proofreader
Cathy Cumberlidge

Graphics
Geetanjali Sawant

Production Coordinator
Melwyn D'sa

Cover Work
Melwyn D'sa

About the Author

David Heffelfinger is the Chief Technology Officer of Ensode Technology, LLC—a software consulting firm based in the greater Washington DC area. He has been architecting, designing, and developing software professionally since 1995, and has been using Java as his primary programming language since 1996. He has worked on many large scale projects for several clients, including the US Department of Homeland Security, Freddie Mac, Fannie Mae, and the US Department of Defense. He has a Masters degree in Software Engineering from Southern Methodist University. David is the Editor-in-Chief of Ensode.net (`http://www.ensode.net`), a website about Java, Linux, and other technology topics.

I would like to thank everyone who helped in making this book a reality. I would like to thank the Development Editors, Mehul Shetty and Dhiraj Chandiramani, and the Project Coordinators, Shubhanjan Chatterjee and Pallabi Chatterjee.

I would also like to thank the Technical Reviewers, Allan Bond and Arun Gupta for their insightful comments and suggestions.

Additionally, I would like to thank the GlassFish team at Oracle (formerly Sun Microsystems) for developing such an outstanding application server.

Finally, I would like to thank my wife and daughter for putting up with the long hours of work that kept me away from the family.

About the Reviewers

Allan Bond is a software developer who has been active in the IT industry for over 10 years. His primary focus is systems development using Java and related technologies. He has worked and consulted for a variety of organizations, ranging from small businesses to Fortune 500 companies and government agencies. Allan holds a Masters degree in Information Systems Management from Brigham Young University.

I would like to thank my wife and children for their patience during the nights (and sometimes weekends) I needed to complete the review of this book.

Arun Gupta is a Java EE and GlassFish evangelist working at Oracle. Arun has over 14 years of experience in the software industry working in the Java (TM) platform and several web-related technologies. In his current role, he works to create and foster the community around Java EE 6 and GlassFish. He has participated in several standard bodies and worked amicably with members from other companies. He has been with the Java EE team since its inception and has contributed to all Java EE releases in different capacity. Arun has extensive worldwide speaking experience on a myriad of topics and loves to engage with the community everywhere.

He is a prolific blogger at `http://blogs.sun.com/arungupta`. This blog has over 1,000 blog entries, with frequent visitors from all over the world, and it reaches up to 25,000 hits per day.

Table of Contents

Preface

This book begins with the installation of Glassfish 3 and deploying Java applications. It also explains how to develop, configure, package, and deploy servlets. Additionally, we will learn the processing of HTML forms. As we move on, we will develop Java Server Pages and get to know about implicit JSP objects. We will also get to know about all the JSTL (JSP Standard Tag Library) tag libraries. This book gives us a better understanding on how to manage data from a database through the Java Database Connectivity (JDBC) API and the Java Persistence API (JPA). We will also learn more about the newly introduced features of JPA 2.0 and develop JSF 2.0 applications to learn how to customize them. We will then set up Glassfish for the Java Messaging (JMS) API and understand the working of message queues and message topics. Later, we will use the Context and Dependency Injection (CDI) API to integrate application layers and study the SOAP-based web service development using the JAX-WS specification. Finally, we will learn more about the RESTful web service development using the JAX-RS specification.

The book covers the various Java EE 6 conventions and annotations that can simplify enterprise Java application development. The latest versions of the Servlet, JSF, JPA, EJB, and JAX-WS specifications are covered, as well as new additions to the specification, such as JAX-RS and CDI.

What this book covers

Chapter 1, Getting Started with GlassFish will discuss how to download and install GlassFish. We will look at several methods of deploying a Java EE application through the GlassFish web console, through the `asadmin` command, and by copying the file to the `autodeploy` directory. We will cover basic GlassFish administration tasks such as setting up domains and setting up database connectivity by adding connection pools and data sources.

Chapter 2, Servlet Development and Deployment will cover how to develop, configure, package, and deploy servlets. We will also cover how to process HTML form information by accessing the HTTP request object. Additionally, forwarding HTTP requests from one servlet to another will be explained, as well as redirecting the HTTP response to a different server. We will discuss how to persist objects in memory across requests by attaching them to the servlet context and the HTTP session. Finally, we will look at all the major new features of Servlet 3.0, including configuring web applications via annotations, pluggability through `web-fragment.xml`, programmatic servlet configuration, and asynchronous processing.

Chapter 3, JavaServer Pages will talk about how to develop and deploy simple JSPs. We will cover how to access implicit objects such as `request`, `session`, and so on, from JSPs. Additionally, we will look at how to set and get the values of JavaBean properties via the `<jsp:useBean>` tag. In addition to that, we will find out how to include a JSP into another JSP at runtime via the `<jsp:include>` tag, and at compilation time via the JSP `include` directive. We will discuss how to write custom JSP tags by extending `javax.servlet.jsp.tagext.SimpleTagSupport` or by writing TAG files. We will also discuss how to access JavaBeans and their properties via the Unified Expression Language. Finally, we will cover the JSP XML syntax that allows us to develop XML-compliant JavaServer Pages.

Chapter 4, JSP Standard Tag Library will cover all JSP Standard Tag Library tags, including the core, formatting, SQL, and XML tags. Additionally, JSTL functions will be explained. Examples illustrating the most common JSTL tags and functions will be provided; additional JSTL tags and functions will be mentioned and described.

Chapter 5, Database Connectivity will talk about how to access data in a database via both the Java Database Connectivity (JDBC) and through the Java Persistence API (JPA). Defining both unidirectional and bidirectional one-to-one, one-to-many, and many-to-many relationships between JPA entities will be covered. Additionally, we will discuss how to use JPA composite primary keys by developing custom primary key classes. We will also discuss how to retrieve entities from a database by using the Java Persistence Query Language (JPQL). We will look at how to build queries programmatically through the JPA 2.0 Criteria API and automating data validation through JPA 2.0's Bean Validation support

Chapter 6, JavaServer Faces will cover how to develop web-based applications using JavaServer Faces—the standard component framework for the Java EE 5 platform. We will talk about how to write a simple application by creating JSPs containing JSF tags and managed beans. We will discuss how to validate user input by using JSF's standard validators and by creating our own custom validators, or by writing validator methods. Additionally, we will look at how to customize standard JSF error messages; both the message text and the message style (font, color, and so on). Finally, we will discuss how to write applications by integrating JSF and the Java Persistence API (JPA).

Chapter 7, Java Messaging Service will talk about how to set up JMS connection factories, JMS message queues, and JMS message topics in GlassFish using the GlassFish web console. We will cover how to send and receive messages to and from a message queue. We will discuss how to send and receive messages to and from a JMS message topic. We will find out how to browse messages in a message queue without removing the messages from the queue. Finally, we will look at how to set up and interact with durable subscriptions to JMS topics.

Chapter 8, Security will talk about how to use GlassFish's default realms to authenticate our web applications. We will cover the file realm, which stores user information in a flat file, and the certificate realm, which requires client-side certificates for user authentication. Additionally, we will discuss how to create additional realms that behave just like the default realms, by using the realm classes included with GlassFish.

Chapter 9, Enterprise JavaBeans will cover how to implement business logic via stateless and stateful session beans. Additionally, we will explain the concept of container-managed transactions and bean-managed transactions. We will look at the life cycles for the different types of Enterprise Java Beans. We will talk about how to have EJB methods invoked periodically by the EJB container, by taking advantage of the EJB timer service. Finally, we will explain how to make sure that EJB methods are only invoked by authorized users.

Chapter 10, Contexts and Dependency Injection will talk about how JSF pages can access CDI named beans as if they were JSF managed beans. We will explain how CDI makes it easy to inject dependencies into our code. We will discuss how we can use qualifiers to determine what specific implementation of dependency to inject into our code. Finally, we will look at all the scopes that a CDI bean can be placed into.

Chapter 11, Web Services with JAX-WS will cover how to develop web services and web service clients via the JAX-WS API. We will discuss how to send attachments to a web service. We will explain how to expose an EJB's methods as web services. Finally, we will look at how to secure web services so that they are not accessible to unauthorized clients.

Chapter 12, RESTful Web Services with Jersey and JAX-RS will discuss how to easily develop RESTful web services using JAX-RS—a new addition to the Java EE specification. We will explain how to automatically convert data between Java and XML by taking advantage of the Java API for XML Binding (JAXB). Finally, we will cover how to pass parameters to our RESTful web services via the `@PathParam` and `@QueryParam` annotations.

What you need for this book

It is required to install the Java Development Kit (JDK) 1.5 or a newer version, and GlassFish v3 or v3.1. Maven 2 is highly recommended, as all of the code examples use it. A Java IDE such as NetBeans, Eclipse, or IntelliJ IDEA is optional.

Who this book is for

If you are a Java developer and wish to become proficient with Java EE 6, then this book is for you. You are expected to have some experience with Java and to have developed and deployed applications in the past, but need no previous knowledge of Java EE or J2EE. You will also learn how to use GlassFish 3 to develop and deploy applications.

Conventions

In this book, you will find a number of styles of text that distinguish between different kinds of information. Here are some examples of these styles, and an explanation of their meaning.

Code words in text are shown as follows: "The `<servlet>` and `<servlet-mapping>` XML tags are used to actually configure our servlet."

A block of code is set as follows:

```
<servlet-mapping>
  <servlet>SimpleServlet</servlet>
  <url-pattern>*.foo</url-pattern>
</servlet-mapping>
```

When we wish to draw your attention to a particular part of a code block, the relevant lines or items are set in bold:

```
<b>Application Menu</b>
<ul>
  <li/> <a href="main.jsp">Main</a>
  <li/> <a href="secondary.jsp">Secondary</a>
</ul>
Current page: <%= pageName %>
```

Any command-line input or output is written as follows:

```
javac -cp /opt/sges-v3/glassfish/lib/javaee.jar
net/ensode/glassfishbook/simpleapp/SimpleServlet.java
```

New terms and **important words** are shown in bold. Words that you see on the screen, in menus or dialog boxes for example, appear in the text like this: "At this point, we should click on the **Deploy an Application** item under the **Deployment** section in the main screen".

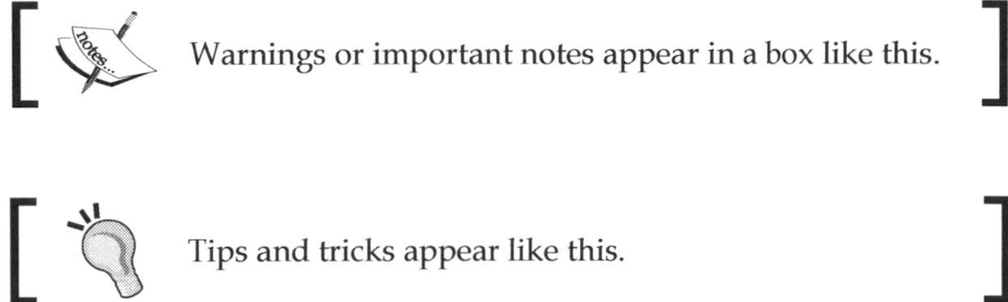

Warnings or important notes appear in a box like this.

Tips and tricks appear like this.

Reader feedback

Feedback from our readers is always welcome. Let us know what you think about this book—what you liked or may have disliked. Reader feedback is important for us to develop titles that you really get the most out of.

To send us general feedback, simply send an e-mail to `feedback@packtpub.com`, and mention the book title via the subject of your message.

If there is a book that you need and would like to see us publish, please send us a note in the **SUGGEST A TITLE** form on `www.packtpub.com` or e-mail `suggest@packtpub.com`.

If there is a topic that you have expertise in and you are interested in either writing or contributing to a book on, see our author guide on `www.packtpub.com/authors`.

Customer support

Now that you are the proud owner of a Packt book, we have a number of things to help you to get the most from your purchase.

Downloading the example code for this book

You can download the example code files for all Packt books you have purchased from your account at `http://www.PacktPub.com`. If you purchased this book elsewhere, you can visit `http://www.PacktPub.com/support` and register to have the files e-mailed directly to you.

Errata

Although we have taken every care to ensure the accuracy of our content, mistakes do happen. If you find a mistake in one of our books—maybe a mistake in the text or the code—we would be grateful if you would report this to us. By doing so, you can save other readers from frustration and help us improve subsequent versions of this book. If you find any errata, please report them by visiting `http://www.packtpub.com/support`, selecting your book, clicking on the **let us know** link, and entering the details of your errata. Once your errata are verified, your submission will be accepted and the errata will be uploaded on our website, or added to any list of existing errata, under the Errata section of that title. Any existing errata can be viewed by selecting your title from `http://www.packtpub.com/support`.

Piracy

Piracy of copyright material on the Internet is an ongoing problem across all media. At Packt, we take the protection of our copyright and licenses very seriously. If you come across any illegal copies of our works, in any form, on the Internet, please provide us with the location address or website name immediately so that we can pursue a remedy.

Please contact us at `copyright@packtpub.com` with a link to the suspected pirated material.

We appreciate your help in protecting our authors, and our ability to bring you valuable content.

Questions

You can contact us at `questions@packtpub.com` if you are having a problem with any aspect of the book, and we will do our best to address it.

1
Getting Started with GlassFish

In this chapter, we will discuss how to get started with GlassFish. Some of the topics discussed in this chapter include:

- Overview of Java EE and GlassFish
- Obtaining GlassFish
- Installing GlassFish
- Verifying the GlassFish installation
- Deploying Java EE applications
- Setting up database connectivity

Overview of Java EE and GlassFish

Java EE (formerly called J2EE) includes a standard set of technologies for server-side Java development. Java EE technologies include Servlets, Java Server Pages (JSPs), Java Server Faces (JSF), Enterprise JavaBeans (EJBs), Java Messaging Service (JMS), Java Persistence API (JPA), Java API for XML Web Services (JAX-WS), and Java API for RESTful Web Services (JAX-RS), among others. Several commercial and open source application servers exist. Java EE application servers allow developers to develop and deploy Java EE-compliant applications; GlassFish being one of them. Other open source Java EE application servers include Red Hat's JBoss, Apache Software Foundation's Geronimo, and ObjectWeb's JOnAS. Commercial application servers include BEA's Weblogic, IBM's Websphere, and Oracle Application Server.

GlassFish is an open source, freely available Java EE application server. GlassFish is licensed under Common Development and Distribution License (CDDL).

> To find out more about GlassFish's license, see `http://www.sun.com/cddl/`.

Like all Java EE-compliant application servers, GlassFish provides the necessary libraries to allow us to develop and deploy Java applications compliant with Java EE specifications.

What's new in Java EE 6

Java EE 6—the latest version of the Java EE specification—includes several improvements and additions to the specification. The following sections list the major improvements to the specification that are of interest to enterprise application developers.

JavaServer Faces (JSF) 2.0

Java EE 6 includes a new version of JSF. JSF 2.0 includes the following notable new features:

- JSF 2.0 adopts Facelets as an official part for the specification. Facelets is a view technology specifically designed for JSF. Some of the advantages of Facelets include the ability to define a view in XHTML, the ability to easily create templates, and the ability to develop JSF components using markup, without having to use any Java code.
- JSF 2.0 also includes the ability to configure JSF applications using annotations, thus greatly reducing, and in many cases eliminating the need to use XML for configuration.

Enterprise JavaBeans (EJB) 3.1

Early versions of the EJB specification gained a reputation of being hard to use.

EJB 3.0 took major strides in greatly simplifying EJB development. EJB 3.1 adds the following additional features to make EJB development even simpler.

- Local interfaces are now optional as an actual bean instance can be injected into local clients.
- Singleton session beans can be used to manage application states.
- Session beans can now be invoked asynchronously, allowing us to use session beans for tasks that were previously reserved for JMS and message-driven beans.

- Improved EJB timer service allows us to schedule jobs declaratively via annotations.
- Enterprise JavaBeans can now be packaged inside a WAR (Web ARchive) file. This feature greatly simplifies EJB packaging, as in the past an EAR (Enterprise ARchive) file was needed to package web functionality and EJB functionality into a single module.

Java Persistence API (JPA) 2.0

JPA was introduced as a standard part of Java EE in version 5 of the specification. JPA was intended to replace Entity Beans as the standard object relational mapping framework for Java EE. JPA adopted ideas from third-party object-relational frameworks such as Hibernate, JDO, and so on, and made them part of the standard.

JPA 2.0 improves over JPA 1.0 in a number of areas:

- Non-entity collections can now be persisted via the `@ElementCollection` and `@CollectionTable` annotations.
- JPA queries can now be built through the new Criteria API, reducing reliance on JPQL.
- The JPA Query Language (JPQL) has improved, adding support for SQL-like CASE expressions, NULLIF and COALESCE operators.

Contexts and Dependency Injection for Java (Web Beans 1.0)

The Context and Dependency Injection is an API that helps simplify enterprise application development. This API helps unify the web and transactional tiers of a Java EE application. For example, Context and Dependency Injection allows Enterprise JavaBeans to be used as JSF Managed Beans.

Java Servlet API 3.0

Servlets are the building blocks of all Java web applications. Early Java web applications relied on the Servlet API directly. Over the years, several APIs have been built on top of the Servlet API, some standard, and some third party. All Java web application frameworks such as JSF, Struts, Wicket, Tapestry, and so on rely on the Servlet API to do its work "behind the scenes". The servlet API itself hadn't changed much over the years. Java EE 6 includes a number of improvements to the Servlet API such as annotations, web fragments, and asynchronous requests.

Java API for RESTful web services (JAX-RS) 1.1

JAX-RS is a Java API for developing RESTful web services. RESTful web services use the Representational State Transfer (REST) architecture.

Java EE 6 adopted JAX-RS as an official part of the Java EE specification.

Java API for XML-based web services (JAX-WS) 2.2

JAX-WS is the Java API for XML web services. JAX-WS is used to develop traditional SOAP-based web services. Java EE 6 includes an updated JAX-WS specification. JAX-WS 2.2 is a maintenance release, with minor improvements and enhancements over JAX-WS 2.0.

Java Architecture for XML Binding (JAXB) 2.2

JAXB is used to map Java classes to XML and back. Java EE 6 includes an updated maintenance release of JAXB.

What's new in GlassFish v3

GlassFish v3 is the first application server to fully support the Java EE 6 specification. This should come as no surprise as GlassFish is the reference implementation of Java EE. Glassfish v3 offers the following notable features:

- GlassFish v3 has a modular architecture based on OSGi. This OSGi-based architecture allows GlassFish to have pluggable modules, allowing us to run GlassFish with only the features we need, and not have to waste resources such as memory and CPU with the features we don't need.
- GlassFish v3 is embeddable; it can be embedded into an existing JVM. It allows us to write Java applications that have GlassFish embedded in them. We would simply need to add the GlassFish libraries to our project to take advantage of this feature.

- GlassFish v3 is extensible; it can be adapted to support additional technologies that are not part of the Java EE specification. Several extensions are available out of the box from the GlassFish update center, for example, support for Grails (a Groovy-based web application framework) and JRuby on Rails. The extensibility features of GlassFish 3 allows application developers and vendors to implement their own GlassFish extensions.

GlassFish advantages

With so many options in Java EE application servers, why choose GlassFish? Besides the obvious advantage of GlassFish being available free of charge, it offers the following benefits:

- **Commercial support available**: Commercial support is available (at a cost). Many software development shops will not use any software for which commercial support is not available, therefore commercial support availability allows GlassFish to be used in environments where it otherwise wouldn't.
- **Java EE reference implementation**: GlassFish is the Java EE reference implementation. This means that other application servers may use GlassFish to make sure their product complies with the specification. GlassFish could theoretically be used to debug other application servers. If an application deployed under another application server is not behaving properly, but it does behave properly when deployed under GlassFish, then more than likely the improper behavior is due to a bug in the other application server.
- **Supports latest versions of the Java EE specification**: As GlassFish is the reference Java EE specification, it tends to implement the latest specifications before any other application server in the market. As a matter of fact, at the time of writing, GlassFish is the only Java EE application server in the market that supports the complete Java EE 6 specification.

Obtaining GlassFish

GlassFish can be downloaded from `https://glassfish.dev.java.net`. On entering this URL into the browser, the following screenshot appears:

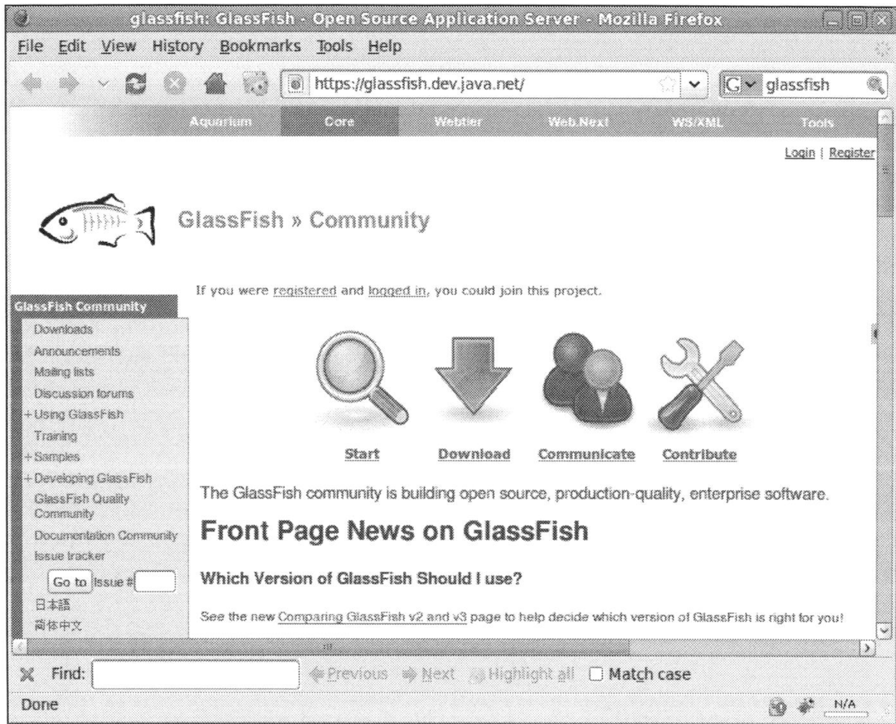

Clicking on the **Download** link takes us to a page containing a table similar to the following screenshot:

GlassFish Server	The GlassFish Server is available in different releases to address different requirements. For more details, check out this **detailed comparison between v2 and v3**.	
GlassFish v2.1	A *final* release based on the **Java EE 5** standard, with clustering, load balancing and high availability and with Update Center. Commercially supported by Sun and recommended for production environments. Community Release | Sun's Supported Release | Quick Start Guide | Documentation | Support | Training	Download
GlassFish v3 Preview	An *unsupported, early access* release implementing the latest version of the **Java EE 6** standard. Includes an extensible core based on OSGi, Admin Console and Update Center. It does not have HA, clustering and other features. Community Release | Java EE 6 SDK Preview | Quick Start Guide | Installation Guide | Documentation	Download
GlassFish v3 Prelude	A *final* release implementing the web layer of the **Java EE 5** standard. It is based on the same core as GF v3 Preview; it does not have production features but it is more stable. Community Release | Sun's Supported Release | Quick Start Guide | Installation Guide | Documentation | Support | Patches	Download

At the time of writing, GlassFish 3 has not been officially released yet, but as can be seen in the previous screenshot, there is a Java EE 6-compliant preview version available. Clicking on the **Download** link for this version takes us to the following page:

How do I get GlassFish v3 Preview?

GlassFish v3 Preview Community Distributions

GlassFish v3 Preview (en)	Size (MB)	GlassFish v3 Web Profile Preview (en)	Size (MB)	Description
Windows Installer File	50	Windows Installer File	30	GUI-based installer for Windows
Self-Extracting Installer File	50	Self-Extracting Installer File	30	GUI-based installer for Solaris, Linux and MacOS X
Zip File	71	Zip File	40	Platform-independent download file

Required JDK Version

Installations require JDK 6. The minimum (and certified) version of the JDK software that is required depends on t operating system:

- For supported operating systems except MacOS, the minimum required version is 1.6.0_13.
- For the MacOS operating system, the minimum required version is 1.6.0_7.

As we can see, the page has download links for all officially supported platforms (Windows, Solaris, Linux, and MacOS X), plus a platform-independent ZIP file.

To download GlassFish, simply click on the link for your platform—the file should start downloading immediately. After the file finishes downloading, we should have a file called something such as `glassfish-v3-preview-unix.sh`, `glassfish-v3-preview-windows.exe`, or `glassfish-v3-preview.zip`. The exact filename will depend on the exact GlassFish version and platform.

Installing GlassFish

We will use the Unix installer to illustrate the installation process. This installer works under Linux, Solaris, and MacOS X. Windows installation is very similar.

Installing GlassFish is an easy process. However, GlassFish assumes some dependencies are present on your system.

NetBeans 6.8 comes bundled with GlassFish 3. By installing the NetBeans Java bundle, GlassFish is automatically installed as well.

GlassFish dependencies

In order to install GlassFish 3, a recent version of the Java Development Kit (JDK) must be installed on your workstation (JDK 1.6 or a newer version required), and the Java executable must be in your system path. The latest JDK can be downloaded from `http://java.sun.com/`. Please refer to the JDK installation instructions for your particular platform at `http://java.sun.com/javase/6/webnotes/install/index.html`.

Performing the installation

Once the JDK has been installed, installation can begin by simply executing the downloaded file (permissions may have to be modified to make it executable):

```
../glassfish-v3-preview-unix.sh
```

The actual filename will depend on the version of GlassFish downloaded. The following steps need to be performed in order to successfully install GlassFish:

1. After running the previous command, the GlassFish installer will start initializing:

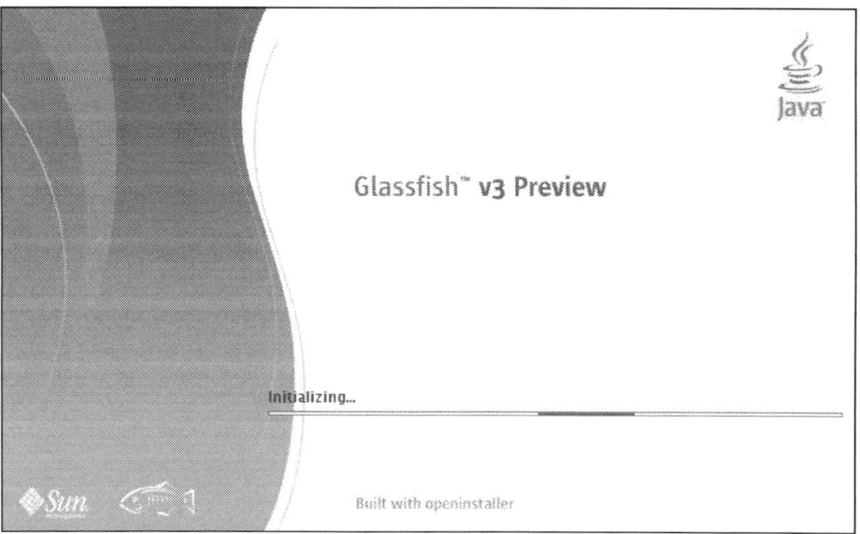

2. After a few seconds, we should see the installer's welcome screen:

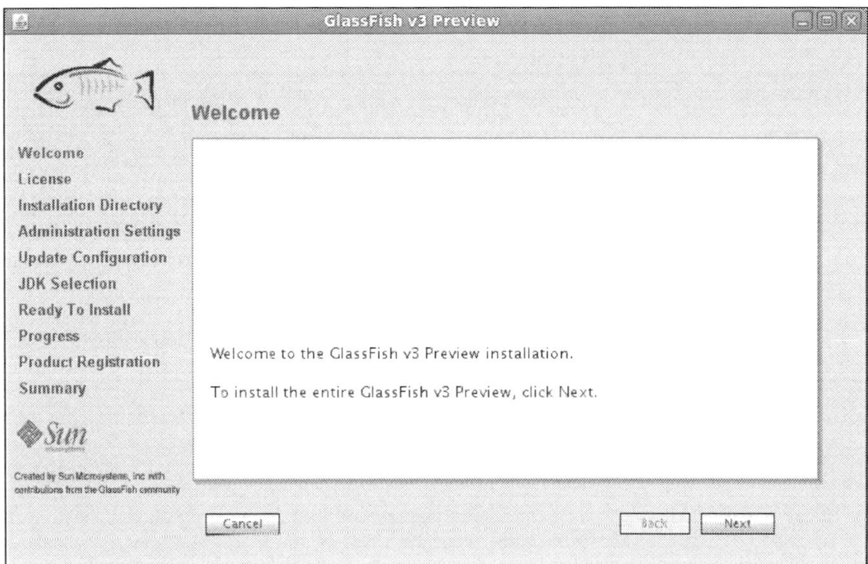

3. After clicking **Next**, we are prompted to accept the license terms:

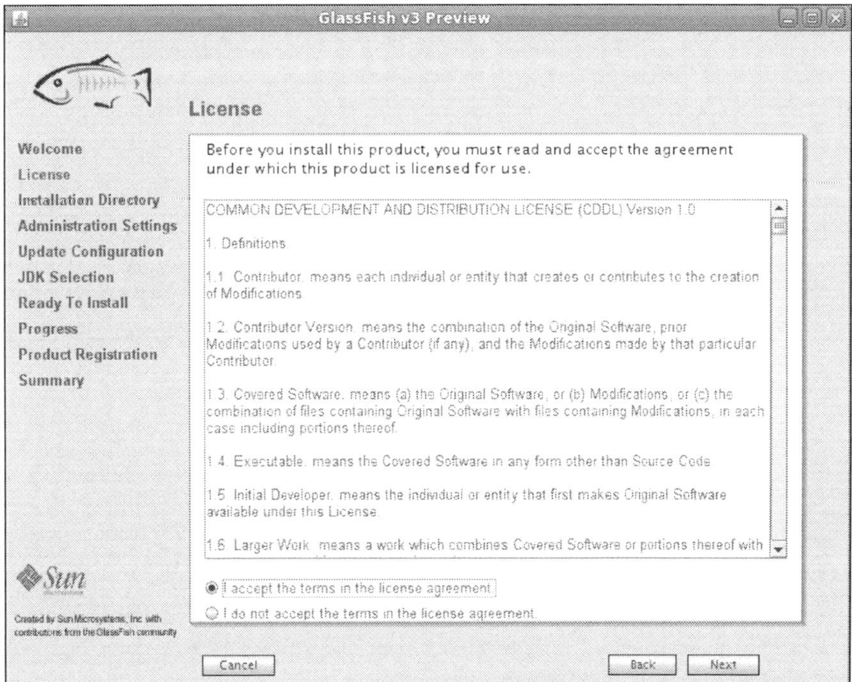

4. The next screen in the installer prompts us for an installation directory. The installation directory defaults to a directory called `glassfishv3` under our home directory. It is a reasonable default, but we are free to change it.

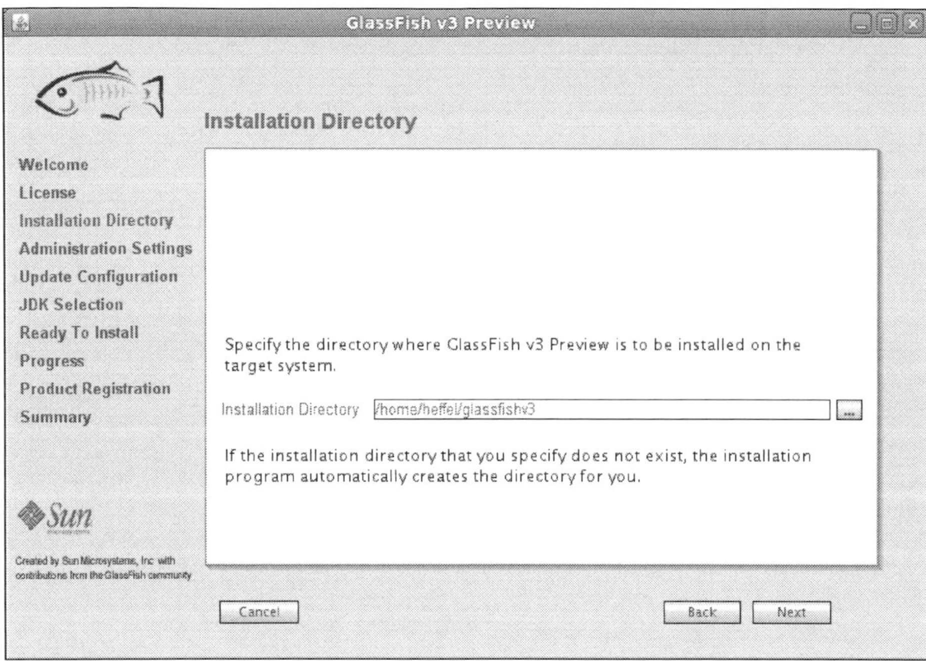

5. The next page in the installer allows us to customize Glassfish's administration and HTTP ports. Additionally, it allows us to provide a username and password for the administrative user. By default, no username and password combination is required to log into the admin console. This default behavior is appropriate for development boxes. We can override this behavior by choosing to provide a username and password in this step in the installation wizard.

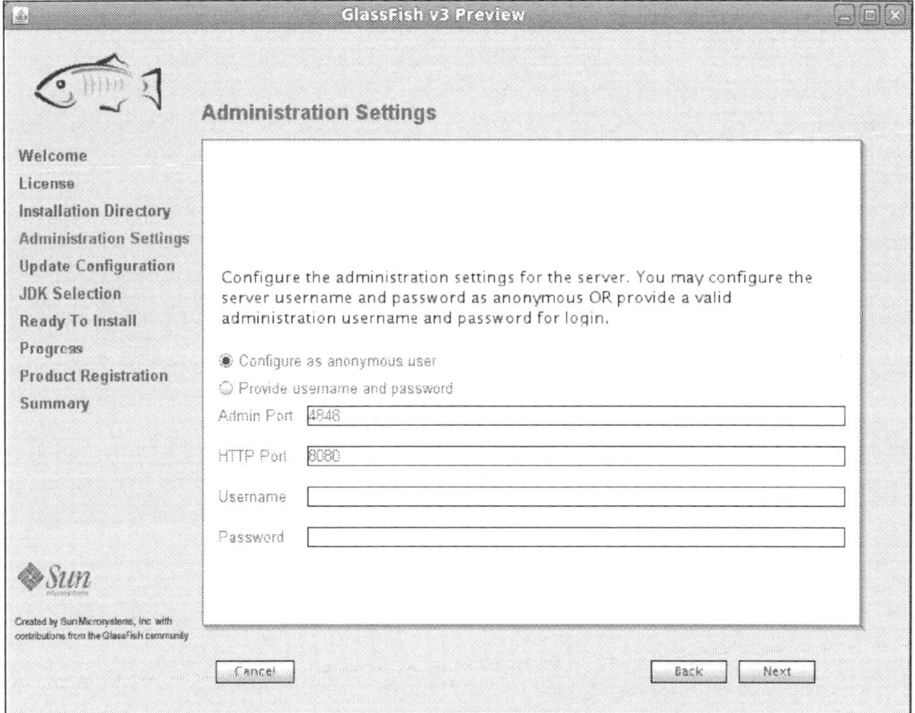

6. At this point in the installation, we need to indicate if we would like to install the GlassFish update tool. The update tool allows us to easily install additional GlassFish modules. Therefore, unless disk space is a concern, it is recommended to install it. If we access the internet through a proxy server, we can enter its host name or IP address and port at this point in the installation.

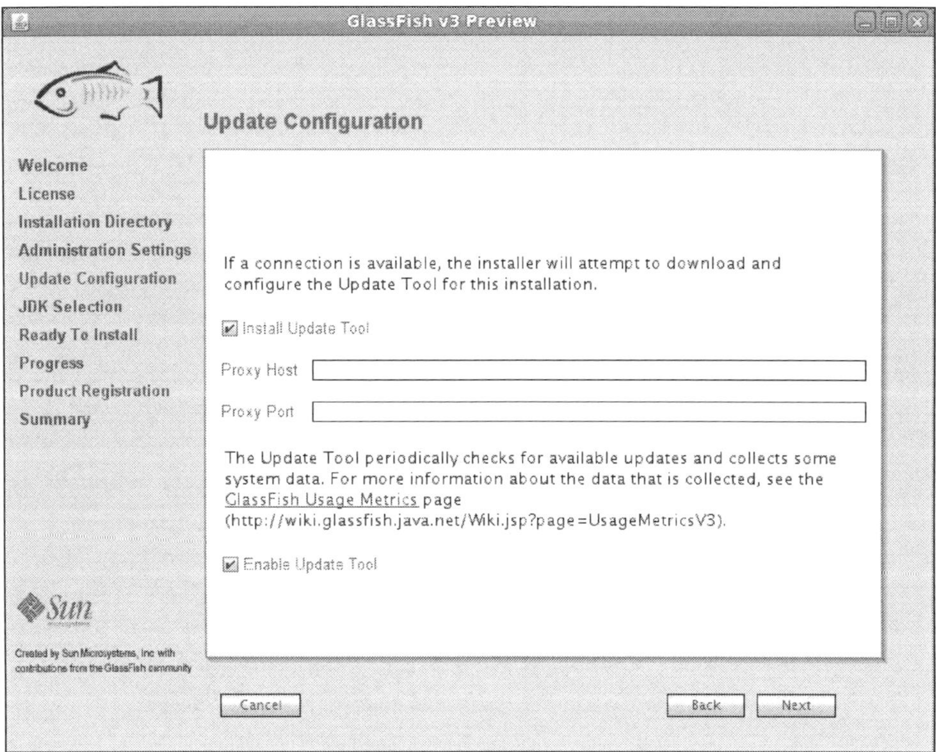

7. Now, we are prompted to either select an automatically detected Java SDK or type in the location of the SDK. By default, the Java SDK matching the value of the JAVA_HOME environment variable is selected.

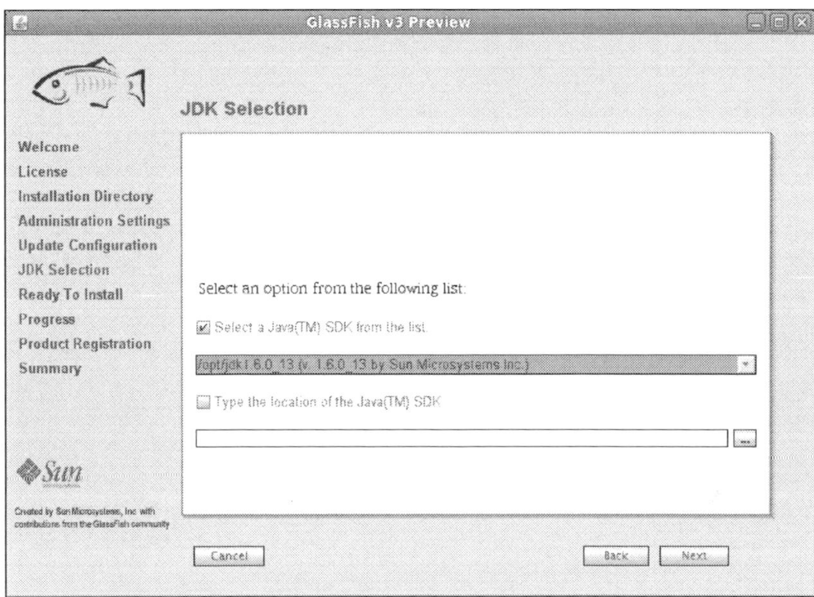

8. At this point, the installer summarizes the steps it is about to take. Clicking on the **Install** button causes the installation to begin:

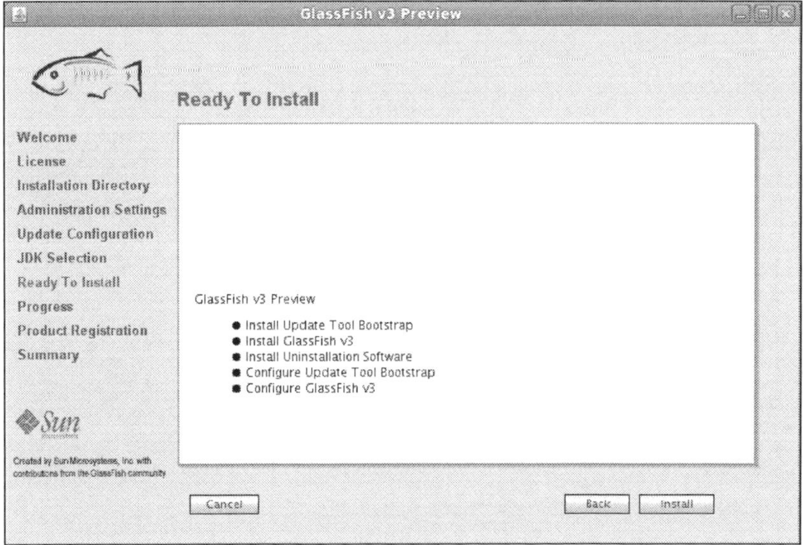

9. The progress of the installation is shown in the next screenshot:

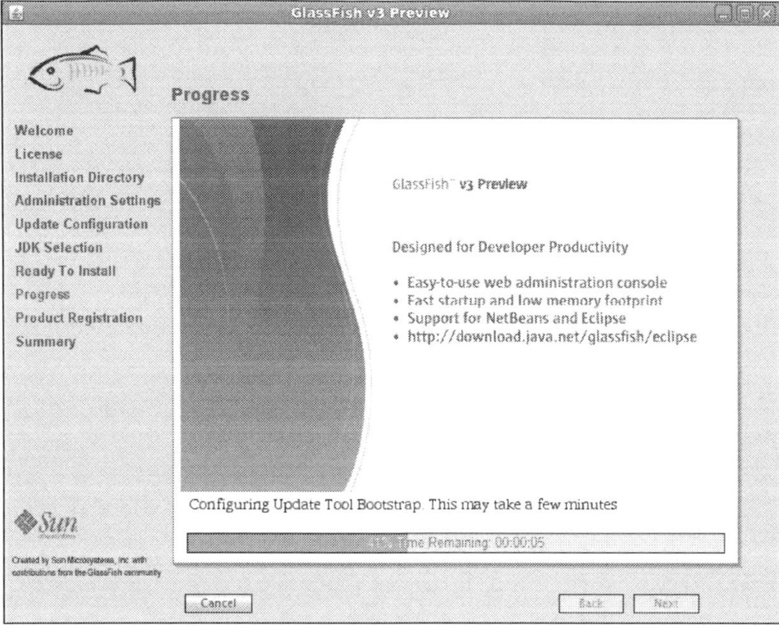

10. After installation finishes, we are asked to register our copy of GlassFish. At this point, we can link our GlassFish installation to an existing Sun Online Account, create a new Sun Online Account or skip installation:

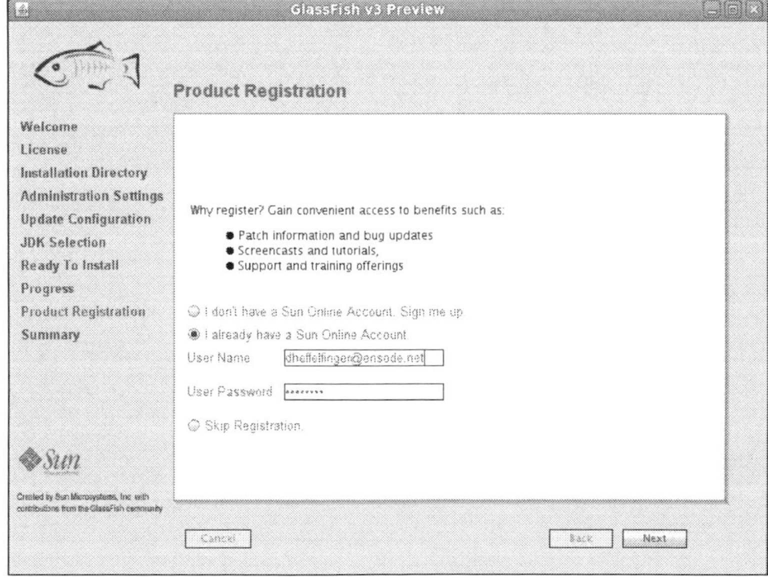

11. The next page in the installer shows an installation summary. Now, we simply need to click on the **Exit** button to exit the installer:

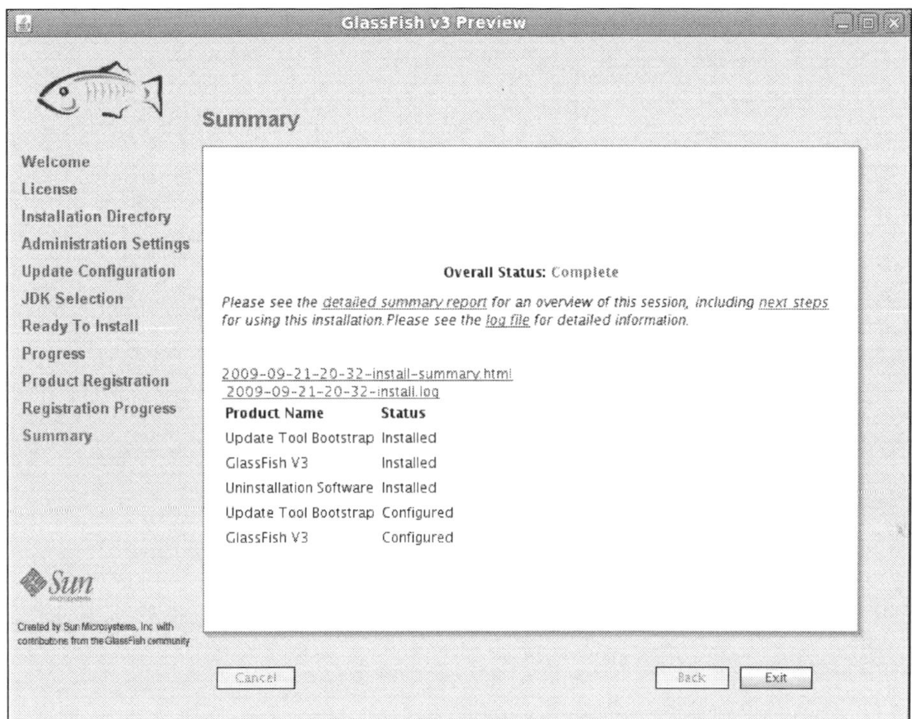

Verifying the installation

To start GlassFish, change the directory to `[glassfish installation directory]/glassfishv3/bin` and execute the following command:

```
./asadmin start-domain domain1
```

This command and most commands shown in this chapter assume a Unix or Unix-like operating system. For windows systems, the initial "./" is not necessary.

A few seconds after executing the previous command, we should see a message similar to the following at the bottom of the terminal:

```
Name of the domain started: [domain1] and
its location: [/home/heffel/glassfishv3/glassfish/domains/domain1].
Admin port for the domain: [4848].
```

We can then open a browser window and type the following URL in the browser's location text field: `http://localhost:8080`.

If everything went well, we should see a page similar to the following screenshot:

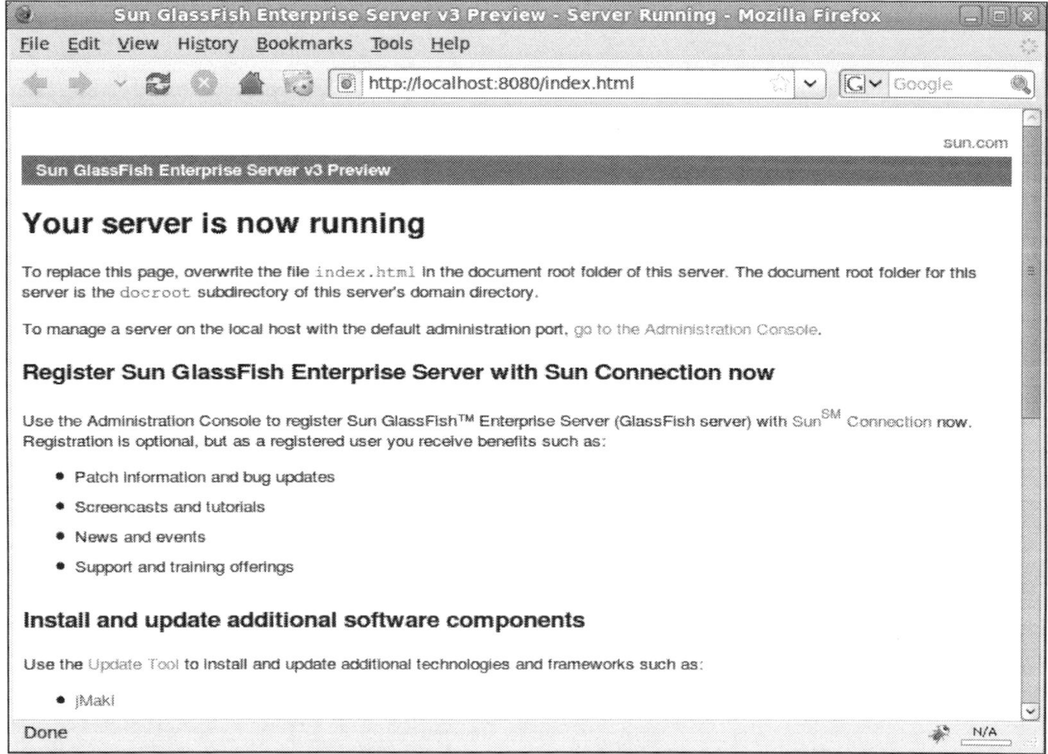

Getting Help

If any of the previous steps fail or for help with GlassFish in general, a great resource is the GlassFish forum, which can be found at `http://forums.java.net/jive/forum.jspa?forumID=56`.

Deploying our first Java EE application

To further test that our GlassFish installation is running properly, we will deploy a WAR (Web ARchive) file and make sure it deploys and executes properly. Before moving on, please download the file `simpleapp.war` from this book's website.

Deploying an application through the Web Console

To deploy simpleapp.`war`, open a browser and navigate to the following URL: `http://localhost:4848`. You should be greeted with a login screen that looks like the following screenshot:

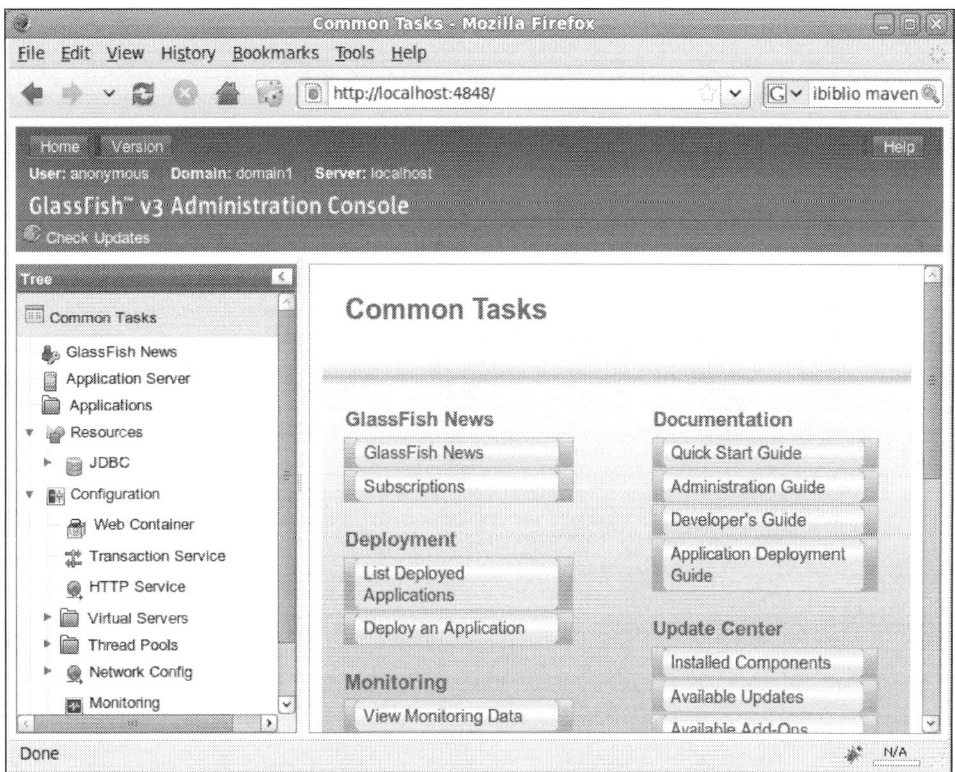

If GlassFish was configured as anonymous user, then we will see the previous page directly. Otherwise, we will see it after entering the administrator credentials entered during installation.

At this point, we should click on the **Deploy an Application** item under the **Deployment** section in the main screen.

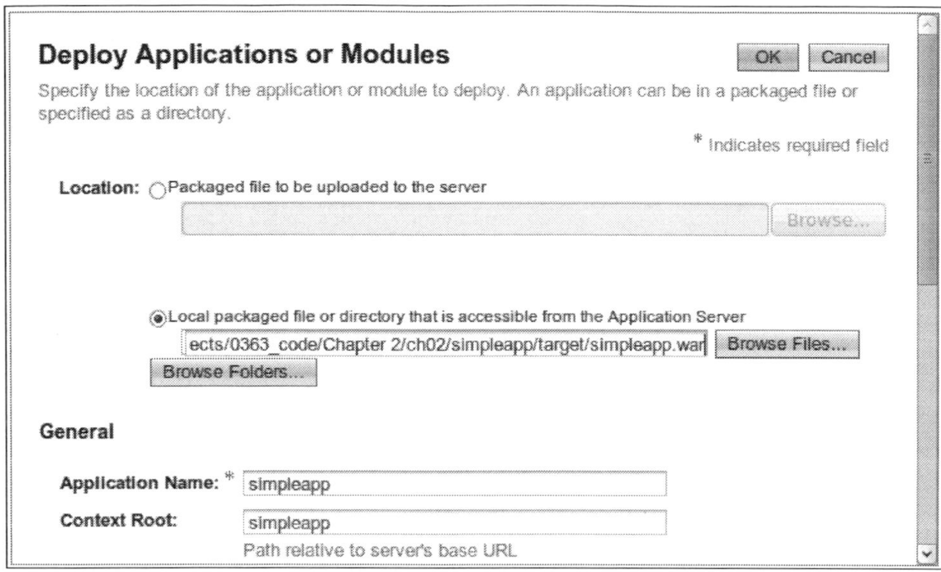

We should select the **Local packaged file or directory that is accessible from the Application Server** radio button, and either type the path to our WAR file or select it by clicking on the **Browse Files...** button.

After we have selected our WAR file, we simply click on the **OK** button to deploy it.

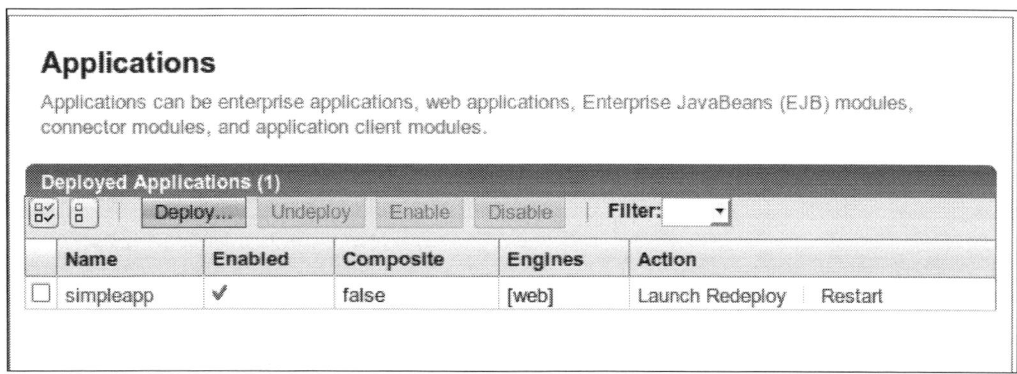

As can be seen in the previous screenshot, our `simpleapp` application has now been deployed.

To execute the `simpleapp` application, type the following URL in the browser's location text field: `http://localhost:8080/simpleapp/simpleservlet`. The resulting page should look as follows:

That's it! We have successfully deployed our first Java EE application.

Undeploying an application through the Web Console

In the next section, we explain how to deploy a web application through the command line. For the instructions in the next section to work, we need to undeploy `simpleapp.war`.

To undeploy the application we deployed in the previous section, log into the GlassFish Admin Console by typing the following URL in the browser's location text field: `http://localhost:4848`.

Then, either click on the **Applications** menu item near the top left of the page or click on the **List Deployed Applications** item on the administration console's home page.

Either way should take us to the application management page:

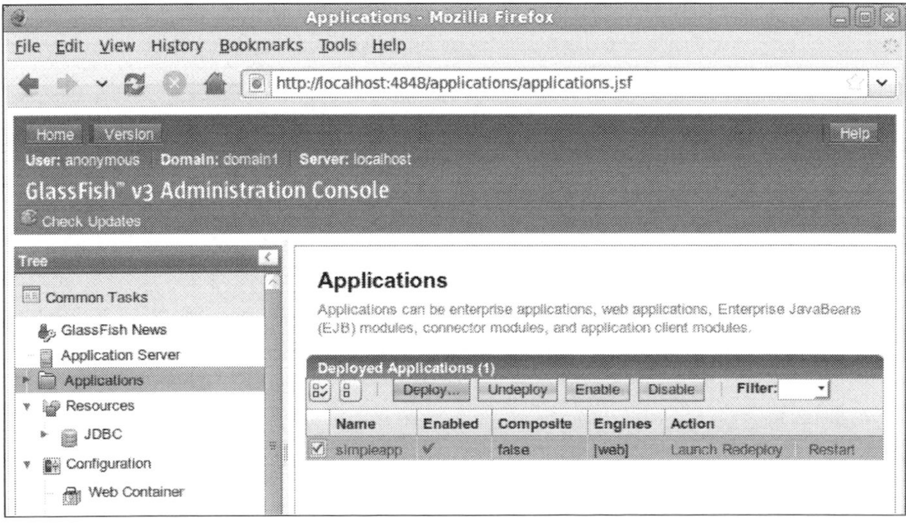

The application can be undeployed simply by selecting it from the list of deployed applications and clicking on the **Undeploy** button. After undeploying the application, the application management page looks as follows:

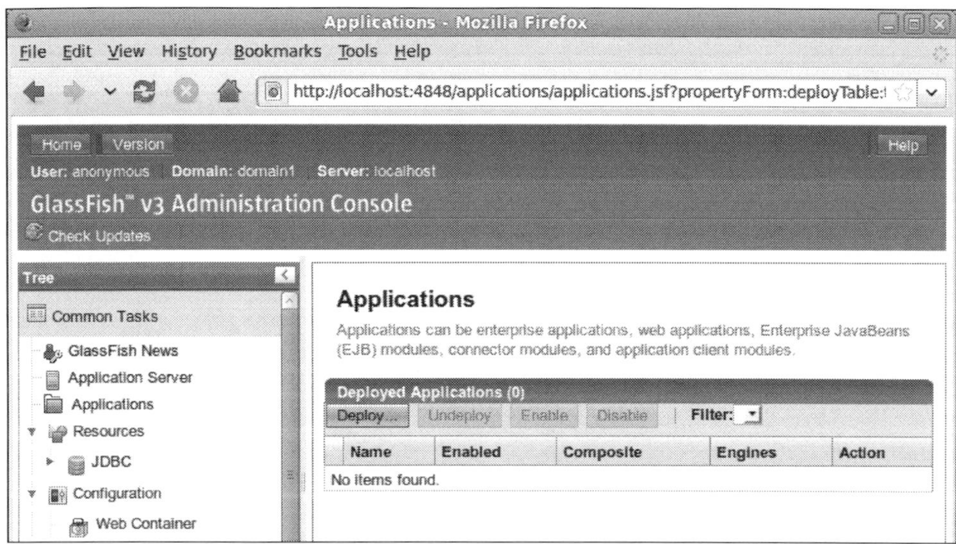

Deploying an application through the command line

There are two ways by which an application can be deployed through the command line: it can be done by copying the artifact we want to deploy to an `autodeploy` directory or by using GlassFish's `asadmin` command line utility.

The autodeploy directory

Now that we have undeployed the `simpleapp.war` file, we are ready to deploy it using the command line. To deploy the application in this manner, simply copy `simpleapp.war` to `[glassfish installation directory]/glassfishv3/glassfish/domains/domain1/autodeploy`. The application will be automatically deployed just by copying it to this directory.

We can verify that the application has been successfully deployed by looking at the server log. The server log can be found at `[glassfish installation directory]/glassfishv3/glassfish/domains/domain1/logs/server.log`. The last few lines of this file should look as follows:

```
[#|2009-09-23T19:26:39.463-0400|INFO|glassfish|javax.enterprise.
system.tools.deployment.org.glassfish.deployment.common|_ThreadID=20;_
ThreadName=Thread-1;|[AutoDeploy] Selecting file /home/heffel/
glassfishv3/glassfish/domains/domain1/autodeploy/simpleapp.war for
autodeployment.|#]
```

```
[#|2009-09-23T19:26:39.635-0400|INFO|glassfish|null|_ThreadID=20;_
ThreadName=Thread-1;|Deployment expansion took 64|#]


[#|2009-09-23T19:26:41.132-0400|INFO|glassfish|null|_ThreadID=20;_
ThreadName=Thread-1;|DOL Loading time938|#]


[#|2009-09-23T19:26:41.190-0400|INFO|glassfish|org.apache.catalina.
loader.WebappLoader|_ThreadID=20;_ThreadName=Thread-1;|Unknown loader
org.glassfish.internal.api.DelegatingClassLoader@55d866c5 class org.
glassfish.internal.api.DelegatingClassLoader|#]


[#|2009-09-23T19:26:41.610-0400|INFO|glassfish|javax.enterprise.system.
container.web.com.sun.enterprise.web|_ThreadID=20;_ThreadName=Thread-
1;|Loading application simpleapp at /simpleapp|#]


[#|2009-09-23T19:26:41.808-0400|INFO|glassfish|javax.enterprise.system.
tools.admin.org.glassfish.server|_ThreadID=20; ThreadName=Thread-
1;|Deployment of simpleapp done is 2,239 ms|#]


[#|2009-09-23T19:26:41.810-0400|INFO|glassfish|javax.enterprise.
system.tools.deployment.org.glassfish.deployment.common|_ThreadID=20;_
ThreadName=Thread-1;|[AutoDeploy] Successfully autodeployed : /home/
heffel/glassfishv3/glassfish/domains/domain1/autodeploy/simpleapp.war.|#]
```

We can of course also verify the deployment by navigating to the URL for the application, which will be the same one we used when deploying through the web console: `http://localhost:8080/simpleapp/simpleservlet`. The application should execute properly.

An application deployed this way can be undeployed by simply deleting the artifact (in our case, the WAR file) from the `autodeploy` directory. After deleting the file, we should see a message similar to the following in the server log:

```
[#|2009-09-23T19:29:09.835-0400|INFO|glassfish|javax.enterprise.
system.tools.deployment.org.glassfish.deployment.common|_ThreadID=20;_
ThreadName=Thread-1;|Autoundeploying application :simpleapp|#]


[#|2009-09-23T19:29:09.909-0400|INFO|glassfish|javax.enterprise.
system.tools.deployment.org.glassfish.deployment.common|_ThreadID=20;_
ThreadName=Thread-1;|[AutoDeploy] Successfully autoundeployed : /home/
heffel/glassfishv3/glassfish/domains/domain1/autodeploy/simpleapp.war.|#]
```

The asadmin command line utility

An alternate way of deploying an application through the command line is by using the following command:

```
asadmin deploy [path to file]/simpleapp.war
```

The server log file should show a message similar to the following:

```
[#|2009-09-23T19:35:04.012-0400|INFO|glassfish|null|_ThreadID=16;_
ThreadName=Thread-1;|Deployment expansion took 76|#]


[#|2009-09-23T19:35:04.986-0400|INFO|glassfish|null|_ThreadID=16;_
ThreadName=Thread-1;|DOL Loading time707|#]


[#|2009-09-23T19:35:05.025-0400|INFO|glassfish|org.apache.catalina.
loader.WebappLoader|_ThreadID=16;_ThreadName=Thread-1;|Unknown loader
org.glassfish.internal.api.DelegatingClassLoader@55d866c5 class org.
glassfish.internal.api.DelegatingClassLoader|#]


[#|2009-09-23T19:35:05.238-0400|INFO|glassfish|javax.enterprise.system.
container.web.com.sun.enterprise.web|_ThreadID=16;_ThreadName=Thread-
1;|Loading application simpleapp at /simpleapp|#]


[#|2009-09-23T19:35:05.321-0400|INFO|glassfish|javax.enterprise.system.
tools.admin.org.glassfish.server|_ThreadID=16;_ThreadName=Thread-
1;|Deployment of simpleapp done is 1,576 ms|#]
```

The `asadmin` executable can be used to undeploy an application as well by issuing the following command:

```
asadmin undeploy simpleapp
```

The following message should be shown at the bottom of the terminal window:

```
Command undeploy executed successfully.
```

Please note that the file extension is not used to undeploy the application. The argument to `asadmin undeploy` should be the context root for the application (what is typed right after `http://localhost:4848` to access the application through the browser), which defaults to the WAR filename.

In the next chapter, we will see how to change the default context root for an application.

GlassFish domains

The alert reader might have noticed that the `autodeploy` directory is under a `domains/domain1` subdirectory. GlassFish has a concept of **domains**. Domains allow a collection of related applications to be deployed together. Several domains can be started concurrently. They behave like individual GlassFish instances. A default domain called `domain1` is created when installing GlassFish.

Creating domains

Additional domains can be created from the command line by issuing the following command:

```
asadmin create-domain domainname
```

This command takes several parameters to specify ports where the domain will listen to for several services (HTTP, Admin, JMS, IIOP, secure HTTP, and so on). Type the following command in the command line to see these parameters:

```
asadmin create-domain --help
```

If we want several domains to execute concurrently on the same server, these ports must be chosen carefully, as specifying the same ports for different services (or even the same service across domains) will prevent one of the domains from working properly.

The default ports for the default `domain1` domain are listed in the following table:

Service	Port
Admin	4848
HTTP	8080
Java Messaging System (JMS)	7676
Internet Inter-ORB Protocol (IIOP)	3700
Secure HTTP (HTTPS)	8181
Secure IIOP	3820
Mutual Authorization IIOP	3920
Java Management Extensions (JMX) Administration	8686

Please note that when creating a domain, the only port that needs to be specified is the admin port. If the other ports are not specified, the default ports listed in the preceding table will be used. Care must be taken when creating a domain because as explained previously, two domains cannot run concurrently in the same server if any of their services listen for connections on the same port.

An alternate method of creating a domain without having to specify ports for every service is to issue the following command:

```
asadmin createdomain --portbase [port number] domainname
```

The value of the `--portbase` parameter dictates the base port for the domain. Ports for different services will be offsets of the given port number. The following table lists the ports assigned to all the different services:

Service	Port
Admin	`portbase` + 48
HTTP	`portbase` + 80
Java Messaging System (JMS)	`portbase` + 76
Internet Inter-ORB Protocol (IIOP)	`portbase` + 37
Secure HTTP (HTTPS)	`portbase` + 81
Secure IIOP	`portbase` + 38
Mutual Authorization IIOP	`portbase` + 39
Java Management Extensions (JMX) Administration	`portbase` + 86

Of course, care must be taken when choosing the value for `portbase`, making sure that none of the assigned ports collide with any other domain.

As a rule of thumb, creating domains using a `portbase` number greater than 8000 and divisible by 1000 should create domains that don't conflict with each other. For example, it should be safe to create a domain using a `portbase` of 9000, another one using a `portbase` of 10000, so on and so forth.

Deleting domains

Deleting a domain is very simple; it can be accomplished by issuing the following command in the command line:

```
asadmin delete-domain domainname
```

We should see a message like the following on the terminal window:

```
Command delete-domain executed successfully.
```

Please use the previous command with care because once a domain is deleted, it cannot be easily recreated (all deployed applications will be gone, as well as any connection pools, datasources, and so on).

Stopping a domain

A domain that is executing can be stopped by issuing the following command:

```
asadmin stop-domain domainname
```

This command will stop the domain named `domainname`.

If only one domain is running, the `domainname` argument is optional.

This book assumes that the reader is working with the default domain called `domain1` and the default ports. If this is not the case, instructions given need to be modified to match the appropriate domain and port.

Setting up database connectivity

Any non-trivial Java EE application will connect to a Relational Database Management Server (RDBMS). Supported RDBMS systems include JavaDB, Oracle, Derby, Sybase, DB2, Pointbase, MySQL, PostgreSQL, Informix, Cloudscape, and SQL Server. In this section, we will demonstrate how to set up GlassFish to communicate with a MySQL database. The procedure is similar for other RDBMS systems.

GlassFish comes bundled with an RDBMS called JavaDB. This RDBMS is based on Apache Derby. To limit the downloads and configuration needed to follow this book's code, all examples needing an RDBMS will use the embedded JavaDB RDBMS. The instructions in this section are for illustrating how to connect GlassFish to a third-party RDBMS.

Setting up connection pools

The first step to follow when setting up a connection pool is to copy the JAR file containing the JDBC driver for our RDBMS in the `lib` directory of the domain (consult your RDBMS documentation for information on where to obtain this JAR file). If the GlassFish domain where we want to add the connection pool is running when copying the JDBC driver, it must be restarted for the change to take effect. The domain can be restarted by executing `asadmin restart-domain`.

Once the JDBC driver has been copied to the appropriate location and the application server has been restarted, log into the admin console by pointing the browser to `http://localhost:4848`.

Then, click on **Resources** | **JDBC** | **Connection Pools**. The browser should now look something like this:

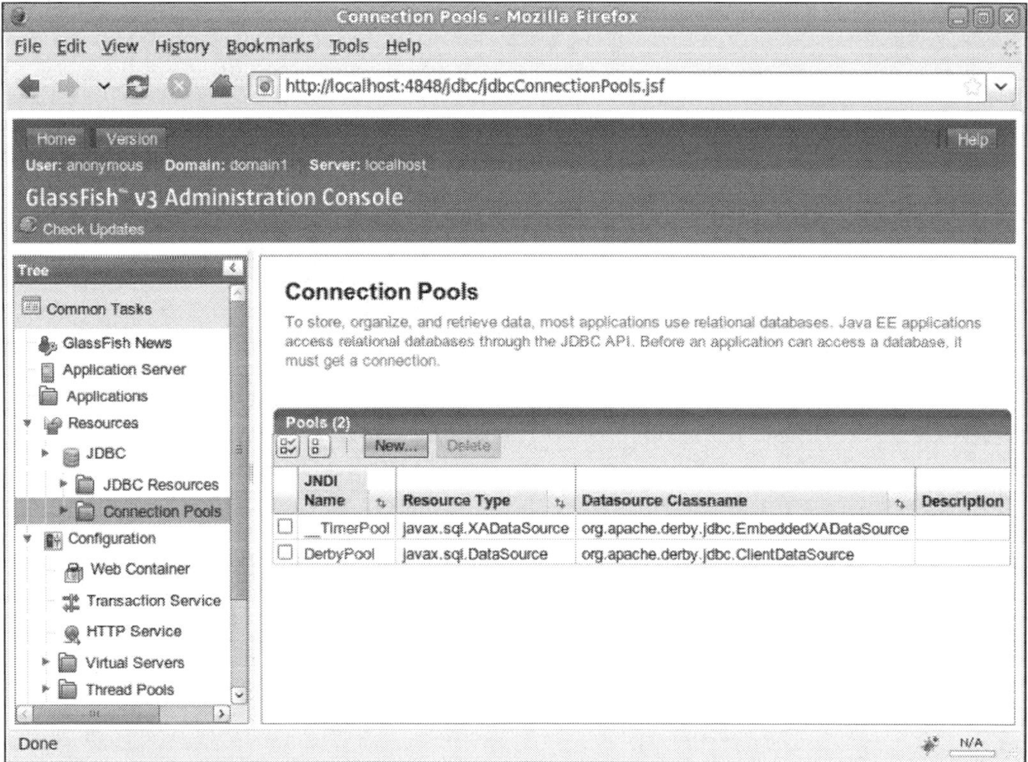

Click on the **New...** button. After entering the appropriate values for our RDBMS, the page should look something like this:

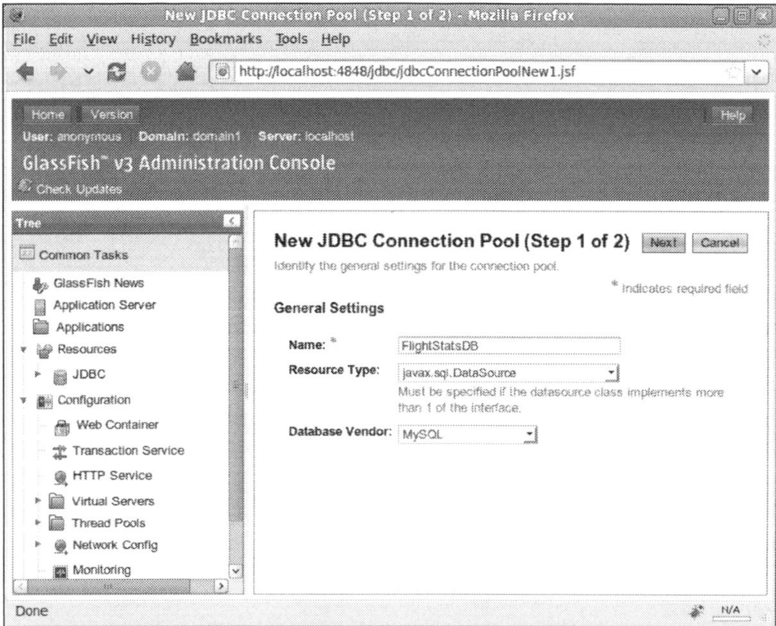

After entering the appropriate data for the RDBMS and clicking on the **Next** button, we should see a page like the following:

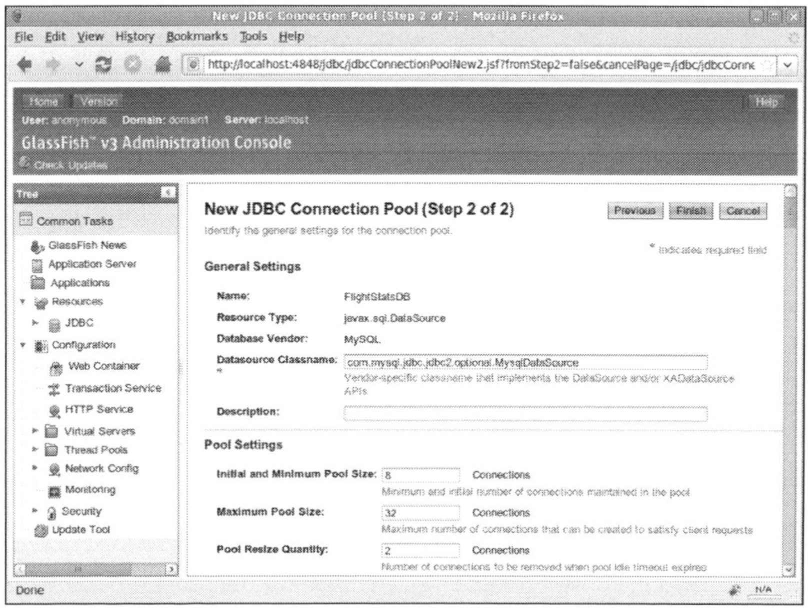

Most of the default values on the top portion of this page are sensible. Scroll all the way down and enter the appropriate data for our RDBMS, then click on the **Finish** button on the top right of the screen.

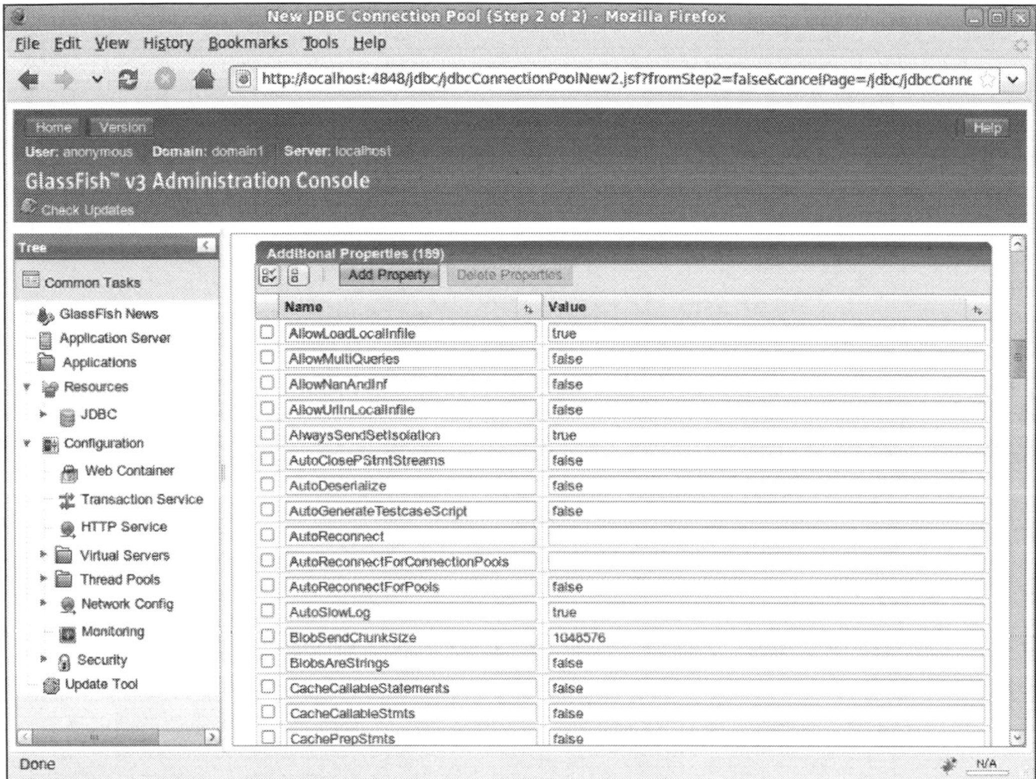

Properties vary depending on the RDBMS we are using, but usually there is a URL property where we should enter the JDBC URL for our database, plus username and password properties where we should enter authentication credentials for our database. The list of properties is shown in the previous screenshot.

Our newly created connection pool should now be visible in the list of connection pools:

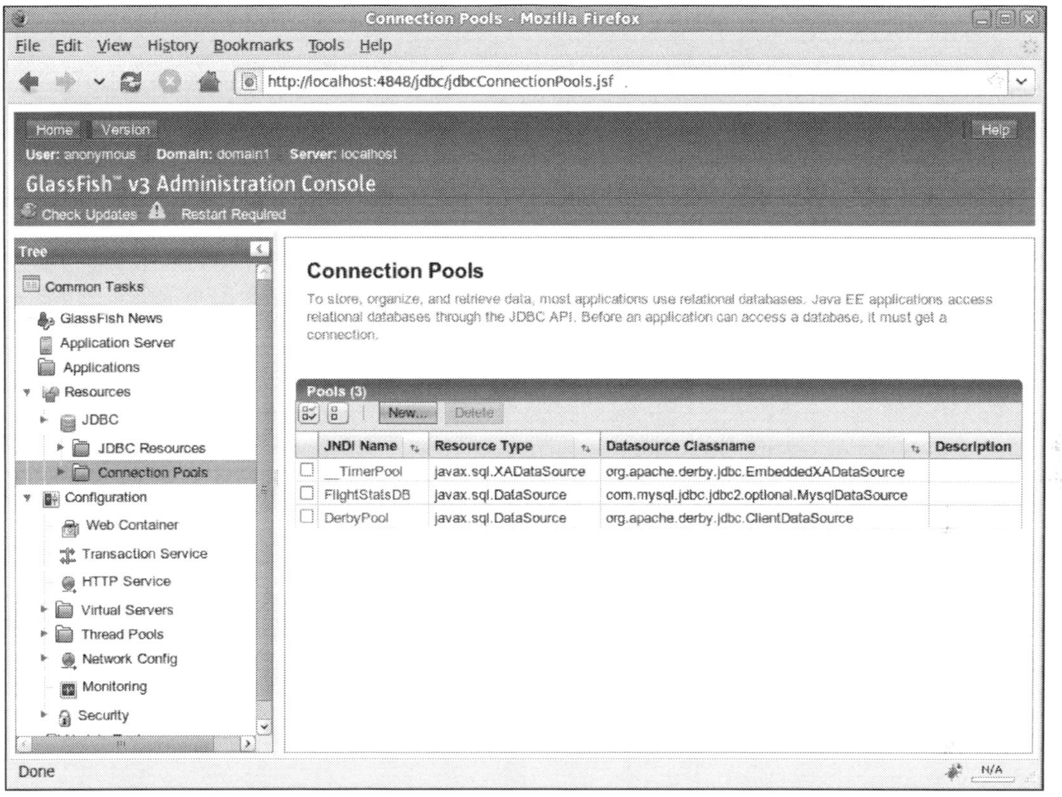

In most cases, GlassFish needs to be restarted after setting up a new connection pool.

After restarting and navigating to the connection pools page, we can verify that our connection pool was successfully set up by clicking on its **JNDI Name** for the new connection pool, and clicking on the **Ping** button on the resulting page:

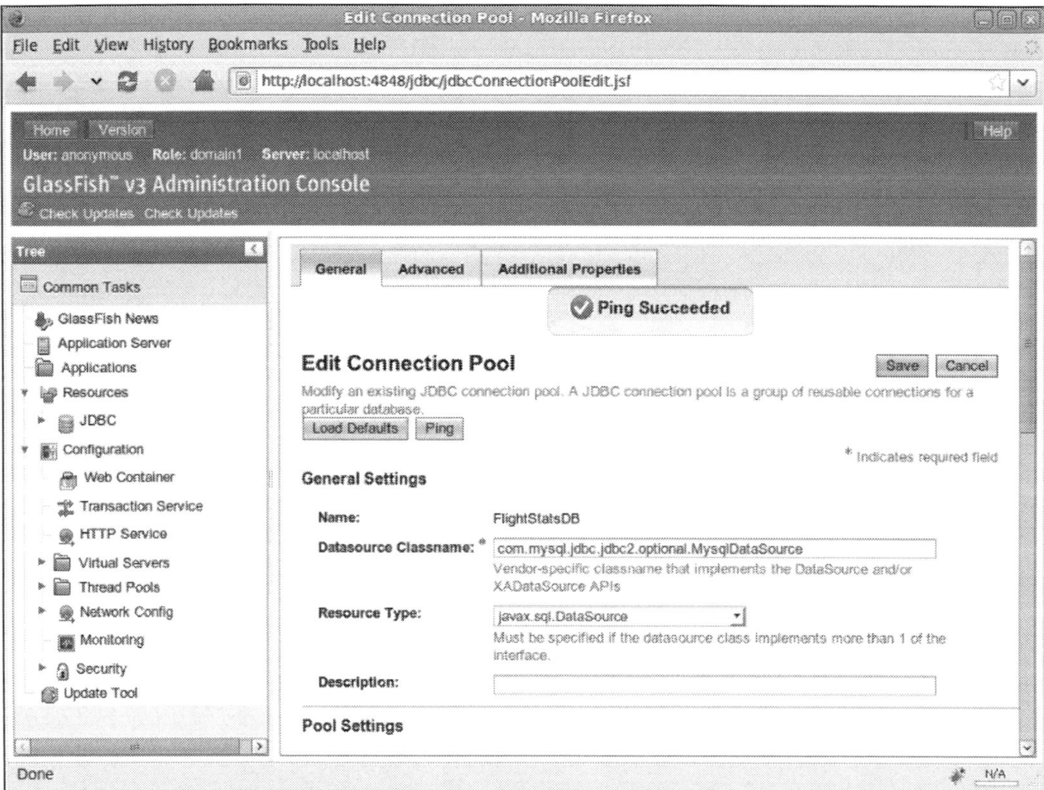

Our connection pool is now ready to be used by our applications.

Setting up data sources

Java EE applications don't access connection pools directly. Instead, they access a data source that points to a connection pool. To set up a new data source, click on the **JDBC Resources** menu item on the left-hand side of the web console, then click on the **New...** button. After filling up the appropriate information for our new data source, we should see a page like the following:

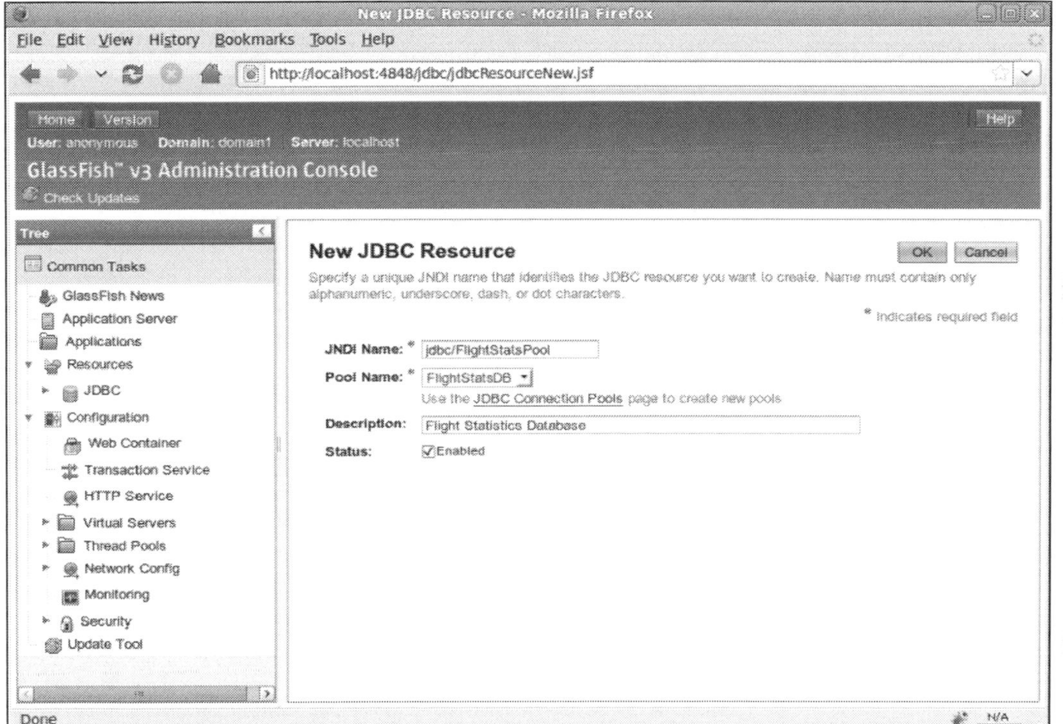

After clicking on the **OK** button, we can see our newly created data source:

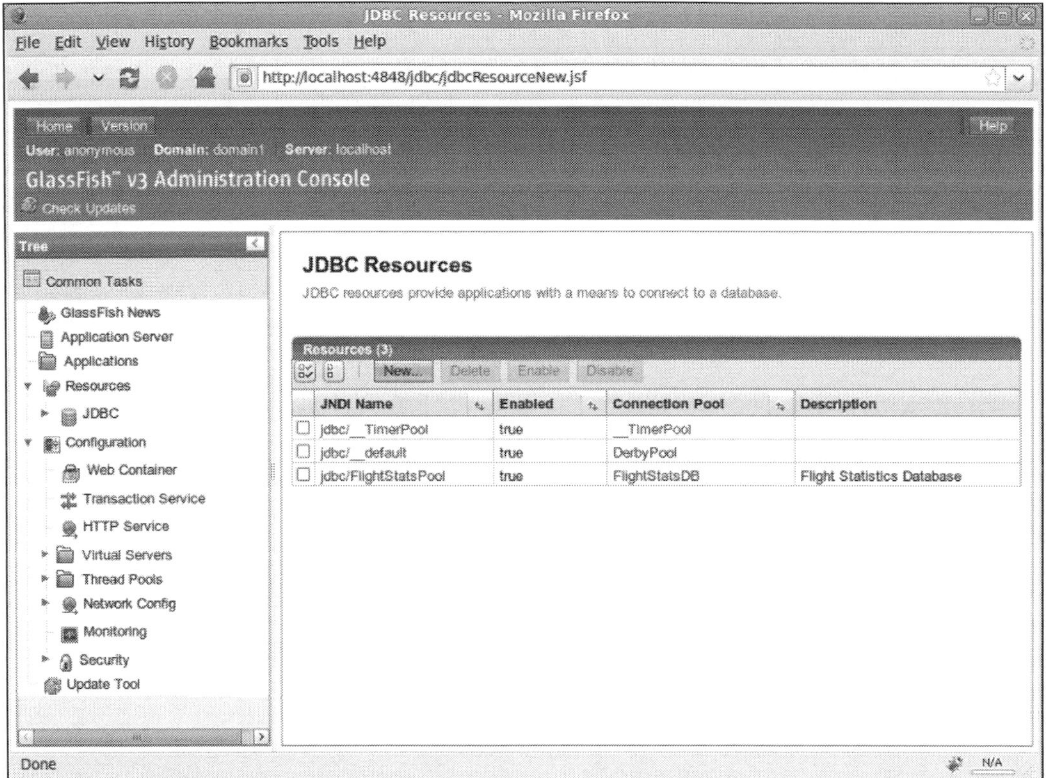

Final notes

Most of the examples in this book are IDE agnostic. However, both the NetBeans and Eclipse IDEs integrate with GlassFish for ease of development and deployment. Readers wishing to use one of these IDEs might want to refer to Appendix B for instructions on how to integrate them with GlassFish.

Summary

In this chapter, we discussed how to download and install GlassFish. We also discussed several methods of deploying a Java EE application through the GlassFish web console, through the `asadmin` command, and by copying the file to the `autodeploy` directory. We also discussed basic GlassFish administration tasks such as setting up domains and setting up database connectivity by adding connection pools and data sources.

2

Servlet Development and Deployment

In this chapter, we will discuss how to develop and deploy Java Servlets. Some of the topics covered include:

- An explanation of what servlets are
- Developing, configuring, packaging, and deploying our first servlet
- HTML form processing
- Forwarding HTTP requests
- Redirecting HTTP responses
- Persisting data across HTTP requests
- New features introduced in Servlet 3.0

What is a servlet?

A servlet is a Java class that is used to extend the capabilities of servers that host applications. Servlets can respond to requests and generate responses. The base class for all servlets is `javax.servlet.GenericServlet`. This class defines a generic, protocol-independent servlet.

By far, the most common type of servlet is an HTTP servlet. This type of servlet is used in handling HTTP requests and generating HTTP responses. An HTTP servlet is a class that extends the `javax.servlet.http.HttpServlet` class, which is a subclass of `javax.servlet.GenericServlet`.

A servlet must implement one or more methods to respond to specific HTTP requests. These methods are overridden from the parent `HttpServlet` class. As can be seen in the following table, these methods are named so that knowing which one to use is intuitive:

HTTP request	HttpServlet method
GET	`doGet(HttpServletRequest request, HttpServletResponse response)`
POST	`doPost(HttpServletRequest request, HttpServletResponse response)`
PUT	`doPut(HttpServletRequest request, HttpServletResponse response)`
DELETE	`doDelete(HttpServletRequest request, HttpServletResponse response)`

Each of these methods take the same two parameters, namely an instance of a class implementing the `javax.servlet.http.HttpServletRequest` interface and an instance of a class implementing the `javax.servlet.http.HttpServletResponse` interface. These interfaces will be covered in detail later in this chapter.

Application developers never call these methods directly. They are called automatically by the application server whenever it receives the corresponding HTTP request.

Of the four methods listed previously, `doGet()` and `doPost()` are by far the most commonly used.

An HTTP GET request is generated whenever a user types the servlet's URL in the browser, when a user clicks on a link pointing to the servlet's URL, or when a user submits an HTML form using the GET method, where the form's action points to the servlet's URL. In any of these cases, the code inside the servlet's `doGet()` method gets executed.

An HTTP POST request is typically generated when a user submits an HTML form using the POST method and an action pointing to the servlet's URL. In this case, the servlet's code inside the `doPost()` method gets executed.

Writing our first servlet

In Chapter 1, we deployed a simple application that printed a message on the browser window. That application basically consisted of a single servlet. In this section, we will see how that servlet was developed, configured, and packaged.

The code for the servlet is as follows:

```
package net.ensode.glassfishbook.simpleapp;
import java.io.IOException;
import java.io.PrintWriter;
import javax.servlet.http.HttpServlet;
import javax.servlet.http.HttpServletRequest;
import javax.servlet.http.HttpServletResponse;

public class SimpleServlet extends HttpServlet
{
  protected void doGet(HttpServletRequest request,
    HttpServletResponse response)
  {
    try
    {
      response.setContentType("text/html");
      PrintWriter printWriter = response.getWriter();
      printWriter.println("<h2>");
      printWriter.println("If you are reading this, your application
        server is good to go!");
      printWriter.println("</h2>");
    }
    catch (IOException ioException)
    {
      ioException.printStackTrace();
    }
  }
}
```

As this servlet is meant to execute when a user enters its URL in the browser window, we need to override the `doGet()` method from the parent `HttpServlet` class. Like we explained previously, this method takes two parameters: an instance of a class implementing the `javax.servlet.http.HttpServletRequest` interface, and an instance of a class implementing the `javax.servlet.http.HttpServletResponse` interface.

> Even though `HttpServletRequest` and `HttpServletResponse` are interfaces, application developers don't typically write classes implementing them. When control goes to a servlet from an HTTP request, the application server (in our case, GlassFish) provides objects implementing these interfaces.

The first thing our `doGet()` method does is set the content type for the `HttpServletResponse` object to "text/html". If we forget to do this, the default content type used is "text/plain", which means that the HTML tags used a couple of lines down will be displayed on the browser, as opposed to them being interpreted as HTML tags.

We then obtain an instance of `java.io.PrintWriter` by calling the `HttpServletResponse.getWriter()` method. We can then send text output to the browser by calling the `PrintWriter.print()` and `PrintWriter.println()` methods (the previous example uses `println()` exclusively). As we set the content type to "text/html", any HTML tags are properly interpreted by the browser.

Compiling the servlet

To compile the servlet, the Java library included with GlassFish must be in the CLASSPATH. This library is called `javaee.jar` and it can be found in the `[glassfish installation directory]/glassfish/lib` folder.

To compile from the command line using the `javac` compiler, a command like the following must be issued (all in one line):

```
javac -cp /opt/sges-v3/glassfish/lib/javaee.jar net/ensode/glassfishbook/
simpleapp/SimpleServlet.java
```

Of course, these days very few developers compile code with the "raw" `javac` compiler. Instead, either a graphical IDE or a command line build tool such as Apache ANT or Apache Maven is used. Consult your IDE or build tool documentation for information on how to add the `javaee.jar` library to its CLASSPATH.

Maven

Apache Maven is a build tool similar to ANT. However, Maven offers a number of advantages over ANT, including automatic download of dependencies and standard commands for compilation and packaging of applications. Maven was the build tool used to compile and package all examples in this book. Therefore, it is recommended to have Maven installed in order to easily build the examples.

When using Maven, the code can be compiled and packaged by issuing the following command in the project's root directory (in this case, `simpleapp`): `mvn package`

Maven can be downloaded from `http://maven.apache.org/`.

Configuring the servlet

Before we can deploy our servlet, we need to configure it. All Java EE web applications can be configured via an XML deployment descriptor named `web.xml` or via annotations. In this section, we will discuss how to configure a Java EE web application via `web.xml`; later in the chapter, we will cover configuration via annotations. The `web.xml` deployment descriptor for our servlet is as follows:

```
<?xml version="1.0" encoding="UTF-8"?>
<web-app xmlns="http://java.sun.com/xml/ns/javaee"
         xmlns:xsi="http://www.w3.org/2001/XMLSchema-instance"
         xsi:schemaLocation="http://java.sun.com/xml/ns/javaee
           http://java.sun.com/xml/ns/javaee/web-app_3_0.xsd"
         version="3.0">
  <servlet>
    <servlet-name>SimpleServlet</servlet-name>
    <servlet-class>
      net.ensode.glassfishbook.simpleapp.SimpleServlet
    </servlet-class>
  </servlet>
  <servlet-mapping>
    <servlet-name>SimpleServlet</servlet-name>
    <url-pattern>/simpleservlet</url-pattern>
  </servlet-mapping>
</web-app>
```

The first few lines are boilerplate XML stating the XML version and encoding, plus the schema used for the XML file and other information. It is safe to just copy and paste these lines and reuse them across applications. The `<servlet>` and `<servlet-mapping>` XML tags are used to actually configure our servlet.

The `<servlet>` tag contains two nested tags: `<servlet-name>` defines a logical name for the servlet and `<servlet-class>` indicates the Java class defining the servlet.

The `<servlet-mapping>` tag also contains two nested tags: `<servlet-name>` matches the value set inside the `<servlet>` tag and `<url-pattern>` sets the URL pattern for which the servlet will execute.

The `<url-pattern>` tag can be specified in one of the following two ways: by using a path prefix (which is what the previous example does) or by specifying an extension suffix.

Path prefix values for `<url-pattern>` indicate that any URL paths starting with the given path will be serviced by the corresponding servlet. Path prefix values must start with a forward slash.

> Java EE web applications run from within a context root. The context root is the first string in the URL that is neither the server name or IP address nor the port. For example, in the URL `http://localhost:8080/simpleapp/simpleservlet`, the string `simpleapp` is the context root. The value for `<url-pattern>` is relative to the application's context root.

Extension suffix values for `<url-pattern>` indicate that any URLs ending in the given suffix will be serviced by the corresponding servlet. In the previous example, we chose to use a path prefix. If we had chosen to use an extension suffix, the `<servlet-mapping>` tag would look something like this:

```
<servlet-mapping>
  <servlet>SimpleServlet</servlet>
  <url-pattern>*.foo</url-pattern>
</servlet-mapping>
```

This would direct any URLs ending with the string `.foo` to our servlet.

The reason the `<servlet-name>` tag is specified twice (once inside the `<servlet>` tag and again inside the `<servlet-mapping>` tag) is because a Java EE web application can have more than one servlet. Each of the servlets must have a `<servlet>` tag in the application's `web.xml` file. The `<servlet>` tag for each must have a corresponding `<servlet-mapping>` tag. The `<servlet-name>` nested tag is used to indicate which `<servlet>` tag corresponds to which `<servlet-mapping>` tag.

A Java EE `web.xml` file can contain many additional XML tags. However, these additional tags are not needed for this simple example. Additional tags will be discussed in future examples when they are needed.

Before we can execute our servlet, we need to package it as part of a web application in a WAR (Web ARchive) file.

Packaging the web application

All Java EE web applications must be packaged in a WAR (Web ARchive) file before they can be deployed. A WAR file is nothing but a compressed file containing our code and configuration. WAR files can be created by any utility that can create files in a ZIP format (for example, WinZip, 7-Zip, and so on). Also, many Java IDEs and build tools such as ANT and Maven automate WAR file creation.

A WAR file must contain the following directories (in addition to its root directory):

- `WEB-INF`
- `WEB-INF/classes`
- `WEB-INF/lib`

The root directory contains JSPs (covered in the next chapter), HTML files, JavaScript files, and CSS files.

`WEB-INF` contains deployment descriptors such as `web.xml`.

`WEB-INF/classes` contains the compiled code (`.class` files) and may optionally contain property files. Just like with any Java classes, the directory structure must match the package structure. Therefore, this directory typically contains several subdirectories corresponding to the classes contained in it.

`WEB-INF/lib` contains JAR files containing any library dependencies our code might have.

The root directory, `WEB-INF` and `WEB-INF/classes` directories can have subdirectories. Any resources on a subdirectory of the root directory (other than `WEB-INF`) can be accessed by prepending the subdirectory name to its filename. For example, if there was a subdirectory called `css` containing a CSS file called `style.css`, this CSS file could be accessed in JSPs and HTML files in the root directory by the following line:

```
<link rel="stylesheet" type="text/css" media="screen"
  href="css/style.css" />
```

Notice the `css` prefix to the filename corresponding to the directory where the CSS file resides.

To create a WAR file from scratch, create the previous directory structure in any directory in your system, then perform the following steps:

1. Copy the `web.xml` file to `WEB-INF`.
2. Create the following directory structure under `WEB-INF/classes`: `net/ensode/glassfishbook/simpleapp`.
3. Copy `SimpleServlet.class` to the `simpleapp` directory from the previous step.
4. From the command line, issue the following command from the directory right above `WEB-INF`: `jar cvf simpleapp.war *`.

You should now have a WAR file ready for deployment.

When using Maven to build the code, the WAR file is automatically generated when issuing the `mvn package` command. The WAR file can be found under the `target` directory. It is named `simpleapp.war`.

Before we can execute our application, it needs to be deployed.

Deploying the web application

Like we discussed in Chapter 1, there are several ways of deploying an application. The easiest and most straightforward way to deploy any Java EE application is to copy the deployment file (in this case, WAR file) to `[glassfish installation directory]/glassfish/domains/domain1/autodeploy`.

After copying the WAR file to the `autodeploy` directory, the system log should show a message similar to the following:

```
[#|2010-04-08T19:39:48.313-0400|INFO|glassfishv3.0|javax.enterprise.
system.tools.deployment.org.glassfish.deployment.common|_ThreadID=28;_
ThreadName=Thread-1;|[AutoDeploy] Successfully autodeployed : /home/
heffel/sges-v3/glassfish/domains/domain1/autodeploy/simpleapp.war.|#]
```

The system log can be found under `[glassfish installation directory]/glassfish/domains/domain1/logs/server.log`.

The last line should contain the string "Successfully autodeployed", indicating that our WAR file was deployed successfully.

Testing the web application

To verify that the servlet has been properly deployed, we need to point our browser to `http://localhost:8080/simpleapp/simpleservlet`. After doing so, we should see a page similar to the following:

Unsurprisingly, this is the same message we saw when deploying the application in Chapter 1, as this is the same application we deployed then.

Earlier in this chapter, we mentioned that URL paths for a Java EE application are relative to their context root. The default context root for a WAR file is the name of the WAR file itself (minus the `.war` extension). As can be seen in the previous screenshot, the context root for our application is `simpleapp`, which happens to match the name of the WAR file. This default can be changed by adding an additional configuration file to the `WEB-INF` directory of the WAR file. The name of this file should be `sun-web.xml`. An example `sun-web.xml` file that will change the context root of our application from the default `simpleapp` to `simple` would look as follows:

```
<?xml version="1.0" encoding="UTF-8"?>
<!DOCTYPE sun-web-app PUBLIC "-//Sun Microsystems, Inc.//DTD
Application Server 8.1 Servlet 2.4//EN" "http://www.sun.com/software/
appserver/dtds/sun-web-app_2_4-1.dtd">
<sun-web-app>
  <context-root>/simple</context-root>
</sun-web-app>
```

As can be seen in this example, the context root for the application must be in the `<context-root>` tag of the `sun-web.xml` configuration file. After redeploying the `simpleapp.war` file, directing the browser to `http://localhost:8080/simple/simpleservlet` will execute our servlet.

[The `sun-web.xml` file can contain a number of additional tags to configure several aspects of the application. Additional tags will be discussed in the relevant sections of this book.]

Processing HTML forms

Servlets are rarely accessed by typing their URL directly in the browser. The most common use of servlets is to process data entered by users in an HTML form. In this section, we illustrate this process.

Before digging into the servlet code and HTML markup, let's take a look at the `web.xml` file for this new application:

```
<?xml version="1.0" encoding="UTF-8"?>
<web-app version="2.4" xmlns="http://java.sun.com/xml/ns/j2ee"
         xmlns:xsi="http://www.w3.org/2001/XMLSchema-instance"
         xsi:schemaLocation="http://java.sun.com/xml/ns/j2ee
           http://java.sun.com/xml/ns/j2ee/web-app_2_4.xsd">
  <servlet>
    <servlet-name>FormHandlerServlet</servlet-name>
    <servlet-class>
      net.ensode.glassfishbook.formhandling.FormHandlerServlet
    </servlet-class>
  </servlet>
  <servlet-mapping>
    <servlet-name>FormHandlerServlet</servlet-name>
    <url-pattern>/formhandlerservlet</url-pattern>
  </servlet-mapping>
  <welcome-file-list>
    <welcome-file>dataentry.html</welcome-file>
  </welcome-file-list>
</web-app>
```

This `web.xml` file is very similar to the one we saw in the previous section. However, it contains an XML tag we haven't seen before, namely the `<welcome-file>` tag. The `<welcome-file>` tag determines which file to direct to when a user types a URL ending in the application's context root (for this example, the URL would be `http://localhost:8080/formhandling`, as we are naming our WAR file `formhandling.war` and not specifying a custom context root). We will name the HTML file containing the form as `dataentry.html`. This way, GlassFish will render it in the browser when the user types our application's URL and does not specify a filename.

> If no `<welcome-file>` is specified in the application's `web.xml` file, GlassFish will look for a file named `index.html` and use it as the welcome file. If it can't find it, it will look for a file named `index.jsp` and use it as the welcome file. If it can't find either one, it will display a directory listing.

The HTML file containing the form for our application looks as follows:

```
<!DOCTYPE html PUBLIC "-//W3C//DTD HTML 4.01 Transitional//EN"
  "http://www.w3.org/TR/html4/loose.dtd">
<html>
  <head>
    <meta http-equiv="Content-Type" content="text/html;
      charset=UTF-8">
    <title>Data Entry Page</title>
  </head>
  <body>
    <form method="post" action="formhandlerservlet">
      <table cellpadding="0" cellspacing="0" border="0">
        <tr>
          <td>Please enter some text:</td>
          <td><input type="text" name="enteredValue" /></td>
        </tr>
        <tr>
          <td></td>
          <td><input type="submit" value="Submit"></td>
        </tr>
      </table>
    </form>
  </body>
</html>
```

Notice how the value for the form's `action` attribute matches the value of the servlet's `<url-pattern>` in the application's `web.xml` file (minus the initial slash). As the value of the form's `method` attribute is `post`, our servlet's `doPost()` method will be executed when the form is submitted.

Let's now take a look at our servlet's code:

```
package net.ensode.glassfishbook.formhandling;
import java.io.IOException;
import java.io.PrintWriter;
import javax.servlet.http.HttpServlet;
import javax.servlet.http.HttpServletRequest;
import javax.servlet.http.HttpServletResponse;

public class FormHandlerServlet extends HttpServlet
{
  protected void doPost(HttpServletRequest request,
    HttpServletResponse response)
  {
    String enteredValue;
    enteredValue = request.getParameter("enteredValue");
    response.setContentType("text/html");
```

```
        PrintWriter printWriter;
        try
        {
          printWriter = response.getWriter();
          printWriter.println("<p>");
          printWriter.print("You entered: ");
          printWriter.print(enteredValue);
          printWriter.print("</p>");
        }
        catch (IOException e)
        {
          e.printStackTrace();
        }
      }
    }
```

As can be seen in this example, we obtain a reference to the value the user typed by calling the `request.getParameter()` method. This method takes a single `String` object as its sole parameter. The value of this string must match the name of the input field in the HTML file. In this case, the HTML file has a text field named `enteredValue`:

```
<input type="text" name="enteredValue" />
```

Therefore, the servlet has a corresponding line:

```
enteredValue = request.getParameter("enteredValue");
```

This line of code is used to obtain the text entered by the user and store it in the string variable named `enteredValue` (the name of the variable does not need to match the input field name, but naming it that way is good practice to make it easy to remember what value the variable is holding).

After packaging the previous three files in a WAR file called `formhandling.war` and deploying the WAR file, we can see the rendered `dataentry.html` file by entering `http://localhost:8080/formhandling` in the browser:

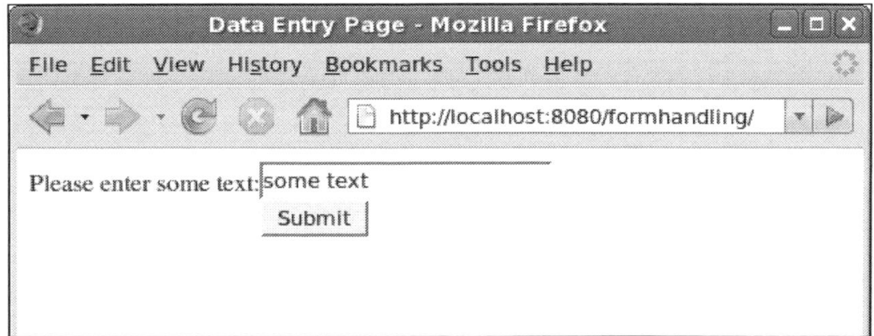

After the user enters **some text** in the text field and submits the form (either by hitting the *Enter* key or clicking on the **Submit** button), we should see the output of the servlet:

The `HttpServletRequest.getParameter()` method can be used to obtain the value of any HTML input field that can return only one value (text boxes, text areas, single selects, radio buttons, hidden fields, and so on). The procedure to obtain any of these fields' values is identical. In other words, the servlet doesn't care if the user typed in the value in a text field, selected it from a set of radio buttons, and so on. As long as the input field's name matches the value passed to the `getParameter()` method, the previous code will work.

> When dealing with radio buttons, all related radio buttons must have the same name. Calling the `HttpServletRequest.getParameter()` method and passing in the name of the radio buttons will return the value of the selected radio button.

Some HTML input fields such as checkboxes and multiple select boxes allow the user to select more than one value. For these fields, instead of using the `HttpServletRequest.getParameter()` method, the `HttpServletRequest.getParameterValues()` method is used. This method also takes a string containing the input field's name as its only parameter and returns an array of strings containing all the values that were selected by the user.

Let's add a second HTML file and a second servlet to our application to illustrate this case. The relevant sections of this HTML tag are shown in the following code:

```
<form method="post" action="multiplevaluefieldhandlerservlet">
<p>Please enter one or more options.</p>
  <table cellpadding="0" cellspacing="0" border="0">
    <tr>
      <td><input name="options" type="checkbox" value="option1" />
```

```
          Option 1
        </td>
      </tr>
      <tr>
        <td><input name="options" type="checkbox" value="option2" />
          Option 2
        </td>
      </tr>
      <tr>
        <td><input name="options" type="checkbox" value="option3" />
          Option 3
        </td>
      </tr>
      <tr>
        <td><input type="submit" value="Submit" /></td>
        <td></td>
      </tr>
    </table>
  </form>
```

The new HTML file contains a simple form having three checkboxes and a submit button. Notice how every checkbox has the same value for its `name` attribute. As we mentioned before, any checkboxes that are clicked by the user will be sent to the servlet.

Let's now take a look at the servlet that will handle this HTML form:

```
package net.ensode.glassfishbook.formhandling;
import java.io.IOException;
import java.io.PrintWriter;
import javax.servlet.http.HttpServlet;
import javax.servlet.http.HttpServletRequest;
import javax.servlet.http.HttpServletResponse;

public class MultipleValueFieldHandlerServlet extends HttpServlet
{
  protected void doPost(HttpServletRequest request,
    HttpServletResponse response)
  {
    String[] selectedOptions = request.getParameterValues("options");
    response.setContentType("text/html");
    try
    {
      PrintWriter printWriter = response.getWriter();
      printWriter.println("<p>");
```

```
            printWriter.print("The following options were selected:");
            printWriter.println("<br/>");
            if (selectedOptions != null)
            {
              for (String option : selectedOptions)
              {
                printWriter.print(option);
                printWriter.println("<br/>");
              }
            }
            else
            {
              printWriter.println("None");
            }
            printWriter.println("</p>");
          }
          catch (IOException e)
          {
            e.printStackTrace();
          }
        }
      }
```

This code calls the `request.getParameterValues()` method and assigns its return value to the `selectedOptions` variable. Further down the `doPost()` method, the code traverses the `selectedOptions` array and prints the selected values in the browser.

The previous code uses the enhanced `for` loop introduced in JDK 1.5. Refer to `http://java.sun.com/j2se/1.5.0/docs/guide/language/foreach.html` for more information.

If no checkboxes are clicked, the `request.getParameterValues()` method will return `null`. Therefore, it's a good idea to check for `null` before attempting to traverse through this method's return values.

Before this new servlet can be deployed, the following lines need to be added to the application's `web.xml` file:

```
<servlet>
  <servlet-name>MultipleValueFieldHandlerServlet</servlet-name>
  <servlet-class>
    net.ensode.glassfishbook.formhandling.MultipleValueFieldHand
      lerServlet
  </servlet-class>
</servlet>
```

We would also need to add the following lines of code:

```
<servlet-mapping>
  <servlet-name>MultipleValueFieldHandlerServlet</servlet-name>
  <url-pattern>/multiplevaluefieldhandlerservlet</url-pattern>
</servlet-mapping>
```

These lines assign a logical name and URL to the new servlet.

After re-creating the `formhandling.war` file by adding the compiled servlet and the HTML file and redeploying it, we can see the changes in action by typing the following URL in the browser window: `http://localhost:8080/formhandling/multiplevaluedataentry.html`.

After submitting the form, control goes to our servlet and the browser window should look something like this:

Of course, the actual message seen in the browser window will depend on which checkboxes the user clicked on.

Request forwarding and response redirection

In many cases, one servlet processes form data, then transfers control to another servlet or JSP to do some more processing or display a confirmation message on the screen. There are two ways of doing this: either the request can be forwarded or the response can be redirected to another servlet or page.

Request forwarding

Notice how the text displayed in the previous section's example matches the value of the `value` attribute of the checkboxes that were clicked, and not the labels displayed on the previous page. This might confuse the users. Let's modify the servlet to change these values so that they match the labels, then forward the request to another servlet that will display the confirmation message on the browser.

The new version of `MultipleValueFieldHandlerServlet` is shown in the following code:

```
package net.ensode.glassfishbook.formhandling;
import java.io.IOException;
import java.util.ArrayList;
import javax.servlet.ServletException;
import javax.servlet.http.HttpServlet;
import javax.servlet.http.HttpServletRequest;
import javax.servlet.http.HttpServletResponse;

public class MultipleValueFieldHandlerServlet extends HttpServlet
{
  protected void doPost(HttpServletRequest request,
    HttpServletResponse response)
  {
    String[] selectedOptions = request.getParameterValues("options");
    ArrayList<String> selectedOptionLabels = null;
    if (selectedOptions != null)
    {
      selectedOptionLabels = new
        ArrayList<String>(selectedOptions.length);
      for (String selectedOption : selectedOptions)
      {
        if (selectedOption.equals("option1"))
        {
          selectedOptionLabels.add("Option 1");
```

```
          }
          else if (selectedOption.equals("option2"))
          {
            selectedOptionLabels.add("Option 2");
          }
          else if (selectedOption.equals("option3"))
          {
            selectedOptionLabels.add("Option 3");
          }
        }
      }
      request.setAttribute("checkedLabels", selectedOptionLabels);
      try
      {
           request.getRequestDispatcher("confirmation
             servlet").forward(request, response);
      }
      catch (ServletException e)
      {
        e.printStackTrace();
      }
      catch (IOException e)
      {
        e.printStackTrace();
      }
    }
  }
```

This version of the servlet iterates through the selected options and adds the corresponding label to an `ArrayList` of strings. This string is then attached to the request object by calling the `request.setAttribute()` method. This method is used to attach any object to the request so that any other code we forward the request to can have access to it later.

The previous code uses generics—a feature introduced to the Java language in JDK 1.5 (see `http://java.sun.com/j2se/1.5.0/docs/guide/language/generics.html` for details).

After attaching the `ArrayList` to the request, we then forward the request to the new servlet using the following line of code:

```
request.getRequestDispatcher("confirmationservlet").forward(
  request, response);
```

The `String` argument to this method must match the value of the `<url-pattern>` tag of the servlet in the application's `web.xml` file.

At this point, control goes to our new servlet. The code for this new servlet is as follows:

```
package net.ensode.glassfishbook.requestforward;
import java.io.IOException;
import java.io.PrintWriter;
import java.util.List;
import javax.servlet.http.HttpServlet;
import javax.servlet.http.HttpServletRequest;
import javax.servlet.http.HttpServletResponse;

public class ConfirmationServlet extends HttpServlet
{
  @Override
  protected void doPost(HttpServletRequest request,
    HttpServletResponse response)
  {
    try
    {
      PrintWriter printWriter;
      List<String> checkedLabels = (List<String>)
        request.getAttribute("checkedLabels");
      response.setContentType("text/html");
      printWriter = response.getWriter();
      printWriter.println("<p>");
      printWriter.print("The following options were selected:");
      printWriter.println("<br/>");
      if (checkedLabels != null)
      {
        for (String optionLabel : checkedLabels)
        {
          printWriter.print(optionLabel);
          printWriter.println("<br/>");
        }
      }
      else
      {
        printWriter.println("None");
      }
      printWriter.println("</p>");
    }
    catch (IOException ioException)
    {
      ioException.printStackTrace();
    }
  }
}
```

This code obtains the `ArrayList` that was attached to the request by the previous servlet. This is accomplished by calling the `request.getAttribute()` method. The parameter for this method must match the value used to attach the object to the request.

Once the previous servlet obtains a list of option labels, it traverses through it and displays them on the browser:

Forwarding a request as described before works only for other resources (servlets and JSP pages) in the same context as the code doing the forwarding. In simple terms, the servlet or JSP we want to forward to must be packaged in the same WAR file as the code invoking the `request.getRequestDispatcher().forward()` method. If we need to direct the user to a page in another context (or even another server), we can do it by redirecting the response object.

Response redirection

One disadvantage of forwarding a request as described in the previous section is that requests can only be forwarded to other servlets or JSPs in the same context. If we need to direct the user to a page on a different context (deployed in another WAR file in the same server or deployed in a different server), we need to use the `HttpServletResponse.sendRedirect()` method.

To illustrate response redirection, let's develop a simple web application that asks the user to select their favorite search engine, then directs the user to his/her search engine of choice. The HTML page for this application would look as follows:

```
<!DOCTYPE html PUBLIC "-//W3C//DTD HTML 4.01 Transitional//EN"
  "http://www.w3.org/TR/html4/loose.dtd">
<html>
  <head>
```

Amazon.com
1850 Mercer Rd.
Lexington, KY 40511

Carlos F S Antunes
5823 SAGEBROOK DR
PARK CITY, UT 84098-6327
United States

Billing Address:
Natalia Antunes
Av do Vagalume 495
Faz. Engenho d'Agua II
Sao Paulo, SP 11630-000
Brazil

DrKk5ZGgR/-1 of 1-/sss-us/5820133 1S

S
C
58
P
U

Your order of November 12, 2010 (Order ID 103-2758131-3854622)

Qty.	Item
	IN THIS SHIPMENT
1	**Java EE 6 with GlassFish 3 Application Server** Heffelfinger, David --- Paperback **(** F-10 **) 1849510369** **1849510369**

Subtotal
Shipping & Handling
Promotional Certificat
Order Total
Paid via Amex
Balance due

This shipment completes your order.

Have feedback on how we packaged your order? Tell us at www.amazon.com/packaging.

60/DrKk5ZGgR/-1 of 1-//1S/sss-us/5820133/1117-02:00/1113-21:23/ljcollin Pack Type: V4

http://www.amazon.com

For detailed information about this and other orders, please visit Your Account. You can also print invoices, change your e–mail address and payment settings, alter your communication preferences, and much more – 24 hours a day – at http://www.amazon.com/your–account.

Thanks for shopping at Amazon.com, and please come again!

ipping Address:
rlos F S Antunes
23 SAGEBROOK DR
RK CITY, UT 84098–6327
ited States

Item Price	Total
$42.20	$42.20

$42.20
$3.99
–$3.99
$42.20
$42.20
$0.00

```
    <meta http-equiv="Content-Type" content="text/html;
      charset=UTF-8">
    <title>Response Redirection Demo</title>
  </head>
  <body>
    <form method="post" action="responseredirectionservlet">
    Please indicate your favorite search engine.
      <table>
        <tr>
          <td><input type="radio" name="searchEngine"
                     value="http://www.google.com">Google</td>
        </tr>
        <tr>
          <td><input type="radio" name="searchEngine"
                     value="http://www.msn.com">MSN</td>
        </tr>
        <tr>
          <td><input type="radio" name="searchEngine"
                     value="http://www.yahoo.com">Yahoo!</td>
        </tr>
        <tr>
          <td colspan="2"><input type="submit" value="Submit" /></td>
        </tr>
      </table>
    </form>
  </body>
</html>
```

The HTML form in this markup code contains three radio buttons. The value for each of them is the URL for the search engine corresponding to the user's selection. Notice how the value for the `name` attribute of each radio button is the same, namely `searchEngine`. The servlet will obtain the value of the selected radio button by calling the `request.getParameter()` method and passing the string `searchEngine` as a parameter. This is demonstrated in the following code:

```
package net.ensode.glassfishbook.responseredirection;
import java.io.IOException;
import java.io.PrintWriter;
import javax.servlet.http.HttpServlet;
import javax.servlet.http.HttpServletRequest;
import javax.servlet.http.HttpServletResponse;

public class ResponseRedirectionServlet extends HttpServlet
{
  @Override
```

```
    protected void doPost(HttpServletRequest request,
      HttpServletResponse response) throws IOException
    {
      String url = request.getParameter("searchEngine");
      if (url != null)
      {
        response.sendRedirect(url);
      }
      else
      {
        PrintWriter printWriter = response.getWriter();
        printWriter.println("No search engine was selected.");
      }
    }
  }
```

By calling `request.getParameter("searchEngine")`, the previous code assigns the URL of the selected search engine to the variable `url`. Then (after checking for `null`, in case the user clicked on the submit button without selecting a search engine), directs the user to the selected search engine by calling `response.sendRedirect()` and passing the `url` variable as a parameter.

The `web.xml` file for this application should be fairly straightforward and is not shown (it is part of this book's code download).

After packaging the code and deploying it, we can see it in action by typing the following URL in the browser: `http://localhost:8080/responseredirection/`.

After clicking on the **Submit** button, the user is directed to their favorite search engine.

It should be noted that redirecting the response as just illustrated creates a new HTTP request to the page we are redirecting to. Therefore, any request parameters and attributes are lost.

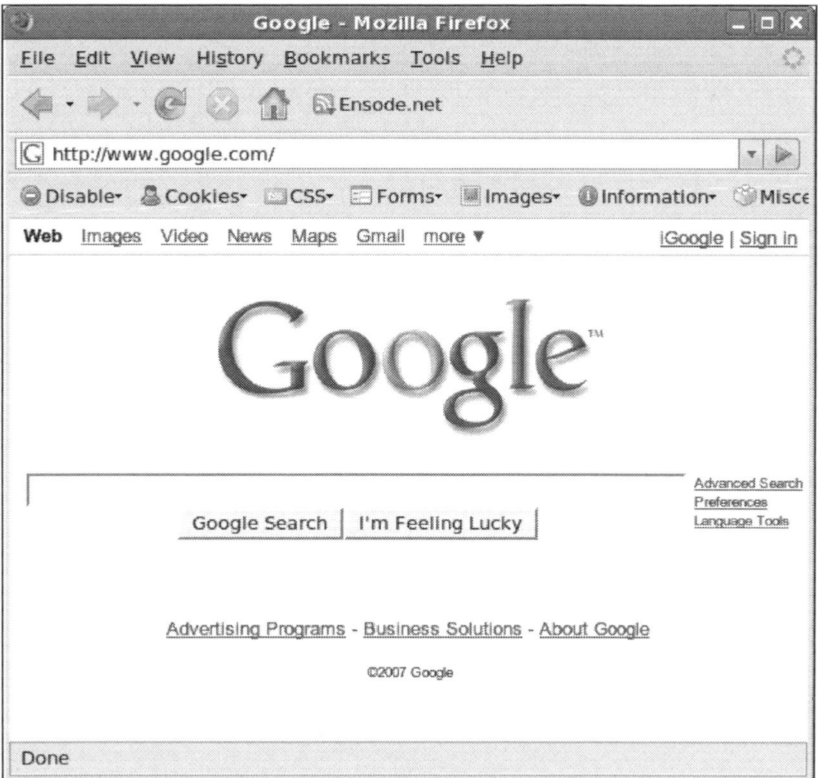

Persisting application data across requests

In the previous section, we saw how it is possible to store an object in the request by invoking the `HttpRequest.setAttribute()` method, and how this object can be retrieved later by invoking the `HttpRequest.getAttribute()` method. This approach only works if the request was forwarded to the servlet by invoking the `getAttribute()` method. If this is not the case, the `getAttribute()` method will return null.

It is possible to persist an object across requests. In addition to attaching an object to the request object, an object can also be attached to the session object or to the servlet context. The difference between these two is that objects attached to the session will not be visible by different users, whereas objects attached to the servlet context are.

Attaching objects to the session and servlet context is very similar to attaching objects to the request. To attach an object to the session, the `HttpServletRequest.getSession()` method must be invoked. This method returns an instance of `javax.servlet.http.HttpSession`. We then call the `HttpSession.setAttribute()` method to attach the object to the session. The following code fragment illustrates the process:

```
protected void doPost(HttpServletRequest request, HttpServletResponse
  response)
{
  .
  .
  .
  Foo foo = new Foo(); //theoretical object
  HttpSession session = request.getSession();
  session.setAttribute("foo", foo);
  .
  .
  .
}
```

We can then retrieve the object from the session by calling the `HttpSession.getAttribute()` method:

```
protected void doPost(HttpServletRequest request, HttpServletResponse
  response)
{
  HttpSession session = request.getSession();
  Foo foo = (Foo)session.getAttribute("foo");
}
```

Notice how the return value of `session.getAttribute()` needs to be casted to the appropriate type. This is necessary as the return value of this method is `java.lang.Object`.

The procedure to attach and retrieve objects to and from the servlet context is very similar. The servlet needs to call the `getServletContext()` method (defined in the class called `GenericServlet`, which is the parent class of `HttpServlet`, which in turn is the parent class of our servlets). This method returns an instance of `javax.servlet.ServletContext`, which defines a `setAttribute()` and a `getAttribute()` method. These methods work the same way as their `HttpServletRequest` and `HttpSessionResponse` counterparts.

The procedure to attach an object to the servlet context is illustrated in the following code snippet:

```
protected void doPost(HttpServletRequest request, HttpServletResponse
  response)
{
  //The getServletContext() method is defined higher in
  //the inheritance hierarchy.
  ServletContext servletContext = getServletContext();
  Foo foo = new Foo();
  servletContext.setAttribute("foo", foo);
  .
  .
  .
}
```

This code attaches the `foo` object to the servlet context. This object will be available to any servlet in our application and will be the same across sessions. It can be retrieved by calling the `ServletContext.getAttribute()` method, as illustrated next:

```
protected void doPost(HttpServletRequest request, HttpServletResponse
  response)
{
  ServletContext servletContext = getServletContext();
  Foo foo = (Foo)servletContext.getAttribute("foo");
  .
  .
  .
}
```

This code obtains the `foo` object from the request context. A cast is again needed as the `ServletContext.getAttribute()` method, like its counterparts, returns an instance of `java.lang.Object`.

Objects attached to the servlet context are said to have a scope of application. Similarly, objects attached to the session are said to have a scope of session, and objects attached to the request are said to have a scope of request.

New features introduced in Servlet 3.0

Java EE 6 includes a new version of the Servlet API—Servlet 3.0. This version of the Servlet API includes several new features that make servlet development easier. Servlet 3.0 also makes it easier to take advantage of modern web application techniques such as Ajax.

In the next several sections, we will discuss some of the most important additions to the Servlet API.

Optional web.xml deployment descriptor

Servlet 3.0 makes the `web.xml` deployment descriptor completely optional. Servlets can be configured via annotations instead of XML.

If a web application is configured both through annotations and through a `web.xml` deployment descriptor, settings in `web.xml` take precedence.

@WebServlet annotation

Servlets can be decorated with the `@WebServlet` annotation to specify their name, URL pattern, initialization parameters, and other configuration items usually specified in the `web.xml` deployment descriptor.

At a minimum, a servlet to be configured via annotations must have a `@WebServlet` annotation specifying the servlet's URL pattern.

Using this new Servlet 3.0 annotation, our first example in this chapter can be rewritten as follows:

```
package net.ensode.glassfishbook.simpleapp;

import java.io.IOException;
import java.io.PrintWriter;

import javax.servlet.annotation.WebServlet;
```

```
import javax.servlet.http.HttpServlet;
import javax.servlet.http.HttpServletRequest;
import javax.servlet.http.HttpServletResponse;

@WebServlet(urlPatterns = {"/simpleservlet"})
public class SimpleServlet extends HttpServlet
{
  @Override
  protected void doGet(HttpServletRequest request,
    HttpServletResponse response)
  {
    try
    {
      response.setContentType("text/html");
      PrintWriter printWriter = response.getWriter();
      printWriter.println("<h2>");
      printWriter.println("If you are reading this, your application
        server " + "is good to go!");
      printWriter.println("</h2>");
    }
    catch (IOException ioException)
    {
      ioException.printStackTrace();
    }
  }
}
```

Notice that all we had to do was annotate our servlet with the `@WebServlet` annotation, and specify its URL pattern as the value of its `urlPatterns` attribute.

Just like with a `web.xml`, we can specify more than one URL pattern for our servlet. All we need to do is separate each URL pattern with a comma. For example, if we wanted our servlet to handle all URLs ending with `.foo` in addition to handling all URLs starting with `/simpleservlet`, we would annotate it as follows:

```
@WebServlet(urlPatterns = {"/simpleservlet", "*.foo"})
```

With this simple change to our code, we avoid having to write a `web.xml` for our application.

After packaging and deploying this new version of the application, it will work just like the previous version.

Passing initialization parameters to a servlet via annotations

It is sometimes useful to pass some initialization parameters to a servlet. This way, we can make said servlet behave differently based on the parameters sent to it. For example, we may want to configure a servlet to behave differently in development and production environments.

Traditionally, servlet initialization parameters were sent via the `<init-param>` parameter in `web.xml`. As of servlet 3.0, initialization parameters can be passed to the servlet as the value of the `initParams` attribute of the `@WebServlet` annotation. The following example illustrates how to do this:

```
package net.ensode.glassfishbook.initparam;
import java.io.IOException;
import java.io.PrintWriter;
import javax.servlet.ServletConfig;
import javax.servlet.ServletException;
import javax.servlet.annotation.WebInitParam;
import javax.servlet.annotation.WebServlet;
import javax.servlet.http.HttpServlet;
import javax.servlet.http.HttpServletRequest;
import javax.servlet.http.HttpServletResponse;

@WebServlet(name = "InitParamsServlet", urlPatterns = {
  "/InitParamsServlet"}, initParams = {
  @WebInitParam(name = "param1", value = "value1"),
  @WebInitParam(name = "param2", value = "value2")})
public class InitParamsServlet extends HttpServlet
{
  @Override
  protected void doGet(HttpServletRequest request,
    HttpServletResponse response) throws ServletException,
    IOException
  {
    ServletConfig servletConfig = getServletConfig();
    String param1Val = servletConfig.getInitParameter("param1");
    String param2Val = servletConfig.getInitParameter("param2");
    response.setContentType("text/html");
    PrintWriter printWriter = response.getWriter();
    printWriter.println("<p>");
    printWriter.println("Value of param1 is " + param1Val);
    printWriter.println("</p>");
    printWriter.println("<p>");
    printWriter.println("Value of param2 is " + param2Val);
    printWriter.println("</p>");
  }
}
```

As we can see, the value of the `initParams` attribute of the `@WebServlet` annotation is an array of `@WebInitParam` annotations. Each `@WebInitParam` annotation has two attributes: `name`, which corresponds to the parameter name and `value`, which corresponds to the parameter value.

We can obtain the values of our parameters by invoking the `getInitParameter()` method on the `javax.servlet.ServletConfig` class. This method takes a single `String` argument as a parameter, corresponding to the parameter name, and returns a `String` corresponding to the parameter value.

Each servlet has a corresponding instance of `ServletConfig` assigned to it. As we can see in this example, we can obtain this instance by invoking `getServletConfig()`, which is a method inherited from `javax.servlet.GenericServlet`—the parent class of `HttpServlet`, which our servlets extend.

After packaging our servlet in a WAR file and deploying it to GlassFish either via the asadmin command line tool (the GlassFish web console) or by copying it to the `autodeploy` directory in our domain, we will see the following page rendered in the browser:

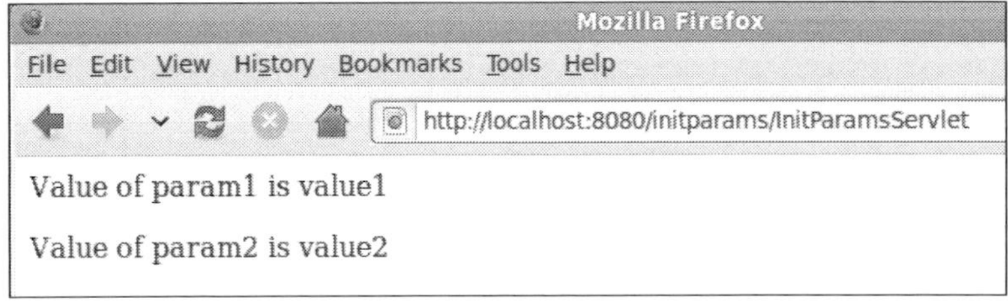

As we can see, the rendered values correspond to the values we set in each `@WebInitParam` annotation.

@WebFilter annotation

Filters were introduced to the servlet specification in version 2.3. A filter is an object that can dynamically intercept a request and manipulate its data before the request is handled by the servlet. Filters can also manipulate a response after a servlet's `doGet()` or `doPost()` method finishes, but before the output is sent to the browser.

The only way to configure a filter in earlier servlet specifications was to use the `<filter-mapping>` tag in `web.xml`. Servlet 3.0 introduced the ability to configure servlets via the `@WebFilter` annotation.

The following code snippet illustrates how to do this:

```
package net.ensode.glassfishbook.simpleapp;
import java.io.IOException;
import java.util.Enumeration;
import javax.servlet.Filter;
import javax.servlet.FilterChain;
import javax.servlet.FilterConfig;
import javax.servlet.ServletContext;
import javax.servlet.ServletException;
import javax.servlet.ServletRequest;
import javax.servlet.ServletResponse;
import javax.servlet.annotation.WebFilter;
import javax.servlet.annotation.WebInitParam;

@WebFilter(filterName = "SimpleFilter", initParams = {
  @WebInitParam(name = "filterparam1", value = "filtervalue1")},
  urlPatterns = {"/InitParamsServlet"})
public class SimpleFilter implements Filter
{
  private FilterConfig filterConfig;

  @Override
  public void init(FilterConfig filterConfig) throws
    ServletException
  {
    this.filterConfig = filterConfig;
  }

  @Override
  public void doFilter(ServletRequest servletRequest,
    ServletResponse servletResponse, FilterChain filterChain)
    throws IOException, ServletException
  {
    ServletContext servletContext = filterConfig.getServletContext();
    servletContext.log("Entering doFilter()");
    servletContext.log("initialization parameters: ");
    Enumeration<String> initParameterNames =
        filterConfig.getInitParameterNames();
    String parameterName;
    String parameterValue;
    while (initParameterNames.hasMoreElements())
    {
      parameterName = initParameterNames.nextElement();
      parameterValue = filterConfig.getInitParameter(parameterName);
      servletContext.log(parameterName + " = " + parameterValue);
    }
    servletContext.log("Invoking servlet...");
```

```
        filterChain.doFilter(servletRequest, servletResponse);
        servletContext.log("Back from servlet invocation");
      }

      @Override
      public void destroy()
      {
        filterConfig = null;
      }
    }
```

As we can see in this code, the `@WebFilter` annotation has several attributes we can use to configure the filter. The `urlPatterns` attribute is of special importance. This attribute takes an array of `String` objects as its value. Each element in the array corresponds to a URL that our filter will intercept. In our example, we are intercepting a single URL pattern that corresponds to the servlet we wrote in the previous section.

Other attributes in the `@WebFilter` annotation include the optional `filterName` attribute, which we can use to give our filter a name. If we don't specify a name for our filter, then the filter name defaults to the filter's class name.

As we can see in the previous code example, we can send initialization parameters to a filter. This is done just like we send initialization parameters to a servlet. The `@WebFilter` annotation has an `initParams` attribute that takes an array of `@WebInitParam` annotations as its value. We can obtain the values of said parameters by invoking the `getInitParameter()` method on `javax.servlet.FilterConfig`, as illustrated in the example.

Our filter is fairly simple. It simply sends some output to the server log before and after the servlet is invoked. Inspecting the server log after deploying our application and pointing the browser to the servlet's URL should reveal our filter's output.

```
[#|2009-09-30T19:38:15.454-0400|INFO|glassfish|javax.enterprise.system.
container.web.com.sun.enterprise.web|_ThreadID=17;_ThreadName=Thread-
1;|PWC1412: WebModule[/servlet30filter] ServletContext.log():Entering
doFilter()|#]

[#|2009-09-30T19:38:15.456-0400|INFO|glassfish|javax.enterprise.
system.container.web.com.sun.enterprise.web|_ThreadID=17;_
ThreadName=Thread-1;|PWC1412: WebModule[/servlet30filter] ServletContext.
log():initialization parameters: |#]

[#|2009-09-30T19:38:15.459-0400|INFO|glassfish|javax.enterprise.system.
container.web.com.sun.enterprise.web|_ThreadID=17;_ThreadName=Thread-
1;|PWC1412: WebModule[/servlet30filter] ServletContext.log():filterparam1
= filtervalue1|#]
```

```
[#|2009-09-30T19:38:15.461-0400|INFO|glassfish|javax.enterprise.system.container.web.com.sun.enterprise.web|_ThreadID=17;_ThreadName=Thread-1;|PWC1412: WebModule[/servlet30filter] ServletContext.log():Invoking servlet...|#]

[#|2009-09-30T19:38:15.471-0400|INFO|glassfish|javax.enterprise.system.container.web.com.sun.enterprise.web|_ThreadID=17;_ThreadName=Thread-1;|PWC1412: WebModule[/servlet30filter] ServletContext.log():Back from servlet invocation|#]
```

Of course, servlet filters have many real uses. They can be used for profiling web applications, for applying security, and for compressing data, among many other uses.

@WebListener annotation

During the lifetime of a typical web application, a number of events take place, such as HTTP requests are created or destroyed, request or session attributes are added, removed, or modified, and so on and so forth.

The Servlet API provides a number of listener interfaces we can implement in order to react to these events. All of these interfaces are in the `javax.servlet` package. The following table summarizes them:

Listener Interface	Description
`ServletContextListener`	Contains methods for handling context initialization and destruction events.
`ServletContextAttributeListener`	Contains methods for reacting to any attributes added, removed, or replaced in the servlet context (application scope).
`ServletRequestListener`	Contains methods for handling request initialization and destruction events.
`ServletRequestAttributeListener`	Contains methods for reacting to any attributes added, removed, or replaced in the request.
`HttpSessionListener`	Contains methods for handling HTTP session initialization and destruction events.
`HttpSessionAttributeListener`	Contains methods for reacting to any attributes added, removed, or replaced in the HTTP session.

All we need to do to handle any of the events handled by the interfaces described in this table is to implement one of these interfaces and annotate it with the `@WebListener` interface or declare it in the `web.xml` deployment descriptor via the `<listener>` tag. Unsurprisingly, the ability to use an annotation to register a listener was introduced in version 3.0 of the Servlet specification.

The API for all of these interfaces is fairly straightforward and intuitive. We will show an example for one of these interfaces; others will be very similar.

The JavaDoc for all of the previous interfaces can be found at `http://java.sun.com/javaee/6/docs/api/javax/servlet/http/package-summary.html`

The following code example illustrates how to implement the `ServletRequestListener` interface, which can be used to perform some action whenever an HTTP request is created or destroyed:

```
package net.ensode.glassfishbook.listener;
import javax.servlet.ServletContext;
import javax.servlet.ServletRequestEvent;
import javax.servlet.ServletRequestListener;
import javax.servlet.annotation.WebListener;

@WebListener()
public class HttpRequestListener implements ServletRequestListener
{
  @Override
  public void requestInitialized(ServletRequestEvent
    servletRequestEvent)
  {
    ServletContext servletContext =
        servletRequestEvent.getServletContext();
    servletContext.log("New request initialized");
  }

  @Override
  public void requestDestroyed(ServletRequestEvent
    servletRequestEvent)
  {
    ServletContext servletContext =
        servletRequestEvent.getServletContext();
    servletContext.log("Request destroyed");
  }
}
```

As we can see, all we need to do to activate our listener class is to annotate it with the `@WebListener` annotation. Our listener must also implement one of the listener interfaces we listed previously. In our example, we chose to implement `javax.servlet.ServletRequestListener`. This interface has methods that are automatically invoked whenever an HTTP request is initialized or destroyed.

The `ServletRequestListener` interface has two methods: `requestInitialized()` and `requestDestroyed()`. In our previous simple implementation, we simply sent some output to the log, but of course we can do anything we need to do in our implementations.

Deploying our previous listener along with the simple servlet we developed earlier in the chapter, we can see the following output in GlassFish's log:

```
[#|2009-10-03T10:37:53.465-0400|INFO|glassfish|javax.enterprise.system.
container.web.com.sun.enterprise.web|_ThreadID=39;_ThreadName=Thread-
2;|PWC1412: WebModule[/nbservlet30listener] ServletContext.log():New
request initialized|#]
[#|2009-10-03T10:37:53.517-0400|INFO|glassfish|javax.enterprise.system.
container.web.com.sun.enterprise.web|_ThreadID=39;_ThreadName=Thread-
2;|PWC1412: WebModule[/nbservlet30listener] ServletContext.log():Request
destroyed|#]
```

Implementing the other listener interfaces is just as simple and straightforward.

Pluggability

When the original Servlet API was released back in the late 1990s, writing servlets was the only way of writing server-side web applications in Java. Since then, several standard Java EE and third-party frameworks have been built on top of the Servlet API. Examples of such standard frameworks include JSP's and JSF, third-party frameworks include Struts, Wicket, Spring Web MVC, and several others.

Nowadays, very few (if any) Java web applications are built using the Servlet API directly. Instead, the vast majority of projects utilize one of the several available Java web application frameworks. All of these frameworks use the Servlet API "under the covers". Therefore, setting up an application to use one of these frameworks has always involved making some configuration in the application's `web.xml` deployment descriptor. In some cases, some applications use more than one framework. This tends to make the `web.xml` deployment descriptor fairly large and hard to maintain.

Servlet 3.0 introduces the concept of pluggability. Web application framework developers now have not one, but two ways to avoid having application developers modify the web.xml deployment descriptor in order to use their framework. Framework developers can choose to use annotations instead of a web.xml to configure their servlets. After doing this, all that is needed to use the framework is to include the library JAR file(s) provided by the framework developers in the application's WAR file. Alternatively, framework developers may choose to include a web-fragment.xml file as part of the JAR file to be included in web applications that use their framework.

web-fragment.xml is almost identical to web.xml. The main difference is that the root element of a web-fragment.xml file is <web-fragment> as opposed to <web-app>. The following code example illustrates a sample web-fragment.xml file:

```
<?xml version="1.0" encoding="UTF-8"?>
<web-fragment version="3.0" xmlns="http://java.sun.com/xml/ns/javaee"
  xmlns:xsi="http://www.w3.org/2001/XMLSchema-instance"
  xsi:schemaLocation="http://java.sun.com/xml/ns/javaee
  http://java.sun.com/xml/ns/javaee/web-fragment_3_0.xsd">
  <servlet>
    <servlet-name>WebFragment</servlet-name>
    <servlet-class>
      net.ensode.glassfishbook.webfragment.WebFragmentServlet
    </servlet-class>
  </servlet>
  <servlet-mapping>
    <servlet-name>WebFragment</servlet-name>
    <url-pattern>/WebFragment</url-pattern>
  </servlet-mapping>
</web-fragment>
```

As we can see, web-fragment.xml is almost identical to a typical web.xml. In this simple example we only use the <servlet> and <servlet-mapping> elements. However, all other usual web.xml elements such as <filter>, <filter-mapping>, and <listener> are available as well.

As specified in our web-fragment.xml file, our servlet can be invoked via its URL pattern, /WebFragment. Therefore, the URL to execute our servlet, once deployed as part of a web application, would be http://localhost:8080/webfragmentapp/WebFragment. Of course, the host name, port, and context root must be adjusted as appropriate.

All we need to do for GlassFish or any Java EE 6-compliant application server to pick up the settings in `web-fragment.xml` is to place the file in the `META-INF` folder of the library where we pack our servlet, filter, and/or listener, then place our library's JAR file in the `lib` directory of the WAR file containing our application.

Configuring web applications programmatically

In addition to allowing us to configure web applications through annotations and through a `web-fragment.xml` file, Servlet 3.0 also allows us to configure our web applications programmatically at runtime.

The `ServletContext` class has new methods to configure servlets, filters, and listeners programmatically. The following example illustrates how to configure a servlet programmatically at runtime, without resorting to the `@WebServlet` annotation or to XML:

```
package net.ensode.glassfishbook.servlet;

import javax.servlet.ServletContext;
import javax.servlet.ServletContextEvent;
import javax.servlet.ServletContextListener;
import javax.servlet.ServletException;
import javax.servlet.ServletRegistration;
import javax.servlet.annotation.WebListener;

@WebListener()
public class ServletContextListenerImpl implements
  ServletContextListener
{
  @Override
  public void contextInitialized(ServletContextEvent
    servletContextEvent)
  {
    ServletContext servletContext =
        servletContextEvent.getServletContext();
    try
    {
      ProgrammaticallyConfiguredServlet servlet = servletContext.
          createServlet(ProgrammaticallyConfiguredServlet.class);
      servletContext.addServlet("ProgrammaticallyConfiguredServlet",
          servlet);
      ServletRegistration servletRegistration =
          servletContext.getServletRegistration(
          "ProgrammaticallyConfiguredServlet");
```

```
        servletRegistration.addMapping(
            "/ProgrammaticallyConfiguredServlet");
      }
      catch (ServletException servletException)
      {
        servletContext.log(servletException.getMessage());
      }
    }
    @Override
    public void contextDestroyed(ServletContextEvent
      servletContextEvent)
    {
    }
  }
```

In this example, we invoke the `createServlet()` method of `ServletContext` to create the servlet that we are about to configure. This method takes an instance of `java.lang.Class` corresponding to our servlet's class. This method returns a class implementing `javax.servlet.Servlet` or any of its child interfaces (thanks to Generics, a Java language feature introduced in Java 5, we don't need to explicitly cast the return value to the actual type of our servlet).

Once we create our servlet, we need to invoke `addServlet()` on our `ServletContext` instance to register our servlet with the servlet container. This method takes two parameters: the first being a `String` corresponding to the servlet name, the second being the servlet instance returned by a call to `createServlet()`.

Once we have registered our servlet, we need to add a URL mapping to it. In order to do this, we need to invoke the `getServletRegistration()` method on our `ServletContext` instance, passing the servlet name as a parameter. This method returns the servlet container's implementation of `javax.servlet.ServletRegistration`. From this object, we need to invoke its `addMapping()` method, passing the URL mapping we wish our servlet to handle.

Our example servlet is very simple. It simply displays a text message on the browser.

```
package net.ensode.glassfishbook.servlet;

import java.io.IOException;
import javax.servlet.ServletException;
import javax.servlet.ServletOutputStream;
import javax.servlet.http.HttpServlet;
import javax.servlet.http.HttpServletRequest;
import javax.servlet.http.HttpServletResponse;
```

```
public class ProgrammaticallyConfiguredServlet extends HttpServlet
{
  @Override
  protected void doGet(HttpServletRequest request,
    HttpServletResponse response) throws ServletException,
    IOException
  {
    ServletOutputStream outputStream = response.getOutputStream();
    outputStream.println("This message was generated from a servlet
      that was " + "configured programmatically.");
  }
}
```

After packing our code in a WAR file, deploying to GlassFish and pointing the browser to the appropriate URL (`http://localhost:8080/programmaticservletwebapp/ProgrammaticallyConfiguredServlet`, assuming we packaged the application in a WAR file named `programmaticservletwebapp.war` and didn't override the default context root), we should see the following message in the browser:

This message was generated from a servlet that was configured programmatically.

The `ServletContext` interface has methods to create and add servlet filters and listeners. They work very similarly to the way the `addServlet()` and `createServlet()` methods work, therefore we won't be discussing them in detail. Refer to the Java EE 6 API documentation at `http://java.sun.com/javaee/6/docs/api/` for details.

Asynchronous processing

Traditionally, servlets have created a single thread per request in Java web applications. After a request is processed, the thread is made available for other requests to use. This model works fairly well for traditional web applications in which HTTP requests are relatively few and far in between. However, most modern web applications take advantage of Ajax (Asynchronous JavaScript and XML), a technique that makes web applications behave much more responsively than traditional web applications. Ajax has the side effect of generating a lot more HTTP requests than traditional web applications. If some of these threads block for a long time waiting for a resource to be ready or are doing anything that takes a long time to process, it is possible our application may suffer from thread starvation.

To alleviate the situation described in the previous paragraph, the Servlet 3.0 specification introduced asynchronous processing. Using this new capability, we are no longer limited to a single thread per request. We can now spawn a separate thread and return the original thread back to the pool to be reused by other clients.

The following example illustrates how to implement asynchronous processing using the new capabilities introduced in Servlet 3.0:

```
package net.ensode.glassfishbook.asynchronousservlet;

import java.io.IOException;
import java.util.logging.Level;
import java.util.logging.Logger;
import javax.servlet.AsyncContext;
import javax.servlet.ServletException;
import javax.servlet.annotation.WebServlet;
import javax.servlet.http.HttpServlet;
import javax.servlet.http.HttpServletRequest;
import javax.servlet.http.HttpServletResponse;

@WebServlet(name = "AsynchronousServlet", urlPatterns = {
  "/AsynchronousServlet"}, asyncSupported = true)
public class AsynchronousServlet extends HttpServlet
{
  @Override
  protected void doGet(HttpServletRequest request,
    HttpServletResponse response) throws ServletException,
    IOException
  {
    final Logger logger =
      Logger.getLogger(AsynchronousServlet.class.getName());
    logger.log(Level.INFO, "--- Entering doGet()");
    final AsyncContext ac = request.startAsync();
    logger.log(Level.INFO, "---- invoking ac.start()");
    ac.start(new Runnable()
    {
      @Override
      public void run()
      {
        logger.log(Level.INFO, "inside thread");
        try
        {
          //simulate a long running process.
          Thread.sleep(10000);
        }
        catch (InterruptedException ex)
        {
          Logger.getLogger(AsynchronousServlet.class.getName()).
            log(Level.SEVERE, null, ex);
        }
        try
        {
```

```
                ac.getResponse().getWriter().println("You should see this
                  after a brief wait");
                ac.complete();
              }
              catch (IOException ex)
              {
                Logger.getLogger(AsynchronousServlet.class.getName()).
                  log(Level.SEVERE, null, ex);
              }
            }
          });
          logger.log(Level.INFO, "Leaving doGet()");
        }
      }
```

The first thing we need to do to make sure our asynchronous processing code works as expected is to set the `asyncSupported` attribute of the `@WebServlet` annotation to `true`.

To actually spawn an asynchronous process, we need to invoke the `startAsync()` method on the instance of `HttpServletRequest` that we receive as a parameter in the `doGet()` or `doPost()` method in our servlet. This method returns an instance of `javax.servlet.AsyncContext`. This class has a `start()` method that takes an instance of a class implementing `java.lang.Runnable` as its sole parameter. In our example, we used an anonymous inner class to implement `Runnable` in line. Of course, a standard Java class implementing `Runnable` can be used as well.

When we invoke the `start()` method of `AsyncContext`, a new thread is spawned and the `run()` method of the `Runnable` instance is executed. This thread runs in the background, the `doGet()` method returns immediately, and the request thread is immediately available to service other clients. It is important to notice that even though the `doGet()` method returns immediately, the response is not committed until after the thread spawned finishes. It can signal it has finished processing by invoking the `complete()` method on `AsyncContext`.

In the previous example, we sent some entries to the GlassFish log file to illustrate better what is going on. Observing the GlassFish log right after our servlet executes, we should notice that all log entries are written to the log within a fraction of a second of each other. The message **You should see this after a brief wait** isn't shown in the browser until after the log entry indicating that we are leaving the `doGet()` method, gets written to the log.

Summary

This chapter covered how to develop, configure, package, and deploy servlets.

We also covered how to process HTML form information by accessing the HTTP request object.

Additionally, forwarding HTTP requests from one servlet to another was covered, as well as redirecting the HTTP response to a different server.

We also discussed how to persist objects in memory across requests by attaching them to the servlet context and the HTTP session.

Finally, we covered all the major new features of Servlet 3.0, including configuring web applications via annotations, pluggability through `web-fragment.xml`, programmatic servlet configuration, and asynchronous processing.

3
JavaServer Pages

In the previous chapter, we saw how to develop Java servlets. Servlets are great for handling form input, but servlet code that outputs HTML markup to the browser tends to be cumbersome to write, read, and debug. A better way to send output to the browser is through **JavaServer Pages (JSPs)**.

The following topics will be covered in this chapter:

- Developing our first JSP
- Implicit JSP objects
- JSPs and JavaBeans
- Reusing JSP content
- Writing custom tags

Introduction to JavaServer Pages

In the early days, servlets were the only API available to develop server-side web applications in Java. Servlets had a number of advantages over CGI scripts, which were (and to some extent, still are) prevalent in those days. Some of the advantages of servlets over CGI scripts included increased performance and enhanced security.

However, servlets also had one major disadvantage. As the HTML code to be rendered in the browser needed to be embedded in Java code, most servlet code was very hard to maintain. To overcome this limitation, Java Server Pages (JSP) technology was created. JSPs use a combination of static HTML content and dynamic content to generate web pages. As the static content is separate from the dynamic content, JSP pages are a lot easier to maintain than servlets that generate HTML output.

In most modern applications using JSPs, servlets are still used. However, they typically assume the role of a controller in the **Model-View-Controller** (**MVC**) design pattern, with JSPs assuming the role of a view. As controller servlets have no user interface, we don't run into the issue of having HTML markup inside Java code.

In this chapter, we will cover how to develop server-side web applications using JavaServer Pages technology.

Developing our first JSP

JSPs are basically pages containing both static HTML markup and dynamic content. Dynamic content can be generated by using snippets of Java code called scriptlets or by using standard or custom JSP tags. Let's look at a very simple JSP code that displays the current server time in the browser:

```
<%@ page language="java" contentType="text/html; charset=UTF-8"
  pageEncoding="UTF-8"%>
<%@ page import="java.util.Date" %>

<!DOCTYPE html PUBLIC "-//W3C//DTD HTML 4.01 Transitional//EN"
  "http://www.w3.org/TR/html4/loose.dtd">
<html>
  <head>
    <meta http-equiv="Content-Type" content="text/html;
      charset=UTF-8">
    <title>Server Date And Time</title>
  </head>
  <body>
    <p>Server date and time: <% out.print(new Date()); %>
    </p>
  </body>
</html>
```

To deploy this JSP, all that needs to be done is to put it in a WAR file. Like we mentioned before, the easiest way to deploy the WAR file is to copy it to `[glassfish installation directory]/glassfish/domains/domain1/autodeploy`.

Quickly deploying simple JSPs

Simple JSPs can be quickly deployed without having to package them in a WAR file by copying them to `[glassfish installation directory]/glassfish/domains/domain1/docroot/`, and previewed in the browser by pointing them to `http://localhost:8080/jspname.jsp`.

After a successful deployment, pointing the browser to `http://localhost:8080/firstjsp/first.jsp` should result in a page like the following:

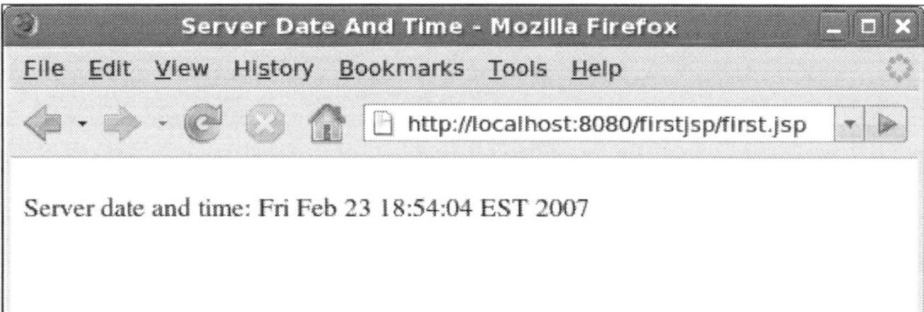

The **Server date and time:** string came from the static text immediately following the `<p>` tag in the JSP page. The actual date and time displayed is the server's date and time. The value came from the output of the code between the `<%` and `%>` delimiters. We can place any valid Java code between these two delimiters. Code inside these delimiters is known as a **scriptlet**. The scriptlet in the previous JSP makes use of the `out` implicit object. JSP implicit objects are objects that can be readily used in any JSP; no need to declare or initialize them. The `out` implicit object is an instance of `javax.servlet.jsp.JspWriter`. It can be thought of as an equivalent of calling the `HttpServletResponse.getWriter()` method.

The first two lines in the previous JSP are **JSP page directives**. A JSP page directive defines attributes that apply to the entire JSP page. A JSP page directive can have several attributes. In the previous example, the first page directive sets the `language`, `contentType`, `charset`, and `PageEncoding` attributes. The second one adds an `import` statement to the page.

As can be seen in the example, JSP page directive attributes can be combined in a single directive, or a separate page directive can be used for each attribute.

The following table lists all attributes for the page directive:

Attribute	Description	Valid values	Default value
`autoFlush`	Determines whether the output buffer should be flushed automatically when it is full.	`true` or `false`	`true`
`buffer`	The output buffer size in kilobytes.	`Nkb`, where `N` is an integer number. `"none"` is also a valid value.	`8kb`
`contentType`	Determines the page's HTTP response MIME type and character encoding.	Any valid MIME type and character encoding combination.	`text/html ; charset= ISO-8859-1`
`deferredSyntaxAllowedAsLiteral`	In earlier versions of the JSP specification, the #{} syntax for the expression language was not reserved. For backwards compatibility purposes, this attribute sets any expressions using this syntax to be string literals.	`true` or `false`	`false`
`errorPage`	Indicates which page to navigate when the JSP throws an exception.	Any valid relative URL to another JSP.	N/A
`extends`	Indicates the class this JSP extends.	The fully qualified name for the JSP's parent class.	N/A

Attribute	Description	Valid values	Default value
`import`	Imports one or more classes to be used in scriptlets.	A fully qualified name of a class to import or the full package name + ".*" to import all necessary classes from the package (for example, `<%@ page import java.util.* %>`).	N/A
`info`	The value for this attribute is incorporated into the compiled JSP. It can later be retrieved by calling the page's `getServletInfo()` method.	Any string.	N/A
`isELIgnored`	Setting this value to `true` prevents expression language expressions from being interpreted.	`true` or `false`	`false`
`isErrorPage`	Determines if the page is an error page.	`true` or `false`	`false`
`isThreadSafe`	Determines whether the page is thread safe.	`true` or `false`	`true`
`language`	Determines the scripting language used in scriptlets, declarations, and expressions in the JSP page.	Any scripting language that can execute in the Java Virtual Machine (groovy, jruby, and so on).	`java`

Attribute	Description	Valid values	Default value
`pageEncoding`	Determines the page encoding, for example, "UTF-8".	Any valid page encoding.	N/A
`session`	Determines whether the page has access to the HTTP session.	`true` or `false`	`true`
`trimDirectiveWhitespaces`	When JSPs are rendered as HTML in the browser, the generated markup frequently has a lot of blank lines in it. Setting this attribute to `true` prevents these extraneous blank lines from being generated in the markup.	`true` or `false`	`false`

Of the attributes in the table, `errorPage`, `import`, and `isErrorPage` are the most commonly used. Others have sensible defaults.

When deployed to the application server, JSPs are translated into (compiled into) servlets. The `extends` attribute of the page directive indicates the generated servlet's parent class. The value of this attribute must be a subclass of `javax.servlet.GenericServlet`.

Although the `language` attribute can accept any language that can execute in the Java Virtual Machine, it is extremely rare to use any language other than Java.

JSP implicit objects

JSP implicit objects are objects that can be used in a JSP without having to be declared or initialized. They are actually declared and initialized behind the scenes by the application server when the JSP is deployed.

In the previous section's example, we used the JSP implicit object `out`. This object, for all practical purposes, is equivalent to calling the `HttpResponse.getWriter()` method in a servlet. In addition to the `out` object, there are several other implicit objects that can be used in JSP scriptlets. These implicit objects are listed in the following table:

Implicit object	Implicit object class	Description
application	javax.servlet.ServletContext	Equivalent to calling the getServletContext() method in a servlet.
config	javax.servlet.ServletConfig	Equivalent to invoking the getServletConfig() method in a servlet.
exception	java.lang.Throwable	Only accessible if the page directive's isErrorPage attribute is set to true. Provides access to the exception that was thrown, that led to the page being invoked.
out	javax.servlet.jsp.JspWriter	Equivalent to the return value of HttpServletResponse.getWriter().
page	java.lang.Object	Provides access to the page's generated servlet.
pageContext	javax.servlet.jsp.PageContext	Provides several methods for managing the various web application scopes (request, session, application). Refer to the JavaDoc for PageContext at http://java.sun.com/javaee/5/docs/api/javax/servlet/jsp/PageContext.html.
request	javax.servlet.ServletRequest	Equivalent to the instance of HttpServletRequest we obtain as a parameter of the doGet() and doPost() methods in a servlet.
response	javax.servlet.ServletResponse	Equivalent to the instance of HttpServletResponse we obtain as a parameter of the doGet() and doPost() methods in a servlet.
session	javax.servlet.http.HttpSession	Equivalent to the return value of the HttpServletRequest.getSession() method.

The following example JSP illustrates the use of several of the JSP implicit objects:

```
<%@ page language="java" contentType="text/html; charset=UTF-8"
  pageEncoding="UTF-8"%>
<!DOCTYPE html PUBLIC "-//W3C//DTD HTML 4.01 Transitional//EN"
  "http://www.w3.org/TR/html4/loose.dtd">
<%@page import="java.util.Enumeration"%>
```

```
<html>
  <head>
    <meta http-equiv="Content-Type" content="text/html;
      charset=UTF-8">
    <title>Implicit Objects Demo</title>
  </head>
  <body>
    <p>This page uses JSP Implicit objects to attach objects to the
      request, session, and application scopes.<br />
      It also retrieves some initialization parameters sent in the
      web.xml configuration file.<br />
      The third thing it does is get the buffer size from the
      implicit response object.<br />
    </p>
    <p>
      <%
        application.setAttribute("applicationAttribute", new String(
          "This string is accessible across sessions."));

        session.setAttribute("sessionAttribute", new String(
          "This string is accessible across requests"));

        request.setAttribute("requestAttribute", new String(
          "This string is accessible in a single request"));

        Enumeration initParameterNames =
          config.getInitParameterNames();

        out.print("Initialization parameters obtained ");
        out.print("from the implicit <br/>");
        out.println("config object:<br/><br/>");
        while (initParameterNames.hasMoreElements())
        {
          String parameterName =
            (String) initParameterNames.nextElement();
          out.print(parameterName + " = ");
          out.print(config.getInitParameter((String) parameterName));
          out.print("<br/>");
        }
        out.println("<br/>");
        out.println("Implicit object <b>page</b> is of type "
          + page.getClass().getName() + "<br/><br/>");
        out.println("Buffer size is: " + response.getBufferSize()
          + " bytes");
      %>
```

```
      </p>
      <p>
        <a href="implicitobjects2.jsp">
          Click here to continue.
        </a>
      </p>
    </body>
  </html>
```

This JSP utilizes most of the implicit objects available to JSP scriptlets. The first thing it does is attach objects to the `application`, `session`, and `request` implicit objects. It then gets all initialization parameters from the implicit `config` object and displays their names and values on the browser by using the implicit `out` object. Next, it displays the fully qualified name of the implicit `page` object. Finally, it displays the buffer size by accessing the implicit `response` object.

JSP (and optionally servlet) initialization parameters are declared in the application's `web.xml` file. For this application, the `web.xml` file looks as follows:

```
<?xml version="1.0" encoding="UTF-8"?>
<web-app version="2.4" xmlns="http://java.sun.com/xml/ns/j2ee"
         xmlns:xsi="http://www.w3.org/2001/XMLSchema-instance"
         xsi:schemaLocation="http://java.sun.com/xml/ns/j2ee
           http://java.sun.com/xml/ns/j2ee/web-app_2_4.xsd">
  <servlet>
    <servlet-name>ImplicitObjectsJsp</servlet-name>
    <jsp-file>/implicitobjects.jsp</jsp-file>
    <init-param>
      <param-name>webxmlparam</param-name>
      <param-value>
        This is set in the web.xml file
      </param-value>
    </init-param>
  </servlet>
  <servlet-mapping>
    <servlet-name>ImplicitObjectsJsp</servlet-name>
    <url-pattern>/implicitobjects.jsp</url-pattern>
  </servlet-mapping>
</web-app>
```

Remember that a JSP gets compiled into a servlet at runtime the first time it is accessed after deployment. As such, we can treat it as a servlet in the `web.xml` file. In order to be able to pass initialization parameters to a JSP, we must treat it like a servlet, as initialization parameters are placed between the `<init-param>` and `</init-param>` XML tags. As shown in the previous `web.xml` file, the parameter name is placed between the `<param-name>` and `</param-name>` tags, and the parameter value is placed between the `<param-value>` and `</param-value>` tags. A servlet (and a JSP) can have multiple initialization parameters. Each initialization parameter must be declared inside a separate `<init-param>` tag.

Notice that in the previous `web.xml` file, we declared a servlet mapping for our JSP. This was necessary to allow GlassFish's web container to pass initialization parameters to the JSP. As we didn't want the URL of the JSP to change, we used the JSP's actual URL as the value for the `<url-pattern>` tag. If we wanted to access the JSP via a different URL (not necessarily one ending in `.jsp`), we could have placed the desired URL inside the `<url-pattern>` tag.

At the bottom of `implicitobjects.jsp`, there is a hyperlink to a second JSP, called `implicitobjects2.jsp`. The markup and code for `implicitobjects2.jsp` looks as follows:

```
<%@ page language="java" contentType="text/html; charset=UTF-8"
  pageEncoding="UTF-8"%>
<!DOCTYPE html PUBLIC "-//W3C//DTD HTML 4.01 Transitional//EN"
  "http://www.w3.org/TR/html4/loose.dtd">
<%@page import="java.util.Enumeration"%>
<html>
  <head>
    <meta http-equiv="Content-Type" content="text/html;
      charset=UTF-8">
    <title>Sanity Check</title>
  </head>
  <body>
    <p>This page makes sure we can retrieve the application, session
      and request attributes set in the previous page. <br />
    </p>
    <p>applicationAttribute value is:
      <%=application.getAttribute("applicationAttribute")%>
      <br />
      sessionAttribute value is:
      <%=session.getAttribute("sessionAttribute")%>
      <br />
      requestAttribute value is:
      <%=request.getAttribute("requestAttribute")%>
      <br />
```

```
    </p>
    <p>
      The following attributes were found at the application scope:
      <br/><br/>
      <%
        Enumeration applicationAttributeNames = pageContext
          .getAttributeNamesInScope(pageContext.APPLICATION_SCOPE);
        while (applicationAttributeNames.hasMoreElements())
        {
          out.println(applicationAttributeNames.nextElement() +
            "<br/>");
        }
      %>
    </p>
    <p><a href="buggy.jsp">This hyperlink points to a JSP that will
      throw an exception.</a></p>
  </body>
</html>
```

In this second JSP, we retrieve the objects that were attached to the application, session, and request objects. The attached objects are obtained by calling the appropriate implicit object's `getAttribute()` method. Notice how all calls to the `getAttribute()` method are nested between the `<%=` and `%>` delimiters. Snippets of code between these delimiters are called **JSP expressions**. JSP expressions are evaluated and their return value is displayed in the browser without having to call the `out.print()` method.

This JSP also retrieves the names of all objects attached to the application scope and displays them in the browser window.

At the bottom of the previous JSP, there is a hyperlink to a third JSP. This third JSP is called `buggy.jsp`. Its only purpose is to demonstrate the `errorPage` attribute of the `page` directive, the `error` attribute of the `page` directive, and the `exception` implicit object. Therefore, it is not terribly complicated.

```
<%@ page language="java" contentType="text/html; charset=UTF-8"
  pageEncoding="UTF-8" errorPage="error.jsp" %>
<!DOCTYPE html PUBLIC "-//W3C//DTD HTML 4.01 Transitional//EN"
  "http://www.w3.org/TR/html4/loose.dtd">
<html>
  <head>
    <meta http-equiv="Content-Type" content="text/html;
      charset=UTF-8">
    <title>Buggy JSP</title>
  </head>
  <body>
```

```
    <p>
      This text will never be seen in the browser since the exception
        will be thrown before the page renders.
      <%
        Object o = null;
        out.println(o.toString()); //NullPointerException thrown
          here.
      %>
    </p>
  </body>
</html>
```

The only thing this JSP does is force a `NullPointerException`, which will result in GlassFish's servlet container directing the user to the page declared as an error page in the `errorPage` attribute of the `page` directive. This page is `error.jsp`; its markup and code is shown next:

```
<%@ page language="java" contentType="text/html; charset=UTF-8"
  pageEncoding="UTF-8" isErrorPage="true"%>
<!DOCTYPE html PUBLIC "-//W3C//DTD HTML 4.01 Transitional//EN"
  "http://www.w3.org/TR/html4/loose.dtd">
<%@page import="java.io.StringWriter"%>
<%@page import="java.io.PrintWriter"%>
<html>
  <head>
    <meta http-equiv="Content-Type" content="text/html;
      charset=UTF-8">
    <title>There was an error in the application</title>
  </head>
  <body>
    <h2>Exception caught</h2>
    <p>Stack trace for the exception is:<br />
      <%
        StringWriter stringWriter = new StringWriter();
        PrintWriter printWriter = new PrintWriter(stringWriter);
        exception.printStackTrace(printWriter);
        out.write(stringWriter.toString());
      %>
    </p>
  </body>
</html>
```

Notice how this page declares itself to be an error page by setting the `isErrorPage` attribute of the `page` directive to `true`. As this page is an error page, it has access to the `exception` implicit object. This page simply calls the `printStackTrace()` method of the `exception` implicit object and sends its output to the browser via the `out` implicit object. In a real application, a user-friendly error message would probably be displayed.

As the previous application consists only of three JSPs, packaging it for deployment simply consists of putting all the JSPs in the root of the WAR file and the `web.xml` file in its usual location (the `WEB-INF` subdirectory in the WAR file).

After deploying and pointing the browser to `http://localhost:8080/jspimplicitobjects/implicitobjects.jsp`, we should see `implicitobjects.jsp` rendered in the browser:

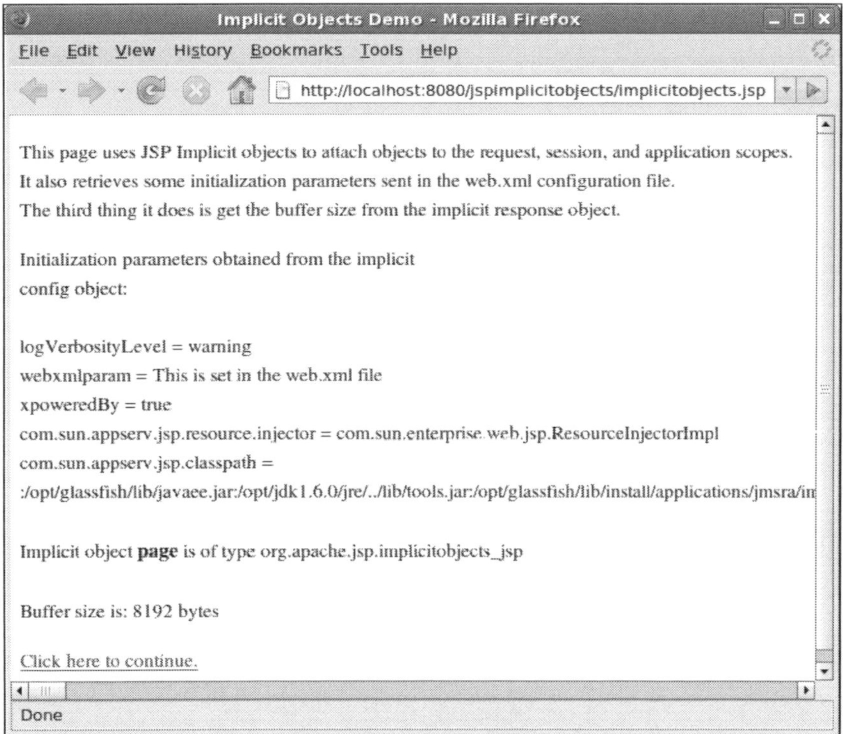

As we can see, the JSP has a number of "mysterious" initialization parameters in addition to the one we set in the application's `web.xml` file. These additional initialization parameters are set automatically by GlassFish's web container.

Clicking on the hyperlink at the bottom of the page takes us to `implicitobjects2.jsp`:

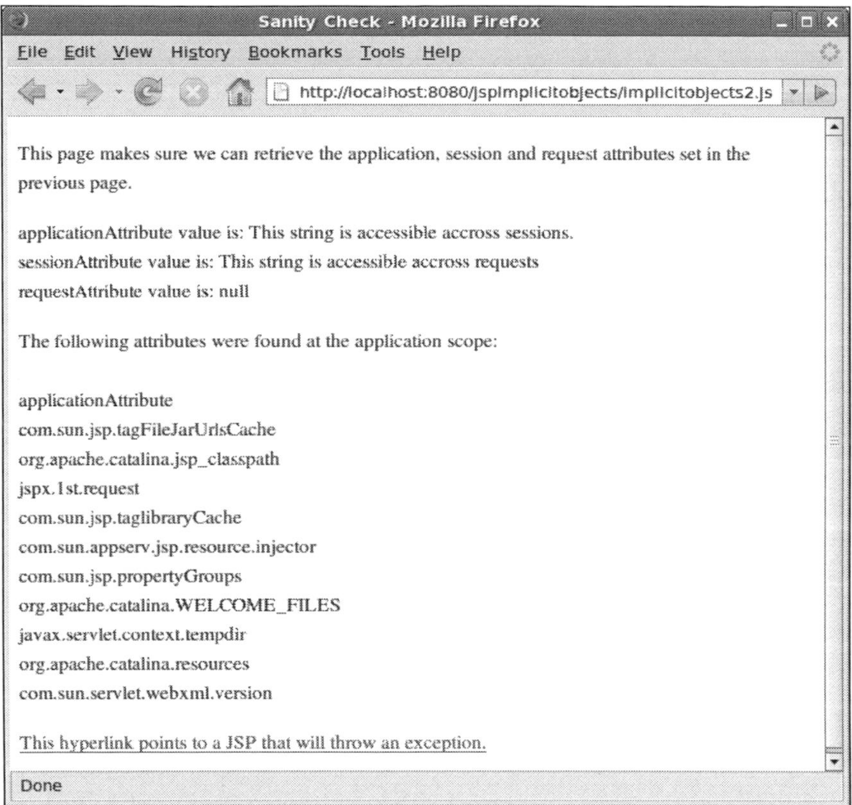

Notice how the value for the request attribute shows up as **null**. The reason for this is that when we clicked on the hyperlink on the previous page, a new HTTP request was created, therefore any attributes attached to the previous request were lost. If we had forwarded the request to this JSP, we would have seen the expected value on the browser window.

Notice how in addition to the attribute we attached to the application, GlassFish also attaches a number of other attributes to this implicit object.

Finally, clicking on the hyperlink at the bottom of the page takes us to the buggy JSP, which does not render. Instead, control is transferred to `error.jsp`:

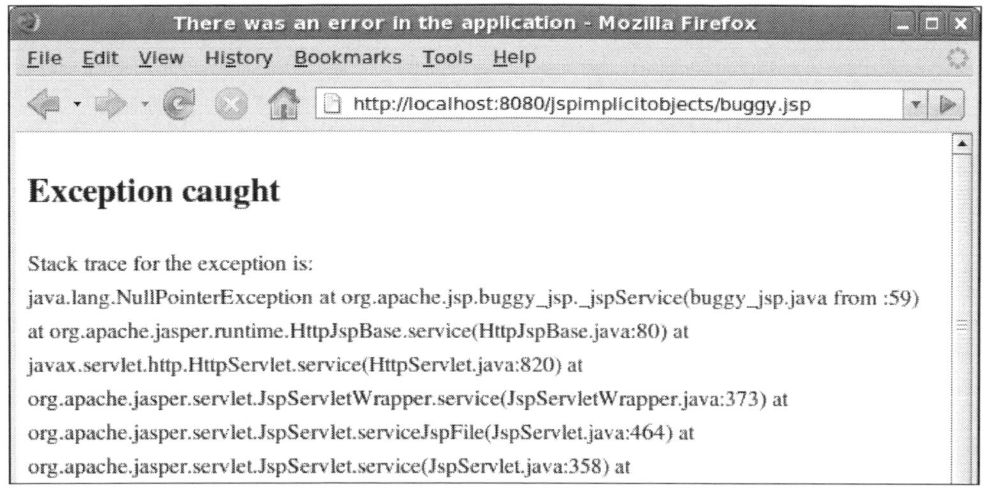

Nothing surprising is displayed here; we see the exception's stack trace as expected.

JSPs and JavaBeans

It is very easy to set and retrieve JavaBean properties with JSPs. A JavaBean is a type of Java class. In order for a class to qualify as a JavaBean, it must possess the following attributes:

- It must have a `public` constructor taking no arguments.
- Its variables must be accessed via getter and setter methods.
- It must implement `java.io.Serializable`.
- Although not a strict requirement, it's good coding practice to make all of JavaBean's member variables `private`.

Do not confuse JavaBeans with Enterprise JavaBeans. They are not the same thing. Enterprise JavaBeans are covered in detail in Chapter 9.

All examples in this section will use the following JavaBean to illustrate JSP and JavaBean integration:

```
package net.ensode.glassfishbook.javabeanproperties;
public class CustomerBean
{
  public CustomerBean()
  {

  }
  String firstName;
  String lastName;
  public String getFirstName()
  {
    return firstName;
  }
  public void setFirstName(String firstName)
  {
    this.firstName = firstName;
  }
  public String getLastName()
  {
    return lastName;
  }
  public void setLastName(String lastName)
  {
    this.lastName = lastName;
  }
}
```

As we can see, this class qualifies as a JavaBean as it meets all the requirements listed previously. Notice how the setter and getter method names follow a naming convention. While getter methods start with the word "get" followed by the property name, setter methods start with the word "set" followed by the property name. The only difference is that the property name is capitalized in the method names. It is important to follow these conventions for the JSP and JavaBean integration to work.

JSPs declare that they will use a JavaBean via the `<jsp:useBean>` tag. JavaBean properties are set via the `<jsp:setProperty>` tag and retrieved via the `<jsp:getProperty>` tag.

In JavaBean terminology, a property simply refers to one of the JavaBean's class variables.

The following example illustrates the use of these tags:

```
<%@ page language="java" contentType="text/html; charset=UTF-8"
  pageEncoding="UTF-8"%>
<jsp:useBean id="customer"
  class="net.ensode.glassfishbook.javabeanproperties.CustomerBean"
  scope="page"></jsp:useBean>
<jsp:setProperty name="customer" property="firstName"
  value="Albert" />
<jsp:setProperty name="customer" property="lastName" value="Chan" />
<!DOCTYPE html PUBLIC "-//W3C//DTD HTML 4.01 Transitional//EN"
  "http://www.w3.org/TR/html4/loose.dtd">
<html>
  <head>
    <meta http-equiv="Content-Type" content="text/html;
      charset=UTF-8">
    <title>JavaBean Properties</title>
  </head>
  <body>
    <form>
      <table cellpadding="0" cellspacing="0" border="0">
        <tr>
          <td align="right">First Name: </td>
          <td>
            <input type="text" name="firstName"
              value='<jsp:getProperty name="customer"
                property="firstName"/>'>
          </td>
        </tr>
        <tr>
          <td align="right">Last Name: </td>
          <td>
            <input type="text" name="lastName"
              value='<jsp:getProperty name="customer"
                property="lastName"/>'>
          </td>
        </tr>
        <tr>
          <td></td>
          <td><input type="submit" value="Submit"></td>
        </tr>
      </table>
    </form>
  </body>
</html>
```

As can be seen in this example, the `<jsp:useBean>` tag is typically used with three attributes: the `id` attribute sets an identifier for the bean so that we can refer to it later, the `class` attribute specifies the fully qualified name of the bean, and the `scope` attribute specifies the scope of the bean. The bean in this example has a scope of `page`. This scope is specific to JSPs and cannot be used with servlets. Objects in this scope can only be accessed by the JSP that declares it. Other valid values for the `scope` attribute are `application`, `session`, and `request`. If an attribute other than `page` is specified, the JSP searches for an object attached to the specified scope with a name matching the specified id. If it finds it, it uses it; otherwise, it attaches the bean to the specified scope. If no scope is specified, then the default scope is `page`. If the attached object is not an instance of the expected class, a `ClassCastException` is thrown.

Bean properties can be set by using the `<jsp:setProperty>` tag. The `name` attribute of this tag identifies the bean for which we are setting the property. Its value must match the value of the `id` attribute of the `<jsp:useBean>` tag. The `property` attribute value must match the name of one of the bean's properties. The `value` attribute determines the value to be assigned to the bean's property. Behind the scenes, the property's setter method is called by the `<jsp:setProperty>` tag..

The `<jsp:getProperty>` tag has two attributes: a `name` attribute and a `property` attribute. The `name` attribute identifies the bean we are obtaining the value from. Its value must match the `id` attribute of the bean's `<jsp:useBean>` tag. The `property` attribute identifies what bean property we want. The `<jsp:getProperty>` invokes the getter method corresponding to the property specified in its `property` attribute.

After packaging and deploying the previous JSP and pointing the browser to `http://localhost:8080/javabeanproperties/beanproperties1.jsp`, we should see a page like the following:

Notice how the form is pre-populated with the bean's properties, as we embedded the `<jsp:getProperty>` tags inside the `value` attribute of the HTML `input` tag.

In the previous example, the JSP itself set the bean's properties from hardcoded values and later accessed them via the `<jsp:getProperty>` tag. More often than not, bean attributes are set from request parameters. If we take the previous JSP and replace the following code fragment:

```
<jsp:setProperty name="customer" property="firstName"
  value="Albert" />
<jsp:setProperty name="customer" property="lastName" value="Chan" />
```

With this one:

```
<jsp:setProperty name="customer" property="firstName" param="fNm" />
<jsp:setProperty name="customer" property="lastName" param="lNm" />
```

The JSP will populate the bean's attributes from request parameters. The only difference between the modified JSP and the original one is that the `value` attribute of the `<jsp:setProperty>` tag has been replaced with the `param` attribute. When the `<jsp:setProperty>` tag has a `param` attribute, it looks for a request parameter name matching its value. If it finds it, it sets the corresponding bean property to the value of the request parameter.

Redeploying the application and pointing the browser to `http://localhost:8080/javabeanproperties/beanproperties2.jsp?fNm=Albert&lNm=Chang` (assuming the modified JSP was saved as `beanproperties2.jsp`) should result in the display of a page identical to the previous screenshot.

If request parameter names match the bean property names, there is no need to explicitly set each property name to the corresponding request attribute. There is a shortcut that will set each bean attribute to its corresponding value in the request. If we modify the JSP once again, this time replacing the code fragment:

```
<jsp:setProperty name="customer" property="firstName"
  param="fNm" />
<jsp:setProperty name="customer" property="lastName"
  param="lNm" />
```

With this one:

```
<jsp:setProperty name="customer" property="*"/>
```

The `<jsp:setProperty>` tag will now look for request parameter names matching bean property names and set the bean properties to the corresponding request parameters. Pointing the browser to `http://localhost:8080/javabeanproperties/beanproperties3.jsp?firstName=Albert&lastName=Chang` (assuming the modified JSP was saved as `beanproperties3.jsp`), we should once again see a page like the one in the previous screenshot displayed in the browser. Notice how in this case the request parameter names match the bean property names.

Even though the examples in this section dealt exclusively with `String` properties, the techniques demonstrated here work with numeric properties as well. Property values from the request or in the `<jsp:setProperty>` tag are automatically converted to the appropriate type.

Reusing JSP content

Most web applications' web pages contain certain areas that are identical across pages. For example, each page may display a company logo at the top or a navigation menu. Copying and pasting the code to generate these common areas is not very maintainable, because if a change needs to be made to one of them, the change must be done on every page.

When using JSPs to develop a web application, it is possible to define each of these areas in a single JSP, then include this JSP as a part of other JSPs. For example, we could have a JSP that renders the site's navigation menu, then have every other JSP include the navigation menu JSP to render the navigation menu. If the navigation menu needs to change, the change needs to be done only once. JSPs including the navigation menu JSP don't need to be changed.

There are two ways by which a JSP can be included in another JSP. It can be done via the `<jsp:include>` tag or via the `include` directive.

The following example illustrates the use of the `include` directive to include a JSP as part of a parent JSP:

```
<%@ page language="java" contentType="text/html; charset=UTF-8"
  pageEncoding="UTF-8"%>
<%! String pageName = "Main"; %>
<!DOCTYPE html PUBLIC "-//W3C//DTD HTML 4.01 Transitional//EN"
  "http://www.w3.org/TR/html4/loose.dtd">
<html>
  <head>
    <meta http-equiv="Content-Type" content="text/html;
      charset=UTF-8">
    <title>Main Page</title>
  </head>
  <body>
    <table cellpadding="0" cellspacing="0" border="1" width="100%"
      height="100%">
      <tr>
        <td width="100">
          <%@ include file="navigation.jspf"%>
        </td>
        <td>This is the main page.</td>
      </tr>
    </table>
  </body>
</html>
```

As can be seen in this example, the `include` directive is very straightforward to use. It takes a single attribute called `file`; the value of this attribute is the file to include. Notice that the included file in the example has an extension of `jspf`. This is the recommended extension for JSP fragments, that is, JSPs that do not render into a proper HTML page.

Notice the following line near the top of the markup:

```
<%! String pageName = "Main"; %>
```

This line is a **JSP declaration**. Any variables (or methods) declared in a JSP declaration are available to the JSP declaring it and to any JSPs included via the `include` directive.

The code and markup for `navigation.jspf` is shown next:

```
<b>Application Menu</b>
<ul>
  <li/> <a href="main.jsp">Main</a>
  <li/> <a href="secondary.jsp">Secondary</a>
</ul>
Current page: <%= pageName %>
```

Notice how `navigation.jspf` accesses the `pageName` variable declared in the parent JSP (in order for this to work, any JSP including `navigation.jspf` must declare a variable called `pageName`).

There is a third file called `secondary.jsp`. This file is almost identical to `main.jsp` and is not shown. The only differences between `main.jsp` and `secondary.jsp` are the values of the `pageName` variable, the page title, and the text inside the second cell in the table.

After packaging and deploying these files into a WAR file and pointing the browser to `http://localhost:8080/jspcontentreuse/main.jsp`, we should see a page like the following:

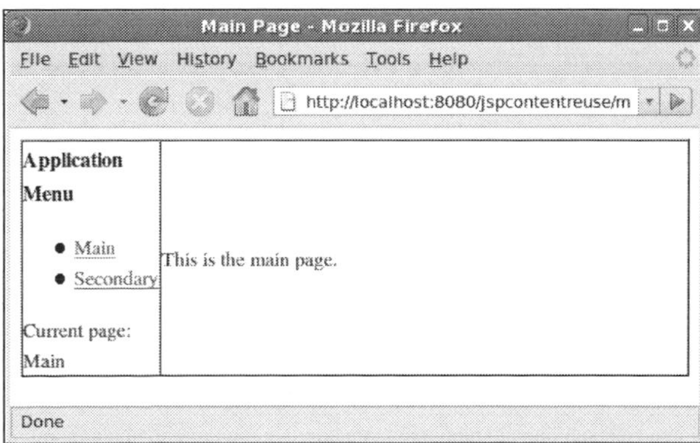

The menu on the left hand side is rendered by `navigation.jspf`. The main area is rendered by `main.jsp`. Clicking on the hyperlink labeled **Secondary** will take us to the secondary page, which is virtually identical to the main page.

We admit we are not using very fancy web design. The reason for this is that we want to keep the HTML as simple as possible, so that we can focus on the topic at hand.

JSP files included via a page directive are included at compile time, that is, when our JSP is translated into a servlet. This is the reason included JSPs have access to variables declared in the parent JSP.

When using the `<jsp:include>` tag, the included JSP is added at runtime. Therefore, it doesn't have access to any variable declared in the parent JSP.

The `<jsp:include>` tag has two attributes: a `page` attribute that sets the page to include and an optional `flush` attribute that determines if any existing buffer should be flushed before reading in the included JSP. Valid values for the `flush` attribute include `true` and `false`; it defaults to `false`.

The previous JSPs can be easily modified to use the `<jsp:include>` tag. All that needs to be done is replace the `include` directive with the equivalent `<jsp:include>` tag, and of course, remove the JSP expression from `navigation.jspf`, as it will be included at runtime and will not have access to it.

JSP custom tags

JSP technology allows software developers to create custom tags. Custom tags can be used in JSP along with standard HTML tags. There are several ways of developing custom tags. In this section, we will discuss the two most popular ways: extending the `javax.servlet.jsp.tagext.SimpleTagSupport` class and creating a tag file.

Extending SimpleTagSupport

One way we can create custom JSP tags is by extending the `javax.servlet.jsp.tagext.SimpleTagSupport` class. This class provides default implementations of all methods in the `javax.servlet.jsp.tagext.SimpleTag` interface plus some methods not defined in this interface. In most cases, all that needs to be done to create a custom tag this way is override the `SimpleTagSupport.doTag()` method.

Let's illustrate this approach with an example. Most HTML forms have an embedded table containing several rows of labels and input fields. Let's create a JSP custom tag that will generate each of these rows (to keep things simple, our tag will only generate text fields):

```
package net.ensode.glassfishbook.customtags;

import java.io.IOException;
import javax.servlet.jsp.JspContext;
import javax.servlet.jsp.JspException;
import javax.servlet.jsp.JspWriter;
import javax.servlet.jsp.tagext.SimpleTagSupport;

public class LabeledTextField extends SimpleTagSupport
{
  private String label;
  private String value = "";
  private String name;

  @Override
  public void doTag() throws JspException, IOException
  {
    JspContext jspContext = getJspContext();
    JspWriter jspWriter = jspContext.getOut();
    jspWriter.print("<tr>");
    jspWriter.print("<td>");
    jspWriter.print("<b>");
    jspWriter.print(label);
    jspWriter.print("</b>");
    jspWriter.print("</td>");
    jspWriter.print("<td>");
    jspWriter.print("<input type=\"text\" name=\"");
    jspWriter.print(name);
    jspWriter.print("\" ");
    jspWriter.print("value=\"");
    jspWriter.print(value);
    jspWriter.print("\"");
    jspWriter.print("/>");
    jspWriter.print("</td>");
    jspWriter.println("</tr>");
  }
```

```
    public String getLabel()
    {
      return label;
    }
    public void setLabel(String label)
    {
      this.label = label;
    }
    public String getName()
    {
      return name;
    }
    public void setName(String name)
    {
      this.name = name;
    }
    public String getValue()
    {
      return value;
    }
    public void setValue(String value)
    {
      this.value = value;
    }
  }
```

This class consists of an overriden version of the `doTag()` method and several attributes. Our `doTag()` method obtains a reference to an instance of `javax.servlet.jsp.JspWriter` by the `getJSPContext()sp` method. This method is defined in the tag's parent class and returns an instance of `javax.servlet.jsp.JspContext`. We then invoke the `getOut()` method of `JspContext`. This method returns an instance of `javax.servlet.jsp.JspWriter` that can be used to send output to the browser via its `print()` and `println()` methods. The rest of the `doTag()` method basically sends output to the browser via these two methods.

Notice how some of the calls to `jspWriter.print()` in the `doTag()` method take instance variables as their parameter. These attributes are set by the JSP containing the tag via the tag's **Tag Library Descriptor** file.

In order to be able to use custom tags in our JSPs, a Tag Library Descriptor (TLD) file must be created. The TLD tag for the previous custom tag is shown next:

```
<taglib xsi:schemaLocation="http://java.sun.com/xml/ns/
          javaee web-jsptaglibrary_2_1.xsd"
        xmlns="http://java.sun.com/xml/ns/javaee"
        xmlns:xsi="http://www.w3.org/2001/XMLSchema-instance"
        version="2.1">
  <tlib-version>1.0</tlib-version>
  <uri>DemoTagLibrary</uri>
  <tag>
    <name>labeledTextField</name>
    <tag-class>
      net.ensode.glassfishbook.customtags.LabeledTextField
    </tag-class>
    <body-content>empty</body-content>
    <attribute>
      <name>label</name>
      <required>true</required>
      <rtexprvalue>true</rtexprvalue>
    </attribute>
    <attribute>
      <name>value</name>
      <rtexprvalue>true</rtexprvalue>
    </attribute>
    <attribute>
      <name>name</name>
      <required>true</required>
      <rtexprvalue>true</rtexprvalue>
    </attribute>
  </tag>
</taglib>
```

A TLD file must contain a `<tlib-version>` element, which indicates the tag library version. It must also contain a `<uri>` element. The `<uri>` element is used in the JSP containing the tag. It is used to uniquely identify the tag library. Finally and most importantly, a TLD file must contain one or more `<tag>` elements. TLD files must be placed in the `WEB-INF` directory of the application's WAR file or one of its subdirectories. As illustrated in the previous example TLD file, the `<tag>` element contains several sub-elements:

- A `<name>` element that assigns a logical name to the custom tag.
- A `<tag-class>` element that identifies the fully qualified name for the custom tag.
- One or more `<attribute>` elements that define attributes for the custom tag.

The `<attribute>` element in turn can contain a number of sub-elements:

- A `<name>` element defining the name of the attribute. The value of this element must match the name of one of the tag's instance variables with a corresponding setter method.
- An optional `<required>` element indicating passing a value for the attribute if required. If this element is set to `true` and no value is sent to the attribute in the JSP, the page will fail to compile. The default value for this element is `false`.
- An optional `<rtexprvalue>` tag indicating if the attribute can contain a runtime expression as its value. If this element is set to `true`, then the tag will accept Unified Expression Language expressions as its value. The Unified Expression Language is discussed in detail later in the chapter.

> We are covering only the most commonly used elements of a TLD file. To see the complete list of TLD file elements, refer to the JSP 2.1 specification at `http://jcp.org/aboutJava/communityprocess/final/jsr245/index.html`.

Once we have the tag code and TLD, we are ready to use the tag in a JSP:

```
<%@ page language="java" contentType="text/html; charset=UTF-8"
  pageEncoding="UTF-8"%>
<%@taglib prefix="d" uri="DemoTagLibrary"%>
<!DOCTYPE html PUBLIC "-//W3C//DTD HTML 4.01 Transitional//EN"
  "http://www.w3.org/TR/html4/loose.dtd">
<html>
  <head>
    <meta http-equiv="Content-Type" content="text/html;
      charset=UTF-8">
    <title>Custom Tag Demo</title>
  </head>
  <body>
    <form>
      <table>
```

```
            <d:labeledTextField label="Line 1" name="line1" value="This
              is line 1"></d:labeledTextField>
            <d:labeledTextField label="Line 2" name="line2">
            </d:labeledTextField>
            <d:labeledTextField label="City" name="city">
            </d:labeledTextField>
            <d:labeledTextField label="State" name="state">
            </d:labeledTextField>
            <d:labeledTextField label="Zip" name="zip">
            </d:labeledTextField>
            <tr>
              <td></td>
              <td><input type="submit" value="Submit"></td>
            </tr>
          </table>
        </form>
      </body>
    </html>
```

This JSP uses our custom tag to generate a rudimentary address data entry form. The first thing we should notice about this JSP is the use of the `taglib` directive. This directive lets the JSP know that we will be using a custom tag library. The `uri` attribute of the `taglib` directive must match the value of the `<uri>` element in the tag library's TLD file. The value of the `prefix` attribute of the `taglib` directive is prepended before the name of any custom tag from the library we use. In the previous example, all `<d:labeledField>` attributes are uses of the custom tag we have developed. The `d` before the `:` in each of those tags corresponds to the value of the `prefix` attribute.

The next thing that should catch our eye in this example is the usage of the custom tag itself. Notice how every time we use the custom tag, we set a value for its `label` and `value` attributes. We must do this because these attributes were declared as `required` in the tag's TLD file. The values we set for the tag's attributes are automatically used to set the values of the tag's Java class instance variables. The name of the attribute matches the corresponding instance variable. Behind the scenes, the tag's class setter method for the appropriate instance variable is called.

After we package and deploy the JSP, custom tag code, and TLD file in a WAR file and deploy it, we should see that the previous JSP should render in the browser as displayed in the following screenshot:

Notice how only the first text field has been pre-populated. This is because it was the only one for which we set the `value` attribute.

If we look at the generated HTML markup from our JSP, we can see the markup that was actually generated from our custom tag:

```
<table>
  <tr>
    <td><b>Line 1</b></td>
    <td><input type="text" name="line1" value="This is line 1"/></td>
  </tr>
  <tr>
    <td><b>Line 2</b></td>
    <td><input type="text" name="line2" value=""/></td>
  </tr>
  <tr>
    <td><b>City</b></td>
    <td><input type="text" name="city" value=""/></td>
  </tr>
  <tr>
    <td><b>State</b></td>
    <td><input type="text" name="state" value=""/></td>
  </tr>
  <tr>
```

```
      <td><b>Zip</b></td>
      <td><input type="text" name="zip" value=""/></td>
    </tr>
    <tr>
      <td></td>
      <td><input type="submit" value="Submit"></td>
    </tr>
  </table>
```

For simplicity and brevity, only a portion of the generated markup is shown. All highlighted lines were generated by the custom tag.

Using tag files to create custom JSP tags

As was shown in the previous section, creating a custom tag by extending the `SimpleTagSupport` class involves writing some Java code to generate HTML markup. Code to accomplish this is usually hard to write and hard to read. An alternate way of creating custom JSP tags is by using tag files. This alternate method does not involve writing any Java code.

A tag file is very similar to a JSP. Tag filenames must end with a `.tag` extension and must be placed in a subdirectory called `tags` under the WAR file's `WEB-INF` directory. The following tag file generates a complete (and less rudimentary) address input field:

```
<%@ tag language="java"%>
<%@ attribute name="addressType" required="true"%>
<jsp:useBean id="address" scope="request"
  class="net.ensode.glassfishbook.customtags.AddressBean" />
<table cellpadding="0" cellspacing="0" border="0">
  <tr>
    <td align="right" width="70"><b>Line 1</b> </td>
    <td><input type="text" name="${addressType}_line1" size="30"
      maxlength="100" value="${address.line1}"></td>
  </tr>
  <tr>
    <td align="right"><b>Line 2</b> </td>
    <td><input type="text" name="${addressType}_line2" size="30"
      maxlength="100" value="${address.line2}"></td>
  </tr>
  <tr>
    <td align="right"><b>City</b> </td>
    <td><input type="text" name="${addressType}_city" size="30"
      value="${address.city}"></td>
```

```
    </tr>
    <tr>
      <td align="right"><b>State</b> </td>
      <td>
        <select name="${addressType}_state">
          <option value=""></option>
          <option value="AL"
            <% if(address.getState().equals("AL"))
              out.print (" selected "); %>>Alabama</option>
          <option value="AK"
            <% if(address.getState().equals("AK"))
              out.print (" selected "); %>>Alaska</option>
          <option value="AZ"
            <% if(address.getState().equals("AZ"))
              out.print (" selected "); %>>Arizona</option>
          <option value="AR"
            <% if(address.getState().equals("AR"))
              out.print (" selected "); %>>Arkansas</option>
          <option value="CA"
            <% if(address.getState().equals("CA"))
              out.print (" selected "); %>>California</option>
          <option value="CO"
            <% if(address.getState().equals("CO"))
              out.print (" selected "); %>>Colorado</option>
          <option value="CT"
            <% if(address.getState().equals("CT"))
              out.print (" selected "); %>>Conneticut</option>
          <option value="DC"
            <% if(address.getState().equals("DC"))
              out.print (" selected "); %>>District of Columbia
          </option>
          <option value="FL"
            <% if(address.getState().equals("FL"))
              out.print (" selected "); %>>Florida</option>
        </select>
      </td>
    </tr>
    <tr>
      <td align="right"><b>Zip</b> </td>
      <td><input type="text" name="${addressType}_zip" size="5"
        value="${address.zip}"></td>
    </tr>
  </table>
```

As can be seen in the example, a tag file is very similar to a JSP file. Just like a JSP, it can contain scriptlets and `set` and `get` JavaBean properties. One difference between tag files and JSPs is that tag files use a `tag` directive instead of a `page` directive. The most commonly used attribute of the `tag` directive is the `import` attribute, which just like in the JSP `page` directive, is used to import individual classes or packages to be used in the tag file.

Tag files can have an `attribute` directive that generates an attribute that can be set by the parent JSP file. The previous example creates a required attribute called `addressType`.

Notice that the value for the `name` attribute of each input field in the example tag file contains text like the following: `${addressType}_line1`. The first part of this string (`${addressType}`) is a special notation to obtain the value of the `addressType` attribute. This notation can also be used to obtain values of JavaBean properties. The syntax to obtain JavaBean properties using this notation is `${<bean name>.<property name>}`. The `value` attribute of each `input` field in the previous example uses this notation to obtain the value of a property of the address bean. The address bean is a simple JavaBean that declares several attributes along with their corresponding setter and getter methods.

> The ${} notation is part of the Unified Expression Language—a new expression language for the JSP 2.1 specification. This notation is compatible with the JSP expression language introduced in JSP 2.0. However, the unified expression language also supports the #{} notation. This new notation is not compatible with previous versions of the JSP specification. The #{} notation will be covered in detail in *Chapter 6, JavaServer Faces*.

As can be seen in the example, tag files can contain scriptlets. The scriptlets in the example compare the value of the state attribute in the state bean to each option in the select element, then set the appropriate element to be selected (for simplicity and brevity, only a small subset of all states was used).

Using a custom tag defined in a tag file is almost identical to using a tag defined using Java code:

```
<%@ page language="java" contentType="text/html; charset=UTF-8"
  pageEncoding="UTF-8"%>
<%@ taglib prefix="ct" tagdir="/WEB-INF/tags"%>
<!DOCTYPE html PUBLIC "-//W3C//DTD HTML 4.01 Transitional//EN"
  "http://www.w3.org/TR/html4/loose.dtd">
<html>
  <head>
```

```
    <meta http-equiv="Content-Type" content="text/html;
      charset=UTF-8">
    <title>Custom Tag Demo</title>
  </head>
  <body>
    <form>
    <h3>Shipping Address</h3>
    <ct:address addressType="shipping" />
  </body>
</html>
```

Notice how the `taglib` directive is used to import the tag library into the JSP. However, in this case, instead of using a `uri` attribute, a `tagdir` attribute is used to indicate the location of the tag library. All tag files located in the same directory are implicitly part of a tag library; no TLD file is necessary. However, it is possible to add a TLD for a tag library composed of tag files. The TLD for such a tag library must be named `implicit.tld` and it must be placed in the same directory as the tag files (in the previous example, `WEB-INF/tags`; tag libraries must be placed in this directory or any subdirectory of the `tags` directory).

In order for the previous JSP to work properly, an instance of `net.ensode.glassfishbook.customtags.AddressBean` must be attached to the request. The following servlet will create an instance of this class. Populate some of its fields and forward the request to the previous JSP.

```
package net.ensode.glassfishbook.customtags;

import java.io.IOException;
import java.io.PrintWriter;
import javax.servlet.ServletException;
import javax.servlet.http.HttpServlet;
import javax.servlet.http.HttpServletRequest;
import javax.servlet.http.HttpServletResponse;

public class CustomTagDemoServlet extends HttpServlet
{
  @Override
  protected void doGet(HttpServletRequest request,
    HttpServletResponse response)
  {
    AddressBean addressBean = new AddressBean();
    addressBean.setLine1("43623 Park Ridge Ct");
    addressBean.setCity("Orlando");
    addressBean.setState("FL");
    addressBean.setZip("00303");
```

```
        request.setAttribute("address", addressBean);
        try
        {
          request.getRequestDispatcher("customtagdemo2.jsp").forward
            (request,response);
        }
        catch (ServletException e)
        {
          e.printStackTrace();
        }
        catch (IOException e)
        {
          e.printStackTrace();
        }
      }
    }
```

Of course, a real application would probably obtain this information from a database. This simple example just instantiates the bean and populates it with some arbitrary attributes.

After packaging this JSP and tag file in a WAR file, deploying the WAR file, and pointing the browser to the servlet's URL (as defined in the `<servlet-mapping>` element of the application's `web.xml` file), we should see a page like the following:

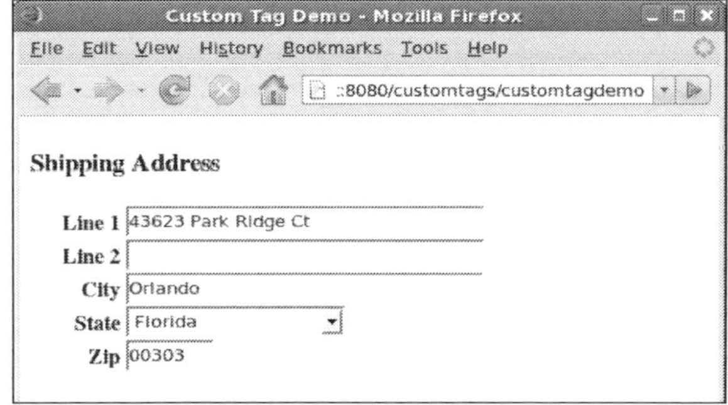

Unified Expression Language

In the previous section, we saw how the Unified Expression Language can be used to retrieve property values from JavaBeans. When JavaBeans properties are accessed this way, GlassFish's web container looks for a JavaBean attached with the given name to the page, request, session, and application scopes, in that order. It uses the first one to find and invoke the getter method corresponding to the property we want to obtain.

If we know in what scope the bean we want is attached to, we can obtain it from that scope directly, as JSP expressions have access to the JSP implicit objects. In the next example, we attach several instances of a JavaBean called `CustomerBean` to the different scopes. Before illustrating the JSP, let's take a look at the source code for this bean:

```
package net.ensode.glassfishbook.unifiedexprlang;

public class CustomerBean
{
  public CustomerBean()
  {

  }
  public CustomerBean(String firstName, String lastName)
  {
    this.firstName = firstName;
    this.lastName = lastName;
  }
  private String firstName;
  private String lastName;
  public String getFirstName()
  {
    return firstName;
  }
  public void setFirstName(String firstName)
  {
    this.firstName = firstName;
  }
  public String getLastName()
  {
    return lastName;
  }
  public void setLastName(String lastName)
  {
    this.lastName = lastName;
  }

  @Override
  public String toString()
  {
    StringBuffer fullNameBuffer = new StringBuffer();
    fullNameBuffer.append(firstName);
    fullNameBuffer.append(" ");
    fullNameBuffer.append(lastName);
    return fullNameBuffer.toString();
  }
}
```

This is a fairly simple JavaBean consisting of two properties and their corresponding setter and getter methods. In order for this class to qualify as a JavaBean, it must have a `public` constructor that takes no arguments. In addition to that constructor, we added a convenience constructor that takes two parameters to initialize the bean's properties. Additionally, the class overrides the `toString()` method so that its output is the customer's first and last names.

Like we mentioned before, the following JSP obtains instances of `CustomerBean` from the different scopes through the Unified Expression Language and shows the corresponding output in the browser window:

Before this JSP is executed, all instances of `CustomerBean` must be attached to the corresponding scope. We wrote a servlet that does this and then forwards the request to the JSP. For brevity, this servlet is not shown, but it is available as part of this book's code download.

```
<%@ page language="java" contentType="text/html; charset=UTF-8"
  pageEncoding="UTF-8"%>

<jsp:useBean scope="page" id="customer6"
  class="net.ensode.glassfishbook.unifiedexprlang.CustomerBean" />

<jsp:setProperty name="customer6" property="firstName"
  value="David" />
<jsp:setProperty name="customer6" property="lastName"
  value="Heffelfinger" />

<!DOCTYPE html PUBLIC "-//W3C//DTD HTML 4.01 Transitional//EN"
  "http://www.w3.org/TR/html4/loose.dtd">
<html>
  <head>
    <meta http-equiv="Content-Type" content="text/html;
      charset=UTF-8">
    <title>Unified Expression Language Demo</title>
  </head>
  <body>
    Customer attached to the application Scope:
    ${applicationScope.customer1}
    <br />
    <br />
    Customer attached to the session scope:
    ${sessionScope.customer2.firstName}
      ${sessionScope.customer2.lastName}
    <br />
    <br />
```

```
        Customer attached to the request scope:
        ${requestScope.customer3}
        <br />
        <br />
        Customer attached to the page scope:
        ${pageScope.customer6}
        <br />
        <br />
        List of customers attached to the session:
        <br />
        ${sessionScope.customerList[0]}
        <br />
        ${sessionScope.customerList[1].firstName}
        ${sessionScope.customerList[1].lastName}
        <br />
        <br />
      </body>
    </html>
```

The first highlighted line in this JSP looks for a bean attached to the application scope, with a name of `customer1`. As we aren't referencing any of the bean's properties, the bean's `toString()` method is invoked at that point.

The next two highlighted lines look for a bean attached to the session scope with a name of `customer2`. In this case, we are accessing individual properties. The first line accesses the `firstName` property and the second line accesses the `lastName` property. Behind the scenes, Glassfish's web container invokes the corresponding getter method for each property.

The next two highlighted lines obtain instances of `CustomerBean` from the request and page scopes respectively. Again, as we aren't accessing individual properties, the bean's `toString()` method is invoked.

The last three highlighted lines illustrate a very nice feature of the Unified Expression Language. In this case, instances of `CustomerBean` were not attached to the session directly. Instead, an `ArrayList` containing instances of `CustomerBean` was attached to the session. This `ArrayList` was attached with a name of `customerList`. As can be seen in these three lines, we can access individual elements of the `ArrayList` by placing the element number in brackets, similar to what we would do with an array in regular Java code. By the way, this technique also works with arrays as well as any other class implementing the `java.util.Collection` interface.

After packaging the previous JSP into a WAR file, deploying it, and pointing the browser to the appropriate URL, we should see it rendered in the browser:

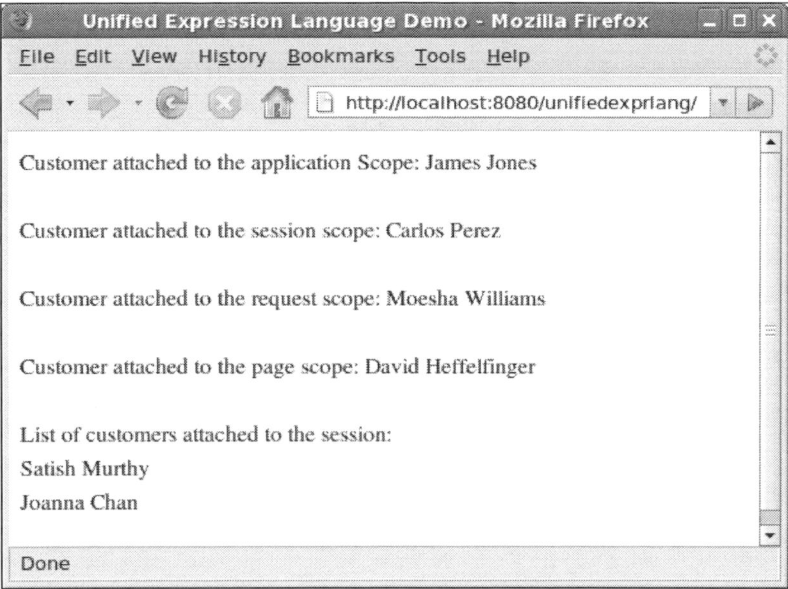

In this particular case, the `toString()` method outputs the customer's first and last names. Therefore, the output is indistinguishable from displaying these two properties next to each other.

Of course, the techniques shown in the example work on every scope. We can access a bean attached to any scope by not specifying any properties. Similarly, we can access bean properties on any scope and, of course, we can access individual elements to a collection or array attached to any scope.

JSP XML syntax

In addition to using the standard JSP syntax that we have been discussing throughout this chapter, JSPs can also be developed using XML syntax. JSPs developed using this alternate syntax are formally known as **JSP documents**. By convention, JSP document filenames end with the `.jspx` extension.

The following table compares the standard JSP syntax with the equivalent XML syntax:

JSP Feature	Standard Syntax Example	XML Syntax Example
Comment	<%-- comment --%>	<!-- comment -->
Declaration	<%! String s; %>	<jsp:declaration> String s; </jsp:declaration>
Expression	<%= new java.util.Date() %>	<jsp:expression> new java.util.Date() </jsp:expression>
Scriptlet	<% x = 5 + y; %>	<jsp:scriptlet> <![CDATA[x = 5 + y;]]> </jsp:scriptlet>
Attribute Directive	<%@ attribute name="addressType" required="true"%>	<jsp:directive.attribute name="addressType" required="true"/>
Include Directive	<%@ include file="navigation.jspf"%>	<jsp:directive.include file="navigation.jspf" />
Page Directive	<%@page import="java.util.Enumeration"%>	<jsp:directive.page import="java.util. Enumeration" />
Tag Directive	<%@ tag language="java"%>	<jsp:directive.tag language="java" />
Taglib Directive	<%@taglib prefix="d" uri="DemoTagLibrary"%>	<jsp:root xmlns:d="DemoTagLibrary">
Variable Directive	<%@ variable name-given="value" %>	<jsp:directive.variable name-given="value" />

As we can see from this table, developing JSPs using XML syntax is fairly easy and straightforward if we already know how to develop JSPs using the traditional syntax. We should note that the tag and attribute directives described in the table can only be used in JSP tags.

To develop a JSP using XML syntax, we simply need to use the XML syntax for all the JSP features we intend to use. Also, as JSP documents need to be valid XML, we need to make sure our JSPs are correctly formatted, making sure that each opening tag has a corresponding closing tag, for instance.

The following JSP document is a modified version of one of the examples we saw in the *JSPs and JavaBeans* section earlier in this chapter:

```
<?xml version="1.0" encoding="UTF-8"?>
<jsp:root xmlns:jsp="http://java.sun.com/JSP/Page" version="2.0">
  <jsp:directive.page language="java" contentType="text/html"
    pageEncoding="UTF-8"/>
    <jsp:useBean id="customer"
     class="net.ensode.glassfishbook.javabeanproperties.CustomerBean"
     scope="page">
    </jsp:useBean>
    <jsp:setProperty name="customer" property="firstName"
                     param="fNm" />
    <jsp:setProperty name="customer" property="lastName"
                     param="lNm" />
    <html>
      <head>
        <title>JavaBean Properties</title>
      </head>
      <body>
        <form>
          <table cellpadding="0" cellspacing="0" border="0">
            <tr>
              <td align="right">First Name: </td>
              <td><input type="text" name="firstName"
                         value='${customer.firstName}'/>
              </td>
            </tr>
            <tr>
              <td align="right">Last Name: </td>
              <td><input type="text" name="lastName"
                         value='${customer.lastName}'/>
              </td>
            </tr>
            <tr>
              <td></td>
              <td><input type="submit" value="Submit"/></td>
            </tr>
          </table>
        </form>
      </body>
    </html>
</jsp:root>
```

Notice that other than some minor changes to make the page XML compliant, all we had to do to use the XML syntax was to add a `<jsp:root>` element and change the page directive to use the XML syntax we described in the table earlier in this section.

Summary

This chapter covered a lot of ground. We talked about how to develop and deploy simple JSPs. We also covered how to access implicit objects such as `request`, `session`, and so on, from JSPs. Additionally, we covered how to set and get the values of JavaBean properties via the `<jsp:useBean>` tag. In addition to that, we covered how to include a JSP into another JSP at runtime via the `<jsp:include>` tag, and at compilation time via the JSP `include` directive. We also covered how to write custom JSP tags by extending `javax.servlet.jsp.tagext.SimpleTagSupport` or by writing TAG files. We also covered how to access JavaBeans and their properties via the Unified Expression Language.

Finally, we covered the JSP XML syntax that allows us to develop XML-compliant JavaServer Pages.

4
JSP Standard Tag Library

The **JSP Standard Tag Library** (**JSTL**) is a collection of standard JSP tags that perform several common tasks. This frees us from having to develop custom tags for these tasks, or from using a mix of tags from several organizations to do our work.

JSTL contains the following tags:

- Core tags that perform conditional logic and iteration through collections, among other things
- Format tags that perform string formatting and internationalization
- SQL tags that interact with a database
- XML tags for XML processing

Additionally, JSTL contains a number of functions that perform several tasks, the vast majority of which are for string manipulation.

In this chapter, we will cover each of the JSTL tag libraries, providing examples for the most commonly used tags and functions. Topics we will cover in this chapter include:

- Core JSTL tag library
- Formatting JSTL tag library
- SQL JSTL tag library
- XML JSTL tag library
- JSTL functions

Core JSTL tag library

Core JSTL tags perform tasks such as writing output to the browser, conditional display of segments in a page, and iterating through collections. Much of what the core JSTL tags do can be accomplished with scriptlets. However, the page is much easier to read and therefore more maintainable if core JSTL tags are used instead of scriptlets.

The following example shows a JSP using some of the most common JSTL core tags:

```
<%@ page language="java" contentType="text/html; charset=UTF-8"
  pageEncoding="UTF-8"%>
<%@taglib uri="http://java.sun.com/jsp/jstl/core" prefix="c"%>
<!DOCTYPE html PUBLIC "-//W3C//DTD HTML 4.01 Transitional//EN"
  "http://www.w3.org/TR/html4/loose.dtd">
<%@page import="java.util.ArrayList"%>
<html>
  <%
    ArrayList<String> nameList = new ArrayList<String>(4);
    nameList.add("David");
    nameList.add("Raymond");
    nameList.add("Beth");
    nameList.add("Joyce");
    request.setAttribute("nameList", nameList);
  %>
  <head>
    <meta http-equiv="Content-Type" content="text/html;
      charset=UTF-8">
    <title>Core Tag Demo</title>
  </head>
  <body>
    <c:set var="name" scope="page" value="${param.name}"></c:set>
    <c:out value="Hello"></c:out>
    <c:choose>
      <c:when test="${!empty name}">
        <c:out value="${name}"></c:out>
      </c:when>
      <c:otherwise>
        <c:out value="stranger"></c:out>
        <br />
        <c:out value="Need a name? Here are a few options:" />
        <br />
        <ul>
          <c:forEach var="nameOption"
                     items="${requestScope.nameList}">
```

```
                <li /><c:out value="${nameOption}"></c:out>
              </c:forEach>
            </ul>
          </c:otherwise>
        </c:choose>
        <c:remove var="name" scope="page" />
      </body>
    </html>
```

In a nutshell, this example looks for a request parameter called `name`. If it finds it, it displays the message "Hello `${name}`" in the browser (`${name}` is actually replaced with the value of the parameter). If the parameter is not found, it prints the message "Hello stranger" and gets a little smart with the user, suggesting a few names. This can be seen in the following screenshot:

The page employs the `taglib` directive to declare that it uses the JSTL core tag library. Although any prefix can be used for this library, using the prefix `c` is standard practice.

Before doing anything with JSTL, the page has a scriptlet that initializes an instance of `java.util.ArrayList` with some strings containing names and attaches `ArrayList` to the request (this would typically be done in a servlet or some other class, not in the JSP itself; it was done this way in the example for simplicity).

The first JSTL tag used in the page is the `<c:set>` tag. This tag sets the result of the expression defined in its `variable` attribute and stores it in a variable in the specified scope. The name of the variable is defined in the tag's `var` attribute. The scope of the variable is defined in the tag's `scope` attribute; if no scope is specified, the page scope is used by default. The expression to be evaluated is defined in the tag's `value` attribute.

Page scope is always the default

A number of JSTL tags contain a `var` attribute to define a variable in a scope specified by a `scope` attribute. In all cases, if no scope is specified, the page scope is used by default.

In the previous example, the expression is looking for the value of a request parameter with a name of "name". `param` is an implicit variable that resolves to a map using request parameter names as keys and request parameter values as values. This implicit variable is equivalent to calling the `getParameterMap()` method on the request. The value after the dot (name in the previous example) corresponds to the key we want to get from the parameter map (which in turn corresponds to the request parameter name).

The next core JSTL tag we see in the example is the `<c:out>` tag. This tag simply displays in the browser the value of the expression defined in its `value` attribute. In this particular case, the expression defined in the `value` attribute is a constant, therefore it is displayed verbatim in the browser output.

Next, we see the `<c:choose>` tag. This tag allows us to perform if/then/else like conditions in the page. The `<c:choose>` tag must contain one or more `<c:when>` tags and optionally a `<c:otherwise>` tag. The `<c:when>` tag contains a `test` attribute that must contain a Boolean expression. Once the expression in one of the `<c:when>` tags nested in a `<c:choose>` tag evaluates to true, the body of the tag is executed and the `test` attribute of other `<c:when>` tags nested inside the same `<c:choose>` tag is not evaluated.

The next new tag we see in the example is the `<c:otherwise>` tag. The body of this optional tag is executed if none of the expressions in any `<c:when>` tag evaluates to true. In the example, the body of the tag is executed when no request parameter with a name of "name" exists in the request, or if the value of the parameter is an empty `String`.

In the previous example, the `<c:when>` tag contains a `!` operator that negates a Boolean expression, just like in Java. The tag also contains an `empty` operator; this operator checks to see if a `String` is null or has a length of zero. The `test` attribute of the `<c:when>` tag can have several logical and/or relational operators that can be combined to build more complex expressions. All relational operators that can be used in the test attribute (or any other Unified Expression Language expression, for that matter) are listed in the following table:

Relational operator	Description
`==` or `eq`	Equals: evaluates to true if the expression on the left of the operator equals the expression on the right of the operator.
`>` or `gt`	Greater than: evaluates to true if the expression on the left of the operator is greater than the expression on the right of the operator.
`<` or `lt`	Less than: evaluates to true if the expression on the left of the operator is less than the expression on the right of the operator.
`>=` or `ge`	Greater than or equal: evaluates to true if the expression on the left of the operator is greater than or equal to the expression on the right of the operator.
`<=` or `le`	Less than or equal: evaluates to true if the expression on the left of the operator is less than or equal to the expression on the right of the operator.
`!=` or `ne`	Not equal: evaluates to true if the expression on the left of the operator is not equal to the expression on the right of the operator.

All of these symbolic operators work the same way as their equivalent Java operators, therefore, their use should be natural to any Java developer. In addition to allowing us to use the symbolic operators in the Unified Expression Language, all symbolic operators have a textual equivalent. These textual equivalents are used if we need our page to be valid XML, as using the symbolic operators typically results in an invalid XML markup.

In addition to relational operators, logical operators can also be used in Unified Expression Language expressions. Valid logical operators are listed in the following table:

<table>
<tr><th>Logical operator</th><th>Description</th></tr>
<tr><td><code>&&</code> or <code>and</code></td><td>And: evaluates to true if both the expression on the left of the operator and the one on the right of the operator are true.</td></tr>
<tr><td><code>||</code> or <code>or</code></td><td>Or: evaluates to true if either the expression on the left of the operator or the one on the right of the operator is true (or both).</td></tr>
<tr><td><code>!</code> or <code>not</code></td><td>Not: negates the expression on the right of the operator. If the expression evaluates to true, this operator makes it evaluate to false, and vice versa.</td></tr>
<tr><td><code>empty</code></td><td>Empty: evaluates to true if the value to the right of the operator is null or empty. The value to the right of the operator must be a <code>String</code> or a <code>Collection</code>.</td></tr>
<tr><td><code>E1?E2:E3</code></td><td>Conditional expression: if <code>E1</code> is true, evaluates to <code>E2</code>; otherwise, it evaluates to <code>E3</code>.</td></tr>
</table>

Just like with relational operators, logical operators work the same way as their Java equivalents. All of them, except the ternary operator and `empty`, have a symbolic and textual variant.

The Unified Expression Language also contains arithmetic operators. These are listed in the following table:

Arithmetic operator	Description
+	Addition: adds the values on the left and right of the operator.
- (binary)	Subtraction: subtracts the value on the right of the operator from the value on the left of the operator.
*	Multiplication: multiplies the values on the left and right of the operator
/ or `div`	Division: divides the values on the left (dividend) and right (divisor) of the operator.
`%` or `mod`	Modulo: divides the values on the left (dividend) and right (divisor) of the operator and returns the remainder.
- (unary)	Minus: multiplies the value to the right of the operator by -1.

All arithmetic operators must be used with numerical values.

After our brief discussion of the Unified Expression Language operators, we can now get back to discussing the example. The next new tag we see in the example is the `<c:forEach>` tag. This tag iterates through a `Collection`, array, or `Map`. In the example, it iterates through an instance of `java.util.ArrayList` attached to the request in the scriptlet defined earlier in the page. The `var` attribute of the `<c:forEach>` tag defines a variable to be used to access the current element in the collection. This variable is only visible inside the body of the tag. The `items` attribute of the `<c:forEach>` tag indicates the array, collection, or map to iterate through. The `<c:forEach>` tag has additional attributes that are not shown in the example: the `begin` attribute indicates the index of the first item to iterate from and the `end` attribute indicates the last item to iterate to. If the `begin` attribute is not set, iteration begins at the first item in the `Collection`, array, or `Map`. If the `end` attribute is not set, iteration ends at the last element of the `Collection`, array, or `Map`. An additional attribute of the `<c:forEach>` tag is the `step` attribute. It indicates the increment from one index to the next and defaults to 1. In addition to iterating through a `Collection`, array, or `Map`, the `<c:forEach>` tag can be used to execute its body a number of times. To use the `<c:forEach>` tag this way, its `items` attribute is omitted and its `begin` and `end` attributes are required.

The next new tag we see in the example is the `<c:remove>` tag. This tag is used to remove a variable attached to the scope specified in its `scope` attribute. If no scope is specified, the `<c:remove>` tag uses a default scope of page.

There are some additional core JSTL tags not shown in the example. These remaining tags are explained next.

The `<c:if>` tag is similar to the `<c:when>` tag; its body is executed if the expression defined by its `test` attribute is true. The `<c:if>` tag has two optional attributes: a `var` attribute that defines the name of a `Boolean` variable storing the results of the tag's `test` attribute, and a `scope` attribute defining the scope of the `var` attribute. The `<c:if>` tag should not be nested in a `<c:choose>` tag. Unlike the `<c:when>` tag, the expression defined in the `test` attribute of multiple `<c:if>` tags is evaluated, regardless of whether a previous `<c:if>` expression resolved to `true` or not.

The `<c:forTokens>` tag iterates over a delimiter separated string. The `<c:forTokens>` tag has two required attributes: `items` and `delims`. The `items` attribute value must be an expression resolving to a `String` or a `String` constant. The value of the `delims` attribute must be an expression or a `String` constant indicating the characters to be used as delimiters. Each individual character in the `delims` attribute will be used as a delimiter for the value of the item, similar to the way the `java.util.StringTokenizer` class works. Additionally, the `<c:forTokens>` tag has a `var` attribute that works essentially the same way as the `var` attribute of the `<c:forEach>` tag. That is, it defines a name for the current item in its `items` attribute, allowing it to be accessed in the body of the `<c:forTokens>` tag.

The `<c:import>` tag is similar to `<jsp:include>`. It includes the contents of a relative or absolute URL into the rendered JSP. Optionally, this tag can store the contents of the included URL in a `String` or in an instance of `java.io.Reader`. The `<c:import>` tag has one required attribute called `url`; the value of this attribute is a `String` expression containing the URL to be imported. If we wish to store the contents of the included URL in a `String`, then the `var` attribute must be used. The value of this attribute is the name of the `String` that will hold the contents of the included URL. If we wish to include the contents of the included URL in an instance of `java.io.Reader`, then the `varReader` attribute must be used. The value of this attribute is the name of the variable that will hold the contents of the included URL. The `<c:import>` tag has an optional scope attribute that defines the scope of the variable defined by the `var` or `varReader` attributes. If this attribute is not used, the `var` or `varReader` variable will have a default scope of page.

The `<c:redirect>` tag redirects the browser to the URL specified in its `url` attribute. It is equivalent to calling the `sendRedirect()` method of an instance of `javax.servlet.http.HttpServletResponse`.

The `<c:url>` tag constructs a URL from the value of its `url` attribute and stores it in a `String` whose name is defined in the tag's `var` attribute. The default scope of the variable defined by the `var` attribute is page. This can be changed by using the tag's `scope` attribute.

It is possible to pass parameters to the URL defined in the `url` attribute of the `<c:import>`, `<c:redirect>`, or `<c:url>` tags. This is done by using the `<c:param>` tag. This tag must be nested inside one of the mentioned three tags. The `<c:param>` tag has two attributes: a required `name` attribute defining the parameter name and a `value` attribute defining the parameter value.

The last core JSTL tag is the `<c:catch>` tag. This tag catches any `java.lang.Throwable` thrown inside its body.

> `java.lang.Throwable` is the parent class of `java.lang.Exception` and `java.lang.Error`. Therefore, any `Exception` or `Error` thrown inside the body of the `<c:catch>` tag is also caught.

If a `Throwable` is thrown inside the body of the `<c:catch>` tag, control goes to the line immediately following the closing `</c:catch>` tag. Any lines inside the body of the `<c:catch>` tag, that were processed before the `Throwable` is thrown, are processed. The `<c:catch>` tag has a single optional attribute named `var`. This attribute defines a variable to hold the `Throwable` that was thrown inside the body of the `<c:catch>` tag. This variable always has a scope of page.

The following table lists all of the JSTL core tag libraries:

Tag	Description	Example

`<c:catch>`	Catches any `Exception`, `Error`, or `Throwable` thrown inside its body.	`<c:catch var="e">`
		`  <c:out value="1/0"/>`
		`    <c:if test="e!=null">`
		`      <c:out value=`
		`        "e.message"/>`
		`    </c:if>`
		`</c:catch>`

`<c:choose>`	Used to wrap the `<c:when>` and (optionally) `<c:otherwise>` tags. The body of the first `<c:when>` tag containing a test expression that evaluates to `true` is executed. If none of the `<c:when>` tags contain a test expression that evaluates to true, then the body of the `<c:otherwise>` tag is executed.	`<c:choose>`
		`  <c:when test="empty o">`
		`    <c:out value="o is`
		`      empty"/>`
		`  </c:when>`
		`  <c:otherwise>`
		`    <c:out value="o is`
		`      not empty"/>`
		`  </c:otherwise>`
		`</c:choose>`

Tag	Description	Example
<c:forEach>	Iterates over an array, Collection, or Map.	<c:forEach items="${session.array OrCollection}" var="item"> <c:out value="item" = ${item}> </c:forEach>
<c:if>	Its body gets executed if the test expression evaluates to true.	<c:if test="${a>b}"> <c:out value="a is greater than b"/> </c:if>
<c:import>	Imports content from the URL indicated in the url attribute into the rendered page.	<c:import url="http://foo.com/ somePage.jsp"> <c:param name="someName" value="some val"/> </c:import>
<c:out>	Outputs the value of the value expression.	<c:out value="> is the greater than symbol" escapeXml="true"/>
<c:otherwise>	Its body gets executed if none of the test expressions in the <c:when> tags nested in the same <c:choose> tag evaluate to true.	See example for <c:choose>
<c:param>	Sets a parameter for a URL defined in the <c:url> or <c:import> tag.	See example for <c:import>
<c:redirect>	Redirects to the specified URL.	<c:redirect url="http://ensode.net"/>
<c:remove>	Removes a variable from the page scope or the specified scope.	<c:remove var="varName" scope="session"/>
<c:set>	Sets a variable in the page scope or the specified scope.	<c:set var="varName" value="foo" scope="session"/>
<c:url>	Creates a URL variable.	<c:url value="http://foo.com" var="fooUrl"/>
<c:when>	Its body gets executed when its test expression evaluates to true.	See example for <c:choose>

Formatting JSTL tag library

The formatting JSTL tag library provides tags that ease internationalization and localization of web applications. This tag library allows displaying a page in different languages, based on the user's locale. It also allows locale specific formatting of dates and currency.

The following example illustrates the use of the formatting JSTL tag library:

```
<%@ page language="java" contentType="text/html; charset=UTF-8"
  pageEncoding="UTF-8"%>
<%@ taglib uri="http://java.sun.com/jsp/jstl/fmt" prefix="fmt"%>

<!DOCTYPE html PUBLIC "-//W3C//DTD HTML 4.01 Transitional//EN"
  "http://www.w3.org/TR/html4/loose.dtd">
<html>
  <head>
    <meta http-equiv="Content-Type" content="text/html;
      charset=UTF-8">
    <title>Format Tag Demo</title>
  </head>
  <body>
    <jsp:useBean id="today" class="java.util.Date" />
    <fmt:setLocale value="en_US" />
    <fmt:bundle basename="ApplicationResources">
      <fmt:message key="greeting" />,<br />
      <fmt:message key="proposal" />
      <fmt:formatNumber type="currency" value="42000" />.<br />
      <fmt:message key="offer_ends" />
      <fmt:formatDate value="${today}" type="date"
        dateStyle="full" />.
    </fmt:bundle>
    <br />
    <br />
    <fmt:setLocale value="es_ES" />
    <fmt:bundle basename="ApplicationResources">
      <fmt:message key="greeting" />,<br />
      <fmt:message key="proposal" />
      <fmt:formatNumber type="currency" value="42000" />.<br />
      <fmt:message key="offer_ends" />
      <fmt:formatDate value="${today}" type="date"
        dateStyle="full" />
    </fmt:bundle>
  </body>
</html>
```

This page display basically greets the user, then proceeds to make a proposal (sales pitch), followed by a price, and an offer end date:

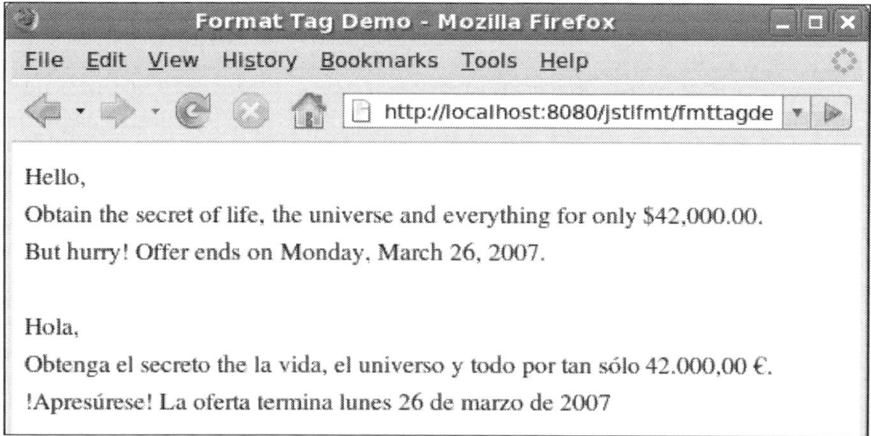

As this page is internationalized, the actual text of the page is stored in a property file called a resource bundle. The resource bundle for the page is called `ApplicationResources.properties`. This is set in the page via the `<fmt:bundle>` tag.

The page displays the same message in English and Spanish. Therefore, two resource bundles are needed; one for each locale. The locale to use is defined in the `value` attribute of the `<fmt:setLocale>` tag.

A real application would not simultaneously display the same messages in two different languages. Instead, it would detect the user's locale from the request and use the appropriate resource bundle. If the user's locale doesn't match any of the available resource bundles, then the default one would be used.

The English (and default) version of `ApplicationResources.properties` looks as follows:

```
greeting=Hello
proposal=Obtain the secret of life, the universe and everything for
  only
offer_ends=But hurry! Offer ends on
```

The Spanish version of the resource bundle is called `ApplicationResources_es.properties`:

```
greeting=Hola
proposal=Obtenga el secreto the la vida, el universo y todo por tan
  sólo
offer_ends=!Apresúrese! La oferta termina
```

As we can see, a resource bundle is nothing but a property file with keys and values. The keys in each localized resource bundle must be the same; the value should vary according to the locale. In order to be accessible to JSP pages and Java code, resource bundles need to be placed in any directory in the `WEB-INF/classes` directory folder or any of its subdirectories in the WAR file where the application is deployed. If they are placed in a subdirectory of the `WEB-INF/classes` directory, then the `basename` attribute of the `<fmt:bundle>` tag must include each directory under this directory, separated by dots. For example, if `ApplicationResources.properties` and `ApplicationResources_es.properties` were placed under `WEB-INF/classes/net/ensode`, the `<fmt:bundle>` tag would look like this:

```
<fmt:bundle basename="net.ensode.ApplicationResources">
```

As we can see, this looks like a fully qualified class name, but in reality we are pointing to the resource bundle.

Resource bundle names for each locale must have the same base name as the base resource bundle (in this case, `ApplicationProperties`), followed by an underscore, followed by an appropriate locale (in this case, `es`). The locale can only specify a language (for example, `en` or `es`), or a language and country (for example, `en_US` or `es_ES`). If no country is specified in the locale, any country whose primary language matches the locale will use the resource bundle for that language.

[The previous example uses `es_ES` as the locale, assuming every page that is in Spanish comes from Spain. Obviously, this wouldn't work in a real application and was done this way for simplicity.]

The `<fmt:message>` tag looks for a key in the resource bundle matching its `key` attribute and displays its value on the page. Although not illustrated in the example, sometimes resource bundle values can have parameters that are substituted at runtime with appropriate values. Parameters are designated by an integer between curly braces. This is illustrated in the following example:

```
personalGreeting=Hello {0}
```

The {0} in this property is a parameter. Parameters can be substituted by the appropriate values at runtime by using the <fmt:param> tag. This tag must be nested inside a <fmt:message> tag. The <fmt:param> tag has an attribute named value. The value of this attribute can be a String constant or Unified Expression Language expression. It is used to substitute the parameter with this value. Resource bundle values can have more than one parameter, in which case, the number of <fmt:param> tags nested inside <fmt:message> must match the number of parameters. The order of the <fmt:param> tags determines which parameter gets substituted. The first <fmt:param> tag will replace the parameter indexed at 0, the second <fmt:param> tag will replace the parameter indexed at 1, and so on and so forth.

The next formatting tag we see in the example is the <fmt:formatNumber> tag. This tag formats a number according to the locale. Some locales use a comma to separate thousands and a dot as a decimal separator, while for others it is the other way around. As can be seen in the previous screenshot, the <fmt:formatNumber> tag will take care of this for us. Another useful attribute of the <fmt:formatNumber> tag is the type attribute. This attribute has three valid values: number, percent, or currency. As can be seen in the example, if the type attribute is set to currency, then the appropriate currency symbol for the locale is automatically added to the number.

The next new formatting tag we see in the example is the <fmt:formatDate> tag. This tag will take a Date object specified by its value attribute and format it appropriately for the given locale. In addition to translating the date into the appropriate language, this tag will place the day of the week, the day of the month, the month, and the year in the appropriate place for the corresponding locale. It will also use the correct capitalization for the first letter of the month. The dateStyle attribute of the <fmt:formatDate> tag has the following valid values: full, long, medium, short, and default. If no value is specified, default is used.

The format tag library tags we have covered so far are the most commonly used tags. The following table lists all the JSTL formatting library tags:

Tag	Description	Example
<fmt:bundle>	Loads a resource bundle to be used inside its body.	<fmt:bundle basename="resbund"> <fmt:message key="greeting"> </fmt:bundle>
<fmt:formatDate>	Formats the date specified by its value attribute optionally using a specified pattern.	<fmt:formatDate value="${today}" pattern= "MM/dd/yyyy"/>

Tag	Description	Example
`<fmt:formatNumber>`	Formats the number specified by its `value` attribute according to the current locale. Can be used to format the number as currency or percentage, depending on the value of its optional `type` attribute.	`<fmt:formatNumber value="42000" />`
`<fmt:message>`	Displays a localized message corresponding to the key defined in its `key` attribute.	`<fmt:message key="offer_ends" />`
`<fmt:param>`	Substitutes a parameter in the enclosing `<fmt:message>` tag.	`<fmt:param value="someVal"/>`
`<fmt:parseDate>`	Parses a string containing a date into a `Date` object.	`<fmt:parseDate value="03/31/2007" pattern= "MM/dd/yyyy" var="parsedDate"/>`
`<fmt:parseNumber>`	Parses a numeric string into a `Long` or `Double` object.	`<fmt:parseNumber value="42,000.00" var= "parsedNumber"/>`
`<fmt:requestEncoding>`	Sets the character encoding of the request.	`<fmt:requestEncoding key="ISO-8859-1"/>`
`<fmt:setBundle>`	Sets the resource bundle to use in the specified scope. Default scope is `page`.	`<fmt:setBundle baseName="resbund" var="bundle" scope="session"/>`
`<fmt:setLocale>`	Sets the locale to use in the specified scope. Default scope is `page`.	`<fmt:setLocale value="en_US" />`
`<fmt:setTimeZone>`	Sets the time zone to use in the specified scope. Default scope is `page`.	`<fmt:setTimeZone value="EST" var= "sessionTimeZone" scope="session"/>`
`<fmt:timeZone>`	Sets the time zone to use inside its body.	`<fmt:timeZone value="EST"> <fmt:formatDate value="${today}"/> </fmt:timeZone>`

SQL JSTL tag library

The SQL JSTL tag library allows us to execute SQL queries from JSP pages. As this tag library mixes presentation and database access code, it should only be used for prototyping and for writing simple "throwaway" applications. For more complex applications, it is always a good idea to follow the DAO and MVC design patterns.

The following example illustrates the most commonly used tags in the SQL JSTL tag library:

```
<%@ page language="java" contentType="text/html; charset=UTF-8"
  pageEncoding="UTF-8"%>
<%@ taglib uri="http://java.sun.com/jsp/jstl/sql" prefix="sql"%>
<%@ taglib uri="http://java.sun.com/jsp/jstl/core" prefix="c"%>
<!DOCTYPE html PUBLIC "-//W3C//DTD HTML 4.01 Transitional//EN"
  "http://www.w3.org/TR/html4/loose.dtd">
<html>
  <head>
    <meta http-equiv="Content-Type" content="text/html;
      charset=UTF-8">
    <title>SQL Tag Demo</title>
  </head>
  <body>
    <sql:setDataSource dataSource="jdbc/__CustomerDBPool" />
    <sql:transaction>
      <sql:update>
        insert into CUSTOMERS (CUSTOMER_ID, FIRST_NAME, LAST_NAME)
        values (((select max(CUSTOMER_ID) from customers) + 1), ?, ?)
        <sql:param value="${param.firstName}" />
        <sql:param value="${param.lastName}" />
      </sql:update>
    </sql:transaction>
    <p>Successfully inserted the following row into the CUSTOMERS
      table:</p>
    <sql:query var="selectedRows"
      sql="select FIRST_NAME, LAST_NAME from customers where
        FIRST_NAME = ? and LAST_NAME = ?">
      <sql:param value="${param.firstName}" />
      <sql:param value="${param.lastName}" />
    </sql:query>
    <table border="1" cellpadding="0" cellspacing="0">
      <tr>
        <td>First Name</td>
        <td>Last Name</td>
      </tr>
```

```
        <c:forEach var="currentRow" items="${selectedRows.rows}">
          <tr>
            <td><c:out value="${currentRow.FIRST_NAME}" /></td>
            <td><c:out value="${currentRow.LAST_NAME}" /></td>
          </tr>
        </c:forEach>
      </table>
    </body>
  </html>
```

After packaging this JSP in a WAR file, deploying the WAR file, and pointing the browser to the JSP's URL (and passing the parameters that the page expects), we should see a page like the following:

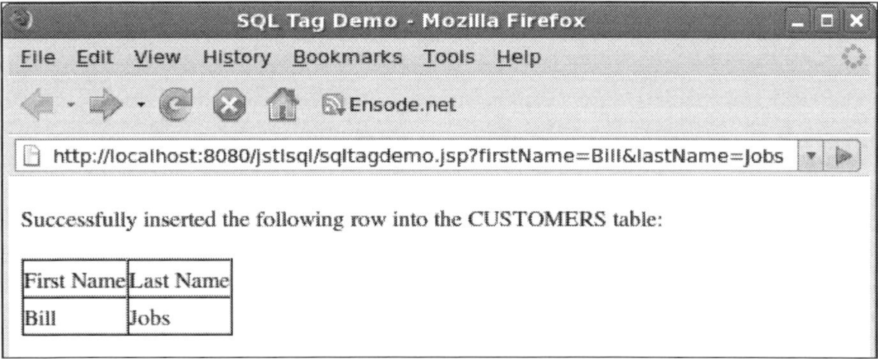

Like most of our examples, the previous page is pretty simplistic and does not necessarily represent what would be done in an actual application. The page inserts a row into the CUSTOMERS table and then queries the table for rows matching the values inserted. A real application (keeping in mind that the SQL tag library should only be used for very simple applications) would typically insert values obtained from request parameters into the database. It would be unlikely for the same page to query the database for the data just inserted. This would probably be done in a separate page.

The first JSTL SQL tag we see in the example is the `<sql:setDataSource>` tag. This tag sets the datasource to be used for database access. The datasource can either be obtained via JNDI by using its JNDI name as the value of this tag's `datasource` attribute, or by specifying a JDBC URL, username, and password via the `url`, `user`, and `password` attributes. The previous example uses the first approach. In order for this approach to work correctly, a `<resource-ref>` element must be added to the application's `web.xml` file.

```
<web-app xmlns="http://java.sun.com/xml/ns/javaee" version="2.5"
  xmlns:xsi="http://www.w3.org/2001/XMLSchema-instance"
  xsi:schemaLocation="http://java.sun.com/xml/ns/javaee
    http://java.sun.com/xml/ns/javaee/web-app_2_5.xsd">
  <resource-ref>
    <res-ref-name>jdbc/__CustomerDBPool</res-ref-name>
    <res-type>javax.sql.DataSource</res-type>
    <res-auth>Container</res-auth>
  </resource-ref>
</web-app>
```

The `<res-ref-name>` subelement of the `<resource-ref>` element contains the JNDI name of a JDBC datasource. This needs to be set up in the application server. The procedure to set up a JDBC datasource is covered in detail in the next chapter.

The `<res-type>` subelement of the `<resource-ref>` element contains the fully qualified name of the resource to be obtained via JNDI. For datasources, this will always be `javax.sql.DataSource`.

The `<res-auth>` subelement of the `<resource-ref>` element should have a value of `Container` when using the `<resource-ref>` element to define a datasource as a resource. This allows the application server to use the credentials set up in the connection pool corresponding to the datasource to log into the database.

No suitable driver SQL exception

Sometimes, the `<sql:setDataSource>` tag will result in a `java.sql.SQLException: No suitable driver` exception when using its `datasource` attribute to locate the datasource via JNDI. This typically means that we forgot to modify the application's `web.xml` file, as described previously.

Like we mentioned before, an alternate way of using the `<sql:setDataSource>` tag is to specify the database connection URL and credentials. If we had used this approach in the previous example, the `<sql:setDataSource>` tag would have looked like this:

```
<sql:setDataSource url="jdbc:derby://localhost:1527/customerdb"
  user="dev" password="dev" />
```

The attributes used are self-explanatory. The `url` attribute should contain the JDBC URL for the connection. The `user` and `password` attributes should contain the username and password used to log into the database respectively.

The next JSTL SQL tag we see in the example is the `<sql:transaction>` tag. Unsurprisingly, this tag wraps any `<sql:query>` and `<sql:update>` tags it contains in a transaction.

Next, we see the `<sql:update>` tag that is used to execute any queries that modify the data in the database. It can be used for `INSERT`, `UPDATE`, or `DELETE` SQL statements. As can be seen in the example, queries inside this tag can have one or more parameters. Just like when using JDBC Prepared Statements, question marks are used as placeholders for parameters. The `<sql:param>` tag is used to set the value of any parameter in a query defined in a `<sql:update>` or `<sql:query>` tag. The `<sql:param>` tag sets the value for its containing tag via its value attribute that may contain a `String` constant or a Unified Expression Language expression.

The `<sql:query>` tag is used to query data from the database via a `SELECT` statement. The query's result set is stored in a variable defined by this tag's `var` attribute. By default, the `var` attribute has a scope of page. This can be changed by using the `<sql:query>` scope attribute and setting its value to the appropriate scope (`page`, `request`, `session`, or `application`). As can be seen in the example, we can iterate through the variable defined by this tag's `var` attribute by using a `<c:forEach>` tag.

The following table lists all the JSTL SQL tags:

Tag	**Description**	**Example**
`<sql:dateParam>`	Sets the value for a date parameter in a `<sql:query>` or `<sql:update>` tag.	See example for `<sql:query>`.
`<sql:param>`	Sets the value for a text or numeric parameter in a `<sql:query>` or `<sql:update>` tag.	See example for `<sql:update>`.

Tag	Description	Example

<sql:query>	Executes the SQL query defined in its sql attribute and optionally attaches the resulting result set into the specified scope, using the specified variable name.	<sql:query
		  sql="select * from
		    table
		    where
		    last_update < ?"
		 var="selectedRows">
		  <sql:dateParam
		    value=
		     "${someDate}"/>
		</sql:query>

<sql:setDataSource>	Defines the datasource to be used at the specified scope. If no scope is specified, the default scope is page. Datasource can be obtained via a JNDI lookup or by specifying a JDBC URL through the url, user, and password attributes..	<sql:setDataSource dataSource="jdbc/ __CustomerDBPool" />

<sql:transaction>	Wraps any <sql:query> and <sql:update> tags inside its body in a transaction.	<sql:transaction>
		  <sql:update
		    sql="update
		      table set
		      some_col = ?">
		    <sql:param
		      value=
		       "someValue"/>
		  </sql:update>
		  <sql:update
		    sql="update
		      table2 set
		      some_col = ?">
		    <sql:param
		      value=
		       "someValue"/>
		  </sql:update>
		</sql:transaction>

<sql:update>	Executes an SQL INSERT, UPDATE, or DELETE statement.	<sql:update
		  sql="update table
		  set some_col = ?">
		  <sql:param
		    value=
		      "someValue"/>
		</sql:update>

XML JSTL tag library

The XML JSTL tag library provides an easy way to parse XML documents and to do Extensible Stylesheet Language Transformations (XSLT). This tag library uses XPath expressions to navigate through elements in an XML document.

XPath is an expression language used for finding information in an XML document, or for making calculations based on the content of an XML document. For more information about XPath, refer to `http://www.w3.org/TR/xpath`.

The following example illustrates the most commonly used tags in the XML JSTL tag library:

```
<%@ page language="java" contentType="text/html; charset=UTF-8"
  pageEncoding="UTF-8"%>
<%@ taglib uri="http://java.sun.com/jsp/jstl/xml" prefix="x"%>
<%@ taglib uri="http://java.sun.com/jsp/jstl/core" prefix="c"%>

<c:import url="customers.xml" var="xml" />
<x:parse doc="${xml}" var="doc" />
<!DOCTYPE html PUBLIC "-//W3C//DTD HTML 4.01 Transitional//EN"
  "http://www.w3.org/TR/html4/loose.dtd">
<html>
  <head>
    <meta http-equiv="Content-Type" content="text/html;
      charset=UTF-8">
    <title>XML Tag Demo</title>
  </head>
  <body>
    <table cellpadding="0" cellspacing="0" border="1">
      <tr>
        <td>First Name</td>
        <td>Last Name</td>
        <td>Email</td>
      </tr>
      <x:forEach select="$doc/customers/customer">
        <tr>
          <td>
            <x:out select="firstName" />
          </td>
          <td>
            <x:out select="lastName" />
          </td>
```

```
          <td>
            <x:choose>
              <x:when select="email">
                <x:out select="email" />
              </x:when>
              <x:otherwise>
                <c:out value="N/A" />
              </x:otherwise>
            </x:choose>
          </td>
        </tr>
      </x:forEach>
    </table>
  </body>
</html>
```

The first thing we should notice in this example is the use of the `<c:import>` core JSTL tag to import an XML file from a URL. The value of the URL attribute defines the URL where the XML file can be located; it can be a relative or absolute URL. In the example, the `customers.xml` file is in the same directory as the JSP, therefore a relative path is used to obtain it. The `customers.xml` file has customer information including first name, last name, and email, as shown next:

```
<?xml version="1.0" encoding="UTF-8"?>
<customers>
  <customer>
    <firstName>Karl</firstName>
    <lastName>Smith</lastName>
    <email>karls@nonexistent.org</email>
  </customer>
  <customer>
    <firstName>Jenny</firstName>
    <lastName>Conte</lastName>
    <email>jenny@notreal.com</email>
  </customer>
  <customer>
    <firstName>Rhonda</firstName>
    <lastName>Benedict</lastName>
  </customer>
</customers>
```

After packaging the previous two files in a WAR file and visiting the JSP's URL, we should see a page like the following:

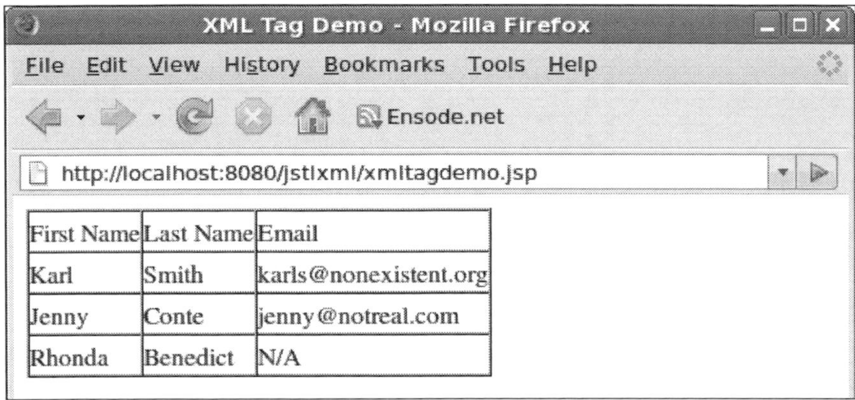

The first JSTL XML tag we see in the example is the `<x:parse>` tag. This tag parses an XML document and stores it in the variable defined by its `var` attribute. The XML document to parse is defined in its `doc` attribute.

The XML JSTL tag library contains several tags that are analogous to similar tags in the Core JSTL tag libraries. These tags include `<x:if>`, `<x:choose>`, `<x:when>`, `<x:otherwise>`, `<x:forEach>`, `<x:param>`, and `<x:set>`. Usage of these tags is very similar to their core tag counterparts. The main difference is that these tags contain a `select` attribute containing an XPath expression to evaluate, instead of the `value` attribute that the corresponding core tags contain. The example illustrates the usage of most of these tags.

The next JSTL XML tag we see in the example is the `<x:forEach>` tag. This tag iterates over the elements of an XML document. Elements to iterate over are specified as an XPath expression through the `select` attribute.

The next JSTL XML tag we see in the example is the `<x:out>` tag, which outputs the value of the XPath expression defined in its `select` attribute.

Next, we see the `<x:choose>` tag, which is the parent tag of the `<x:when>` and (optionally) `<x:otherwise>` tags. The body of the first nested `<x:when>` tag containing an XPath expression evaluating to true as its `select` attribute is executed. `select` expressions for subsequent `<x:when>` attributes are not evaluated after one of them evaluates to true. If no `select` attributes for any of the `<x:when>` tags evaluate to true, the body of the optional `<x:otherwise>` tag is executed.

An additional XML JSTL tag is the `<x:transform>` tag, which is used to do XSLT transformations on XML documents. This tag is typically used with two attributes. The `xml` attribute indicates the location of the XML document to transform. It can be imported via the `<c:import>` tag, as illustrated in the example. The `xslt` attribute indicates the XSL stylesheet used to transform the document. This stylesheet can also be imported via the `<c:import>` tag.

The following table lists all of the JSTL XML tags:

<table>
<tr><th>Tag</th><th>Description</th><th>Example</th></tr>
<tr><td><code><x:choose></code></td><td>Used to wrap the <code><x:when></code> and (optionally) <code><x:otherwise></code> tags. The body of the first <code><x:when></code> tag containing a select expression that evaluates to <code>true</code> is executed. If none of the <code><x:when></code> tags contain a test expression that evaluates to true, then the body of the <code><x:otherwise></code> tag is executed.</td><td>See example for <code><x:forEach></code>.</td></tr>
<tr><td><code><x:forEach></code></td><td>Iterates over the elements of an XML document. The elements to iterate over are specified through the <code>select</code> attribute.</td><td><pre><x:forEach select=
  "$doc/customers/customer">
  <tr>
    <td>
      <x:out
        select="firstName" />
    </td>
    <td>
      <x:out
        select="lastName" />
    </td>
    <td>
      <x:choose>
        <x:when
          select="email">
          <x:out
            select="email" />
        </x:when>
        <x:otherwise>
          <c:out
            value="N/A" />
        </x:otherwise>
      </x:choose>
    </td>
  </tr>
</x:forEach></pre></td></tr>
</table>

Tag	Description	Example
`<x:otherwise>`	Its body gets executed if none of the test expressions in the `<x:when>` tags nested in the same `<x:choose>` tag evaluate to `true`.	See example for `<x:forEach>`.
`<x:out>`	Outputs an XPath expression defined by the `select` attribute.	See example for `<x:forEach>`.
`<x:param>`	Adds a parameter to the containing `<x:transform>` tag.	See example for `<x:transform>`.
`<x:parse>`	Parses an XML document and stores it in the variable defined by its `var` attribute.	`<x:parse doc="${xml}" var="doc" />`
`<x:set>`	Saves the result of the XPath expression defined in its `select` attribute into a variable in the specified scope. If no scope is defined, a default scope of `page` is used.	`<x:set var="custEmail" select="email"/>`

`<x:transform>`	Transforms the XML document defined by the `xml` attribute using the XSL stylesheet defined by the `xslt` attribute.	`<x:transform xml="${someXmlDoc}" xslt="${xslt}">`
		`<x:param name="paramName" value="${paramValue}"/>`
		`</x:transform>`

`<x:when>`	Its body gets executed when its select expression evaluates to `true`.	See example for `<x:forEach>`.

JSTL functions

JSTL contains a number of functions that take Unified Expression Language expressions as parameters. All JSTL functions except one are used exclusively for `String` manipulation. An exception is the `fn:length()` function, which can take a `String`, `Collection`, or array as a parameter. It returns the length of the `String`, the size of the `Collection`, or the length of the array, depending on what parameter is passed to it. The following JSP illustrates the use of JSTL functions:

```
<%@ page language="java" contentType="text/html; charset=UTF-8"
  pageEncoding="UTF-8"%>
<%@ taglib uri="http://java.sun.com/jsp/jstl/functions" prefix="fn"%>
<%@ taglib uri="http://java.sun.com/jsp/jstl/core" prefix="c"%>
```

```
<!DOCTYPE html PUBLIC "-//W3C//DTD HTML 4.01 Transitional//EN"
  "http://www.w3.org/TR/html4/loose.dtd">
<html>
  <head>
    <meta http-equiv="Content-Type" content="text/html;
      charset=UTF-8">
    <title>Function Tag Demo</title>
  </head>
  <body>
    <c:set var="nameArr"
           value="${fn:split('Kevin,Danielle,Alex,Beatrice',',')}" />
    We have a list of ${fn:length(nameArr)} names, here they are:
    <br />
    <ol>
      <c:forEach var="currentName" items="${nameArr}">
        <li />
          ${fn:toUpperCase(currentName)}
        <br />
      </c:forEach>
    </ol>
  </body>
</html>
```

After packaging this JSP in a WAR file, deploying it and pointing the browser to its URL, we should see a page like the following:

This JSP illustrates the use of some of the JSTL functions. The `fn:split()` function splits a `String` into an array of strings using the character specified by its second parameter as a delimiter.

Notice that the strings inside the `fn:split()` function are enclosed inside single quotes. JSTL allows this as using double quotes for the strings would have resulted in illegal syntax, as the `fn:split()` function is already inside double quotes.

In the example, the `fn:length()` function returns the number of elements in the array we created when the `fn:split()` function was executed. Like we mentioned earlier, the `fn:length()` function can also take a `Collection` or a `String` as a parameter. When applied to a `Collection`, the function returns the number of elements in it. When applied to a `String`, the function returns the number of characters in the `String`.

The next function illustrated in the example is `fn:toUpperCase()`, which simply makes every alphabetical character in the `String` it takes as a parameter uppercase. There are many other JSTL functions, all of them are very intuitive to use. The following table lists all the JSTL functions:

Function	Description	Example
`fn:contains(String, String)`	Returns a boolean indicating if the second parameter is contained in the first one.	`${fn:contains("environment", "iron")}`
`fn:containsIgnoreCase(String, String)`	Case-insensitive version of `fn:contains()`.	`${fn:containsIgnoreCase("environment", "Iron")}`
`fn:endsWith(String, String)`	Returns a boolean indicating if the first parameter ends with a string equal to the second parameter.	`${fn:endsWith("Glass Fish", "Fish")}`
`fn:escapeXml(String)`	Returns a string with all XML characters in the parameter escaped into their respective XML character entity code.	`${fn:escapeXml("<html>")}`
`fn:indexOf(String, String)`	Returns an int indicating the index of the second parameter in the first parameter. Returns -1 if the second parameter is not a substring of the first parameter.	`${fn:indexOf("GlassFish", "Fish")}`

Function	Description	Example
`fn:join(String[], String)`	Returns a string composed of the elements in the first parameter, using the second parameter as a delimiter.	`${fn:join(arrayVar," , ")}`
`fn:length(Object)`	Returns the length of an array, the size of a collection, or the length of a string, depending on the type of the parameter.	`${fn:length("String, Collection or Array")}`
`fn:replace(String, String, String)`	Returns a string replacing every instance of the second parameter on the first parameter with the third parameter.	`${fn:replace("CrystalFish", "Glass")}`
`fn:startsWith(String, String)`	Returns a boolean indicating if the first parameter starts with the first parameter.	`${fn:startsWith("GlassFish", "Glass")}`
`fn:split(String, String)`	Returns an array of strings containing elements in the first parameter as delimited by the second parameter.	`${fn:split("Eeny, meeny", ",")}`
`fn:substring(String, int, int)`	Returns a string containing the substring in the first parameter, starting at the index indicated by the second parameter and ending just before the index indicated by the second parameter.	`${fn:substring( "0123456789", 3, 6)}`
`fn:substringAfter (String, String)`	Returns a string containing the substring in the first parameter, starting after the first occurrence of the second parameter until the end of the first parameter.	`${fn:substringAfter( "GlassFish", "Glass")}`
`fn:substringBefore (String, String)`	Returns a string containing the substring in the first parameter, starting before the first occurrence of the second parameter until the end of the first parameter.	`${fn:substringBefore ("GlassFish", "Fish")}`

Function	Description	Example
`fn:toLowerCase (String)`	Returns a string containing a version of the parameters with all alphabetical characters as lowercase.	`${fn:toLowerCase( "GlassFish")}`
`fn:toUpperCase (String)`	Returns a string containing a version of the parameters with all alphabetical characters as uppercase.	`${fn:toUpperCase (" GlassFish ")}`
`fn:trim(String)`	Returns a string containing a modified version of the parameter with all whitespace at the beginning and end of the parameter removed.	`${fn:trim("  Gla ssFish  ")}`

Summary

This chapter covered all JSP Standard Tag Library tags, including the core, formatting, SQL, and XML tags. Additionally, JSTL functions were covered. Examples illustrating the most common JSTL tags and functions were provided; additional JSTL tags and functions were mentioned and described.

5

Database Connectivity

Any non-trivial Java EE application will persist data to a relational database. In this chapter, we will cover how to connect to a database and perform CRUD operations (Create, Read, Update, and Delete). There are two Java EE APIs that can be used to interact with a relational database: the **Java Database Connectivity** (**JDBC**) API and the **Java Persistence API** (**JPA**). Both these APIs will be discussed in this chapter.

Some of the topics covered in this chapter include:

- Retrieving data from a database through JDBC
- Inserting data into a database through JDBC
- Updating data in a database through JDBC
- Deleting data in a database through JDBC
- Retrieving data from a database through JPA
- Inserting data into a database through JPA
- Updating data in a database through JPA
- Deleting data in a database through JPA
- Building queries programmatically through the JPA 2.0 Criteria API
- Automating data validation through JPA 2.0's Bean Validation support

The CustomerDB database

Examples in this chapter will use a database called `CUSTOMERDB`. This database contains tables to track customer and order information for a fictitious store. The database uses JavaDB for its RDBMS as it comes bundled with GlassFish.

A script is included with this book's code download to create this database and pre-populate some of its tables. Instructions on how to execute the script and add a connection pool and datasource to access it are included in the download as well.

The schema for the CUSTOMERDB database is depicted in the following image:

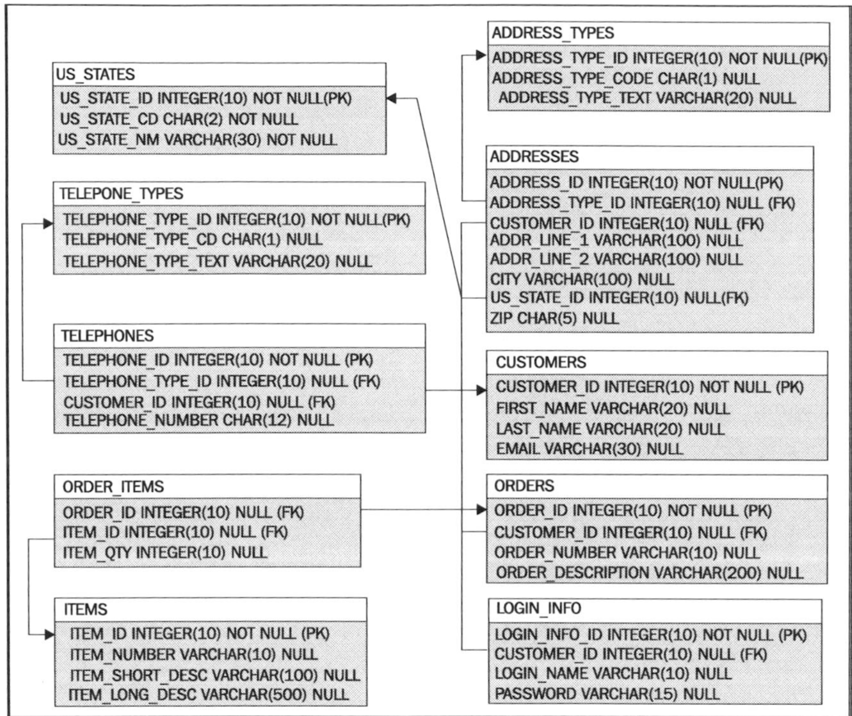

As can be seen in the image, the database contains tables to store customer information such as name, address, and email address. It also contains tables to store order and item information.

The ADDRESS_TYPES table will store values such as "Home", "Mailing", and "Shipping" to distinguish the type of address in the ADDRESSES table. Similarly, the TELEPHONE_TYPES table stores the values "Cell", "Home", and "Work". These two tables are pre-populated when creating the database as well as the US_STATES table.

For simplicity's sake, our database only deals with U.S. addresses.

JDBC

The Java Database Connectivity (JDBC) API is the standard API used for Java applications to interact with a database. Although JDBC is not part of the Java EE specification, it is used very frequently in Java EE applications.

JDBC allows us to send queries to a database to perform select, insert, update, and delete operations. The most common way of interacting with a database through JDBC is through the `java.sql.PreparedStatement` interface. Using prepared statements through this interface offers a number of benefits over using standard JDBC statement objects. Some of the benefits of prepared statements include:

- Prepared statements are compiled into the RDBMS the first time they are executed, therefore increasing performance
- Prepared statements are immune to SQL injection attacks
- Prepared statements free us from explicitly adding single quotes (') to our SQL statements to handle character values

The `java.sql.PreparedStatement` interface has two methods that are very frequently used to send queries to the database: `executeQuery()` and `executeUpdate()`. The `executeQuery()` method is used to issue `select` statements to the database and returns an instance of `java.sql.ResultSet` containing the rows returned from the query. The `executeUpdate()` method is used to issue `insert`, `update`, and `delete` statements to the database. It returns an `int` value corresponding to the number of rows affected by the query. In the following sections, we illustrate database interaction through these two methods.

Retrieving data from a database

As we mentioned in the previous section, the `executeQuery()` method of the `java.sql.PreparedStatement` interface is used to send `select` statements to the database and retrieve data from it. The following example code illustrates this process:

```
package net.ensode.glassfishbook.jdbcselect;

import java.io.IOException;
import java.sql.Connection;
import java.sql.PreparedStatement;
import java.sql.ResultSet;
import java.sql.SQLException;
import java.util.ArrayList;

import javax.naming.InitialContext;
import javax.naming.NamingException;
import javax.servlet.ServletException;
import javax.servlet.http.HttpServlet;
import javax.servlet.http.HttpServletRequest;
import javax.servlet.http.HttpServletResponse;
import javax.sql.DataSource;
```

```
public class JDBCSelectServlet extends HttpServlet
{
  @Override
  protected void doGet(HttpServletRequest request,
    HttpServletResponse response) throws ServletException,
    IOException
  {
    String sql = "select us_state_nm, " +
      "us_state_cd from us_states order by us_state_nm";
    ArrayList<UsStateBean> stateList = new ArrayList<UsStateBean>();
    try
    {
      InitialContext initialContext = new InitialContext();

      DataSource dataSource = (DataSource) initialContext .lookup
        ("jdbc/__CustomerDBPool");
      Connection connection = dataSource.getConnection();
      PreparedStatement preparedStatement =
            connection.prepareStatement(sql);
      ResultSet resultSet = preparedStatement.executeQuery();
      while (resultSet.next())
      {
        stateList.add(new
          UsStateBean(resultSet.getString("us_state_nm"),
          resultSet.getString("us_state_cd")));
      }
      resultSet.close();
      preparedStatement.close();
      connection.close();
      request.setAttribute("stateList", stateList);
      request.getRequestDispatcher("us_states.jsp").forward(request,
        response);
    }
    catch (NamingException namingException)
    {
      namingException.printStackTrace();
    }
    catch (SQLException sqlException)
    {
      sqlException.printStackTrace();
    }
  }
}
```

In this servlet, we create a `String` containing the `select` statement we will be sending to the database.

We then create an instance of `javax.naming.InitialContext`. This instance is then used to perform a **JNDI (Java Naming and Directory Interface)** lookup for the `javax.sql.DataSource` interface corresponding to the database we wish to connect to. This is accomplished by calling the `InitialContext.lookup()` method. The string argument to this method must match the name of the datasource we set up in GlassFish (refer to Chapter 1). This method returns an instance of `java.lang.Object`. Its return value must be casted to the appropriate type (in this case, `javax.sql.DataSource`).

Once we obtain a reference to the `DataSource` object by performing a JNDI lookup, we can obtain a connection from the connection pool by invoking the `getConnection()` method defined in the `javax.sql.DataSource` interface. This method returns an instance of `java.sql.Connection`.

Once we get a connection from a connection pool, we obtain an instance of a class implementing the `java.sql.PreparedStatement` interface by invoking the `prepareStatement()` method on the instance of `java.util.Connection` we obtained in the previous step. The `prepareStatement()` method takes a string containing the SQL query as its sole argument.

Once we get an instance of a class implementing `java.sql.PreparedStatement`, we can finally query the database by invoking its `executeQuery()` method. The `PreparedStatement.executeQuery()` method returns an instance of a class implementing the `java.sql.ResultSet` interface. This instance contains the results of our query.

The servlet then iterates through the result set and populates an `ArrayList` with instances of a JavaBean of type `net.ensode.glassfishbook.jdbcselect.UsStateBean`.

Finally, we close the result set and the prepared statement by invoking their `close()` methods, and the connection is released back to the connection pool by calling the `close()` method on the `java.sql.Connection` instance we were using.

> Calling the `close()` method on the connection does not actually close the connection; it is released back to the connection pool so that other applications can use it.

The previously populated `ArrayList` is then attached to the request and the request is forwarded to a JSP called `us_states.jsp`.

For brevity, source for `UsStateBean.java` and `us_states.jsp` are not shown as these files don't illustrate anything we haven't seen before. Both files are part of this book's code download.

After packaging the code in a WAR file, and deploying and pointing the browser to the appropriate URL, we should see the following page rendered in the browser:

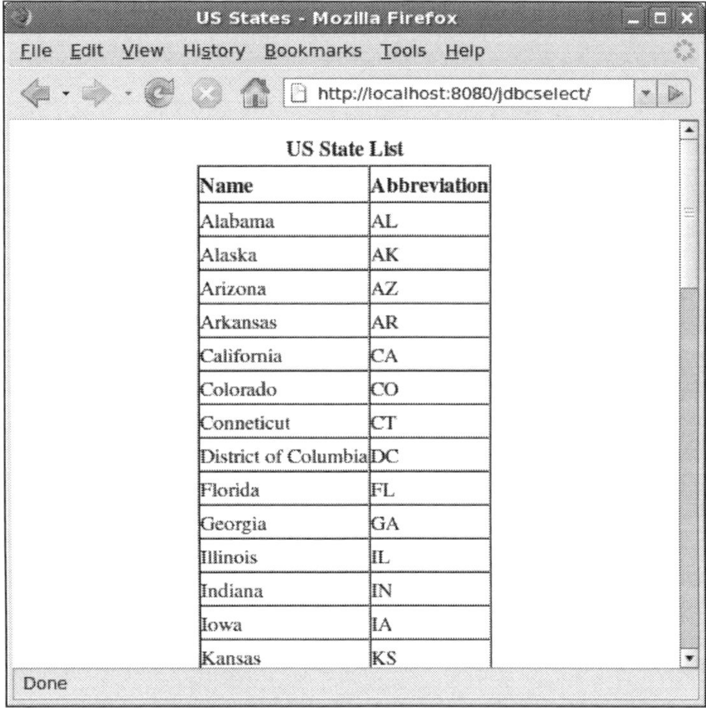

US States - Mozilla Firefox
File Edit View History Bookmarks Tools Help
http://localhost:8080/jdbcselect/
US State List
Name
Abbreviation
Alabama AL
Alaska AK
Arizona AZ
Arkansas AR
California CA
Colorado CO
Conneticut CT
District of Columbia DC
Florida FL
Georgia GA
Illinois IL
Indiana IN
Iowa IA
Kansas KS
Done

All the U.S. state data displayed in the page was retrieved from the database.

As can be seen in the example, the `ResultSet` interface has a `next()` method. This method returns a boolean indicating if the result set has more rows. An instance of a class implementing `ResultSet` has a cursor pointing to the current row. Before any calls to the `next()` method, the cursor is positioned before the first row. When the `next()` method is called for the first time, the cursor points to the first row in the result set. Subsequent calls to the `next()` method move the cursor to the next row. When the cursor is pointing to the last row in the `ResultSet`, a call to `next()` will return false, indicating that there are no more rows in the `ResultSet`.

The `ResultSet.next()` method is commonly used as a condition in a `while` loop. The loop will execute until this method returns false. Inside the loop, operations can be performed on the current row in the result set. The example uses this technique to populate a simple JavaBean with the values for the current row. As can be seen in the code, the `ResultSet` interface contains a method called `getString()`. The `getString()` method returns the value of the column indicated by its sole parameter, which is a `String` corresponding to the column we would like to obtain the value for.

In addition to the `getString()` method, the `ResultSet` interface contains a series of methods for obtaining other types of data. The following table illustrates the most commonly used ones (for the complete list, refer to the JavaDoc documentation for the `ResultSet` interface at `http://java.sun.com/javase/6/docs/api/index.html`):

Method name	Return type
`getBoolean()`	`boolean`
`getDate()`	`java.sql.Date`
`getDouble()`	`double`
`getFloat()`	`float`
`getInt()`	`int`
`getLong()`	`long`
`getShort()`	`short`
`getString()`	`java.lang.String`
`getTime()`	`java.sql.Time`
`getTimeStamp()`	`java.sql.Timestamp`

There are two overloaded versions of each of the methods listed in the table. One version takes a `String` indicating the column name as a parameter, the other version takes an `int` indicating the position of the column in the query. For example, in the following query:

```
select column1, column2, column3 from table
```

The column called `column1` has a position of 1, `column2` has a position of 2, and `column3` has a position of 3. Using the version of the previous methods, taking an `int` usually results in code that is harder to read and understand than using a version taking a `String`, therefore its usage is discouraged.

The `PreparedStatement` instance obtained by calling `Connection.prepareStatement()` contains not just an SQL statement, but a precompiled SQL statement. An SQL statement is given to the `PreparedStatement` instance and this SQL statement is sent to the RDBMS for compilation. This means that when the `PreparedStatement` instance is executed, the RDBMS can run the `PreparedStatement` SQL statement without compiling it and the subsequent calls for execution are faster. Although this is nice for static queries like the one in the previous example, where it really shines is when queries are created dynamically by passing parameters to them. The following example is a modified version of the previous servlet illustrating this concept:

```
package net.ensode.glassfishbook.jdbcselect;

import java.io.IOException;
import java.sql.Connection;
import java.sql.PreparedStatement;
import java.sql.ResultSet;
import java.sql.SQLException;
import java.util.ArrayList;

import javax.annotation.Resource;
import javax.servlet.ServletException;
import javax.servlet.http.HttpServlet;
import javax.servlet.http.HttpServletRequest;
import javax.servlet.http.HttpServletResponse;

public class JDBCSelectServlet2 extends HttpServlet
{
  @Resource(name = "jdbc/__CustomerDBPool")
  private javax.sql.DataSource dataSource;
  @Override
  protected void doGet(HttpServletRequest request,
    HttpServletResponse response) throws ServletException,
    IOException
  {
    String sql = "select us_state_nm, us_state_cd " +
          "from us_states where us_state_nm like ? " +
          "or us_state_nm like ? order by us_state_nm";
    ArrayList<UsStateBean> stateList = new ArrayList<UsStateBean>();
    try
    {
      Connection connection = dataSource.getConnection();
      PreparedStatement preparedStatement =
            connection.prepareStatement(sql);
```

```
        preparedStatement.setString(1, "North%");
        preparedStatement.setString(2, "South%");
        ResultSet resultSet = preparedStatement.executeQuery();
        response.setContentType("text/html");
        while (resultSet.next())
        {
          stateList.add(new
              UsStateBean(resultSet.getString("us_state_nm"),
              resultSet.getString("us_state_cd")));
        }
        resultSet.close();
        preparedStatement.close();
        connection.close();
        request.setAttribute("stateList", stateList);
        request.getRequestDispatcher("us_states.jsp").forward(request,
          response);
      }
      catch (SQLException sqlException)
      {
        sqlException.printStackTrace();
      }
    }
  }
```

In this version of the servlet, we modified the SQL query to limit the result set according to some parameters. Notice the question marks in the SQL statements. These question marks are placeholders for query parameters and are not actually sent to the database.

In the previous example, the `setString()` method of the `PreparedStatement` interface is used to substitute the query parameters with the actual values that will be sent to the database. This method takes two arguments: the first one is the parameter index for the substitution and the second one is the value to use as a substitute. After replacing the parameters with the values, the query in the previous code will retrieve data for all states whose names start with the word "North" or start with the word "South".

Notice that unlike with arrays or collections, the index of the first parameter is 1, not 0.

After compiling the code, packaging in a WAR file and deploying it, and pointing the browser to its URL, we should see a page displaying the following table in the browser:

US State List	
Name	Abbreviation
North Carolina	NC
North Dakota	ND
South Carolina	SC
South Carolina	SC
South Dakota	SD

In addition to the `setString()` method, the `PreparedStatement` interface contains many similar methods that allow us to set parameters of different types. The following table illustrates the most commonly used ones (for the complete list, refer to the JavaDoc documentation for the `PreparedStatement` interface at `http://java.sun.com/javase/6/docs/api/index.html`):

PreparedStatement Method Name
`setBoolean(int parameterIndex, boolean b)`
`setDate(int parameterIndex, java.sql.Date d)`
`setDouble(int parameterIndex, double d)`
`setFloat(int parameterIndex, float f)`
`setInt(int parameterIndex, int i)`
`setLong(int parameterIndex, long l)`
`setShort(int parameterIndex, short s)`
`setString(int parameterIndex, String s)`
`setTime(int parameterIndex, java.sql.Time t)`
`setTimeStamp(int parameterIndex, java.sql.TimeStamp t)`

In all these methods, the first argument defines the parameter index (starting with 1) and the second argument contains the value for the parameter.

In addition to modifying the query to accept parameters, we made an additional, unrelated change to the servlet. Instead of creating an instance of `javax.naming.InitialContext` and performing a JNDI lookup to obtain a reference to the `DataSource`, we used **dependency injection** to obtain the said instance.

Dependency injection is a design pattern in which an object's dependencies are injected at runtime by a container. This design pattern was made popular in the Java world by the Spring framework. Java EE uses the `@Resource` annotation to implement the pattern.

We accomplished this by moving the declaration of the `dataSource` object out of the `doGet()` method and making it a field. We then decorated it with the `@Resource` annotation. The `@Resource` annotation has an element called name. This element is used to indicate the JNDI name of the resource we want to obtain.

The `@Resource` annotation can be used to look up any kind of resources available through JNDI, not only `DataSources`.

Modifying database data

In the previous section, we saw how we can use the `executeQuery()` method of the `java.sql.PreparedStatement` interface to read data from the database. In this section, we will see how we can use the `executeUpdate()` method of this interface to insert, update, or delete data from the database. The `executeUpdate()` method is illustrated in the following example:

```
package net.ensode.glassfishbook.jdbcupdate;

import java.io.IOException;
import java.sql.Connection;
import java.sql.PreparedStatement;
import java.sql.SQLException;

import javax.annotation.Resource;
import javax.servlet.ServletException;
import javax.servlet.http.HttpServlet;
import javax.servlet.http.HttpServletRequest;
import javax.servlet.http.HttpServletResponse;
import javax.sql.DataSource;

public class JdbcUpdateServlet extends HttpServlet
{
  @Resource(name = "jdbc/__CustomerDBPool")
  private DataSource dataSource;
  @Override
  protected void doGet(HttpServletRequest request,
    HttpServletResponse response) throws ServletException,
    IOException
```

```
{
  String insertCustomerSql = "insert into " +
      "customers (customer_id, first_name, " +
      "last_name, email) values (?,?,?,?)";
  String updateCustomerLastNameSql = "update customers " +
      "set last_name = ? where customer_id = ?";
  String deleteCustomerSql = "delete from customers " +
      "where customer_id = ?";

  PreparedStatement insertCustomerStatement;
  PreparedStatement updateCustomerLastNameStatement;
  PreparedStatement deleteCustomerStatement;
  try
  {
    Connection connection = dataSource.getConnection();
    insertCustomerStatement =
      connection.prepareStatement(insertCustomerSql);
    updateCustomerLastNameStatement =
      connection.prepareStatement(updateCustomerLastNameSql);
    deleteCustomerStatement =
      connection.prepareStatement(deleteCustomerSql);

    insertCustomerStatement.setInt(1, 1);
    insertCustomerStatement.setString(2, "Leo");
    insertCustomerStatement.setString(3, "Smith");
    insertCustomerStatement.setString(4, "lsmith@fake.com");
    insertCustomerStatement.executeUpdate();

    insertCustomerStatement.setInt(1, 2);
    insertCustomerStatement.setString(2, "Jane");
    insertCustomerStatement.setString(3, "Davis");
    insertCustomerStatement.setString(4, null);
    insertCustomerStatement.executeUpdate();

    updateCustomerLastNameStatement.setString(1, "Jones");
    updateCustomerLastNameStatement.setInt(2, 2);
    updateCustomerLastNameStatement.executeUpdate();

    deleteCustomerStatement.setInt(1, 1);
    deleteCustomerStatement.executeUpdate();

    deleteCustomerStatement.close();
    updateCustomerLastNameStatement.close();
```

```
            insertCustomerStatement.close();
            connection.close();
            response.getWriter().println("Database Updated Successfully");
        }
        catch (SQLException e)
        {
            e.printStackTrace();
        }
    }
}
```

In this servlet, all SQL statements modify the data in the database. Just as in the previous example, we obtain a reference to the datasource by using dependency injection. We then obtain a connection from the connection pool by calling the `getConnection()` method defined in the `javax.sql.DataSource` interface.

Next, we obtain an instance of a class implementing the `javax.sql.PreparedStatement` interface for each SQL statement. We do this by calling the `prepareStatement()` method defined in the `java.sql.Connection` interface.

Just like before, we set the values for each parameter by calling the appropriate methods defined in the `PreparedStatement` interface (in the example, `setInt()` and `setString()`). After each parameter is set, we call the `executeUpdate()` method. At this point, the statement is actually executed in the database.

After performing all four updates to the database, the servlet simply prints the message "Database Updated Successfully" in the browser.

The Java Persistence API

The **Java Persistence API (JPA)** was introduced to Java EE in version 5 of the specification. Like its name implies, it is used to persist data to a Relational Database Management System. JPA replaced entity beans in Java EE 5 (of course, for backwards compatibility, entity beans are still supported). Java EE Entities are regular Java classes. The Java EE container knows these classes are entities because they are decorated with the `@Entity` annotation. Let's look at an entity mapping to the `CUSTOMER` table in the `CUSTOMERDB` database:

```
package net.ensode.glassfishbook.jpa;

import java.io.Serializable;

import javax.persistence.Column;
import javax.persistence.Entity;
```

```
import javax.persistence.Id;
import javax.persistence.Table;

@Entity
@Table(name = "CUSTOMERS")
public class Customer implements Serializable
{
  @Id
  @Column(name = "CUSTOMER_ID")
  private Long customerId;

  @Column(name = "FIRST_NAME")
  private String firstName;

  @Column(name = "LAST_NAME")
  private String lastName;

  private String email;

  public Long getCustomerId()
  {
    return customerId;
  }
  public void setCustomerId(Long customerId)
  {
    this.customerId = customerId;
  }
  public String getEmail()
  {
    return email;
  }
  public void setEmail(String email)
  {
    this.email = email;
  }
  public String getFirstName()
  {
    return firstName;
  }
  public void setFirstName(String firstName)
  {
    this.firstName = firstName;
  }
  public String getLastName()
```

```
    {
      return lastName;
    }
    public void setLastName(String lastName)
    {
      this.lastName = lastName;
    }
  }
```

In this example, the `@Entity` annotation lets GlassFish (or for that matter, any other Java EE-compliant application server) know that this class is an entity.

The `@Table(name = "CUSTOMERS")` annotation lets the application server know what table to map the entity to. The value of the `name` element contains the name of the database table that the entity maps to. This annotation is optional. If the name of the class maps the name of the database table, then it isn't necessary to specify what table the entity maps to.

The `@Id` annotation indicates that the `customerId` field maps to the primary key.

The `@Column` annotation maps each field to a column in the table. If the name of the field matches the name of the database column, then this annotation is not needed. This is the reason why the `email` field is not annotated.

That is pretty much all we need to do to create a Java EE Entity. Compare this to entity beans, where the bean had to implement a number of life cycle methods that were rarely used. We also had to write a local and/or remote interface, a local and/or remote home interface, plus a deployment descriptor in order to develop a single entity bean.

The `EntityManager` class is used to persist entities to a database. The following example illustrates its usage:

```
package net.ensode.glassfishbook.jpa;

import java.io.IOException;

import javax.annotation.Resource;
import javax.persistence.EntityManager;
import javax.persistence.EntityManagerFactory;
import javax.persistence.PersistenceUnit;
import javax.servlet.ServletException;
import javax.servlet.http.HttpServlet;
import javax.servlet.http.HttpServletRequest;
import javax.servlet.http.HttpServletResponse;
import javax.transaction.HeuristicMixedException;
```

```
import javax.transaction.HeuristicRollbackException;
import javax.transaction.NotSupportedException;
import javax.transaction.RollbackException;
import javax.transaction.SystemException;
import javax.transaction.UserTransaction;

public class JpaDemoServlet extends HttpServlet
{
  @PersistenceUnit
  private EntityManagerFactory entityManagerFactory;
  @Resource
  private UserTransaction userTransaction;
  @Override
  protected void doGet(HttpServletRequest request,
    HttpServletResponse response) throws ServletException,
    IOException
  {
    EntityManager entityManager =
      entityManagerFactory.createEntityManager();
    Customer customer = new Customer();
    Customer customer2 = new Customer();
    Customer customer3;

    customer.setCustomerId(3L);
    customer.setFirstName("James");
    customer.setLastName("McKenzie");
    customer.setEmail("jamesm@notreal.com");

    customer2.setCustomerId(4L);
    customer2.setFirstName("Charles");
    customer2.setLastName("Jonson");
    customer2.setEmail("cjohnson@phony.org");
    try
    {
      userTransaction.begin();
      entityManager.persist(customer);
      entityManager.persist(customer2);

      customer3 = entityManager.find(Customer.class, 4L);
      customer3.setLastName("Johnson");
      entityManager.persist(customer3);

      entityManager.remove(customer);
      userTransaction.commit();
```

```
        }
        catch (NotSupportedException e)
        {
          e.printStackTrace();
        }
        catch (SystemException e)
        {
          e.printStackTrace();
        }
        catch (SecurityException e)
        {
          e.printStackTrace();
        }
        catch (IllegalStateException e)
        {
          e.printStackTrace();
        }
        catch (RollbackException e)
        {
          e.printStackTrace();
        }
        catch (HeuristicMixedException e)
        {
          e.printStackTrace();
        }
        catch (HeuristicRollbackException e)
        {
          e.printStackTrace();
        }
        response.getWriter().println("Database Updated Successfully");
      }
    }
```

This servlet obtains an instance of a class implementing the `javax.persistence.EntityManagerFactory` interface via dependency injection. This is done by decorating the `EntityManagerFactory` variable with the `@PersistenceUnit` annotation. The `EntityManagerFactory` instance is used to obtain a reference to an instance of a class implementing the `javax.persistence.EntityManager` interface.

An instance of a class implementing the `javax.transaction.UserTransaction` interface is then injected via the `@Resource` annotation. This object is necessary as without wrapping calls to persist entities to the database, the code would throw a `javax.persistence.TransactionRequiredException`.

`EntityManager` performs many of the duties that home interfaces performed for entity beans, such as finding entities in a database, updating them, or deleting them. We obtain an instance of a class implementing `EntityManager` by invoking the `createEntityManager()` method on `EntityManagerFactory`.

As JPA entities are plain old Java objects (POJOs), they can be instantiated via the `new` operator. We call methods on them directly, unlike with entity beans where methods on an instance of a class implementing their remote interface is used.

> The call to the `setCustomerId()` method takes advantage of autoboxing—a feature added to the Java language in JDK 1.5. Notice that the method takes an instance of `java.lang.Long` as its parameter, but we are using `long` primitives. The code compiles and executes properly thanks to this feature.

Calls to the `persist()` method on `EntityManager` must be in a transaction, therefore it is necessary to start one by calling the `begin()` method on `UserTransaction`.

We then insert two new rows to the `CUSTOMERS` table by calling the `persist()` method on `entityManager` for the two instances of the `Customer` class we populated earlier in the code.

After persisting the data contained in the `customer` and `customer2` objects, we search the database for a row in the `CUSTOMERS` table with a primary key of 4. We do this by invoking the `find()` method on `entityManager`. This method takes the class of the entity we are searching for as its first parameter, and the primary key of the row corresponding to the object we want to obtain. This method is roughly equivalent to the `findByPrimaryKey()` method on an entity bean's home interface.

The primary key we set for the `customer2` object was 4, therefore what we have now is a copy of this object. The last name for this customer was misspelled when we originally inserted his data into the database. We now correct Mr. Johnson's last name by invoking the `setLastName()` method on `customer3`, then updating the information in the database by invoking `entityManager.persist()`.

We then delete the information for the `customer` object by invoking `entityManager.remove()` and passing the `customer` object as a parameter.

Finally, we commit the changes to the database by invoking the `commit()` method on `userTransaction`.

In order for the previous code to work as expected, an XML configuration file named persistence.xml must be deployed in the WAR file containing the previous servlet. This file must be placed in the WEB-INF/classes/META-INF/ directory inside the WAR file. Contents of this file for the previous code are shown next:

```
<?xml version="1.0" encoding="UTF-8"?>
<persistence version="1.0"
  xmlns="http://java.sun.com/xml/ns/persistence"
  xmlns:xsi="http://www.w3.org/2001/XMLSchema-instance"
  xsi:schemaLocation="http://java.sun.com/xml/ns/persistence
    http://java.sun.com/xml/ns/persistence/persistence_1_0.xsd">
  <persistence-unit name="customerPersistenceUnit">
    <jta-data-source>jdbc/__CustomerDBPool</jta-data-source>
  </persistence-unit>
</persistence>
```

persistence.xml must contain at least one <persistence-unit> element. Each <persistence-unit> element must provide a value for its name attribute and contain a <jta-data-source> child element whose value is the JNDI name of the datasource to be used for the persistence unit.

The reason more than one <persistence-unit> element is allowed is because an application may access more than one database. A <persistence-unit> element is required for each database the application will access. If the application defines more than one <persistence-unit> element, then the @PersistenceUnit annotation used to inject the EntityManagerFactory interface must provide a value for its unitName element. The value for this element must match the name attribute of the corresponding <persistence-unit> element in persistence.xml.

Cannot persist detached object exception

Frequently, an application will retrieve a JPA entity via the EntityManager.find() method, then pass this entity to a business or user interface layer where it will be potentially modified, and later the database data corresponding to the entity will be updated. In cases like this, invoking EntityManager.persist() will result in an exception. In order to update JPA entities this way, we need to invoke EntityManager.merge(). This method takes an instance of the JPA entity as its single argument and updates the corresponding row in the database with the data stored in it.

Entity relationships

In the previous section, we saw how to retrieve, insert, update, and delete single entities from the database. Entities are rarely isolated; in the vast majority of cases, they are related to other entities.

Entities can have one-to-one, one-to-many, many-to-one, and many-to-many relationships.

For example, in the CustomerDB database, there is a one-to-one relationship between the LOGIN_INFO and CUSTOMERS tables. This means that each customer has exactly one corresponding row in the LOGIN_INFO table. There is also a one-to-many relationship between the CUSTOMERS table and the ORDERS table. This is because a customer can place many orders. Additionally, there is a many-to-many relationship between the ORDERS table and the ITEMS table. This is because an order can contain many items and an item can be found in many orders.

In the next few sections, we discuss how to establish relationships between JPA entities.

One-to-one relationships

One-to-one relationships occur when an instance of an entity can have zero or one corresponding instance of another entity.

One-to-one entity relationships can be bidirectional (each entity is aware of the relationship) or unidirectional (only one of the entities is aware of the relationship). In the CUSTOMERDB database, one-to-one mapping between the LOGIN_INFO and CUSTOMERS tables is unidirectional, as the LOGIN_INFO table has a foreign key to the CUSTOMERS table, but not the other way around. As we will soon see, this fact does not stop us from creating a bidirectional one-to-one relationship between the Customer entity and the LoginInfo entity.

The source code for the LoginInfo entity that maps to the LOGIN_INFO table can be seen next:

```
package net.ensode.glassfishbook.entityrelationships;

import javax.persistence.Column;
import javax.persistence.Entity;
import javax.persistence.Id;
import javax.persistence.JoinColumn;
import javax.persistence.Table;

@Entity
```

```
@Table(name = "LOGIN_INFO")
public class LoginInfo
{
  @Id
  @Column(name = "LOGIN_INFO_ID")
  private Long loginInfoId;

  @Column(name = "LOGIN_NAME")
  private String loginName;

  private String password;

  @OneToOne
  @JoinColumn(name="CUSTOMER_ID")
  private Customer customer;

  public Long getLoginInfoId()
  {
    return loginInfoId;
  }
  public void setLoginInfoId(Long loginInfoId)
  {
    this.loginInfoId = loginInfoId;
  }
  public String getPassword()
  {
    return password;
  }
  public void setPassword(String password)
  {
    this.password = password;
  }
  public String getLoginName()
  {
    return loginName;
  }
  public void setLoginName(String userName)
  {
    this.loginName = userName;
  }
  public Customer getCustomer()
  {
    return customer;
  }
  public void setCustomer(Customer customer)
  {
    this.customer = customer;
  }
}
```

The code for this entity is very similar to the code for the `Customer` entity. It defines fields that map to database columns. Each field whose name does not match the database column name is decorated with the `@Column` annotation. In addition to that, the primary key is decorated with the `@Id` annotation.

Where this code gets interesting is in the declaration of the `customer` field. As can be seen in the code, the `customer` field is decorated with the `@OneToOne` annotation. This lets the application server (GlassFish) know that there is a one-to-one relationship between this entity and the `Customer` entity. The `customer` field is also decorated with the `@JoinColumn` annotation. This annotation lets the container know what column in the `LOGIN_INFO` table is the foreign key corresponding to the primary key in the `CUSTOMER` table. Since `LOGIN_INFO`, the table that the `LoginInfo` entity maps to has a foreign key to the `CUSTOMER` table, the `LoginInfo` entity owns the relationship. If the relationship was unidirectional, we wouldn't have to make any changes to the `Customer` entity. However, as we would like to have a bidirectional relationship between these two entities, we need to add a `LoginInfo` field to the `Customer` entity along with the corresponding getter and setter methods.

Like we mentioned before, in order to make the one-to-one relationship between the `Customer` and `LoginInfo` entities bidirectional, we need to make a few simple changes to the `Customer` entity:

```
package net.ensode.glassfishbook.entityrelationships;

import java.io.Serializable;
import java.util.Set;

import javax.persistence.CascadeType;
import javax.persistence.Column;
import javax.persistence.Entity;
import javax.persistence.Id;
import javax.persistence.OneToMany;
import javax.persistence.OneToOne;
import javax.persistence.Table;

@Entity
@Table(name = "CUSTOMERS")
public class Customer implements Serializable
{
  @Id
  @Column(name = "CUSTOMER_ID")
  private Long customerId;

  @Column(name = "FIRST_NAME")
  private String firstName;
```

```
    @Column(name = "LAST_NAME")
    private String lastName;

    private String email;

    @OneToOne(mappedBy = "customer")
    private LoginInfo loginInfo;

    public Long getCustomerId()
    {
      return customerId;
    }
    public void setCustomerId(Long customerId)
    {
      this.customerId = customerId;
    }
    public String getEmail()
    {
      return email;
    }
    public void setEmail(String email)
    {
      this.email = email;
    }
    public String getFirstName()
    {
      return firstName;
    }
    public void setFirstName(String firstName)
    {
      this.firstName = firstName;
    }
    public String getLastName()
    {
      return lastName;
    }
    public void setLastName(String lastName)
    {
      this.lastName = lastName;
    }
    public LoginInfo getLoginInfo()
    {
      return loginInfo;
    }
    public void setLoginInfo(LoginInfo loginInfo)
    {
      this.loginInfo = loginInfo;
    }
  }
```

The only change we need to make to the `Customer` entity to make the one-to-one relationship bidirectional is to add a `LoginInfo` field to it along with the corresponding setter and getter methods. The `loginInfo` field is decorated with the `@OneToOne` annotation. As the `Customer` entity does not own the relationship (the table it maps to does not have a foreign key to the corresponding table), the `mappedBy` element of the `@OneToOne` annotation needs to be added. This element specifies what field in the corresponding entity has the other end of the relationship. In this particular case, the customer field in the `LoginInfo` entity corresponds to the other end of this one-to-one relationship.

The following servlet illustrates the use of this entity:

```
package net.ensode.glassfishbook.entityrelationships;

import java.io.IOException;

import javax.annotation.Resource;
import javax.persistence.EntityManager;
import javax.persistence.EntityManagerFactory;
import javax.persistence.PersistenceUnit;
import javax.servlet.ServletException;
import javax.servlet.http.HttpServlet;
import javax.servlet.http.HttpServletRequest;
import javax.servlet.http.HttpServletResponse;
import javax.transaction.HeuristicMixedException;
import javax.transaction.HeuristicRollbackException;
import javax.transaction.NotSupportedException;
import javax.transaction.RollbackException;
import javax.transaction.SystemException;
import javax.transaction.UserTransaction;

public class OneToOneRelationshipDemoServlet extends HttpServlet
{
  @PersistenceUnit(unitName = "customerPersistenceUnit")
  private EntityManagerFactory entityManagerFactory;

  @Resource
  private UserTransaction userTransaction;

  @Override
  protected void doGet(HttpServletRequest request,
    HttpServletResponse response) throws ServletException,
    IOException
  {
    EntityManager entityManager =
```

```
            entityManagerFactory.createEntityManager();
        Customer customer;
        LoginInfo loginInfo = new LoginInfo();
        loginInfo.setLoginInfoId(1L);
        loginInfo.setLoginName("charlesj");
        loginInfo.setPassword("iwonttellyou");
        try
        {
          userTransaction.begin();
          customer = entityManager.find(Customer.class, 4L);
          loginInfo.setCustomer(customer);
          entityManager.persist(loginInfo);
          userTransaction.commit();
          response.getWriter().println("Database updated successfully.");
        }
        catch (NotSupportedException e)
        {
          e.printStackTrace();
        }
        catch (SystemException e)
        {
          e.printStackTrace();
        }
        catch (SecurityException e)
        {
          e.printStackTrace();
        }
        catch (IllegalStateException e)
        {
          e.printStackTrace();
        }
        catch (RollbackException e)
        {
          e.printStackTrace();
        }
        catch (HeuristicMixedException e)
        {
          e.printStackTrace();
        }
        catch (HeuristicRollbackException e)
        {
          e.printStackTrace();
        }
      }
    }
```

In this example, we first create an instance of the `LoginInfo` entity and populate it with some data. We then obtain an instance of the `Customer` entity from the database by invoking the `find()` method of `EntityManager` (data for this entity was inserted into the CUSTOMERS table in one of the JDBC examples). We then invoke the `setCustomer()` method on the `LoginInfo` entity, passing the customer object as a parameter. Finally, we invoke the `EntityManager.persist()` method to save the data in the database.

What happens behind the scenes is that the CUSTOMER_ID column of the LOGIN_INFO table gets populated with the primary key of the corresponding row in the CUSTOMERS table. This can be easily verified by querying the CUSTOMERDB database.

Notice how the call to `EntityManager.find()` to obtain the `Customer` entity is inside the same transaction where we call `EntityManager.persist()`. This must be the case, otherwise the database will not be updated successfully.

One-to-many relationships

With JPA, one-to-many entity relationships can be bidirectional (one entity contains a many-to-one relationship and the corresponding entity contains an inverse one-to-many relationship).

With SQL, one-to-many relationships are defined by foreign keys in one of the tables. The "many" part of the relationship is the one containing a foreign key to the "one" part of the relationship. One-to-many relationships defined in an RDBMS are typically unidirectional, as making them bidirectional usually results in denormalized data.

Just like when defining a unidirectional one-to-many relationship in an RDBMS, in JPA the "many" part of the relationship is the one that has a reference to the "one" part of the relationship. Therefore, the annotation used to decorate the appropriate setter method is `@ManyToOne`.

In the CUSTOMERDB database, there is a unidirectional one-to-many relationship between customers and orders. We define this relationship in the `Order` entity:

```
package net.ensode.glassfishbook.entityrelationships;

import javax.persistence.Column;
import javax.persistence.Entity;
import javax.persistence.Id;
import javax.persistence.JoinColumn;
import javax.persistence.ManyToOne;
```

```
import javax.persistence.Table;

@Entity
@Table(name = "ORDERS")
public class Order
{
  @Id
  @Column(name = "ORDER_ID")
  private Long orderId;

  @Column(name = "ORDER_NUMBER")
  private String orderNumber;

  @Column(name = "ORDER_DESCRIPTION")
  private String orderDescription;

  @ManyToOne
  @JoinColumn(name = "CUSTOMER_ID")
  private Customer customer;

  public Customer getCustomer()
  {
    return customer;
  }
  public void setCustomer(Customer customer)
  {
    this.customer = customer;
  }
  public String getOrderDescription()
  {
    return orderDescription;
  }
  public void setOrderDescription(String orderDescription)
  {
    this.orderDescription = orderDescription;
  }
  public Long getOrderId()
  {
    return orderId;
  }
  public void setOrderId(Long orderId)
  {
    this.orderId = orderId;
  }
```

```
    public String getOrderNumber()
    {
      return orderNumber;
    }
    public void setOrderNumber(String orderNumber)
    {
      this.orderNumber = orderNumber;
    }
  }
```

If we were to define a unidirectional many-to-one relationship between the `Orders` entity and the `Customer` entity, we wouldn't need to make any changes to the `Customer` entity. To define a bidirectional one-to-many relationship between the two entities, a new field decorated with the `@OneToMany` annotation needs to be added to the `Customer` entity:

```
package net.ensode.glassfishbook.entityrelationships;

import java.io.Serializable;
import java.util.Set;

import javax.persistence.Column;
import javax.persistence.Entity;
import javax.persistence.Id;
import javax.persistence.OneToMany;
import javax.persistence.Table;

@Entity
@Table(name = "CUSTOMERS")
public class Customer implements Serializable
{
  @Id
  @Column(name = "CUSTOMER_ID")
  private Long customerId;

  @Column(name = "FIRST_NAME")
  private String firstName;

  @Column(name = "LAST_NAME")
  private String lastName;

  private String email;

  @OneToOne(mappedBy = "customer")
  private LoginInfo loginInfo;

  @OneToMany(mappedBy="customer")
  private Set<Order> orders;
```

```
    public Long getCustomerId()
    {
      return customerId;
    }
    public void setCustomerId(Long customerId)
    {
      this.customerId = customerId;
    }
    public String getEmail()
    {
      return email;
    }
    public void setEmail(String email)
    {
      this.email = email;
    }
    public String getFirstName()
    {
      return firstName;
    }
    public void setFirstName(String firstName)
    {
      this.firstName = firstName;
    }
    public String getLastName()
    {
      return lastName;
    }
    public void setLastName(String lastName)
    {
      this.lastName = lastName;
    }
    public LoginInfo getLoginInfo()
    {
      return loginInfo;
    }
    public void setLoginInfo(LoginInfo loginInfo)
    {
      this.loginInfo = loginInfo;
    }
    public Set<Order> getOrders()
    {
      return orders;
    }
    public void setOrders(Set<Order> orders)
    {
      this.orders = orders;
    }
  }
```

The only difference between this version of the `Customer` entity and the previous one is the addition of the orders field and the related getter and setter methods. Of special interest is the `@OneToMany` annotation decorating this field. The `mappedBy` attribute must match the name of the corresponding field in the entity corresponding to the "many" part of the relationship. In simple terms, the value of the `mappedBy` attribute must match the name of the field decorated with the `@ManyToOne` annotation in the bean at the other side of the relationship.

The following servlet illustrates how to persist one-to-many relationships to the database:

```
package net.ensode.glassfishbook.entityrelationships;

import java.io.IOException;

import javax.annotation.Resource;
import javax.persistence.EntityManager;
import javax.persistence.EntityManagerFactory;
import javax.persistence.PersistenceUnit;
import javax.servlet.ServletException;
import javax.servlet.http.HttpServlet;
import javax.servlet.http.HttpServletRequest;
import javax.servlet.http.HttpServletResponse;
import javax.transaction.HeuristicMixedException;
import javax.transaction.HeuristicRollbackException;
import javax.transaction.NotSupportedException;
import javax.transaction.RollbackException;
import javax.transaction.SystemException;
import javax.transaction.UserTransaction;

public class OneToManyRelationshipDemoServlet extends HttpServlet
{
  @PersistenceUnit(unitName = "customerPersistenceUnit")
  private EntityManagerFactory entityManagerFactory;

  @Resource
  private UserTransaction userTransaction;

  @Override
  protected void doGet(HttpServletRequest request,
    HttpServletResponse response) throws ServletException,
    IOException
  {
    EntityManager entityManager =
      entityManagerFactory.createEntityManager();
```

```
Customer customer;
Order order1;
Order order2;

order1 = new Order();
order1.setOrderId(1L);
order1.setOrderNumber("SFX12345");
order1.setOrderDescription("Dummy order.");

order2 = new Order();
order2.setOrderId(2L);
order2.setOrderNumber("SFX23456");
order2.setOrderDescription("Another dummy order.");

try
{
  userTransaction.begin();
  customer = entityManager.find(Customer.class, 4L);
  order1.setCustomer(customer);
  order2.setCustomer(customer);
  entityManager.persist(order1);
  entityManager.persist(order2);
  userTransaction.commit();
  response.getWriter().println("Database updated successfully.");
}
catch (NotSupportedException e)
{
  e.printStackTrace();
}
catch (SystemException e)
{
  e.printStackTrace();
}
catch (SecurityException e)
{
  e.printStackTrace();
}
catch (IllegalStateException e)
{
  e.printStackTrace();
}
catch (RollbackException e)
{
  e.printStackTrace();
```

```
        }
        catch (HeuristicMixedException e)
        {
          e.printStackTrace();
        }
        catch (HeuristicRollbackException e)
        {
          e.printStackTrace();
        }
      }
    }
```

This code is pretty similar to the previous example. It instantiates two instances of the `Order` entity, populates them with some data, then in a transaction, an instance of the `Customer` entity is located and used as a parameter of the `setCustomer()` method of both instances of the `Order` entity. We then persist both `Order` entities by invoking `EntityManager.persist()` for each one of them.

Just like when dealing with one-to-one relationships, what happens behind the scenes is that the CUSTOMER_ID column of the ORDERS table in the CUSTOMERDB database is populated with the primary key corresponding to the related row in the CUSTOMERS table.

As the relationship is bidirectional, we can obtain all orders related to a customer by invoking the `getOrders()` method on the `Customer` entity.

Many-to-many relationships

In the CUSTOMERDB database, there is a many-to-many relationship between the ORDERS table and the ITEMS table. We can map this relationship by adding a new `Collection<Item>` field to the `Order` entity and decorating it with the `@ManyToMany` annotation.

```
package net.ensode.glassfishbook.entityrelationships;

import java.util.Collection;

import javax.persistence.Column;
import javax.persistence.Entity;
import javax.persistence.Id;
import javax.persistence.JoinColumn;
import javax.persistence.JoinTable;
import javax.persistence.ManyToMany;
import javax.persistence.ManyToOne;
import javax.persistence.Table;
```

```
@Entity
@Table(name = "ORDERS")
public class Order
{
  @Id
  @Column(name = "ORDER_ID")
  private Long orderId;

  @Column(name = "ORDER_NUMBER")
  private String orderNumber;

  @Column(name = "ORDER_DESCRIPTION")
  private String orderDescription;

  @ManyToOne
  @JoinColumn(name = "CUSTOMER_ID")
  private Customer customer;

  @ManyToMany
  @JoinTable(name = "ORDER_ITEMS",
    joinColumns = @JoinColumn(name = "ORDER_ID",
      referencedColumnName = "ORDER_ID"),
    inverseJoinColumns = @JoinColumn(name = "ITEM_ID",
      referencedColumnName = "ITEM_ID"))
  private Collection<Item> items;

  public Customer getCustomer()
  {
    return customer;
  }
  public void setCustomer(Customer customer)
  {
    this.customer = customer;
  }
  public String getOrderDescription()
  {
    return orderDescription;
  }
  public void setOrderDescription(String orderDescription)
  {
    this.orderDescription = orderDescription;
  }
  public Long getOrderId()
```

```
    {
      return orderId;
    }
    public void setOrderId(Long orderId)
    {
      this.orderId = orderId;
    }
    public String getOrderNumber()
    {
      return orderNumber;
    }
    public void setOrderNumber(String orderNumber)
    {
      this.orderNumber = orderNumber;
    }
    public Collection<Item> getItems()
    {
      return items;
    }
    public void setItems(Collection<Item> items)
    {
      this.items = items;
    }
  }
```

As we can see in this code, in addition to being decorated with the `@ManyToMany` annotation, the items field is also decorated with the `@JoinTable` annotation. Like its name suggests, this annotation lets the application server know what table is used as a join table to create the many-to-many relationship between the two entities. This annotation has three relevant elements: the `name` element that defines the name of the join table, and the `joinColumns` and `inverseJoinColumns` elements that define the columns that serve as foreign keys in the join table pointing to the entities' primary keys. Values for the `joinColumns` and `inverseJoinColumns` elements are yet another annotation—the `@JoinColumn` annotation. This annotation has two relevant elements: the `name` element that defines the name of the column in the join table, and the `referencedColumnName` element that defines the name of the column in the entity table.

The `Item` entity is a simple entity mapping to the ITEMS table in the CUSTOMERDB database:

```
package net.ensode.glassfishbook.entityrelationships;

import java.util.Collection;
```

```
import javax.persistence.Column;
import javax.persistence.Entity;
import javax.persistence.Id;
import javax.persistence.ManyToMany;
import javax.persistence.Table;

@Entity
@Table(name = "ITEMS")
public class Item
{
  @Id
  @Column(name = "ITEM_ID")
  private Long itemId;

  @Column(name = "ITEM_NUMBER")
  private String itemNumber;

  @Column(name = "ITEM_SHORT_DESC")
  private String itemShortDesc;

  @Column(name = "ITEM_LONG_DESC")
  private String itemLongDesc;

  @ManyToMany(mappedBy="items")
  private Collection<Order> orders;

  public Long getItemId()
  {
    return itemId;
  }
  public void setItemId(Long itemId)
  {
    this.itemId = itemId;
  }
  public String getItemLongDesc()
  {
    return itemLongDesc;
  }
  public void setItemLongDesc(String itemLongDesc)
  {
    this.itemLongDesc = itemLongDesc;
  }
  public String getItemNumber()
  {
```

```
        return itemNumber;
    }
    public void setItemNumber(String itemNumber)
    {
        this.itemNumber = itemNumber;
    }
    public String getItemShortDesc()
    {
        return itemShortDesc;
    }
    public void setItemShortDesc(String itemShortDesc)
    {
        this.itemShortDesc = itemShortDesc;
    }
    public Collection<Order> getOrders()
    {
        return orders;
    }
    public void setOrders(Collection<Order> orders)
    {
        this.orders = orders;
    }
}
```

Just like the one-to-one and one-to-many relationships, many-to-many relationships can be unidirectional or bidirectional. As we would like the many-to-many relationship between the `Order` and `Item` entities to be bidirectional, we added a `Collection<Order>` field and decorated it with the `@ManyToMany` annotation. As the corresponding field in the `Order` entity already has the join table defined, it is not necessary to do it again here. The entity containing the `@JoinTable` annotation is said to own the relationship. In a many-to-many relationship, either entity can own the relationship. In our example, the `Order` entity owns it as its `Collection<Item>` field is decorated with the `@JoinTable` annotation.

Just like with the one-to-one and one-to-many relationships, the `@ManyToMany` annotation in the non-owning side of a bidirectional many-to-many relationship must contain a `mappedBy` element indicating what field in the owning entity defines the relationship.

Now that we have seen the changes necessary to establish a bidirectional many-to-many relationship between the `Order` and `Item` entities, we can see the relationship in action in the following example:

```
package net.ensode.glassfishbook.entityrelationships;

import java.io.IOException;
import java.util.ArrayList;
import java.util.Collection;

import javax.annotation.Resource;
import javax.persistence.EntityManager;
import javax.persistence.EntityManagerFactory;
import javax.persistence.PersistenceUnit;
import javax.servlet.ServletException;
import javax.servlet.http.HttpServlet;
import javax.servlet.http.HttpServletRequest;
import javax.servlet.http.HttpServletResponse;
import javax.transaction.HeuristicMixedException;
import javax.transaction.HeuristicRollbackException;
import javax.transaction.NotSupportedException;
import javax.transaction.RollbackException;
import javax.transaction.SystemException;
import javax.transaction.UserTransaction;

public class ManyToManyRelationshipDemoServlet extends HttpServlet
{
  @PersistenceUnit(unitName = "customerPersistenceUnit")
  private EntityManagerFactory entityManagerFactory;

  @Resource
  private UserTransaction userTransaction;

  @Override
  protected void doGet(HttpServletRequest request,
    HttpServletResponse response) throws ServletException,
    IOException
  {
    EntityManager entityManager =
      entityManagerFactory.createEntityManager();
    Order order;
    Collection<Item> items = new ArrayList<Item>();
    Item item1 = new Item();
    Item item2 = new Item();

    item1.setItemId(1L);
    item1.setItemNumber("BCD1234");
    item1.setItemShortDesc("Notebook Computer");
    item1.setItemLongDesc("64 bit Quad core CPU, 4GB memory");
```

```
      item2.setItemId(2L);
      item2.setItemNumber("CDF2345");
      item2.setItemShortDesc("Cordless Mouse");
      item2.setItemLongDesc("Three button, infrared, "
        + "vertical and horizontal scrollwheels");

      items.add(item1);
      items.add(item2);
      try
      {
        userTransaction.begin();
        entityManager.persist(item1);
        entityManager.persist(item2);
        order = entityManager.find(Order.class, 1L);
        order.setItems(items);
        entityManager.persist(order);
        userTransaction.commit();
        response.getWriter().println("Database updated successfully");
      }
      catch (NotSupportedException e)
      {
        e.printStackTrace();
      }
      catch (SystemException e)
      {
        e.printStackTrace();
      }
      catch (SecurityException e)
      {
        e.printStackTrace();
      }
      catch (IllegalStateException e)
      {
        e.printStackTrace();
      }
      catch (RollbackException e)
      {
        e.printStackTrace();
      }
      catch (HeuristicMixedException e)
      {
        e.printStackTrace();
      }
      catch (HeuristicRollbackException e)
      {
        e.printStackTrace();
      }
    }
  }
```

This code creates two instances of the `Item` entity and populates them with some data. It then adds these two instances to a collection. A transaction is then started and the two `Item` instances are persisted to the database. Then, an instance of the `Order` entity is retrieved from the database. The `setItems()` method of the `Order` entity instance is then invoked, passing the collection containing the two `Item` instances as a parameter. The `Customer` instance is then persisted into the database. At this point, two rows are created behind the scenes in the ORDER_ITEMS table, which is the join table between the ORDERS and ITEMS tables.

Composite primary keys

Most tables in the CUSTOMERDB database have a column with the sole purpose of serving as a primary key (this type of primary key is sometimes referred to as a surrogate primary key or as an artificial primary key). However, some databases are not designed this way. Instead, a column in the database that is known to be unique across rows is used as the primary key. If there is no column whose value is not guaranteed to be unique across rows, then a combination of two or more columns is used as the table's primary key. It is possible to map this kind of primary key to JPA entities by using a primary key class.

There is one table in the CUSTOMERDB database that does not have a surrogate primary key—the ORDER_ITEMS table. This table serves as a join table between the ORDERS and the ITEMS tables. In addition to having foreign keys for these two tables, this table has an additional column called ITEM_QTY, which stores the quantity of each item in an order. As this table does not have a surrogate primary key, the JPA entity mapping to it must have a custom primary key class. In this table, the combination of the ORDER_ID and ITEM_ID columns must be unique. Therefore, this is a good combination for a composite primary key.

```
package net.ensode.glassfishbook.compositekeys;

import java.io.Serializable;

public class OrderItemPK implements Serializable
{
  public Long orderId;
  public Long itemId;

  public OrderItemPK()
  {

  }
  public OrderItemPK(Long orderId, Long itemId)
  {
```

```
        this.orderId = orderId;
        this.itemId = itemId;
    }
    @Override
    public boolean equals(Object obj)
    {
        boolean returnVal = false;
        if (obj == null)
        {
            returnVal = false;
        }
        else if (!obj.getClass().equals(this.getClass()))
        {
            returnVal = false;
        }
        else
        {
            OrderItemPK other = (OrderItemPK) obj;
            if (this == other)
            {
                returnVal = true;
            }
            else if (orderId != null && other.orderId != null
                && this.orderId.equals(other.orderId))
            {
                if (itemId != null && other.itemId != null
                    && itemId.equals(other.itemId))
                {
                    returnVal = true;
                }
            }
            else
            {
                returnVal = false;
            }
        }
        return returnVal;
    }
    @Override
    public int hashCode()
    {
        if (orderId == null || itemId == null)
        {
            return 0;
```

```
        }
        else
        {
          return orderId.hashCode() ^ itemId.hashCode();
        }
      }
    }
```

A custom primary key class must satisfy the following requirements:

- The class must be `public`
- It must implement `java.io.Serializable`
- It must have a `public` constructor that takes no arguments
- Its fields must be `public` or `protected`
- Its field names and types must match those of the entity
- It must override the default `hashCode()` and `equals()` methods defined in the `java.lang.Object` class

The `OrderPK` class meets all of these requirements. It also has a convenience constructor that takes two `Long` objects meant to initialize its `orderId` and `itemId` fields. This constructor was added for convenience. This is not a requirement for the class to be used as a primary key class.

When an entity uses a custom primary key class, it must be decorated with the `@IdClass` annotation. As the `OrderItem` class uses `OrderItemPK` as its custom primary key class, it must be decorated with said annotation.

```
package net.ensode.glassfishbook.compositekeys;

import javax.persistence.Column;
import javax.persistence.Entity;
import javax.persistence.Id;
import javax.persistence.IdClass;
import javax.persistence.Table;

@Entity
@Table(name = "ORDER_ITEMS")
@IdClass(value = OrderItemPK.class)
public class OrderItem
{
  @Id
  @Column(name = "ORDER_ID")
  private Long orderId;
```

```
    @Id
    @Column(name = "ITEM_ID")
    private Long itemId;

    @Column(name = "ITEM_QTY")
    private Long itemQty;

    public Long getItemId()
    {
      return itemId;
    }
    public void setItemId(Long itemId)
    {
      this.itemId = itemId;
    }
    public Long getItemQty()
    {
      return itemQty;
    }
    public void setItemQty(Long itemQty)
    {
      this.itemQty = itemQty;
    }
    public Long getOrderId()
    {
      return orderId;
    }
    public void setOrderId(Long orderId)
    {
      this.orderId = orderId;
    }
  }
```

There are two differences between this entity and the previous entities we have seen. The first difference is that this entity is decorated with the `@IdClass` annotation, indicating the primary key class corresponding to it. The second difference is that this entity has more than one field decorated with the `@Id` annotation. As this entity has a composite primary key, each field that is part of the primary key must be decorated with this annotation.

Obtaining a reference of an entity with a composite primary key is not much different than obtaining a reference to an entity with a primary key consisting of a single field. The following example demonstrates how to do this:

```
package net.ensode.glassfishbook.compositekeys;

import java.io.IOException;
import java.io.PrintWriter;

import javax.persistence.EntityManager;
import javax.persistence.EntityManagerFactory;
import javax.persistence.PersistenceUnit;
import javax.servlet.ServletException;
import javax.servlet.http.HttpServlet;
import javax.servlet.http.HttpServletRequest;
import javax.servlet.http.HttpServletResponse;

public class CompositeKeyDemoServlet extends HttpServlet
{
  @PersistenceUnit(unitName = "customerPersistenceUnit")
  private EntityManagerFactory entityManagerFactory;

  @Override
  protected void doGet(HttpServletRequest request,
    HttpServletResponse response) throws ServletException,
    IOException
  {
    PrintWriter printWriter = response.getWriter();
    EntityManager entityManager =
      entityManagerFactory.createEntityManager();
    OrderItem orderItem;
    orderItem = entityManager.find(OrderItem.class, new
      OrderItemPK(1L, 2L));
    response.setContentType("text/html");
    if (orderItem != null)
    {
      printWriter.println("Found an instance of Order Item for the
        supplied primary key:<br/>");
      printWriter.println("OrderItem order id: " +
        orderItem.getOrderId() + "<br/>");
      printWriter.println("OrderItem item id: " +
        orderItem.getItemId() + "<br/>");
    }
    else
    {
      printWriter.println("No instance of OrderItem found for the
        supplied primary key.");
    }
  }
}
```

As can be seen in this example, the only difference between locating an entity with a composite primary key and an entity with a primary key consisting of a single field is that an instance of the custom primary key class must be passed as a second argument of the `EntityManager.find()` method. Fields for this instance must be populated with the appropriate values for each field that is part of the primary key.

Java Persistence Query Language

All of our examples that obtain entities from the database so far have conveniently assumed that the primary key for the entity is known ahead of time. We all know that frequently this is not the case. Whenever we need to search for an entity by a field other than the entity's primary key, we must use the **Java Persistence Query Language (JPQL)**.

JPQL is an SQL-like language used for retrieving, updating, and deleting entities in a database. The following example illustrates how to use JPQL to retrieve a subset of states from the US_STATES table in the CUSTOMERDB database:

```
package net.ensode.glassfishbook.jpaquerylang;

import java.io.IOException;
import java.io.PrintWriter;
import java.util.List;

import javax.persistence.EntityManager;
import javax.persistence.EntityManagerFactory;
import javax.persistence.PersistenceUnit;
import javax.persistence.Query;
import javax.servlet.ServletException;
import javax.servlet.http.HttpServlet;
import javax.servlet.http.HttpServletRequest;
import javax.servlet.http.HttpServletResponse;

public class SelectQueryDemoServlet extends HttpServlet
{
  @PersistenceUnit(unitName = "customerPersistenceUnit")
  private EntityManagerFactory entityManagerFactory;

  @Override
  protected void doGet(HttpServletRequest request,
    HttpServletResponse response) throws ServletException,
    IOException
  {
    PrintWriter printWriter = response.getWriter();
    List<UsState> matchingStatesList;
    EntityManager entityManager =
      entityManagerFactory.createEntityManager();
```

```
        Query query = entityManager.createQuery(
          "SELECT s FROM UsState s WHERE s.usStateNm " +
          "LIKE :name");

        query.setParameter("name", "New%");
        matchingStatesList = query.getResultList();
        response.setContentType("text/html");
        printWriter.println("The following states match " +
          "the criteria:<br/>");
        for (UsState state : matchingStatesList)
        {
          printWriter.println(state.getUsStateNm() + "<br/>");
        }
      }
    }
```

This code invokes the `EntityManager.createQuery()` method, passing a `String` containing a JPQL query as a parameter. This method returns an instance of `javax.persistence.Query`. The query retrieves all `UsState` entities whose name start with the word "New".

As can be seen in this code, JPQL is similar to SQL. However, there are some differences that may confuse readers having SQL knowledge. The equivalent SQL code for the query in the code would be:

```
SELECT * from US_STATES s where s.US_STATE_NM like 'New%'
```

The first difference between JPQL and SQL is that in JPQL, we always reference entity names, whereas in SQL, table names are referenced. The "s" after the entity name in the JPQL query is an alias for the entity. Table aliases are optional in SQL, but entity aliases are required in JPQL. Keeping these differences in mind, the JPQL query should now be a lot less confusing.

The `:name` in the query is a named parameter. Named parameters are meant to be substituted with actual values. This is done by invoking the `setParameter()` method in the instance of `javax.persistence.Query` returned by the call to `EntityManager.createQuery()`. A JPQL query can have multiple named parameters.

To actually run the query and retrieve the entities from the database, the `getResultList()` method must be invoked in an instance of `javax.persistence.Query` obtained from `EntityManager.createQuery()`. This method returns an instance of a class implementing the `java.util.List` interface. This list contains the entities matching the query criteria. If no entities match the criteria, then an empty list is returned.

If we are certain that the query will return a single entity, then the `getSingleResult()` method may be alternatively called on `Query`. This method returns an `Object` that must be casted to the appropriate entity.

The previous example uses the LIKE operator to find entities whose name start with the word "New". This is accomplished by substituting the query's named parameter with the value "New%". The percent sign at the end of the parameter value means that any number of characters after the word "New" will match the expression. The percent sign can be used anywhere in the parameter value. For example, a value of "%Dakota" would match any entities whose name end in "Dakota", a value of "A%a" would match any states whose name start with a capital "A" and end with a lowercase "a". There can be more than one percent sign in a parameter value. The underscore sign (_) can be used to match a single character. All the rules for the percent sign apply to the underscore sign as well.

In addition to the `LIKE` operator, there are other operators that can be used to retrieve entities from the database:

- The `=` operator will retrieve entities whose field at the left of the operator exactly matches the value at the right of the operator.
- The `>` operator will retrieve entities whose field at the left of the operator is greater than the value at the right of the operator.
- The `<` operator will retrieve entities whose field at the left of the operator is less than the value at the right of the operator.
- The `>=` operator will retrieve entities whose field at the left of the operator is greater than or equal to the value at the right of the operator.
- The `<=` operator will retrieve entities whose field at the left of the operator is less than or equal to the value at the right of the operator.

All of these operators work the same way as the equivalent operators in SQL. Just like in SQL, these operators can be combined with the "AND" and "OR" operators. Conditions combined with the "AND" operator match if both conditions are true, conditions combined with the "OR" operator match if at least one of the conditions is true.

If we intend to use a query many times, it can be stored in a **named query**. Named queries can be defined by decorating the relevant entity class with the `@NamedQuery` annotation. This annotation has two elements: a `name` element used to set the name of the query and a `query` element defining the query itself. To execute a named query, the `createNamedQuery()` method must be invoked in an instance of `EntityManager`. This method takes a `String` containing the query name as its sole parameter and returns an instance of `javax.persistence.Query`.

In addition to retrieving entities, JPQL can be used to modify or delete entities. However, entity modification and deletion can be done programmatically via the `EntityManager` interface. Doing so results in code that tends to be more readable than when using JPQL. Due to this, we will not cover entity modification and deletion via JPQL. Readers interested in writing JPQL queries to modify and delete entities, as well as readers wishing to know more about JPQL are encouraged to review the Java Persistence 2.0 specification. This specification can be downloaded from `http://jcp.org/en/jsr/detail?id=317`.

In the examples of this chapter, we showed database access done directly from servlets. We did this to get the point across without bogging ourselves down with details. However, in general, this is not a good practice. Database access code should be encapsulated in Data Access Objects (DAOs).

For more information on the DAO design pattern, refer to `http://java.sun.com/blueprints/corej2eepatterns/Patterns/DataAccessObject.html`.

Also, our examples showed servlets that did pretty much nothing but database access. Servlets typically serve as controllers when following the Model View Controller (MVC) design pattern. We chose not to add any user interface code to our examples as it is irrelevant to the topic at hand. However, for real applications, we would of course have entities populated from user interface components, most likely input fields in a JSP. These fields would be in an HTML form that when submitted, would pass control to a servlet, which would then populate entities from the data entered by the user and pass the entities to a DAO, which would then persist the data to the database.

For more information about the MVC design pattern, refer to `http://java.sun.com/blueprints/patterns/MVC.html`.

New features introduced in JPA 2.0

Version 2.0 of the JPA specification introduces some new features to make working with JPA even easier. In the following sections, we discuss some of these new features:

Criteria API

One of the main additions to JPA in the 2.0 specification is the introduction of the **Criteria API**. The Criteria API is meant as a complement to the Java Persistence Query Language (JPQL).

Although JPQL is very flexible, it has some problems that make working with it more difficult than necessary. For starters, JPQL queries are stored as strings and the compiler has no way of validating JPQL syntax. Additionally, JPQL is not type safe. We could write a JPQL query in which our `where` clause could have a string value for a numeric property and our code would compile and deploy just fine.

To get around the JPQL limitations described in the previous paragraph, the Criteria API was introduced to JPA in version 2.0 of the specification. The Criteria API allows us to write JPA queries programmatically, without having to rely on JPQL.

The following code example illustrates how to use the Criteria API in our Java EE 6 applications:

```
package net.ensode.glassfishbook.criteriaapi;

import java.io.IOException;
import java.io.PrintWriter;
import java.util.List;

import javax.persistence.EntityManager;
import javax.persistence.EntityManagerFactory;
import javax.persistence.PersistenceUnit;
import javax.persistence.TypedQuery;
import javax.persistence.criteria.CriteriaBuilder;
import javax.persistence.criteria.CriteriaQuery;
import javax.persistence.criteria.Path;
import javax.persistence.criteria.Predicate;
import javax.persistence.criteria.Root;
import javax.persistence.metamodel.EntityType;
import javax.persistence.metamodel.Metamodel;
import javax.persistence.metamodel.SingularAttribute;
import javax.servlet.ServletException;
import javax.servlet.annotation.WebServlet;
import javax.servlet.http.HttpServlet;
import javax.servlet.http.HttpServletRequest;
import javax.servlet.http.HttpServletResponse;

@WebServlet(urlPatterns = {"/criteriaapi"})
public class CriteriaApiDemoServlet extends HttpServlet
```

```
{
  @PersistenceUnit(unitName = "customerPersistenceUnit")
  private EntityManagerFactory entityManagerFactory;

  @Override
  protected void doGet(HttpServletRequest request,
    HttpServletResponse response) throws ServletException,
    IOException
  {
    PrintWriter printWriter = response.getWriter();
    List<UsState> matchingStatesList;
    EntityManager entityManager =
      entityManagerFactory.createEntityManager();
    CriteriaBuilder criteriaBuilder =
      entityManager.getCriteriaBuilder();
    CriteriaQuery<UsState> criteriaQuery =
      criteriaBuilder.createQuery(UsState.class);
    Root<UsState> root = criteriaQuery.from(UsState.class);

    Metamodel metamodel = entityManagerFactory.getMetamodel();
    EntityType<UsState> usStateEntityType =
              metamodel.entity(UsState.class);
    SingularAttribute<UsState, String> usStateAttribute =
      usStateEntityType.getDeclaredSingularAttribute("usStateNm",
      String.class);
    Path<String> path = root.get(usStateAttribute);
    Predicate predicate = criteriaBuilder.like(path, "New%");
    criteriaQuery = criteriaQuery.where(predicate);
    TypedQuery typedQuery = entityManager.createQuery(criteriaQuery);

    matchingStatesList = typedQuery.getResultList();
    response.setContentType("text/html");
    printWriter.println("The following states match the
      criteria:<br/>");
    for (UsState state : matchingStatesList)
    {
      printWriter.println(state.getUsStateNm() + "<br/>");
    }
  }
}
```

This example is equivalent to the JPQL example we saw earlier in this chapter. However, this example takes advantage of the Criteria API instead of relying on JPQL.

When writing code using the Criteria API, the first thing we need to do is to obtain an instance of a class implementing the `javax.persistence.criteria.CriteriaBuilder` interface. As we can see in the previous example, we need to obtain said instance by invoking the `getCriteriaBuilder()` method on our `EntityManager`.

From our `CriteriaBuilder` implementation, we need to obtain an instance of a class implementing the `javax.persistence.criteria.CriteriaQuery` interface. We do this by invoking the `createQuery()` method in our `CriteriaBuilder` implementation. Notice that `CriteriaQuery` is generically typed. The generic type argument dictates the type of result that our `CriteriaQuery` implementation will return upon execution. By taking advantage of generics in this way, the Criteria API allows us to write type safe code.

Once we have obtained a `CriteriaQuery` implementation, from it we can obtain an instance of a class implementing the `javax.persistence.criteria.Root` interface. The `Root` implementation dictates what JPA entity we will be querying from. It is analogous to the `FROM` query in JPQL (and SQL).

The next two lines in our example take advantage of another new addition to the JPA specification—the **Metamodel API**. In order to take advantage of the Metamodel API, we need to obtain an implementation of the `javax.persistence.metamodel.Metamodel` interface by invoking the `getMetamodel()` method on our `EntityManagerFactory`.

From our `Metamodel` implementation, we can obtain a generically typed instance of the `javax.persistence.metamodel.EntityType` interface. The generic type argument indicates the JPA entity our `EntityType` implementation corresponds to. `EntityType` allows us to browse the persistent attributes of our JPA entities at runtime. This is exactly what we do in the next line in our example. In our case, we are getting an instance of `SingularAttribute`, which maps to a simple, singular attribute in our JPA entity. `EntityType` has methods to obtain attributes that map to collections, sets, lists, and maps. Obtaining these types of attributes is very similar to obtaining a `SingularAttribute`, therefore we won't be covering those directly. Refer to the Java EE 6 API documentation at `http://java.sun.com/javaee/6/docs/api/` for more information.

As we can see in our example, `SingularAttribute` contains two generic type arguments. The first argument dictates the JPA entity we are working with and the second one indicates the type of attribute. We obtain our `SingularAttribute` by invoking the `getDeclaredSingularAttribute()` method on our `EntityType` implementation and passing the attribute name (as declared in our JPA entity) as a `String`.

Once we have obtained our `SingularAttribute` implementation, we need to obtain an `import javax.persistence.criteria.Path` implementation by invoking the `get()` method in our `Root` instance and passing our `SingularAttribute` as a parameter.

In our example, we will get a list of all the "new" states in the United States (that is, all states whose names start with "New"). Of course, this is the job of a "like" condition. We can do this with the Criteria API by invoking the `like()` method on our `CriteriaBuilder` implementation. The `like()` method takes our `Path` implementation as its first parameter and the value to search for as its second parameter.

`CriteriaBuilder` has a number of methods that are analogous to SQL and JPQL clauses such as `equals()`, `greaterThan()`, `lessThan()`, `and()`, `or()`, and so on and so forth (for the complete list, refer to the Java EE 6 documentation at `http://java.sun.com/javaee/6/docs/api/`). These methods can be combined to create complex queries via the Criteria API.

The `like()` method in `CriteriaBuilder` returns an implementation of the `javax.persistence.criteria.Predicate` interface, which we need to pass to the `where()` method in our `CriteriaQuery` implementation. This method returns a new instance of `CriteriaBuilder` which we assign to our `criteriaBuilder` variable.

At this point, we are ready to build our query. When working with the Criteria API, we deal with the `javax.persistence.TypedQuery` interface, which can be thought of as a type-safe version of the `Query` interface we use with JPQL. We obtain an instance of `TypedQuery` by invoking the `createQuery()` method in `EntityManager` and passing our `CriteriaQuery` implementation as a parameter.

To obtain our query results as a list, we simply invoke `getResultList()` on our `TypedQuery` implementation. It is worth reiterating that the Criteria API is type safe. Therefore, attempting to assign the results of `getResultList()` to a list of the wrong type would result in a compilation error.

After building, packaging, and deploying our code, then pointing the browser to our servlet's URL, we should see all the "New" states displayed in the browser.

Bean Validation support

Another new feature introduced in JPA 2.0 is support for JSR 303, Bean Validation. Bean Validation support allows us to annotate our JPA entities with Bean Validation annotations. These annotations allow us to easily validate user input and perform data sanitation.

Taking advantage of Bean Validation is very simple, all we need to do is annotate our JPA entity fields or getter methods with any of the validation annotations defined in the `javax.validation.constraints` package. Once our fields are annotated as appropriate, the `EntityManager` will prevent non-validating data from being persisted.

The following code example is a modified version of the `Customer` JPA entity we saw earlier in this chapter. It has been modified to take advantage of Bean Validation in some of its fields.

```
package net.ensode.glassfishbook.jpa.beanvalidation;

import java.io.Serializable;

import javax.persistence.Column;
import javax.persistence.Entity;
import javax.persistence.Id;
import javax.persistence.Table;
import javax.validation.constraints.NotNull;
import javax.validation.constraints.Size;

@Entity
@Table(name = "CUSTOMERS")
public class Customer implements Serializable
{
  @Id
  @Column(name = "CUSTOMER_ID")
  private Long customerId;

  @Column(name = "FIRST_NAME")
  @NotNull
  @Size(min=2, max=20)
  private String firstName;

  @Column(name = "LAST_NAME")
  @NotNull
  @Size(min=2, max=20)
  private String lastName;

  private String email;

  public Long getCustomerId()
  {
    return customerId;
```

```
    }
    public void setCustomerId(Long customerId)
    {
      this.customerId = customerId;
    }
    public String getEmail()
    {
      return email;
    }
    public void setEmail(String email)
    {
      this.email = email;
    }
    public String getFirstName()
    {
      return firstName;
    }
    public void setFirstName(String firstName)
    {
      this.firstName = firstName;
    }
    public String getLastName()
    {
      return lastName;
    }
    public void setLastName(String lastName)
    {
      this.lastName = lastName;
    }
  }
```

In this example, we used the `@NotNull` annotation to prevent the `firstName` and `lastName` of our entity from being persisted with `null` values. We also used the `@Size` annotation to restrict the minimum and maximum length of these fields.

This is all we need to do to take advantage of Bean Validation in JPA. If our code attempts to persist or update an instance of our entity that does not pass the declared validation, an exception of type `javax.validation.ConstraintViolationException` will be thrown and the entity will not be persisted.

As we can see, Bean Validation pretty much automates data validation, freeing us from having to manually write validation code.

In addition to the two annotations discussed in the previous example, the `javax.validation.constraints` package contains several additional annotations that we can use to automate validation on our JPA entities. Refer to the Java EE 6 API documentation at `http://java.sun.com/javaee/6/docs/api/` for the complete list.

Summary

This chapter covered how to access data in a database via both the Java Database Connectivity (JDBC) and through the Java Persistence API (JPA).

We covered how to obtain data from the database by using JDBC via the `executeQuery()` method defined in the `java.sql.PreparedStatement` interface. We also covered how to insert, update, and delete data in the database via the `executeUpdate()` method defined in the same interface. Additionally, using dependency injection to inject a DataSource into an object was also covered.

Setting a Java class as an entity by decorating it with the `@Entity` annotation was also covered. Additionally, we covered how to map an entity to a database table via the `@Table` annotation. We also covered how to map entity fields to database columns via the `@Column` annotation, as well as declaring an entity's primary key via the `@Id` annotation.

Using the `javax.persistence.EntityManager` interface to find, persist, and update JPA entities was also covered.

Defining both unidirectional and bidirectional one-to-one, one-to-many, and many-to-many relationships between JPA entities was covered as well.

Additionally, we covered how to use JPA composite primary keys by developing custom primary key classes.

We also covered how to retrieve entities from a database by using the Java Persistence Query Language (JPQL).

We then discussed some new JPA 2.0 features such as the Criteria API that allows us to build JPA queries programmatically, the Metamodel API that allows us to take advantage of Java's type safety when working with JPA, and Bean Validation that allows us to easily validate input by simply annotating our JPA entity fields.

6
JavaServer Faces

In this chapter we will cover **JavaServer Faces (JSF)**, the standard component framework of the Java EE platform. Java EE 6 includes JSF 2.0 (the latest version of JSF) as its standard user interface component framework. Readers familiar with earlier versions of JSF will notice that JSF 2.0 includes a number of new features to make JSF application development simpler. Notably, JSF 2.0 relies a lot on convention over configuration. If we follow JSF conventions, then we don't need to write a lot of configuration. In most cases, we don't need to write any configuration at all. This fact, combined with the fact that `web.xml` is optional in servlet 3.0, means that in many cases we can write complete web applications without having to write a single line of XML configuration. This means it is no longer necessary to write either a `web.xml` or a `faces-config.xml` file.

Introduction to JSF 2.0

JSF 2.0 introduces a number of enhancements to make JSF application development easier. In the following few sections, we explain some of these new features.

> Readers who are not familiar with earlier versions of JSF may not understand the following few sections completely. There's nothing to worry about, everything will be perfectly clear by the end of this chapter.

Facelets

One notable difference between JSF 2.0 and earlier versions is that Facelets is now the preferred view technology for JSF. Earlier versions of JSF used JSP as their default view technology. As JSP technology predates JSF, sometimes using JSP with JSF felt unnatural or created problems. For example, the lifecycle of JSPs is different from the lifecycle of JSF. This mismatch introduced some problems for JSF 1.x application developers.

JSF was designed from the beginning to support multiple view technologies. To take advantage of this capability, Jacob Hookom wrote a new view technology specifically for JSF. He named his view technology "Facelets". Facelets was so successful that it became a de-facto standard for JSF. The JSF 2.0 expert group recognized Facelets' popularity and made it the official view technology for JSF 2.0.

Optional faces-config.xml

J2EE applications have suffered what some have considered to be excessive XML configuration.

Java EE 5 took some measures to reduce XML configuration considerably. Java EE 6 reduces the required configuration even further, making the JSF configuration file, `faces-config.xml`, optional in the latest version of JSF.

In JSF 2.0, JSF managed beans can be configured via the new `@ManagedBean` annotation, obviating the need to configure them in `faces-config.xml`.

Additionally, there is a convention for JSF navigation. If the value of the action attribute of a JSF 2.0 command link or command button matches the name of a facelet (minus the XHTML extension), then by convention the application will navigate to the facelet matching the action name. This convention allows us to avoid having to configure application navigation in `faces-config.xml`.

For most JSF 2.0 applications, `faces-config.xml` is completely unnecessary.

Standard resource locations

JSF 2.0 introduces standard resource locations. Resources are artifacts a page or JSF component needs to render properly. Resource examples include CSS stylesheets, Javascript files, and images.

In JSF 2.0, resources can be placed in a subdirectory under a folder called `resources`, either at the root of a WAR file or under META-INF. By convention, JSF components know that they can retrieve resources from one of these two locations.

In order to avoid cluttering the `resources` directory, resources are typically placed in a subdirectory. This subdirectory is referred to from the `library` attribute of JSF components.

For example, we could place a CSS stylesheet called `styles.css` under `/resources/css/styles.css`.

In our JSF pages, we could retrieve this CSS file using the `<h:outputStylesheet>` tag as follows:

```
<h:outputStylesheet library="css" name="styles.css"/>
```

The value of the `library` attribute must match the subdirectory where our stylesheet is located.

Similarly, we could have a javascript file under `/resources/scripts/somescript.js` and an image under `/resources/images/logo.png`. We could access these resources as follows:

```
<h:graphicImage library="images" name="logo.png"/>
```

And:

```
<h:outputScript library="scripts" name="somescript.js"/>
```

Notice that in each case the value of the `library` attribute matches the corresponding subdirectory name under the `resources` directory, and the value of the `name` attribute matches the resource's filename.

Developing our first JSF 2.0 application

To illustrate basic JSF concepts, we will develop a simple application consisting of two Facelet pages and a single managed bean.

Facelets

Like we mentioned in this chapter's introduction, the default view technology for JSF 2.0 is Facelets. Facelets need to be written using standard XML. The most popular way of developing Facelet pages is to use XHTML in conjunction with JSF specific XML namespaces. The following example shows how a typical Facelet page looks like:

```
<?xml version='1.0' encoding='UTF-8' ?>
<!DOCTYPE html PUBLIC "-//W3C//DTD XHTML 1.0 Transitional//EN"
  "http://www.w3.org/TR/xhtml1/DTD/xhtml1-transitional.dtd">
<html xmlns="http://www.w3.org/1999/xhtml"
      xmlns:h="http://java.sun.com/jsf/html"
      xmlns:f="http://java.sun.com/jsf/core">
  <h:head>
    <title>Enter Customer Data</title>
  </h:head>
  <h:body>
    <h:outputStylesheet library="css" name="styles.css"
      target="body"/>
    <h:form>
```

```
        <h:messages></h:messages>
        <h:panelGrid columns="2"
                     columnClasses="rightAlign,leftAlign">
          <h:outputText value="First Name:">
          </h:outputText>
          <h:inputText label="First Name"
                       value="#{customer.firstName}"
                       required="true">
            <f:validateLength minimum="2" maximum="30">
            </f:validateLength>
          </h:inputText>
          <h:outputText value="Last Name:"></h:outputText>
          <h:inputText label="Last Name"
                       value="#{customer.lastName}"
                       required="true">
            <f:validateLength minimum="2" maximum="30">
            </f:validateLength>
          </h:inputText>
          <h:outputText value="Email:">
          </h:outputText>
          <h:inputText label="Email" value="#{customer.email}">
            <f:validateLength minimum="3" maximum="30">
            </f:validateLength>
          </h:inputText>
          <h:panelGroup></h:panelGroup>
          <h:commandButton action="confirmation" value="Save">
          </h:commandButton>
        </h:panelGrid>
      </h:form>
    </h:body>
</html>
```

The following screenshot illustrates how this page renders in the browser:

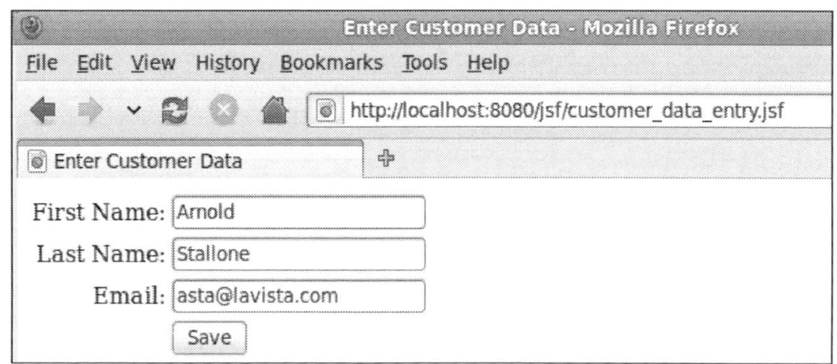

Of course, this screenshot was taken after entering some data in every text field; originally each text field was blank.

Any Facelet JSF page will include the two namespaces illustrated in the example. The first namespace (`xmlns:h="http://java.sun.com/jsf/html"`) is for tags that render HTML components. By convention, the prefix "h" (for "HTML") is used when using this tag library.

The second namespace (`xmlns:f="http://java.sun.com/jsf/core"`) is the core JSF tag library. By convention, the prefix "f" (for "faces") is used when using this tag library.

The first JSF-specific tags we see in the previous example are the `<h:head>` and the `<h:body>` tags. These tags are analogous to the standard HTML `<head>` and `<body>` tags and are rendered as such when the page is displayed in the browser.

The `<h:outputStylesheet>` tag is also a new JSF 2.0 tag. It is used to load a CSS stylesheet from a well-known location. (JSF 2.0 standardizes the locations of resources such as CSS stylesheets and javascript files. This will be discussed in detail later in the chapter.) The value of the `library` attribute must correspond to the directory where the CSS file resides (this directory must be under the `resources` directory). The `name` attribute must correspond to the name of the CSS stylesheet we wish to load.

The next tag we see is the `<h:form>` tag. This tag generates an HTML form when the page is rendered. As can be seen in the example, there is no need to specify an `action` or `method` attribute for this tag. As a matter of fact, there is neither an `action` attribute nor a `method` attribute for this tag. The `action` attribute for the rendered HTML form will be generated automatically and the `method` attribute will always be `"post"`.

The next tag we see is the `<h:messages>` tag. Like its name implies, this tag is used to display any messages. As we will see shortly, JSF can automatically generate validation messages that will be displayed inside this tag. Additionally, arbitrary messages can be added programmatically via the `addMessage()` method defined in `javax.faces.context.FacesContext`.

The next JSF tag we see is `<h:panelGrid>`. This tag is roughly equivalent to an HTML table, but it works a bit differently. Instead of declaring rows and columns, the `<h:panelGrid>` tag has a `columns` attribute. The value of this attribute indicates the number of columns in the table rendered by this tag. As we place components inside this tag, they will be placed in a row until the number of columns defined in the `columns` attribute is reached, then the next component will be placed in the next row. In the example, the value of the `columns` attribute is two. Therefore, the first two tags will be placed in the first row, the next two will be placed in the second row, and so on.

Another interesting attribute of `<h:panelGrid>` is the `columnClasses` attribute. This attribute assigns a CSS class to each column in the rendered table. In the example, two CSS classes (separated by a comma) are used as the value for this attribute. This has the effect of assigning the first CSS class to the first column and the second one to the second column. Had there been three or more columns, the third one would have gotten the first CSS class, the fourth one would have the second CSS class, and so on, alternating between the first one and the second one. To clarify how this works, the next code snippet illustrates a portion of the source of the HTML markup generated by the previous page.

```
<table>
  <tbody>
    <tr>
      <td class="rightAlign">
        First Name:
      </td>
      <td class="leftAlign">
        <input type="text" name="j_idt8:j_idt12" />
      </td>
    </tr>
    <tr>
      <td class="rightAlign">
        Last Name:
      </td>
      <td class="leftAlign">
        <input type="text" name="j_idt8:j_idt14" />
      </td>
    </tr>
    <tr>
      <td class="rightAlign">
        Email:
      </td>
      <td class="leftAlign">
        <input type="text" name="j_idt8:j_idt16" />
      </td>
    </tr>
    <tr>
      <td class="rightAlign"></td>
      <td class="leftAlign">
        <input type="submit" name="j_idt8:j_idt18" value="Save" />
      </td>
    </tr>
  </tbody>
</table>
```

Notice how each `<td>` tag has an alternating CSS tag of `"rightAlign"` or `"leftAlign"`. We achieved this by assigning the value `"rightAlign,leftAlign"` to the `columnClasses` attribute of `<h:panelGrid>`. We should note that the CSS classes we are using in our example are defined in the CSS stylesheet we loaded via the `<h:outputStylesheet>` tag we discussed earlier.

At this point in the example, we start adding components inside `<h:panelGrid>`. These components will be rendered inside the table rendered by `<h:panelGrid>`. Like we mentioned before, the number of columns in the rendered table is defined by the columns attribute of `<h:panelGrid>`. Therefore, we don't need to worry about columns (or rows). We just start adding components and they will be placed in the right place.

The next tag we see is the `<h:outputText>` tag. This tag is similar to the core JSTL `<c:out>` tag. It outputs the text or expression in its `value` attribute to the rendered page.

Next, we see the `<h:inputText>` tag. This tag generates a text field in the rendered page. Its `label` attribute is used for any validation messages. It lets the user know what field the message refers to.

> Although it is not required for the value of the `label` attribute of `<h:inputText>` to match the label displayed on the page, it is highly recommended to use this value. In case of an error, this will let the user know exactly what field the message is referring to.

Of particular interest is the tag's `value` attribute. What we see as the value for this attribute is a **value binding expression**. What this means is that this value is tied to a property of one of the application's managed beans. In the example, this particular text field is tied to a property called `firstName` in a managed bean called `customer`. When a user enters a value for this text field and submits the form, the corresponding property in the managed bean is updated with this value. The tag's `required` attribute is optional and valid values for it are `true` or `false`. If this attribute is set to `true`, the container will not let the user submit the form until the user enters some data in the text field. If the user attempts to submit the form without entering a required value, the page will be reloaded and an error message will be displayed inside the `<h:messages>` tag.

This can be seen in the following screenshot:

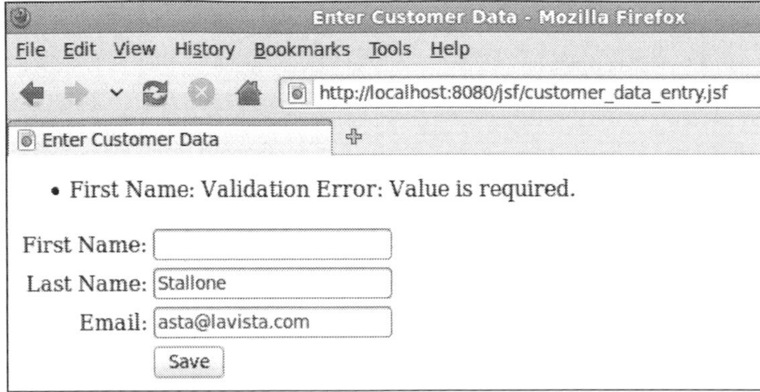

This screenshot illustrates the default error message shown when the user attempts to save the form in the example without entering a value for the customer's first name. The first part of the message ("First Name") is taken from the value of the `label` attribute of the corresponding `<h:inputTextField>` tag. The text of the message can be customized as well as its style (font, color, and so on). We will cover how to do this later in this chapter.

Project stages

Having an `<h:messages>` tag on every JSF page is a good idea. Without it, the user might not see validation messages and will have no idea of why the form submission is not going through. By default, JSF validation messages do not generate any output in the GlassFish log. A common mistake new JSF developers make is failing to add an `<h:messages>` tag to their pages. Without it, if validation fails, then the navigation seems to fail for no reason (the same page is rendered if navigation fails, and without an `<h:messages>` tag, no error messages are displayed in the browser).

To avoid the situation described in the previous paragraph, JSF 2.0 introduces the concept of **project stages**.

The following project stages are defined in JSF 2.0:

- Production
- Development
- UnitTest
- SystemTest

We can define the project stage as an initialization parameter to the faces servlet in the `web.xml` file or as a custom JNDI resource. As `web.xml` is now optional and as altering it makes it relatively easy to use the wrong project stage, if we forget to modify it when we move our code from one environment to another, the preferred way of setting the project stage is through a custom JNDI resource.

With GlassFish, we can do this by logging into the web console, navigating to **JNDI | Custom Resources**, and clicking on the **New...** button.

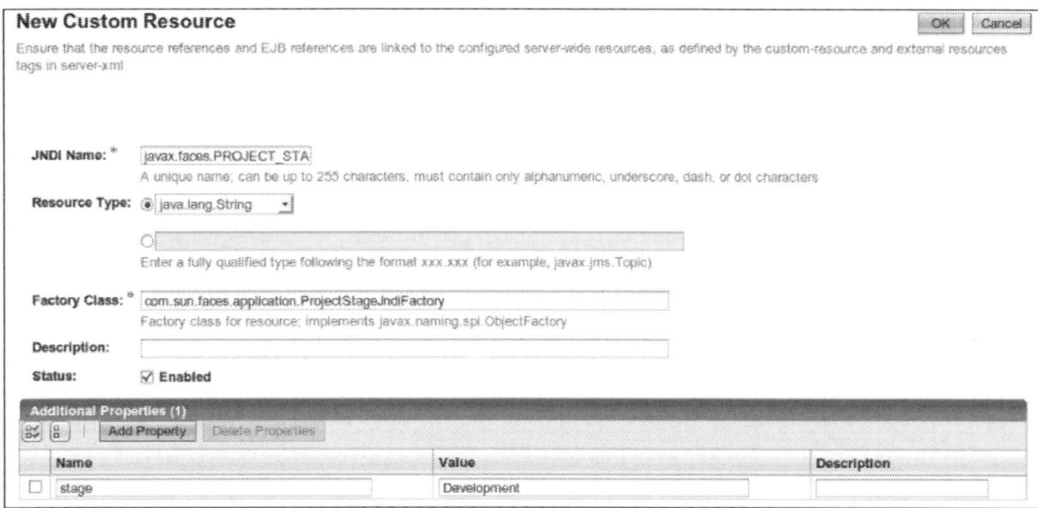

In the resulting page, we need to enter the following information

JNDI Name	`javax.faces.PROJECT_STAGE`
Resource Type	`java.lang.String`
Factory Class	`com.sun.faces.application.ProjectStageJndiFactory`

Then, add a new property with a name of **stage** and a value corresponding to the project stage we wish to use.

Setting the project stage allows us to perform some logic only if we are running in a specific stage. For instance, in one of our managed beans, we could have code that looks as follows:

```
FacesContext facesContext = FacesContext.getCurrentInstance();
Application application = facesContext.getApplication();
if (application.getProjectStage().equals(ProjectStage.Production))
{
  //do production stuff
```

```
}
else if (application.getProjectStage().equals(
  ProjectStage.Development))
{
  //do development stuff
}
else if (application.getProjectStage().equals(ProjectStage.UnitTest))
{
  //do unit test stuff
} else if (application.getProjectStage().equals(
  ProjectStage.SystemTest))
{
  //do system test stuff
}
```

As we can see, project stages allow us to modify our code's behavior for different environments. More importantly, setting the project stage allows the JSF engine to behave a bit differently based on the project stage setting. Relevant to our discussion, setting the project stage to `development` results in additional logging statements in the application server log. Therefore, if we forget to add an `<h:messages>` tag to our page, if our project stage is Development, and validation fails, we will see log entries similar to the following in the GlassFish server log:

```
INFO: WARNING: FacesMessage(s) have been enqueued, but may not have been displayed.
sourceId=j_idt8:j_idt11[severity=(ERROR 2), summary=(First Name: Validation Error: Value is required.), detail=(First Name: Validation Error: Value is required.)]
sourceId=j_idt8:j_idt13[severity=(ERROR 2), summary=(Last Name: Validation Error: Value is required.), detail=(Last Name: Validation Error: Value is required.)]
sourceId=j_idt8:j_idt15[severity=(ERROR 2), summary=(Email: Validation Error: Value is less than allowable minimum of '3'), detail=(Email: Validation Error: Value is less than allowable minimum of '3')]
```

In the default Production stage, this output is not sent to the log, leaving us confused as to why our page navigation doesn't seem to be working.

Validation

Notice that each `<h:inputField>` tag has a nested `<f:validateLength>` tag. As its name implies, this tag validates that the entered value for a text field is between a minimum and maximum length. Minimum and maximum values are defined by the tag's `minimum` and `maximum` attributes. `<f:validateLength>` is one of the standard validators included with JSF. Just like with the `required` attribute of `<h:inputText>`, JSF will automatically display a default error message when a user attempts to submit a form with a value that does not validate.

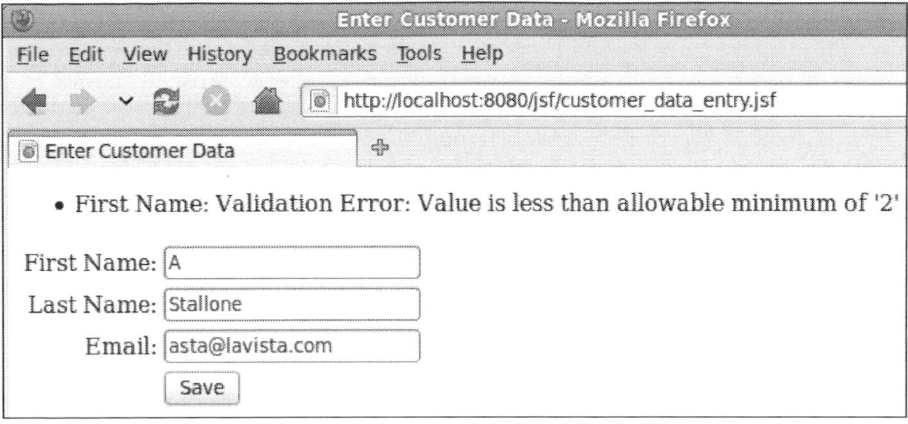

The default message and style can be overridden. We will cover how to do this in the next section.

In addition to `<f:validateLength>`, JSF includes other standard validators. These are listed in the following table:

Validation tag	Description
`<f:validateBean>`	Bean Validation allows us to validate managed bean values by using annotations in our managed beans, without having to add validators to our JSF tags. This tag allows us to fine-tune Bean Validation if necessary.
`<f:validateDoubleRange>`	Validates that the input is a valid `Double` value between the two values specified by the tag's `minimum` and `maximum` attributes, inclusive.
`<f:validateLength>`	Validates that the input's length is between the values specified by the tag's `minimum` and `maximum` values, inclusive.
`<f:validateLongRange>`	Validates that the input is a valid `Double` value between the values specified by the tag's `minimum` and `maximum` attributes, inclusive.
`<f:validateRegex>`	Validates that the input matches a regular expression pattern specified in the tag's `pattern` attribute.
`<f:validateRequired>`	Validates that the input is not empty. This tag is equivalent to setting the `required` attribute to `true` in the parent input field.

Notice that in the description for `<f:validateBean>`, we briefly mentioned Bean Validation. The Bean Validation JSR aims to standardize JavaBean validation. JavaBeans are used across several other APIs that up until recently, had to implement their own validation logic. Just like JPA 2.0, JSF 2.0 adopts the Bean Validation standard to help validate managed bean properties.

If we wish to take advantage of Bean Validation, all we need to do is annotate the desired field with the appropriate Bean Validation annotation, without having to explicitly use a JSF validator.

For the complete list of Bean Validation annotations, refer to the `javax.validation.constraints` package in the Java EE 6 API at `http://java.sun.com/javaee/6/docs/api/`.

Grouping components

`<h:panelGroup>` is the next new tag in the example. Typically, `<h:panelGroup>` is used to group several components together so that they occupy a single cell in an `<h:panelGrid>`. This can be accomplished by adding components inside `<h:panelGroup>` and adding `<h:panelGroup>` to `<h:panelGrid>`. As can be seen in the example, this particular instance of `<h:panelGroup>` has no child components. In this particular case, the purpose of `<h:panelGroup>` is to have an "empty" cell and have the next component, `<h:commandButton>`, align with all other input fields in the form.

Form submission

`<h:commandButton>` renders an HTML submit button in the browser. Just like with standard HTML, its purpose is to submit the form. Its `value` attribute simply sets the button's label. This tag's `action` attribute is used for navigation. The next page to show is based on the value of this attribute. The `action` attribute can have a `String` constant or a **method binding expression**, meaning that it can point to a method in a managed bean that returns a string. Later in this chapter, we will see an example of a `<h:commandButton>` tag whose `action` attribute is a method binding expression.

JSF 2.0 introduces a new convention. If the base name of a page in our application matches the value of the `action` attribute of a `<h:commandButton>` tag, then we navigate to this page when clicking the button. This new JSF 2.0 feature frees us from having to define navigation rules, like we had to do in JSF 1.x. In our example, our confirmation page is called `confirmation.xhtml`. Therefore, by convention this page will be shown when the button is clicked, as the value of its `action` attribute ("confirmation") matches the base name of the page.

Even though the label of the button reads **Save**, in our simple example, clicking on the button won't actually save any data. Later in this chapter, we will see a more advanced version of this application that will actually implement this functionality.

Managed beans

In earlier versions of JSF, we used to have to define our managed beans in a configuration file named `faces-config.xml`. JSF 2.0 introduces new annotations we can use in our managed beans, freeing us from having to maintain a separate configuration file. The following is the managed bean for our example:

```
package net.ensode.glassfishbook.jsf;
import javax.faces.bean.ManagedBean;

@ManagedBean
public class Customer
{
  private String firstName;
  private String lastName;
  private String email;
  public String getEmail()
  {
    return email;
  }
  public void setEmail(String email)
  {
    this.email = email;
  }
  public String getFirstName()
  {
    return firstName;
  }
  public void setFirstName(String firstName)
  {
    this.firstName = firstName;
  }
  public String getLastName()
  {
    return lastName;
  }
  public void setLastName(String lastName)
  {
    this.lastName = lastName;
  }
}
```

The `@ManagedBean` class annotation designates this bean as a JSF managed bean. This annotation has an optional `name` attribute we can use to give our bean a logical name to use in our JSF pages. However, by convention, the value of this attribute is the same as the class name (in our case, `Customer`), with its first character switched to lowercase. In our example, we let this default behavior take place. Therefore, we access our bean's properties via the `customer` logical name. Notice the value of any of the input fields to see this logical name in action.

Notice that other than the `@ManagedBean` annotation, there is nothing special about this bean. It is a standard JavaBean with `private` properties and corresponding getter and setter methods.

Managed bean scopes

Managed beans always have a scope. A managed bean scope defines the lifespan of an application. The managed bean scope is defined by a class level annotation. The following table lists all valid managed bean scopes:

Managed bean scope annnotation	Description
`@ApplicationScoped`	The same instance of application scoped managed beans is available to all of our application's clients. If one client modifies the value of an application scoped managed bean, the change is reflected across clients.
`@SessionScoped`	An instance of each session scoped managed bean is assigned to each of our application's clients. A session scoped managed bean can be used to hold client-specific data across requests.
`@RequestScoped`	Request scoped managed beans only live through a single HTTP request.
`@ViewScoped`	View scoped managed beans are associated with a particular view (page). They are destroyed once the user navigates to a different view.
`@NoneScoped`	None scoped managed beans are instantiated when they are accessed by another managed bean, typically as a managed property.
`@CustomScoped`	JSF 2.0 introduces the ability for us to create custom scopes for our managed beans. The `value` attribute of the `@CustomScoped` annotation must resolve to a session-scoped map.

If no scope is specified in a managed bean (like in our example), then a default scope of request is used.

Navigation

As can be seen in our input page, when clicking on the "save" button in the `customer_data_entry.xhtml` page, our application will navigate to a page called `confirmation.xhtml`. This happens because we are taking advantage of JSF 2.0's convention over configuration feature, in which if the value of the `action` attribute of a command button or link matches the base name of another page, then this navigation takes us to this page.

Same page reloading when clicking on a button or link that should navigate to another page?

When JSF does not recognize the value of the `action` attribute of a command button or command link, it will by default navigate to the same page that was displayed in the browser when the user clicked on a button or link that is meant to navigate to another page.

If navigation does not seem to be working properly, chances are there is a typo in the value of this attribute. Remember that, by convention, JSF will look for a page whose base name matches the value of the `action` attribute of a command button or link.

The source for `confirmation.xhtml` looks as follows:

```
<?xml version='1.0' encoding='UTF-8' ?>
<!DOCTYPE html PUBLIC "-//W3C//DTD XHTML 1.0 Transitional//EN"
  "http://www.w3.org/TR/xhtml1/DTD/xhtml1-transitional.dtd">
<html xmlns="http://www.w3.org/1999/xhtml"
      xmlns:h="http://java.sun.com/jsf/html">
  <h:head>
    <title>Customer Data Entered</title>
  </h:head>
  <h:body>
    <h:panelGrid columns="2" columnClasses="rightAlign,leftAlign">
      <h:outputText value="First Name:"></h:outputText>
      <h:outputText value="#{customer.firstName}"></h:outputText>
      <h:outputText value="Last Name:"></h:outputText>
      <h:outputText value="#{customer.lastName}"></h:outputText>
      <h:outputText value="Email:"></h:outputText>
      <h:outputText value="#{customer.email}"></h:outputText>
    </h:panelGrid>
  </h:body>
</html>
```

There are no tags we haven't seen before in this page. One thing to notice about it is that it is using value binding expressions as the value for all of its `<h:outputText>` tags. As these value binding expressions are the same expressions used in the previous page for the `<h:inputText>` tags, their values will correspond to the data the user entered.

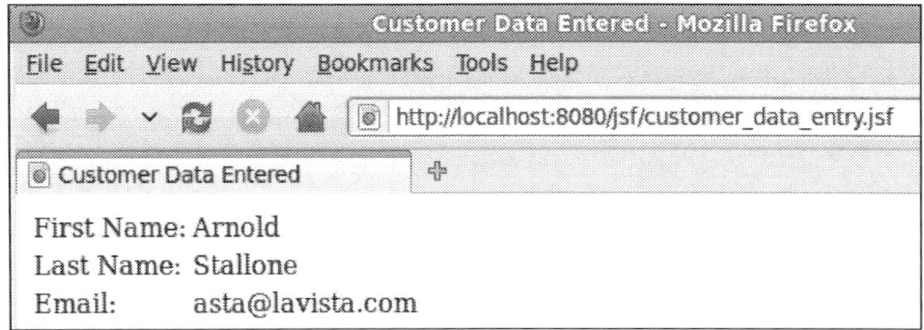

In traditional Java web applications, we define URL patterns to be processed by a specific servlet. Specifically for JSF, the suffixes `.jsf` or `.faces` were commonly used. Another commonly used URL mapping for JSF was the `/faces` prefix. By default, GlassFish automatically adds all three of these mappings to the faces servlet. Therefore, if we wish to use one of these mappings, we don't have to specify any URL mapping at all. If for any reason we need to specify a different mapping, then we need to add a `web.xml` configuration file to our application. However, the defaults will suffice in most cases.

The URL we used for the pages in our application was the name of our Facelets pages, substituting the `.xhtml` suffix with `.jsf`. This takes advantage of the default URL mapping. We could also access our pages by using the `.faces` extension or the `/faces/` prefix.

Custom data validation

In addition to providing standard validators for our use, JSF allows us to create custom validators. This can be done in one of two ways: creating a custom validator class or by adding validation methods to our managed beans.

Creating custom validators

In addition to the standard validators, JSF allows us to create custom validators by creating a Java class implementing the `javax.faces.validator.Validator` interface.

The following class implements an email validator that we will use to validate the email text input field in our customer data entry screen:

```
package net.ensode.glassfishbook.jsfcustomval;

import javax.faces.application.FacesMessage;
import javax.faces.component.UIComponent;
import javax.faces.component.html.HtmlInputText;
import javax.faces.context.FacesContext;
import javax.faces.validator.FacesValidator;
import javax.faces.validator.Validator;
import javax.faces.validator.ValidatorException;
import org.apache.commons.lang.StringUtils;

@FacesValidator(value = "emailValidator")
public class EmailValidator implements Validator
{
  @Override
  public void validate(FacesContext facesContext, UIComponent
    uiComponent, Object value) throws ValidatorException
  {
    org.apache.commons.validator.EmailValidator emailValidator =
      org.apache.commons.validator.EmailValidator.getInstance();
    HtmlInputText htmlInputText = (HtmlInputText) uiComponent;

    String email = (String) value;
    if (!StringUtils.isEmpty(email))
    {
      if (!emailValidator.isValid(email))
      {
        FacesMessage facesMessage = new FacesMessage(
          htmlInputText.getLabel() + ": email format is not valid");
        throw new ValidatorException(facesMessage);
      }
    }
  }
}
```

The `@FacesValidator` annotation registers our class as a JSF custom validator class. The value of its `value` attribute is the logical name that JSF pages can use to refer to it.

As can be seen in the example, the only method we need to implement when implementing the `Validator` interface is a method called `validate()`. This method takes three parameters: an instance of `javax.faces.context.FacesContext`, an instance of `javax.faces.component.UIComponent`, and an object. Typically, application developers only need to be concerned with the last two. The second parameter is the component whose data we are validating, the third parameter is the actual value. In the example, we cast `uiComponent` to `javax.faces.component.html.HtmlInputText`. This way, we get access to its `getLabel()` method, which we can use as part of the error message.

If the entered value is not a valid email address format, a new instance of `javax.faces.application.FacesMessage` is created, passing the error message to be displayed in the browser as its constructor parameter. We then throw a new `javax.faces.validator.ValidatorException`. The error message is then displayed in the browser. How it gets there is done behind the scenes by the JSF API.

Apache Commons Validator

The previous validator uses Apache Commons Validator to do the actual validation. This library includes many common validations such as dates, credit card numbers, ISBN numbers, and e-mails. When implementing a custom validator, it is worth investigating if this library already has a validator that we can use.

In order to use our validator in our page, we need to use the `<f:validator>` JSF tag. The following Facelet page is a modified version of the customer data entry screen. This version uses the `<f:validator>` tag to validate e-mail:

```
<?xml version='1.0' encoding='UTF-8' ?>
<!DOCTYPE html PUBLIC "-//W3C//DTD XHTML 1.0 Transitional//EN"
  "http://www.w3.org/TR/xhtml1/DTD/xhtml1-transitional.dtd">
<html xmlns="http://www.w3.org/1999/xhtml"
      xmlns:h="http://java.sun.com/jsf/html"
      xmlns:f="http://java.sun.com/jsf/core">
  <h:head>
    <title>Enter Customer Data</title>
  </h:head>
  <h:body>
    <h:outputStylesheet library="css" name="styles.css"
      target="body"/>
    <h:form>
      <h:messages></h:messages>
      <h:panelGrid columns="2"
                   columnClasses="rightAlign,leftAlign">
        <h:outputText value="First Name:">
        </h:outputText>
```

```
        <h:inputText label="First Name"
                     value="#{customer.firstName}"
                     required="true">
          <f:validateLength minimum="2" maximum="30">
          </f:validateLength>
        </h:inputText>
        <h:outputText value="Last Name:"></h:outputText>
        <h:inputText label="Last Name"
                     value="#{customer.lastName}"
                     required="true">
          <f:validateLength minimum="2" maximum="30">
          </f:validateLength>
        </h:inputText>
        <h:outputText value="Email:">
        </h:outputText>
        <h:inputText label="Email" value="#{customer.email}">
          <f:validator validatorId="emailValidator" />
        </h:inputText>
        <h:panelGroup></h:panelGroup>
        <h:commandButton action="confirmation" value="Save">
        </h:commandButton>
      </h:panelGrid>
    </h:form>
  </h:body>
</html>
```

After writing our custom validator and modifying our page to take advantage of it, we can see our validator in action:

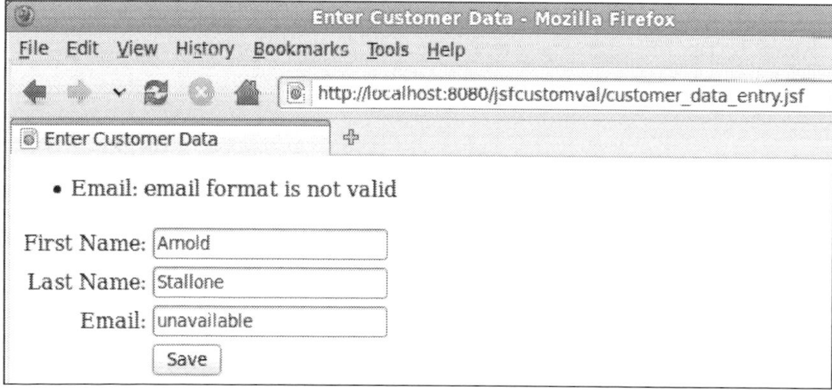

Validator methods

Another way we can implement custom validation is by adding validation methods to one or more of the application's managed beans. The following Java class illustrates the use of validator methods for JSF validation:

```
package net.ensode.glassfishbook.jsfcustomval;

import javax.faces.application.FacesMessage;
import javax.faces.bean.ManagedBean;
import javax.faces.component.UIComponent;
import javax.faces.component.html.HtmlInputText;
import javax.faces.context.FacesContext;
import javax.faces.validator.ValidatorException;

import org.apache.commons.lang.StringUtils;

@ManagedBean
public class AlphaValidator
{
  public void validateAlpha(FacesContext facesContext, UIComponent
    uiComponent, Object value) throws ValidatorException
  {
    if (!StringUtils.isAlphaSpace((String) value))
    {
      HtmlInputText htmlInputText = (HtmlInputText) uiComponent;
      FacesMessage facesMessage = new FacesMessage(
        htmlInputText.getLabel() + ": only alphabetic characters are
        allowed.");
      throw new ValidatorException(facesMessage);
    }
  }
}
```

In this example, the class contains only the validator method. We can give our validator method any name we want. However, its return value must be void and it must take the three parameters illustrated in the example, in that order. In other words, except for the method name, the signature of a validator method must be identical to the signature of the `validate()` method defined in the `javax.faces.validator.Validator` interface.

As we can see, the body of this validator method is nearly identical to the body of our custom validator's `validate()` method. We check the value entered by the user to make sure it contains only alphabetic characters and/or spaces. If it does not, we throw a `ValidatorException` passing an instance of `FacesMessage` containing an appropriate error message string.

StringUtils

In the example, we used `org.apache.commons.lang.StringUtils` to perform the actual validation logic. In addition to the method used in the example, this class contains several methods for verifying that a string is numeric or alphanumeric. This class, part of the Apache commons-lang library, is very useful when writing custom validators.

As every validator method must be in a managed bean, we need to make sure that the class containing our validator method is annotated with the `@ManagedBean` annotation, as illustrated in our example.

The last thing we need to do to use our validator method is to bind it to our component via the tag's `validator` attribute:

```
<?xml version='1.0' encoding='UTF-8' ?>
<!DOCTYPE html PUBLIC "-//W3C//DTD XHTML 1.0 Transitional//EN"
  "http://www.w3.org/TR/xhtml1/DTD/xhtml1-transitional.dtd">
<html xmlns="http://www.w3.org/1999/xhtml"
      xmlns:h="http://java.sun.com/jsf/html"
      xmlns:f="http://java.sun.com/jsf/core">
  <h:head>
    <title>Enter Customer Data</title>
  </h:head>
  <h:body>
    <h:outputStylesheet library="css" name="styles.css"
      target="body"/>
    <h:form>
      <h:messages></h:messages>
      <h:panelGrid columns="2"
                   columnClasses="rightAlign,leftAlign">
        <h:outputText value="First Name:">
        </h:outputText>
        <h:inputText label="First Name"
                     value="#{customer.firstName}"
                     required="true"
                     validator="#{alphaValidator.validateAlpha}">
          <f:validateLength minimum="2" maximum="30">
          </f:validateLength>
        </h:inputText>
        <h:outputText value="Last Name:"></h:outputText>
        <h:inputText label="Last Name"
                     value="#{customer.lastName}"
                     required="true"
                     validator="#{alphaValidator.validateAlpha}">
```

```
            <f:validateLength minimum="2" maximum="30">
            </f:validateLength>
          </h:inputText>
          <h:outputText value="Email:">
          </h:outputText>
          <h:inputText label="Email" value="#{customer.email}">
            <f:validateLength minimum="3" maximum="30">
            </f:validateLength>
            <f:validator validatorId="emailValidator" />
          </h:inputText>
          <h:panelGroup></h:panelGroup>
          <h:commandButton action="confirmation" value="Save">
          </h:commandButton>
        </h:panelGrid>
      </h:form>
    </h:body>
  </html>
```

As neither the First Name nor the Last Name fields should accept anything other than alphabetic characters or spaces, we added our custom validator method to both these fields.

Notice that the value of the validator attribute of the `<h:inputText>` tag is a JSF expression language using the default managed bean name for the bean containing our validation method. `alphaValidator` is the name of our bean and `validateAlpha` is the name of our validator method.

After modifying our page to use our custom validator, we can now see it in action:

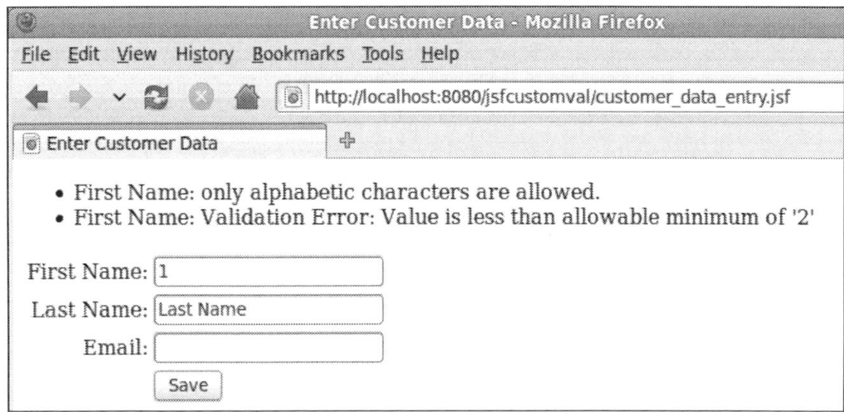

Notice how for the **First Name** field, both our custom validator message and the standard length validator were executed.

Implementing validator methods has the advantage of not having the overhead of creating a whole class just for a single validator method (our example does just that, but in many cases, validator methods are added to an existing managed bean containing other methods). However, the disadvantage is that each component can only be validated by a single validator method. When using validator classes, several `<f:validator>` tags can be nested inside the tag to be validated. Therefore, multiple validations, both custom and standard, can be done on the field.

Customizing JSF's default messages

Like we mentioned in the previous section, it is possible to customize the style (font, color, text, and so on) of JSF default validation messages. Additionally, it is possible to modify the text of the default JSF validation messages. In the following sections, we will explain how to modify error message formatting and text.

Customizing message styles

Customizing message styles can be done via Cascading Style Sheets (CSS). This can be accomplished by using the `<h:message>` `style` or `styleClass` attributes. The `style` attribute is used when we want to declare the CSS style inline. The `styleClass` attribute is used when we want to use a predefined style in a CSS stylesheet or inside a `<style>` tag in our page.

The following markup illustrates using the `styleClass` attribute to alter the style of error messages. It is a modified version of the input page we saw in the previous section.

```
<?xml version='1.0' encoding='UTF-8' ?>
<!DOCTYPE html PUBLIC "-//W3C//DTD XHTML 1.0 Transitional//EN"
  "http://www.w3.org/TR/xhtml1/DTD/xhtml1-transitional.dtd">
<html xmlns="http://www.w3.org/1999/xhtml"
      xmlns:h="http://java.sun.com/jsf/html"
      xmlns:f="http://java.sun.com/jsf/core">
  <h:head>
    <title>Enter Customer Data</title>
  </h:head>
  <h:body>
    <h:outputStylesheet library="css" name="styles.css"
      target="body"/>
    <h:form>
      <h:messages styleClass="errorMsg"></h:messages>
      <h:panelGrid columns="2"
                   columnClasses="rightAlign,leftAlign">
        <h:outputText value="First Name:">
```

```
            </h:outputText>
            <h:inputText label="First Name"
                         value="#{customer.firstName}"
                         required="true"
                         validator="#{alphaValidator.validateAlpha}">
              <f:validateLength minimum="2" maximum="30">
              </f:validateLength>
            </h:inputText>
            <h:outputText value="Last Name:"></h:outputText>
            <h:inputText label="Last Name"
                         value="#{customer.lastName}"
                         required="true"
                         validator="#{alphaValidator.validateAlpha}">
              <f:validateLength minimum="2" maximum="30">
              </f:validateLength>
            </h:inputText>
            <h:outputText value="Email:">
            </h:outputText>
            <h:inputText label="Email" value="#{customer.email}">
              <f:validator validatorId="emailValidator" />
            </h:inputText>
            <h:panelGroup></h:panelGroup>
            <h:commandButton action="confirmation" value="Save">
            </h:commandButton>
          </h:panelGrid>
        </h:form>
      </h:body>
    </html>
```

As we can see, the only difference between this page and the previous one is the use of the `styleClass` attribute of the `<h:messages>` tag. Like we mentioned earlier, the value of the `styleClass` attribute must match the name of a CSS style defined in a cascading stylesheet our page has access to.

In our case, we defined a CSS style for messages as follows:

```
errorMsg
{
  color: red;
}
```

We then used this style as the value of the `styleClass` attribute of our `<h:messages>` tag.

The following screenshot illustrates how the validation error messages look after implementing this change:

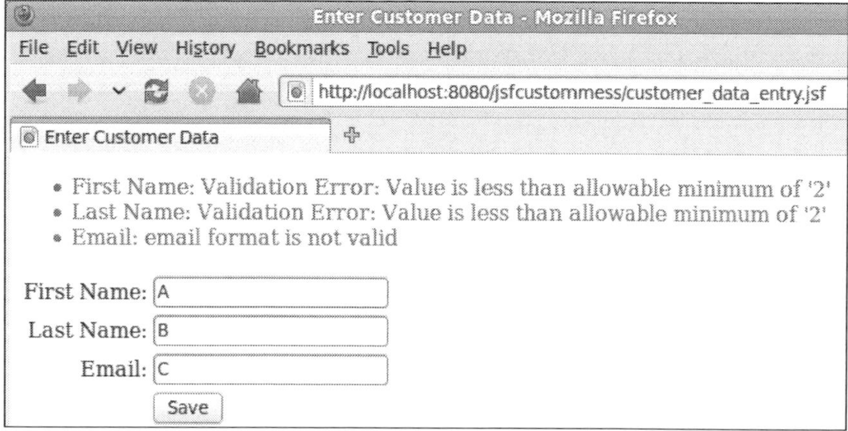

In this particular case, we just set the color of the error message text to red, but we are only limited by CSS capabilities in setting the style of the error messages.

Any standard JSF component has both a `style` and a `styleClass` attribute that can be used to alter its style. The former is used for predefined CSS styles, the latter is used for inline CSS.

Customizing message text

It is sometimes desirable to override JSF's default validation errors. Default validation errors are defined in a resource bundle called `Messages.properties`. This file can be found inside the `jsf-api.jar` file under `[glassfish installation directory]/glassfish/modules`. It can be found under the `javax.faces` folder inside the JAR file. The file contains several messages; we are only interested in validation errors at this point. The default validation error messages are defined as follows:

```
javax.faces.validator.DoubleRangeValidator.MAXIMUM={1}: Validation
Error: Value is greater than allowable maximum of "{0}"

javax.faces.validator.DoubleRangeValidator.MINIMUM={1}: Validation
Error: Value is less than allowable minimum of ''{0}''

javax.faces.validator.DoubleRangeValidator.NOT_IN_RANGE={2}: Validation
Error: Specified attribute is not between the expected values of {0} and
{1}.

javax.faces.validator.DoubleRangeValidator.TYPE={0}: Validation Error:
Value is not of the correct type
```

```
javax.faces.validator.LengthValidator.MAXIMUM={1}: Validation Error:
Value is greater than allowable maximum of ''{0}''

javax.faces.validator.LengthValidator.MINIMUM={1}: Validation Error:
Value is less than allowable minimum of ''{0}''

javax.faces.validator.LongRangeValidator.MAXIMUM={1}: Validation Error:
Value is greater than allowable maximum of ''{0}''

javax.faces.validator.LongRangeValidator.MINIMUM={1}: Validation Error:
Value is less than allowable minimum of ''{0}''

javax.faces.validator.LongRangeValidator.NOT_IN_RANGE={2}: Validation
Error: Specified attribute is not between the expected values of {0} and
{1}.

javax.faces.validator.LongRangeValidator.TYPE={0}: Validation Error:
Value is not of the correct type.

javax.faces.validator.NOT_IN_RANGE=Validation Error: Specified attribute
is not between the expected values of {0} and {1}.

javax.faces.validator.RegexValidator.PATTERN_NOT_SET=Regex pattern must
be set.

javax.faces.validator.RegexValidator.PATTERN_NOT_SET_detail=Regex
pattern must be set to non-empty value.

javax.faces.validator.RegexValidator.NOT_MATCHED=Regex Pattern not
matched

javax.faces.validator.RegexValidator.NOT_MATCHED_detail=Regex pattern of
''{0}'' not matched

javax.faces.validator.RegexValidator.MATCH_EXCEPTION=Error in regular
expression.

javax.faces.validator.RegexValidator.MATCH_EXCEPTION_detail=Error in
regular expression, ''{0}''

javax.faces.validator.BeanValidator.MESSAGE={0}
```

In order to override the default error messages, we need to create our own resource bundle using the same keys as used in the default one, but altering the values to suit our needs. The following is a very simple customized resource bundle for our application:

```
javax.faces.validator.LengthValidator.MINIMUM={1}: minimum allowed
  length is ''{0}''
```

In this resource bundle, we override the error message for when the value entered for a field validated by the `<f:validateLength>` tag is less than the allowed minimum. In order to let our application know that we have a custom resource bundle for message properties, we need to modify the application's `faces-config.xml` file.

```
<?xml version='1.0' encoding='UTF-8'?>
<faces-config version="2.0"
  xmlns="http://java.sun.com/xml/ns/javaee"
  xmlns:xsi="http://www.w3.org/2001/XMLSchema-instance"
  xsi:schemaLocation="http://java.sun.com/xml/ns/javaee
    http://java.sun.com/xml/ns/javaee/web-facesconfig_2_0.xsd">
  <application>
    <message-bundle>net.ensode.Messages</message-bundle>
  </application>
</faces-config>
```

As we can see, the only thing we need to do to the application's `faces-config.xml` file is to add a `<message-bundle>` element indicating the name and location of the resource bundle containing our custom messages.

Custom error message text definitions is one of the few cases in which we still need to define a `faces-config.xml` file for JSF 2.0 applications. However, notice how simple our `faces-config.xml` file is. It is a far cry from a typical `faces-config.xml` file for JSF 1.x that typically contains managed bean definitions, navigation rules, JSF validator definitions, and so on.

After adding our custom message resource bundle and modifying the application's `faces-config.xml` file, we can see our custom validation message in action:

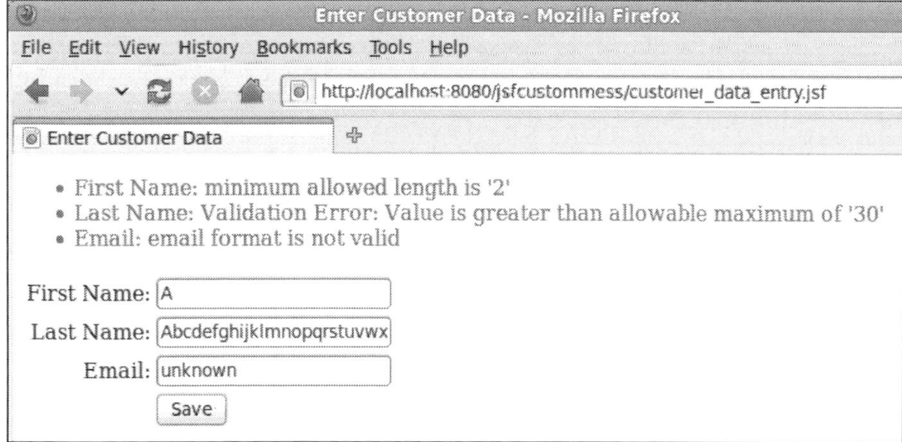

As we can see, if we haven't overridden a validation message, the default error message will still be displayed. In our resource bundle, we only overrode the minimum length validation error message, therefore our custom error message is shown for the **First Name** text field. As we didn't override the error message for data entry going over the maximum allowed length, the default error message is shown. The e-mail validator is the custom validator we developed previously in this chapter. As it is a custom validator, its error message is not affected.

Integrating JSF and JPA

So far we have covered many of the features of JSF. However, our example application does not actually save any data yet. In this section, we will cover how JavaServer Faces and the Java Persistence API can be easily integrated to save user input to a database.

We will also cover additional JSF and JPA features. Regarding JSF, we will cover how to perform some logic in the server before navigating to another page, and how to automatically populate a managed bean's property through the `@ManagedProperty` annotation. As far as JPA, we will cover how to automatically generate primary keys.

Like we have seen in this chapter, JSF managed beans are nothing but standard JavaBeans. In Chapter 5, we saw that JPA uses standard JavaBeans for object-relational mapping. As both JSF managed beans and JPA beans are standard JavaBeans, there is nothing stopping us from using JPA beans as JSF managed beans.

Like we covered earlier, JSF tags can contain value binding expressions that are used to automatically populate managed beans when the form is submitted. If we use a JPA bean as a managed bean, the bean's properties are populated this way. We can then simply call the `EntityManager.persist()` method to save the data into the database.

The first thing we need to do is use a JPA bean as a managed bean to be used for value binding expressions.

```
package net.ensode.glassfishbook.jsfjpa;

import java.io.Serializable;
import javax.faces.bean.ManagedBean;

import javax.persistence.Column;
import javax.persistence.Entity;
import javax.persistence.GeneratedValue;
import javax.persistence.Id;
import javax.persistence.Table;
```

```
@ManagedBean
@Entity
@Table(name = "CUSTOMERS")
public class Customer implements Serializable
{
  @Id
  @GeneratedValue
  @Column(name = "CUSTOMER_ID")
  private Long customerId;
  @Column(name = "FIRST_NAME")
  private String firstName;
  @Column(name = "LAST_NAME")
  private String lastName;
  private String email;

  public Long getCustomerId()
  {
    return customerId;
  }
  public void setCustomerId(Long customerId)
  {
    this.customerId = customerId;
  }
  public String getEmail()
  {
    return email;
  }
  public void setEmail(String email)
  {
    this.email = email;
  }
  public String getFirstName()
  {
    return firstName;
  }
  public void setFirstName(String firstName)
  {
    this.firstName = firstName;
  }
  public String getLastName()
  {
    return lastName;
  }
  public void setLastName(String lastName)
```

```
    {
      this.lastName = lastName;
    }

    @Override
    public String toString()
    {
      Long localCustomerId = customerId;
      String localFirstName = firstName;
      String localLastName = lastName;
      String localEmail = email;

      if (localCustomerId == null)
      {
        localCustomerId = 0L;
      }
      if (localEmail == null)
      {
        localEmail = "";
      }
      if (localFirstName == null)
      {
        localFirstName = "";
      }
      if (localLastName == null)
      {
        localLastName = "";
      }

      String toString = "customerId = " + customerId + "\n";
      toString += "firstName = " + localFirstName + "\n";
      toString += "lastName = " + localLastName + "\n";
      toString += "email = " + localEmail;
      return toString;
    }
  }
```

This class is almost an exact copy of the `Customer` bean we saw in Chapter 5, the only difference being the package it belongs to and the fact that it is annotated with the `@ManagedBean` annotation. Annotating our JPA entity as a JSF managed bean allows us to use it in value binding expressions in our pages. Therefore, we can populate them from user entered data that we can then persist to the database.

Notice that we annotated our entity's primary key with the `@GeneratedValue` annotation. This allows the primary key field to be generated automatically, freeing us from having to populate it explicitly. JPA has several primary key generation strategies. If we don't specify one, the default one will be used automatically. The default primary key generation strategy varies depending on the RDBMS we are using. In the case of JavaDB, which we used in our example, the default primary key generation strategy is TABLE, which uses an automatically generated database table to generate primary keys.

If we are happy with the default primary key generation strategy, all we need to do to have primary keys is to annotate the primary key field with the `@GeneratedValue` annotation. If for any reason we wish to use a different generation strategy, then we need to specify it via the `strategy` attribute of the `@GeneratedValue` annotation.

The following table lists all the supported primary key generation strategies. Note that not all strategies are supported by all RDBMS systems.

Generation strategy	Description
`GenerationType.AUTO`	A generation strategy is automatically picked for us. The default strategy depends on the RDBMS system and JPA implementation.
`GenerationType.IDENTITY`	A database identity column is used to generate the primary key. Not all RDBMS systems support identities.
`GenerationType.SEQUENCE`	A database sequence is used to generate the primary key. Not all RDBMS systems support sequences.
`GenerationType.TABLE`	The primary key is obtained from a database table. The JPA implementation will automatically manage this table, making sure that we obtain a unique value from it every time a primary key is generated.

Using a primary key generation strategy other than the default one requires simply using the appropriate strategy as the value of the `strategy` attribute of the `@GeneratedValue` annotation. For example, if we wanted to use a database sequence to generate primary keys, all we would need to do would be something like this:

```
@GeneratedValue(strategy=GenerationType.SEQUENCE)
```

Our primary key generation strategy would be changed accordingly.

Our `Customer` bean represents the model (data) in our application; our pages represent the view. We also need to add an additional managed bean to be used as a controller, as it is always a good practice to follow the Model-View-Controller design pattern.

```
package net.ensode.glassfishbook.jsfjpa;

import java.sql.Connection;
import java.sql.PreparedStatement;
import java.sql.ResultSet;
import java.sql.SQLException;

import javax.annotation.Resource;
import javax.faces.bean.ManagedBean;
import javax.faces.bean.ManagedProperty;
import javax.persistence.EntityManager;
import javax.persistence.EntityManagerFactory;
import javax.persistence.PersistenceUnit;
import javax.sql.DataSource;
import javax.transaction.UserTransaction;

@ManagedBean
public class CustomerController
{
  @Resource(name = "jdbc/__CustomerDBPool")
  private DataSource dataSource;
  @PersistenceUnit(unitName = "customerPersistenceUnit")
  private EntityManagerFactory entityManagerFactory;
  @Resource
  private UserTransaction userTransaction;
  @ManagedProperty(value = "#{customer}")
  private Customer customer;

  public String saveCustomer()
  {
    String returnValue = "customer_saved";
    EntityManager entityManager =
      entityManagerFactory.createEntityManager();
    try
    {
      userTransaction.begin();
      entityManager.persist(customer);
      userTransaction.commit();
    }
    catch (Exception e)
```

```
        {
          e.printStackTrace();
          returnValue = "error_saving_customer";
        }
        return returnValue;
      }
      public Customer getCustomer()
      {
        return customer;
      }
      public void setCustomer(Customer customer)
      {
        this.customer = customer;
      }
    }
```

The `saveCustomer()` method in this class will be called whenever a user clicks on the **Save** button on the HTML form. A slight modification needs to be made to the page containing the form; we will cover this shortly. This method simply saves the data contained in the `Customer` bean in the database. Refer to Chapter 5 for details.

Of special interest are the `setCustomer()` and `getCustomer()` methods. These methods are not meant to be invoked directly by an application developer. Instead, they should be invoked by GlassFish's JSF implementation with the appropriate instance of the `Customer` bean. We need to declare the `customer` property of the previous controller as a **managed property**. JSF 2.0 introduces the `@ManagedProperty` annotation that can be used to declare a managed bean's property.

As can be seen in the previous example, all we need to do to make a property managed is to annotate it with the `@ManagedProperty` annotation, and specify the logical name of the bean to bind to the property as a JSF expression language expression matching the bean's name. In our case, as we didn't specify a name for our `Customer` bean, the default behavior—which is to use the bean's class name with its first letter changed to lowercase—takes place. Therefore, our `Customer` bean's name is `customer`, which is the value we used for the `value` attribute of the `@ManagedBeanProperty` annotation.

Finally, in order for the `saveCustomer()` method to be called whenever the user submits the form and all fields validate correctly, we need to make a slight modification to the customer data entry page:

```
<?xml version='1.0' encoding='UTF-8' ?>
<!DOCTYPE html PUBLIC "-//W3C//DTD XHTML 1.0 Transitional//EN"
  "http://www.w3.org/TR/xhtml1/DTD/xhtml1-transitional.dtd">
<html xmlns="http://www.w3.org/1999/xhtml"
```

```
    xmlns:h="http://java.sun.com/jsf/html"
    xmlns:f="http://java.sun.com/jsf/core">
<h:head>
  <title>Save Customer</title>
</h:head>
<h:body>
  <h:form>
    <h:messages></h:messages>
    <table cellpadding="0" cellspacing="0" border="0">
      <tr>
        <td align="right">First Name:</td>
        <td align="left">
          <h:inputText label="First Name"
                       value="#{customer.firstName}"
                       required="true">
            <f:validateLength minimum="2" maximum="30">
            </f:validateLength>
          </h:inputText>
        </td>
      </tr>
      <tr>
        <td align="right">Last Name:</td>
        <td align="left">
          <h:inputText label="Last Name"
                       value="#{customer.lastName}"
                       required="true">
            <f:validateLength minimum="2" maximum="30">
            </f:validateLength>
          </h:inputText>
        </td>
      </tr>
      <tr>
        <td align="right">Email:</td>
        <td align="left">
          <h:inputText label="Email"
                       value="#{customer.email}">
            <f:validateLength minimum="2" maximum="30">
            </f:validateLength>
          </h:inputText>
        </td>
      </tr>
      <tr>
        <td></td>
        <td align="left">
          <h:commandButton
```

```
                action="#{customerController.saveCustomer}"
                value="Save">
              </h:commandButton>
            </td>
          </tr>
        </table>
      </h:form>
    </h:body>
</html>
```

The only significant difference between this version of the page and previous versions is that the `action` attribute of the `<h:commandButton>` tag was changed to point to the `saveCustomer()` method of the `CustomerController` managed bean. As can be seen in the source code for this bean (shown earlier in this section), this method returns the `String` `"customer_saved"` if the data was saved successfully, or `"error_saving_customer"` if there was any problem saving the data. These two values match the base names of the pages we wish to navigate to when a customer was saved successfully and when there was a problem saving the data.

There are a few more changes made to this version of the data entry page that are unrelated to the task at hand. First, for simplicity we removed some of the features we covered earlier in the chapter (custom validators, error message styling, and so on). Additionally, and slightly more interesting, we replaced the `<h:panelGrid>` component with a standard HTML table. Most server-side Java developers are at least somewhat familiar with HTML. Therefore, using standard HTML components whenever possible leverages this knowledge and potentially makes the page markup more readable. In previous versions of the JSF specification, it wasn't recommended to mix standard HTML and JSF tags in a JSF page as doing so sometimes resulted in unexpected results. This restriction was lifted in JSF 1.2 as JSF JSP tags were modified to avoid the unexpected issues experienced in earlier versions of JSF. Facelets never had the issue to begin with. As Facelets is now the preferred view technology for JSF, it makes even more sense to use standard HTML components whenever possible.

Ajax enabling JSF 2.0 applications

JSF 1.x did not include native Ajax support. Custom JSF library vendors were forced to implement Ajax in their own way. Unfortunately, this state of events introduced incompatibilities between JSF component libraries. JSF 2.0 standardizes Ajax support, thanks to the newly introduced `<f:ajax>` tag.

The following code illustrates typical usage of the `<f:ajax>` tag:

```
<?xml version='1.0' encoding='UTF-8' ?>
<!DOCTYPE html PUBLIC "-//W3C//DTD XHTML 1.0 Transitional//EN"
  "http://www.w3.org/TR/xhtml1/DTD/xhtml1-transitional.dtd">
<html xmlns="http://www.w3.org/1999/xhtml"
      xmlns:h="http://java.sun.com/jsf/html"
      xmlns:f="http://java.sun.com/jsf/core">
  <h:head>
    <title>JSF Ajax Demo</title>
  </h:head>
  <h:body>
    <h2>JSF Ajax Demo</h2>
    <h:form>
      <h:messages/>
      <h:panelGrid columns="2">
        <h:outputText value="Echo input:"/>
        <h:inputText id="textInput" value="#{controller.text}">
          <f:ajax render="textVal" event="keyup"/>
        </h:inputText>
        <h:outputText value="Echo output:"/>
        <h:outputText id="textVal" value="#{controller.text}"/>
      </h:panelGrid>
      <hr/>
      <h:panelGrid columns="2">
        <h:panelGroup/>
        <h:panelGroup/>
        <h:outputText value="First Operand:"/>
        <h:inputText id="first" value="#{controller.firstOperand}"
          size="3"/>
        <h:outputText value="Second Operand:"/>
        <h:inputText id="second" value="#{controller.secondOperand}"
          size="3"/>
        <h:outputText value="Total:"/>
        <h:outputText id="sum" value="#{controller.total}"/>
        <h:commandButton
            actionListener="#{controller.calculateTotal}"
            value="Calculate Sum">
          <f:ajax execute="first second" render="sum"/>
        </h:commandButton>
      </h:panelGrid>
    </h:form>
  </h:body>
</html>
```

After deploying our application, this code renders as illustrated in the next screenshot:

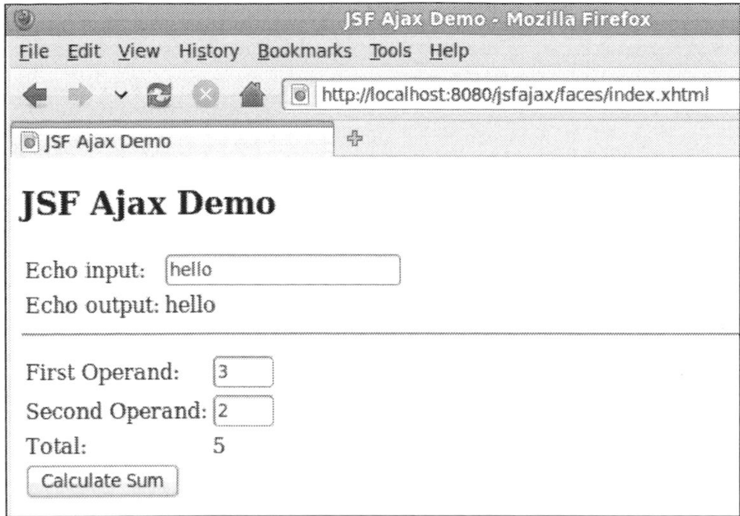

The previous code illustrates two uses of the `<f:ajax>` tag. The first time we use this tag we are implementing a typical Ajax Echo example, in which we have an `outputText` component updating itself with the value of an `inputText` component. Whenever any character is entered into the input field, the value of the `outputText` component is automatically updated.

To implement the functionality described in the previous paragraph, we put an `<f:ajax>` tag inside an `<h:inputText>` tag. The value of the `render` attribute of the `<f:ajax>` tag must correspond to the id of a component we wish to update after the Ajax request finishes. In our particular example, we wish to update the `outputText` component with an id of `"textVal"`, therefore this is the value we use for the `render` attribute of our `<f:ajax>` tag.

In some cases, we may need to render more than one JSF component after an Ajax event finishes. In order to accommodate for this, we can add several IDs as the value of the `render` attribute. We simply need to separate them by spaces.

The other `<f:ajax>` attribute we used in this instance is the `event` attribute. This attribute indicates the Javascript event that triggers the Ajax event. In this particular case, we need to trigger the event any time a key is released while a user is typing into the input field. Therefore, the appropriate event to use is `"keyup"`.

The following table lists all supported Javascript events:

Event	Description
`blur`	The component loses focus.
`change`	The component loses focus and its value gets modified.
`click`	The component is clicked on.
`dblclick`	The component is double-clicked on.
`focus`	The component gains focus.
`keydown`	A key is depressed while the component has focus.
`keypress`	A key is pressed or held down while the component has focus.
`keyup`	A key is released while the component has focus.
`mousedown`	The mouse button is depressed while the component has focus.
`mousemove`	The mouse pointer is moved over the component.
`mouseout`	The mouse pointer leaves the component.
`mouseover`	The mouse pointer is placed over the component.
`mouseup`	The mouse button is released while the component has focus.
`select`	The component's text is selected.
`valueChange`	Equivalent to `change`, the component loses focus and its value gets modified.

We use the `<f:ajax>` once again farther down in the page, to Ajax-enable a command button component. In this instance, we want to recalculate a value based on the value of two input components. In order to have the values on the server updated with the latest user input, we used the `execute` attribute of `<f:ajax>`, this attribute takes a space separated list of component ids to use as input. We then use the `render` attribute just like before to specify which components need to be re-rendered after the Ajax request finishes.

Notice we are using the `actionListener` attribute of `<h:commandButton>`. This attribute is typically used whenever we don't need to navigate to another page after clicking the button. The value for this attribute is an action listener method we wrote in one of our managed beans. Action listener methods must return void, and take an instance of `javax.faces.event.ActionEvent` as it's sole parameter.

The managed bean for our application looks as follows:

```
package net.ensode.glassfishbook.jsfajax;

import javax.faces.bean.ManagedBean;
import javax.faces.bean.ViewScoped;
import javax.faces.event.ActionEvent;
```

```
@ManagedBean
@ViewScoped
public class Controller
{
  private String text;
  private int firstOperand;
  private int secondOperand;
  private int total;
  public Controller()
  {

  }
  public void calculateTotal(ActionEvent actionEvent)
  {
    total = firstOperand + secondOperand;
  }
  public String getText()
  {
    return text;
  }
  public void setText(String text)
  {
    this.text = text;
  }
  public int getFirstOperand()
  {
    return firstOperand;
  }
  public void setFirstOperand(int firstOperand)
  {
    this.firstOperand = firstOperand;
  }
  public int getSecondOperand()
  {
    return secondOperand;
  }
  public void setSecondOperand(int secondOperand)
  {
    this.secondOperand = secondOperand;
  }
  public int getTotal()
  {
    return total;
  }
  public void setTotal(int total)
  {
    this.total = total;
  }
}
```

Notice that we didn't have to do anything special in our managed bean to enable Ajax in our application. It is all controlled by the `<f:ajax>` tag on the page.

As we can see from this example, Ajax enabling JSF 2.0 applications is very simple. We simply need to use a single tag to Ajax to enable our page, without having to write a single line of Javascript, JSON or XML code.

JSF standard components

JSF includes several standard components, we have only covered a set of these components so far. The following sections cover all available JSF components.

JSF core components

JSF core components are components that are not tied to HTML rendering or any other rendering mechanism. They provide functionality like type conversion and validation, among others. In this section, we will cover all core JSF components.

The <f:actionListener> tag

Executes the `processAction()` method of the action listener defined by the tag's `type` attribute. The value of the `type` attribute must be the fully qualified name of a class implementing the `javax.faces.event.ActionListener` interface. This tag is typically a child tag of `<h:commandButton>` or `<h:commandLink>`. When a user clicks on the parent component, the `processAction()` method of the declared `ActionListener` implementation is automatically executed. The following markup segment illustrates how this tag is typically used:

```
<h:commandButton action="save" value="Save">
  <f:actionListener type="net.ensode.CustomActionListener"/>
</h:commandButton>
```

The <f:ajax> tag

Enables Ajax behavior. This tag is typically nested inside another JSF tag such as `<h:commandButton>`. When this tag is present, the parent component is automatically "ajaxified". For example, an Ajax-enabled button does not refresh the whole page, instead it triggers a partial page refresh. This behavior makes our applications much more responsive.

```
<h:commandButton actionListener="#{controller.calculateTotal}"
                 value="Calculate Sum">
  <f:ajax execute="first second" render="sum"/>
</h:commandButton>
```

The value of the execute attribute is a space-separated list of component IDs to be used as input when the Ajax request starts. The value of the render attribute is a space-separated list of components to re-render after the Ajax request completes.

The <f:attribute> tag

Sets an attribute on the parent component, with a key defined by the tag's name attribute and a value defined by the tag's value attribute. All component attributes can later be programmatically retrieved as a map by invoking the getAttributes() method of the appropriate instance of javax.faces.component.UIComponent. This tag is frequently used in conjunction with the <f:actionListener> class to pass parameters to the action listener.

The following markup segment illustrates typical use of this tag:

```
<h:commandButton action="save" value="Save">
  <f:actionListener type="net.ensode.CustomActionListener"/>
  <f:attribute name="someAttribute" value="someValue"/>
</h:commandButton>
```

The processAction() method of our CustomActionListener class would look something like this:

```
public void processAction(ActionEvent actionEvent)
{
  String attribute = (String)
    actionEevent.getComponent().getAttributes().get("attrname1");
  //processing continues...
}
```

The <f:convertDateTime> tag

Converts the value of the parent component into an instance of java.util.Date. This tag allows a correctly formatted user-entered string to be assigned to a date field in a managed bean. The following markup segment illustrates typical usage of this tag:

```
<h:inputText value="#{customer.birthDate}">
  <f:convertDateTime dateStyle="short"/>
</h:inputText>
```

The <f:convertNumber> tag

Converts the value of the parent component into an instance of `java.lang.Number`. This tag allows a correctly formatted user-entered string to be assigned to a numeric field in a managed bean. As `java.lang.Number` is the parent class of `java.lang.Integer`, `java.lang.Long`, `java.lang.Float`, and `java.lang.Double` (among other numeric types), this tag can be used to convert pretty much any type of numeric data entry field into an appropriate type.

The following markup segment illustrates typical usage of this tag:

```
<h:inputText value="#{customer.age}">
  <f:convertNumber/>
</h:inputText>
```

The <f:converter> tag

Registers the custom converter specified by the tag's `converterId` attribute with the parent tag. The specified converter must be a class implementing the `javax.faces.convert.Converter` interface, and it must be either decorated with the `@FacesConverter` annotation or registered in the application's `faces-config.xml` file via the `<converter>` tag.

Suppose we have created a custom class named `TelephoneNumber` to store telephone numbers, and a managed bean named `Customer` has a field called `telephone` of type `TelephoneNumber`. We could create a custom validator to convert a user-entered telephone number into an instance of the `TelephoneNumber` class.

```
<h:inputText value="#{customer.telephone}">
  <f:converter converterId="telephoneConverter"/>
</h:inputText>
```

The `TelephoneConverter` class would have to implement the `javax.faces.convert.Converter` interface.

The <f:event> tag

Allows a managed bean method to be invoked whenever a specific event occurs. This tag must be nested inside another JSF tag. The event to register for is specified as the value of the `type` attribute of `<f:event>`. Valid values include `preRenderComponent`, which is triggered just before the parent component is rendered, `PostAddToView`, which is triggered after the parent component is added to the view, `preValidate`, which is triggered just before the value of the parent component is validated, and `postValidate`, which is triggered just after the parent component is validated.

The value of the listener attribute of <f:event> must be a value binding expression that resolves to a managed bean method that is public, returns void and takes an instance of javax.faces.event.ComponentSystemEvent as its sole parameter. This method will be automatically invoked when the event is fired.

```
<h:outputText>
  <f:event type="preRenderComponent"
           action="#{myManagedBean.doSomething}" />
</h:outputText>
```

The <f:facet> tag

Registers a facet on the parent component. A facet is a special child component that can be accessed via the UIComponent.getFacet() method. This method can be overridden for custom components; it allows components inside a facet to be treated differently. For example, the standard <h:dataTable> tag can have a facet named "header" that is used to render all components in the <f:facet> tag as the header of the rendered HTML table.

The following markup segment illustrates typical usage of this tag:

```
<h:dataTable value="{Order.items}" var="item">
  <h:column>
    <f:facet name="header">
      <h:outputText value="Item Number" />
    </f:facet>
    <h:outputText value="#{item.itemNumber}" />
  </h:column>
  <h:column>
    <f:facet name="header">
      <h:outputText value="Item Description" />
    </f:facet>
    <h:outputText value="#{item.itemShortDesc}" />
  </h:column>
</h:dataTable>
```

The <f:loadBundle> tag

Loads a resource bundle into the request scope. The resource bundle name is specified by the tag's basename attribute. The variable to use to access the resource bundle properties is defined by the tag's var attribute.

The following markup segment illustrates typical usage of this tag:

```
<f:view locale="#{facesContext.externalContext.request.locale}">
  <f:loadBundle basename="net.ensode.Messages" var="mess"/>
  <h:outputText value="#{mess.greeting}"/>
</f:view>
```

The <f:metadata> tag

This tag is primarily used as a parent tag to `<f:viewParam>`, which is used to map GET request parameters to managed bean values.

```
<f:metadata>
  <f:viewParam name="someParam" value="#{someBean.someProperty}" />
</f:metadata>
```

The <f:param> tag

When this tag is a child of `<h:commandLInk>`, it generates a request parameter defined by its `name` and `value` attributes. When this tag is a child of `<h:outputFormat>`, it substitutes a parameter in the string defined by the `value` attribute of `<h:outpufFormat>`.

The following markup segment illustrates typical usage of this tag:

```
<h:outputFormat value="Hello, {0}">
  <f:param value="#{customer.firstName}"/>
</h:outputFormat>
```

The <f:phaseListener> tag

Registers a phase listener to the current page. The phase listener must be an instance of a class implementing `javax.faces.event.PhaseListener`. This class is defined by the tag's `type` attribute.

The following markup segment illustrates typical usage of this tag:

```
<f:view>
  <f:phaseListener type="net.ensode.CustomPhaseListener"/>
</f:view>
```

The <f:selectItem> tag

Adds a selectable item belonging to the parent component. The way this component is rendered depends on the parent component. It can be used as a child component of `<h:selectManyCheckBox>`, `<h:selectManuListBox>`, `<h:selectManyMenu>`, `<h:selectOneListbox>`, `<h:selectOneMenu>`, and `<h:selectOneRadio>`.

The following markup segment illustrates typical usage of this tag:

```
<h:selectManyCheckBox value="#{order.items}">
  <f:selectItem itemValue="#{item1}"
                itemLabel="Wireless keyboard"/>
  <f:selectItem itemValue="#{item1}"
                itemLabel="Wireless mouse"/>
</h:selectManyCheckBox>
```

The <f:selectItems> tag

Adds a series of selectable items belonging to the parent tag. This tag's `value` attribute must be a deferred value expression resolving to an array or a list of `javax.faces.model.SelectItem` objects.

The following markup segment illustrates typical usage of this tag:

```
<h:selectManyCheckBox value="#{order.items}">
  <f:selectItems value="#{valueContainer.allItems} "/>
</h:selectManyCheckBox>
```

The <f:setPropertyActionListener> tag

This tag can be a child tag of `<h:commandLink>` or `<h:commandButton>`. When the button or link is clicked, this tag sets an attribute in a managed bean defined by the tag's `target` attribute with the value of the tag's `value` attribute.

The following markup segment illustrates typical usage of this tag:

```
<h:commandButton value="Save" action="#{controller.save}">
  <f:setPropertyActionListener
    target="#{order.lastUpdUserId}" value="#{user.userId}"/>
</h:commandButton>
```

The <f:subview> tag

This tag is meant to be used only when using JSP as the JSF view technology. Any included JSPs via a `<jsp:include>` tag or JSTL's `<c:import>` tag must be inside a `<f:subview>` tag.

The following markup segment illustrates typical usage of this tag:

```
<f:view>
  <table>
    <tr>
      <td width="30%">
        <f:subview>
```

```
            <jsp:include page="menu.jsp">
          </f:subview>
        </td>
        <td>
          Additional content here.
        </td>
      </tr>
    </table>
  </f:view>
```

The <f:validateBean> tag

This tag is used to fine-tune JSR-303 Bean Validation. It can be used to disable Bean Validation in a case-by-case basis or to assign JSR-303 Bean Validation groups to the components to be validated.

The following markup segment illustrates typical usage of this tag:

```
<h:inputText value="#{someManagedBean.someProperty}">
  <f:validateBean disabled="#{anotherManagedBean.booleanProperty}"/>
</h:inputText>
```

In this example, it is assumed that the `someProperty` property of `someManagedBean` is decorated with a Bean Validation annotation such as `@NotNull` or `@Pattern`. In this case, `<f:validateBean>` is used to disable Bean Validation if the `booleanProperty` in `anotherManagedBean` resolves to `true`.

The <f:validateDoubleRange> tag

Validates that the value for the parent component is an instance of `java.lang.Double` that is between the values defined by the tag's `minimum` and `maximum` attributes.

The following markup segment illustrates typical usage of this tag:

```
<h:inputText value="#{item.price}">
  <f:validateDoubleRange minimum="1.0" maximum="100.0"/>
</h:inputText>
```

The <f:validateLength> tag

Validates that the value for the parent component is a string whose length is between the values defined by the tag's `minimum` and `maximum` attributes (both values inclusive).

The following markup segment illustrates typical usage of this tag:

```
<h:inputText label="First Name"
             value="#{customer.firstName}"
             required="true">
  <f:validateLength minimum="2"
                    maximum="30">
  </f:validateLength>
</h:inputText>
```

The <f:validateLongRange> tag

Validates that the value for the parent component is an instance of `java.lang.Long` that is between the values defined by the tag's `minimum` and `maximum` attributes.

The following markup segment illustrates typical usage of this tag:

```
<h:inputText value="#{orderItem.quantity}">
  <f:validateDoubleRange minimum="1" maximum="100"/>
</h:inputText>
```

The <f:validateRegex> tag

Validates that the value of the parent tag matches the regular expression specified in its `pattern` attribute.

The following markup segment illustrates typical usage of this tag:

```
<h:inputText value="#{someBean.phoneNumber}">
  <f:validateRegex pattern="\d{3}-\d{3}-\d{4}"/>
</h:inputText>
```

The <f:validateRequired> tag

Ensures that the user entered a value in the parent input component. This tag is equivalent to setting the `required` attribute to `true` in an input component.

The following markup segment illustrates typical usage of this tag:

```
<h:inputText value="#{someBean.someProperty}">
  <f:validateRequired/>
</h:inputText>
```

The <f:validator> tag

Validates the value of the parent component against a custom validator implementing the `javax.faces.validator.Validator` interface. The custom validator must be either decorated with the `@FacesValidator` annotation or declared in the application's `faces-config.xml` file.

The following markup segment illustrates typical usage of this tag:

```
<h:inputText label="Email" value="#{customer.email}">
  <f:validator validatorId="emailValidator" />
</h:inputText>
```

The <f:valueChangeListener> tag

Registers an instance of a class implementing the `javax.faces.event.ValueChangeListener` interface with the parent component. The `ValueChangeListener` implementation will implement a `processValueChange()` method that can perform an action if the value of the parent component changes.

The following markup segment illustrates typical usage of this tag:

```
<h:inputText value="#{orderItem.quantity}">
  <f:valueChangeListener
    type="net.ensode.CustomValueChangeListener"/>
</h:inputText>
```

The <f:verbatim> tag

The content of this tag is passed "as is" to the rendered page. Before JSF 1.2, it was not recommended to have HTML tags inside the JSF `<f:view>` tag, as they would sometimes not render properly. A common workaround to this limitation was to put standard HTML tags inside the `<f:verbatim>` tags. As of JSF 1.2 or when using facelets, this tag is redundant as it is now possible to safely place standard HTML tags inside the JSF pages tag.

The following markup segment illustrates typical usage of this tag:

```
<f:view>
  <f:verbatim><p></f:verbatim>
    This text will be rendered inside an HTML &lt;p&gt; tag.
  <f:verbatim></p></f:verbatim>
</f:view>
```

The <f:view> tag

This tag is the parent tag for all JSF tags, both standard and custom.

The following markup segment illustrates typical usage of this tag:

```
<f:view>
  <h:outputText escape="true"
                value="All JSF components must be inside <f:view>"/>
</f:view>
```

The <f:viewParam> tag

This tag is used to map an HTTP GET request parameter to a managed bean property. The value of its `name` attribute must match the parameter name and the value of its `value` parameter must be a value binding expression corresponding to a managed bean value to be populated by the request parameter.

```
<f:metadata>
  <f:viewParam name="someParam" value="#{someBean.someProperty}" />
</f:metadata>
```

JSF HTML components

In the previous examples, we covered only a subset of the standard JSF HTML components. In this section, we will list all the standard JSF HTML components.

The <h:body> tag

Renders the body of the page. This tag is analogous to the standard HTML `<body>` tag.

```
<h:body>
  <!-- body of the page goes here -->
</h:body>
```

The <h:button> tag

Similar to `<h:commandButton>`. However, a button rendered using this tag generates an HTTP GET request when navigating to the target page.

```
<h:button value="Click" action="next_page"/>
```

The <h:column> tag

This tag is typically nested inside the `<h:dataTable>` tag. Any components inside this tag will be rendered as a single column inside the table rendered by `<h:dataTable>`.

The following markup segment illustrates typical usage of this tag:

```
<h:dataTable value="{Order.items}" var="item">
  <h:column>
    <f:facet name="header">
      <h:outputText value="Item Number" />
    </f:facet>
    <h:outputText value="#{item.itemNumber}" />
  </h:column>
  <h:column>
    <f:facet name="header">
      <h:outputText value="Item Description" />
    </f:facet>
    <h:outputText value="#{item.itemShortDesc}" />
  </h:column>
</h:dataTable>
```

The <h:commandButton> tag

Renders an HTML submit button on the rendered page.

The following markup segment illustrates typical usage of this tag:

```
<h:form>
  <h:inputText label="First Name"
               value="#{customer.firstName}"/>
  <h:commandButton action="save"
                   value="Save">
  </h:commandButton>
</h:form>
```

The <h:commandLink> tag

Renders a link that will submit the form defined by this tag's parent `<h:form>` tag.

The following markup segment illustrates typical usage of this tag:

```
<h:form>
  <h:inputText label="First Name"
               value="#{customer.firstName}"/>
  <h:commandLink action="save"
                 value="Save">
  </h:commandLink>
</h:form>
```

The <h:dataTable> tag

Builds a table dynamically based on the values of a collection. The collection holding the values must be defined by the tag's `value` attribute.

The following markup segment illustrates typical usage of this tag:

```
<h:dataTable value="{Order.items}" var="item">
  <h:column>
    <f:facet name="header">
      <h:outputText value="Item Number" />
    </f:facet>
    <h:outputText value="#{item.itemNumber}" />
  </h:column>
  <h:column>
    <f:facet name="header">
      <h:outputText value="Item Description" />
    </f:facet>
    <h:outputText value="#{item.itemShortDesc}" />
  </h:column>
</h:dataTable>
```

The <h:form> tag

Renders an HTML form on the generated page.

The following markup segment illustrates typical usage of this tag:

```
<h:form>
  <h:inputText label="First Name"
               value="#{customer.firstName}"/>
  <h:commandLink action="save"
                 value="Save">
  </h:commandLink>
</h:form>
```

The <h:graphicImage> tag

Renders an HTML `img` tag.

The following markup segment illustrates typical usage of this tag.

If we would like to load an image from a URL:

```
<h:graphicImage url="/images/logo.png"/>
```

If the image is placed in the JSF 2.0 standard resource folder, the tag could be used like this:

```
<h:graphicImage library="images" name="logo.png"/>
```

The <h:head> tag

JSF-specific version of the standard HTML `<head>` tag.

The following markup segment illustrates how to use this tag:

```
<h:head>
  <title>Page Title</title>
</h:head>
```

The <h:inputHidden> tag

Renders an HTML hidden field.

The following markup segment illustrates typical usage of this tag:

```
<h:inputHidden value="#{customer.id}" />
```

The <h:inputSecret> tag

Renders an HTML `input` field of type `password`.

The following markup segment illustrates typical usage of this tag:

```
<h:inputSecret redisplay="false"
               value="#{user.password}" />
```

The <h:inputText> tag

Renders an HTML `input` field of type `text`.

The following markup segment illustrates typical usage of this tag:

```
<h:inputText label="First Name" value="#{customer.firstName}"/>
```

The <h:inputTextarea> tag

Renders an HTML `textarea` field.

The following markup segment illustrates typical usage of this tag:

```
<h:inputTextarea label="Comments" value="#{order.comments}"/>
```

The <h:link> tag

Similar to `<h:commandLink>`. However, a link rendered using this tag generates an HTTP GET request when navigating to the target page.

```
<h:link value="Click" action="next_page"/>
```

The <h:message> tag

Renders messages for a single component. The component to render messages for must use its `id` attribute to set an identifier for itself. This identifier then needs to be used as this element's `for` attribute.

The following markup segment illustrates typical usage of this tag:

```
<table>
  <tr>
    <td align="right">
      <h:outputLabel value="Login Name:"
                     for="loginField"/>
    </td>
    <td>
      <h:inputText id="loginField"
                   value="#{user.login}"
                   required="true"/>
    </td>
    <td><h:message for="loginField"/></td>
  </tr>
</table>
```

The <h:messages> tag

Outputs messages for all components or global messages. If the tag's `globalOnly` attribute is set to `true`, then only global messages (messages not specific to any component) will be displayed.

The following markup segment illustrates typical usage of this tag:

```
<f:view>
  <h:messages/>
  <h:form>
    <h:inputText label="First Name"
                 value="#{customer.firstName}"/>
    <h:commandButton action="save"
                     value="Save"/>
  </h:form>
</f:view>
```

The <h:outputFormat> tag

Renders parameterized text. Parameters in this tag's `value` attribute are defined in a manner similar to the way they are defined in a resource bundle, that is, by placing integers between curly braces in the parameter locations. Parameters are substituted with values defined in any child `<f:param>` elements.

The following markup segment illustrates typical usage of this tag:

```
<h:outputFormat value="Hello, {0}">
  <f:param value="#{customer.firstName}"/>
</h:outputFormat>
```

The <h:outputLabel> tag

Renders an HTML `label` field.

The following markup segment illustrates typical usage of this tag:

```
<table>
  <tr>
    <td align="right">
      <h:outputLabel value="Login Name:"
                     for="loginField"/>
    </td>
    <td>
      <h:inputText id="loginField"
                   value="#{user.login}"
                   required="true"/>
    </td>
  </tr>
</table>
```

The <h:outputLink> tag

Renders an HTML link as an `anchor` (a) element with an `href` attribute.

The following markup segment illustrates typical usage of this tag:

```
<h:outputLink value="http://ensode.net">
  <h:outputText value="Ensode"/>
</h:outputLink>
```

The <h:outputScript> tag

Used to load a Javascript file from the standard resource location.

The following markup segment illustrates how to use this tag:

```
<h:outputScript library="scripts" name="somescript.js"/>
```

The <h:outputStylesheet> tag

Used to load a CSS stylesheet from the standard resource location.

The following markup segment illustrates typical usage of this tag:

```
<h:outputStylesheet library="css" name="styles.css" />
```

The <h:outputText> tag

If the `dir`, `lang`, `style`, or `styleClass` attributes are defined, this tag renders an HTML `span` element containing the tag's `value` attribute. Otherwise, the value defined by the tag's `value` attribute is rendered, escaping any XML/HTML characters so that they are rendered properly. If the tag's `escape` attribute is set to `false`, then XML/HTML characters are not escaped.

The following markup segment illustrates typical usage of this tag:

```
<h:outputText value="#{customer.firstName}"/>
```

The <h:panelGrid> tag

Renders a static HTML table. The number of columns in the table is specified in the tag's `columns` attribute. Child components are then added to a subsequent row once the number of elements defined in the `columns` attribute has been added to the current row.

The following markup segment illustrates typical usage of this tag:

```
<h:panelGrid columns="2"
             columnClasses="rightAlign,leftAlign">
  <h:outputText value="First Name:">
  </h:outputText>
  <h:inputText label="First Name"
               value="#{customer.firstName}"
               required="true">
    <f:validateLength minimum="2"
                      maximum="30">
    </f:validateLength>
  </h:inputText>
  <h:outputText value="Last Name:"></h:outputText>
  <h:inputText label="Last Name"
               value="#{customer.lastName}"
               required="true">
    <f:validateLength minimum="2"
                      maximum="30">
    </f:validateLength>
```

```
    </h:inputText>
    <h:outputText value="Email:">
    </h:outputText>
    <h:inputText label="Email" value="#{customer.email}">
      <f:validateLength minimum="3"
                        maximum="30">
      </f:validateLength>
    </h:inputText>
    <h:panelGroup></h:panelGroup>
    <h:commandButton action="save"
                     value="Save">
    </h:commandButton>
  </h:panelGrid>
```

The <h:panelGroup> tag

Used to group its child components together in a single cell of a parent `<h:panelGrid>` or `<h:dataTable>` tag. Can also be used to create an "empty" cell in a parent `<h:panelGrid>` tag.

The following markup segment illustrates typical usage of this tag:

```
<h:panelGrid columns="2"
             columnClasses="rightAlign,leftAlign">
  <h:outputText value="First Name:">
  </h:outputText>
  <h:inputText label="First Name"
               value="#{customer.firstName}"
               required="true">
    <f:validateLength minimum="2"
                      maximum="30">
    </f:validateLength>
  </h:inputText>
  <h:outputText value="Last Name:"></h:outputText>
  <h:inputText label="Last Name"
               value="#{customer.lastName}"
               required="true">
    <f:validateLength minimum="2"
                      maximum="30">
    </f:validateLength>
  </h:inputText>
  <h:outputText value="Email:">
  </h:outputText>
  <h:inputText label="Email" value="#{customer.email}">
    <f:validateLength minimum="3"
                      maximum="30">
```

```
      </f:validateLength>
    </h:inputText>
    <h:panelGroup></h:panelGroup>
    <h:commandButton action="save"
                     value="Save">
    </h:commandButton>
  </h:panelGrid>
```

The <h:selectBooleanCheckbox> tag

Renders a single HTML `input` field of type `checkbox`. The `value` attribute for this tag is usually set to a value binding expression mapping to a boolean property in a managed bean.

The following markup segment illustrates typical usage of this tag:

```
<h:selectBooleanCheckbox
  value="#{customer.newsletterOk}" />
<h:outputText
  value="Would you like to receive our newsletter?"/>
```

The <h:selectManyCheckbox> tag

Renders a series of related checkboxes. Values for the user to select are defined in any child `<f:selectItem>` or `<f:selectItems>` tags.

The following markup segment illustrates typical usage of this tag:

```
<h:selectManyCheckBox value="#{order.items}">
  <f:selectItems value="#{valueContainer.allItems} "/>
</h:selectManyCheckBox>
```

The <h:selectManyListbox> tag

Renders an HTML `select` field of variable size that allows multiple selections. Values for the user to select are defined in any child `<f:selectItem>` or `<f:selectItems>` tags. The number of elements displayed at the same time is set by the tag's `size` attribute.

The following markup segment illustrates typical usage of this tag:

```
<h:selectManyListBox value="#{order.items}">
  <f:selectItems value="#{valueContainer.allItems} "/>
</h:selectManyListBox>
```

The <h:selectManyMenu> tag

Renders an HTML `select` field that allows multiple selections. Values for the user to select are defined in any child `<f:selectItem>` or `<f:selectItems>` tags. This tag is identical to `<h:selectManyListbox>` except that it always displays one element at a time. Therefore, it has no `size` attribute.

The following markup segment illustrates typical usage of this tag:

```
<h:selectManyMenu value="#{order.items}">
  <f:selectItems value="#{valueContainer.allItems} "/>
</h:selectManyMenu>
```

The <h:selectOneListbox> tag

Renders an HTML select field of variable size that does not allow multiple selections. Values for the user to select are defined in any child `<f:selectItem>` or `<f:selectItems>` tags. The number of elements displayed at the same time is set by the tag's `size` attribute, which is optional. If the `size` attribute is not set, then all elements are displayed at the same time.

The following markup segment illustrates typical usage of this tag:

```
<h:selectOneListBox value="#{order.selectedItem}">
  <f:selectItems value="#{valueContainer.allItems} "/>
</h:selectOneListBox>
```

The <h:selectOneMenu> tag

Renders an HTML "dropdown", which is to say it renders an HTML `select` field that does not allow multiple selections. Only one element is displayed at a time. Values for the user to select are defined in any child `<f:selectItem>` or `<f:selectItems>` tags.

The following markup segment illustrates typical usage of this tag:

```
<h:selectOneMenu value="#{order.selectedItem}">
  <f:selectItems value="#{valueContainer.allItems} "/>
</h:selectOneMenu>
```

The <h:selectOneRadio> tag

Renders a series of related radio buttons. Values for the user to select are defined in any child `<f:selectItem>` or `<f:selectItems>` tags.

The following markup segments illustrate typical usage of this tag:

```
<h:selectOneRadio value="#{order.selectedItem}">
  <f:selectItems value="#{valueContainer.allItems} "/>
</h:selectOneRadio>
```

Additional JSF component libraries

In addition to the standard JSF component libraries, there are a number of third-party JSF tag libraries available. The following table lists some of the most popular. Please note that at the time of writing, not all of the listed component libraries have been updated to support JSF 2.0.

Tag Library	Distributor	License	URL
MyFaces Trinidad	Apache	Apache 2.0	http://myfaces.apache.org/trinidad/
ICEfaces	ICEsoft	MPL 1.1	http://www.icefaces.org
RichFaces	Red Hat/ JBoss	LGPL	http://www.jboss.org/richfaces
Primefaces	Prime Technology	Apache 2.0	http://primefaces.org

Summary

In this chapter, we covered how to develop web-based applications using JavaServer Faces—the standard component framework for the Java EE 6 platform. We covered how to write a simple application by creating JSPs containing JSF tags and managed beans. We also covered how to validate user input by using JSF's standard validators and by creating our own custom validators or by writing validator methods. Additionally, we covered how to customize standard JSF error messages; both the message text and the message style (font, color, and so on). Finally, we covered how to write applications by integrating JSF and the Java Persistence API (JPA).

7
Java Messaging Service

The **Java Messaging API (JMS)** provides a mechanism for Java EE applications to send messages to each other. JMS applications do not communicate directly, instead message producers send messages to a destination and message consumers receive the message from the destination.

The message destination is a message queue when the point-to-point (PTP) messaging domain is used, or a message topic when the publish/subscribe (pub/sub) messaging domain is used.

In this chapter, we will cover the following topics:

- Setting up GlassFish for JMS
- Working with message queues
- Working with message topics

Setting up GlassFish for JMS

Before we start writing code to take advantage of the JMS API, we need to configure some GlassFish resources. Specifically, we need to set up a **JMS connection factory**, a **message queue**, and a **message topic**.

Setting up a JMS connection factory

The easiest way to set up a JMS connection factory is via GlassFish's web console. Recall from Chapter 1 that the web console can be accessed by starting our domain, by entering the following command in the command line:

```
asadmin start-domain domain1
```

Then point the browser to `http://localhost:4848` and log in:

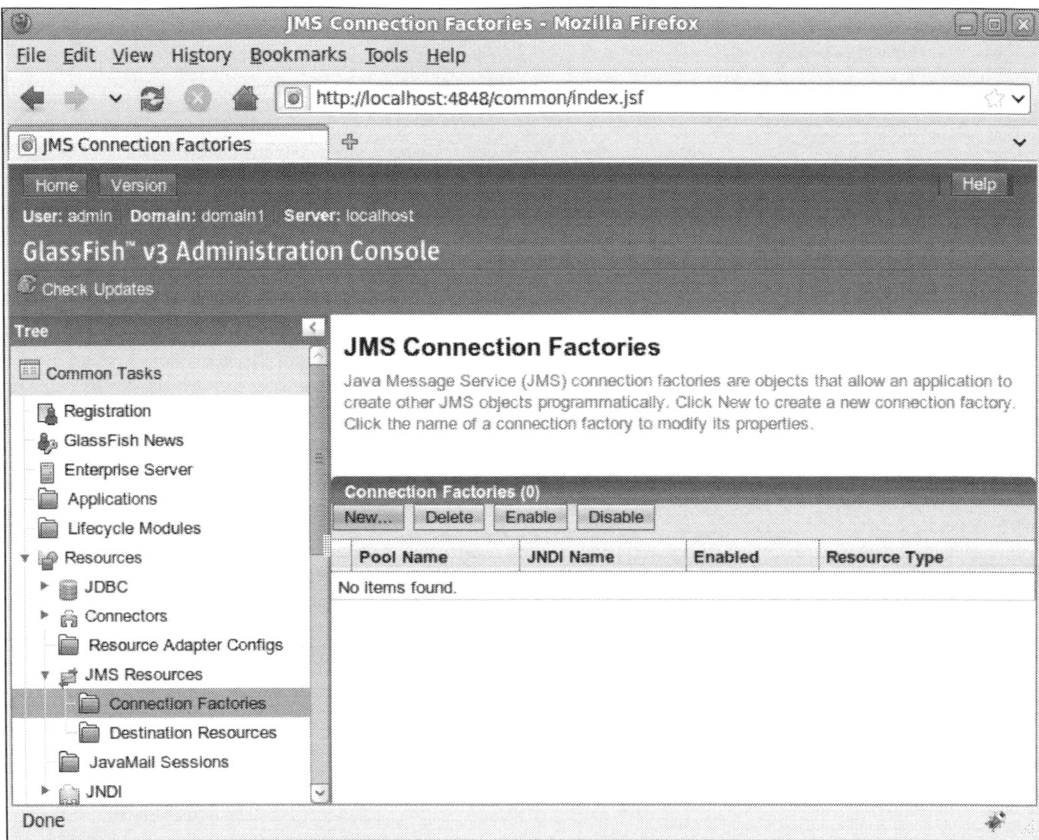

A connection factory can be added by expanding the **Resources** node in the tree at the left-hand side of the web console, expanding the **JMS Resources** node and clicking on the **Connection Factories** node, then clicking on the **New...** button in the main area of the web console.

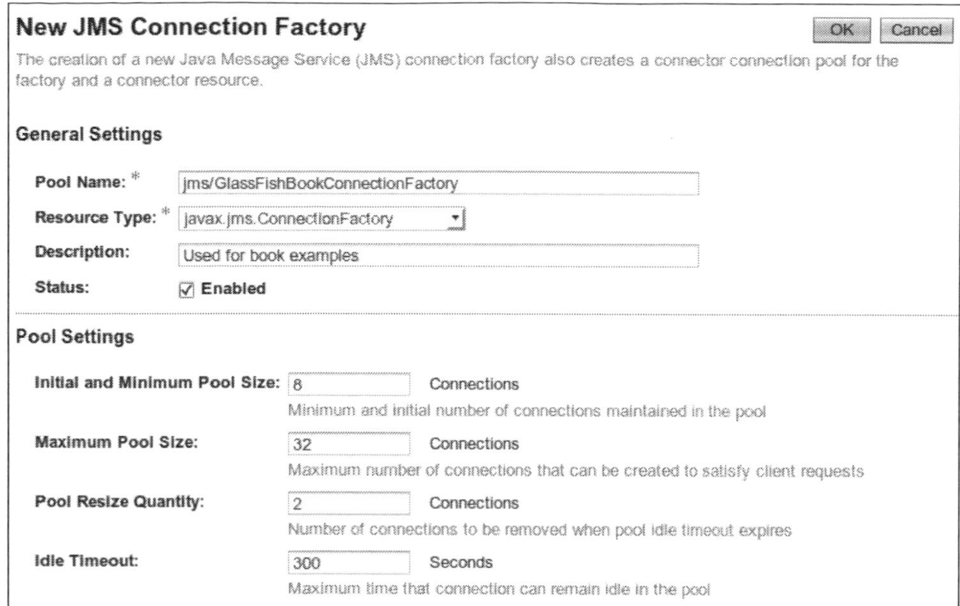

For our purposes, we can take most of the defaults. The only thing we need to do is enter a **Pool Name** and pick a **Resource Type** for our connection factory.

> It is always a good idea to use a **Pool Name** starting with "jms/" when picking a name for JMS resources. This way JMS resources can be easily identified when browsing a JNDI tree.

In the text field labeled **Pool Name**, enter **jms/GlassFishBookConnectionFactory**. Our code examples later in this chapter will use this JNDI name to obtain a reference to this connection factory.

The **Resource Type** drop-down menu has three options:

- **javax.jms.TopicConnectionFactory** - used to create a connection factory that creates JMS topics for JMS clients using the pub/sub messaging domain
- **javax.jms.QueueConnectionFactory** - used to create a connection factory that creates JMS queues for JMS clients using the PTP messaging domain
- **javax.jms.ConnectionFactory** - used to create a connection factory that creates either JMS topics or JMS queues

For our example, we will select **javax.jms.ConnectionFactory**. This way we can use the same connection factory for all our examples, those using the PTP messaging domain and those using the pub/sub messaging domain.

After entering the **Pool Name** for our connection factory, selecting a connection factory type, and optionally entering a description for our connection factory, we must click on the **OK** button for the changes to take effect.

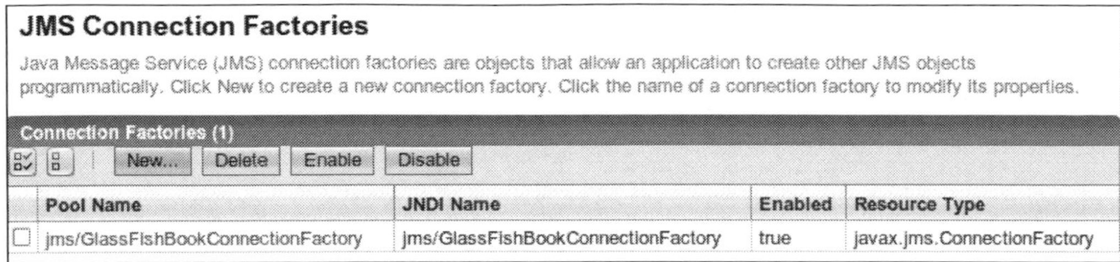
JMS Connection Factories
Java Message Service (JMS) connection factories are objects that allow an application to create other JMS objects programmatically. Click New to create a new connection factory. Click the name of a connection factory to modify its properties.
Connection Factories (1)
New...
Delete
Enable
Disable
Pool Name
JNDI Name
Enabled
Resource Type
jms/GlassFishBookConnectionFactory
jms/GlassFishBookConnectionFactory
true
javax.jms.ConnectionFactory

We should then see our newly created connection factory listed in the main area of the GlassFish web console.

Setting up a JMS message queue

A JMS message queue can be added by expanding the **Resources** node in the tree at the left-hand side of the web console, expanding the **JMS Resources** node and clicking on the **Destination Resources** node, then clicking on the **New...** button in the main area of the web console.

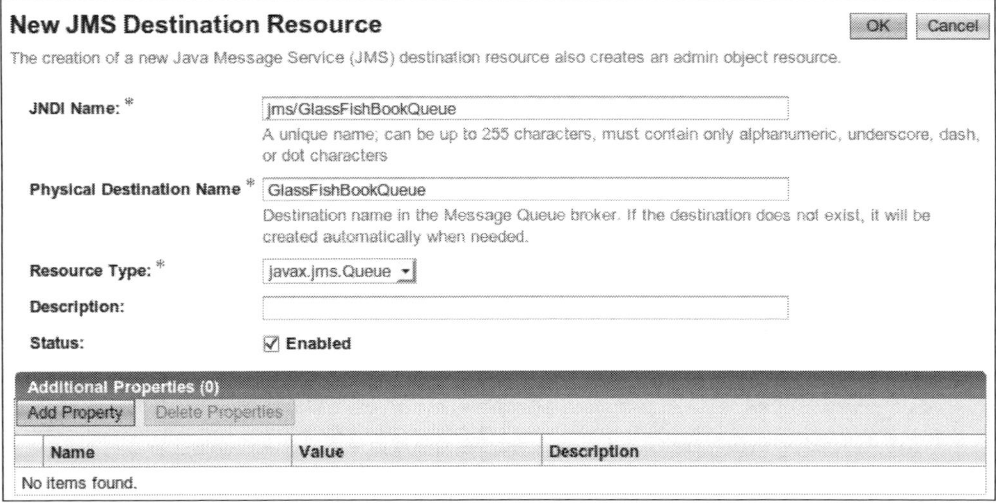
New JMS Destination Resource
OK
Cancel
The creation of a new Java Message Service (JMS) destination resource also creates an admin object resource.
JNDI Name: *
jms/GlassFishBookQueue
A unique name; can be up to 255 characters, must contain only alphanumeric, underscore, dash, or dot characters
Physical Destination Name *
GlassFishBookQueue
Destination name in the Message Queue broker. If the destination does not exist, it will be created automatically when needed.
Resource Type: *
javax.jms.Queue
Description:
Status:
Enabled
Additional Properties (0)
Add Property
Delete Properties
Name
Value
Description
No items found.

In our example, the JNDI name of the message queue is **jms/GlassFishBookQueue**. The resource type for message queues must be **javax.jms.Queue**. Additionally, a **Physical Destination Name** must be entered. In this example, we use **GlassFishBookQueue** as the value for this field.

After clicking on the **New...** button, entering the appropriate information for our message queue, and clicking on the **OK** button, we should see the newly created queue:

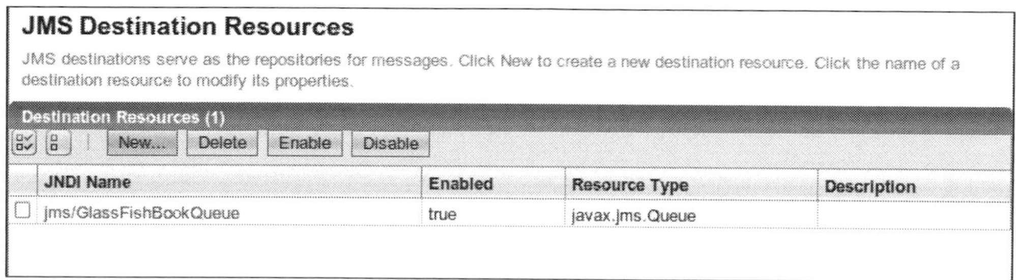
JMS Destination Resources
JMS destinations serve as the repositories for messages. Click New to create a new destination resource. Click the name of a destination resource to modify its properties.
Destination Resources (1)
New...
Delete
Enable
Disable
JNDI Name
Enabled
Resource Type
Description
jms/GlassFishBookQueue
true
javax.jms.Queue

Setting up a JMS message topic

Setting up a JMS message topic in GlassFish is very similar to setting up a message queue.

In the GlassFish web console, expand the **Resources** node in the tree at the left hand side, then expand the **JMS Resouces** node and click on the **Destination** Resources node, then click on the **New...** button in the main area of the web console.

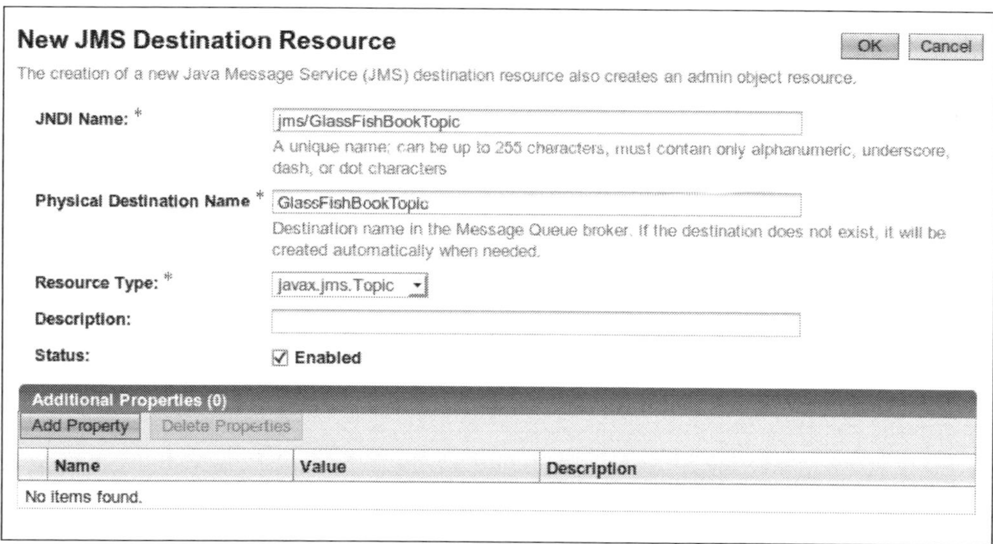
New JMS Destination Resource
OK
Cancel
The creation of a new Java Message Service (JMS) destination resource also creates an admin object resource.
JNDI Name: *
jms/GlassFishBookTopic
A unique name; can be up to 255 characters, must contain only alphanumeric, underscore, dash, or dot characters
Physical Destination Name *
GlassFishBookTopic
Destination name in the Message Queue broker. If the destination does not exist, it will be created automatically when needed.
Resource Type: *
javax.jms.Topic
Description:
Status:
Enabled
Additional Properties (0)
Add Property
Delete Properties
Name
Value
Description
No items found.

Our examples will use a **JNDI Name** of **jms/GlassFishBookTopic**. As this is a message topic, **Resource Type** must be **javax.jms.Topic**. The **Description** field is optional. The **Physical Destination Name** property is required. For our example, we will use **GlassFishBookTopic** as the value for this property.

After clicking on the **OK** button, we can see our newly created message topic:

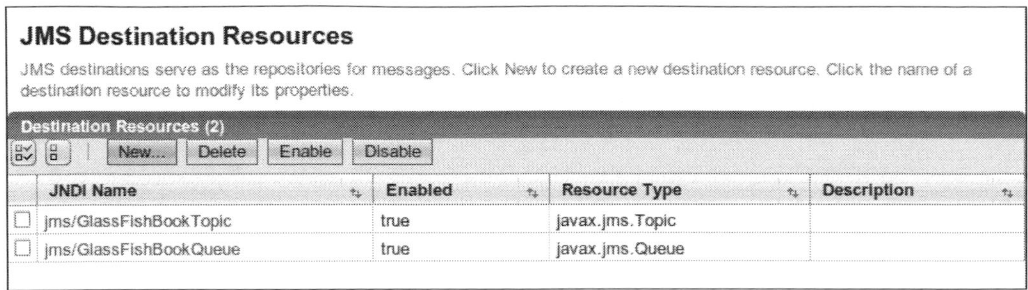

Now that we have set up a connection factory, a message queue, and a message topic, we are ready to start writing code using the JMS API.

Message queues

Like we mentioned earlier, message queues are used when our JMS code uses the point-to-point (PTP) messaging domain. For the PTP messaging domain, there is usually one message producer and one message consumer. The message producer and the message consumer don't need to run concurrently in order to communicate. The messages placed in the message queue by the message producer will stay in the message queue until the message consumer executes and requests the messages from the queue.

Sending messages to a message queue

The following example illustrates how to add messages to a message queue:

```
package net.ensode.glassfishbook;

import javax.annotation.Resource;
import javax.jms.Connection;
import javax.jms.ConnectionFactory;
import javax.jms.JMSException;
import javax.jms.MessageProducer;
import javax.jms.Queue;
import javax.jms.Session;
import javax.jms.TextMessage;

public class MessageSender
{
  @Resource(mappedName = "jms/GlassFishBookConnectionFactory")
  private static ConnectionFactory connectionFactory;
```

```
@Resource(mappedName = "jms/GlassFishBookQueue")
private static Queue queue;

public void produceMessages()
{
  MessageProducer messageProducer;
  TextMessage textMessage;
  try
  {
    Connection connection = connectionFactory.createConnection();
    Session session = connection.createSession(false,
      Session.AUTO_ACKNOWLEDGE);
    messageProducer = session.createProducer(queue);
    textMessage = session.createTextMessage();

    textMessage.setText("Testing, 1, 2, 3. Can you hear me?");
    System.out.println("Sending the following message: "
      + textMessage.getText());
    messageProducer.send(textMessage);

    textMessage.setText("Do you copy?");
    System.out.println("Sending the following message: "
      + textMessage.getText());
    messageProducer.send(textMessage);

    textMessage.setText("Good bye!");
    System.out.println("Sending the following message: "
      + textMessage.getText());
    messageProducer.send(textMessage);

    messageProducer.close();
    session.close();
    connection.close();
  }
  catch (JMSException e)
  {
    e.printStackTrace();
  }
}
public static void main(String[] args)
{
  new MessageSender().produceMessages();
}
}
```

Before delving into the details of this code, alert readers might have noticed that this class is a standalone Java application as it contains a `main` method. As this class is standalone, it executes outside the application server. In spite of this, we can see that some resources are injected into it, specifically the connection factory and queue. The reason we can inject resources into this code, even though it runs outside the application server, is because GlassFish includes a utility called `appclient`.

This utility allows us to "wrap" an executable JAR file and allows it to have access to the application server resources. To execute the previous code, assuming it is packaged in an executable JAR file called `jmsptpproducer.jar`, we would type the following command in the command line:

```
appclient -client jmsptpproducer.jar
```

We would then see, after some GlassFish log entries, the following output on the console:

```
Sending the following message: Testing, 1, 2, 3. Can you hear me?
Sending the following message: Do you copy?
Sending the following message: Good bye!
```

The `appclient` executable can be found under `[GlassFish installation directory]/glassfish/bin`. The previous example assumes this directory is in your PATH variable. If it isn't the complete path to the `appclient` executable, it must be typed in the command line.

With that out of the way, we can now explain the code.

The `produceMessages()` method performs all the necessary steps to send messages to a message queue.

The first thing this method does is obtain a JMS connection by invoking the `createConnection()` method on the injected instance of `javax.jms.ConnectionFactory`. Notice that the `mappedName` attribute of the `@Resource` annotation decorating the connection factory object matches the JNDI name of the connection factory we set up in the GlassFish web console. Behind the scenes, a JNDI lookup is made using this name to obtain the connection factory object.

After obtaining a connection, the next step is to obtain a JMS session from said connection. This can be accomplished by calling the `createSession()` method on the `Connection` object. As can be seen in the previous code, the `createSession()` method takes two parameters.

The first parameter of the `createSession()` method is a Boolean indicating if the session is transacted. If this value is `true`, several messages can be sent as part of a transaction by invoking the `commit()` method in the session object. Similarly, they can be rolled back by invoking its `rollback()` method.

The second parameter of the `createSession()` method indicates how messages are acknowledged by the message receiver. Valid values for this parameter are defined as constants in the `javax.jms.Session` interface.

- `Session.AUTO_ACKNOWLEDGE`: indicates that the session will automatically acknowledge the receipt of a message.
- `Session.CLIENT_ACKNOWLEDGE`: indicates that the message receiver must explicitly call the `acknowledge()` method on the message.
- `Session.DUPS_OK_ACKNOWLEDGE`: indicates that the session will lazily acknowledge the receipt of messages. Using this value might result in some messages being delivered more than once.

After obtaining a JMS session, an instance of `javax.jms.MessageProducer` is obtained by invoking the `createProducer()` method on the session object. The `MessageProducer` object is the one that will actually send messages to the message queue. The injected `Queue` instance is passed as a parameter to the `createProducer()` method. Again, the value of the `mappedName` attribute for the `@Resource` annotation decorating this object must match the JNDI name we gave our message queue when setting it up in the GlassFish web console.

After obtaining an instance of `MessageProducer`, the code creates a series of text messages by invoking the `createTextMessage()` method on the session object. This method returns an instance of a class implementing the `javax.jms.TextMessage` interface. This interface defines a method called `setText()`, which is used to set the actual text in the message. After creating each text message and setting its text, they are sent to the queue by invoking the `send()` method on the `MessageProducer` object.

After sending the messages, the code disconnects from the JMS queue by invoking the `close()` method on the `MessageProducer` object, on the `Session` object, and on the `Connection` object.

Although the previous example sends only text messages to the queue, we are not limited to this type of message. The JMS API provides several types of messages that can be sent and received by JMS applications. All message types are defined as interfaces in the `javax.jms` package.

The following table lists all the available message types:

Message type	Description
BytesMessage	Allows sending an array of bytes as a message.
MapMessage	Allows sending an implementation of `java.util.Map` as a message.
ObjectMessage	Allows sending any Java object implementing `java.io.Serializable` as a message.
StreamMessage	Allows sending an array of bytes as a message. Differs from `BytesMessage` in that it stores the type of each primitive type added to the stream.
TextMessage	Allows sending a `java.lang.String` as a message.

For more information on all of these message types, consult their JavaDoc documentation at `http://java.sun.com/javaee/6/docs/api/`.

Retrieving messages from a message queue

There is no point in sending messages from a queue if nothing is going to receive them. The following example illustrates how to retrieve messages from a JMS message queue:

```
package net.ensode.glassfishbook;

import javax.annotation.Resource;
import javax.jms.Connection;
import javax.jms.ConnectionFactory;
import javax.jms.JMSException;
import javax.jms.MessageConsumer;
import javax.jms.Queue;
import javax.jms.Session;
import javax.jms.TextMessage;

public class MessageReceiver
{
  @Resource(mappedName = "jms/GlassFishBookConnectionFactory")
  private static ConnectionFactory connectionFactory;
  @Resource(mappedName = "jms/GlassFishBookQueue")
  private static Queue queue;

  public void getMessages()
  {
```

```
    Connection connection;
    MessageConsumer messageConsumer;
    TextMessage textMessage;
    boolean goodByeReceived = false;
    try
    {
      connection = connectionFactory.createConnection();
      Session session = connection.createSession(false,
        Session.AUTO_ACKNOWLEDGE);
      messageConsumer = session.createConsumer(queue);
      connection.start();
      while (!goodByeReceived)
      {
        System.out.println("Waiting for messages...");
        textMessage = (TextMessage) messageConsumer.receive();
        if (textMessage != null)
        {
          System.out.print("Received the following message: ");
          System.out.println(textMessage.getText());
          System.out.println();
        }
        if (textMessage.getText() != null
          && textMessage.getText().equals("Good bye!"))
        {
          goodByeReceived = true;
        }
      }
      messageConsumer.close();
      session.close();
      connection.close();
    }
    catch (JMSException e)
    {
      e.printStackTrace();
    }
  }
  public static void main(String[] args)
  {
    new MessageReceiver().getMessages();
  }
}
```

Just like in the previous example, an instance of `javax.jms.ConnectionFactory` and an instance of `javax.jms.Queue` are injected by using the `@Resource` annotation. Getting a connection and a JMS session is exactly the same as in the previous example.

In this example, we obtain an instance of `javax.jms.MessageConsumer` by calling the `createConsumer()` method on the JMS session object. When we are ready to start receiving messages from the message queue, we need to invoke the `start()` method on the JMS connection object.

Code not receiving messages?

A common mistake when writing JMS messages is to fail to call the `start()` method on the JMS connection object. If our code is not receiving messages it should be receiving, we need to make sure we didn't forget to call this method.

Messages are received by invoking the `receive()` method on the instance of `MessageConsumer` obtained from the JMS session. This method returns an instance of a class implementing the `javax.jms.Message` interface. It must be casted to the appropriate type in order to obtain the actual message.

In this particular example, we placed this method call in a `while` loop, as we are expecting a message that will let us know that no more messages are coming. Specifically, we are looking for a message containing the text `"Good bye!"`. Once we receive said message, we break out of the loop and continue processing. In this particular case, there is no more processing to do. Therefore, all we do is call the `close()` method on the message consumer object, on the session object, and on the connection object.

Just like in the previous example, using the `appclient` utility allows us to inject resources into the code and prevents us from having to add any libraries to the CLASSPATH. After executing the code through the `appclient` utility, we should see the following output in the command line:

```
appclient -client target/jmsptpconsumer.jar
Waiting for messages...
Received the following message: Testing, 1, 2, 3. Can you hear me?

Waiting for messages...
Received the following message: Do you copy?

Waiting for messages...
Received the following message: Good bye!
```

This of course assumes that the previous example was already executed and it placed the messages in the message queue.

Asynchronously receiving messages from a message queue

The `MessageConsumer.receive()` method has a disadvantage—it blocks execution until a message is received from the queue. We can avoid this disadvantage by receiving messages asynchronously via an implementation of the `javax.jms.MessageListener` interface.

The `javax.jms.MessageListener` interface contains a single method called `onMessage`. It takes an instance of a class implementing the `javax.jms.Message` interface as its sole parameter. The following example illustrates a typical implementation of this interface:

```
package net.ensode.glassfishbook;

import javax.jms.JMSException;
import javax.jms.Message;
import javax.jms.MessageListener;
import javax.jms.TextMessage;

public class ExampleMessageListener implements MessageListener
{
  @Override
  public void onMessage(Message message)
  {
    TextMessage textMessage = (TextMessage) message;
    try
    {
      System.out.print("Received the following message: ");
      System.out.println(textMessage.getText());
      System.out.println();
    }
    catch (JMSException e)
    {
      e.printStackTrace();
    }
  }
}
```

In this case, the `onMessage()` method simply outputs the message text to the console.

Our main code can now delegate message retrieval to our custom `MessageListener` implementation:

```
package net.ensode.glassfishbook;

import javax.annotation.Resource;
import javax.jms.Connection;
import javax.jms.ConnectionFactory;
import javax.jms.JMSException;
import javax.jms.MessageConsumer;
import javax.jms.Queue;
import javax.jms.Session;

public class AsynchMessReceiver
{
  @Resource(mappedName = "jms/GlassFishBookConnectionFactory")
  private static ConnectionFactory connectionFactory;
  @Resource(mappedName = "jms/GlassFishBookQueue")
  private static Queue queue;

  public void getMessages()
  {
    Connection connection;
    MessageConsumer messageConsumer;
    try
    {
      connection = connectionFactory.createConnection();
      Session session = connection.createSession(false,
        Session.AUTO_ACKNOWLEDGE);
      messageConsumer = session.createConsumer(queue);
      messageConsumer.setMessageListener(new
        ExampleMessageListener());
      connection.start();

      System.out.println("The above line will allow the "
          + "MessageListener implementation to "
          + "receiving and processing messages from the queue.");
      Thread.sleep(1000);
      System.out.println("Our code does not have to block "
          + "while messages are received.");
      Thread.sleep(1000);
      System.out.println("It can do other stuff "
          + "(hopefully something more useful than sending "
          + "silly output to the console. :)");
      Thread.sleep(1000);
```

```
        messageConsumer.close();
        session.close();
        connection.close();
      }
      catch (JMSException e)
      {
        e.printStackTrace();
      }
      catch (InterruptedException e)
      {
        e.printStackTrace();
      }
    }
    public static void main(String[] args)
    {
      new AsynchMessReceiver().getMessages();
    }
  }
```

The only relevant difference between this example and the one in the previous section is that in this case, we are calling the `setMessageListener()` method on the instance of `javax.jms.MessageConsumer` obtained from the JMS session. We pass an instance of our custom implementation of `javax.jms.MessageListener` to this method. Its `onMessage()` method is automatically called whenever there is a message waiting in the queue. By using this approach, the main code does not block while waiting to receive messages.

Executing the previous example (using of course GlassFish's `appclient` utility) results in the following output:

```
appclient -client target/jmsptpasynchconsumer.jar

The above line will allow the MessageListener implementation to receiving
and processing messages from the queue.

Received the following message: Testing, 1, 2, 3. Can you hear me?


Received the following message: Do you copy?


Received the following message: Good bye!


Our code does not have to block while messages are received.

It can do other stuff (hopefully something more useful than sending silly
output to the console. :)
```

Notice how the messages were received and processed while the main thread was executing. We can tell this is the case because the output of the `onMessage()` method of our `MessageListener` can be seen between calls to `System.out.println()` in the primary class.

Browsing message queues

JMS provides a way to browse message queues without actually removing the messages from the queue. The following example illustrates how to do this:

```
package net.ensode.glassfishbook;

import java.util.Enumeration;

import javax.annotation.Resource;
import javax.jms.Connection;
import javax.jms.ConnectionFactory;
import javax.jms.JMSException;
import javax.jms.Queue;
import javax.jms.QueueBrowser;
import javax.jms.Session;
import javax.jms.TextMessage;

public class MessageQueueBrowser
{
  @Resource(mappedName = "jms/GlassFishBookConnectionFactory")
  private static ConnectionFactory connectionFactory;
  @Resource(mappedName = "jms/GlassFishBookQueue")
  private static Queue queue;

  public void browseMessages()
  {
    try
    {
      Enumeration messageEnumeration;
      TextMessage textMessage;
      Connection connection = connectionFactory.createConnection();

      Session session = connection.createSession(false,
        Session.AUTO_ACKNOWLEDGE);
      QueueBrowser browser = session.createBrowser(queue);
      messageEnumeration = browser.getEnumeration();
```

```
        if (messageEnumeration != null)
        {
          if (!messageEnumeration.hasMoreElements())
          {
            System.out.println("There are no messages " + "in the
              queue.");
          }
          else
          {
            System.out.println("The following messages are in the
              queue:");
            while (messageEnumeration.hasMoreElements())
            {
              textMessage =
                (TextMessage) messageEnumeration.nextElement();
              System.out.println(textMessage.getText());
            }
          }
        }
        session.close();
        connection.close();
      }
      catch (JMSException e)
      {
        e.printStackTrace();
      }
    }
    public static void main(String[] args)
    {
      new MessageQueueBrowser().browseMessages();
    }
  }
```

As we can see, the procedure to browse messages in a message queue is straightforward. We obtain a JMS connection and a JMS session the usual way, then invoke the `createBrowser()` method on the JMS session object. This method returns an implementation of the `javax.jms.QueueBrowser` interface. This interface contains a `getEnumeration()` method that we can invoke to obtain an enumeration containing all messages in the queue. To examine the messages in the queue, we simply traverse this enumeration and obtain the messages one by one. In the previous example, we simply invoke the `getText()` method of each message in the queue.

Message topics

Message topics are used when our JMS code uses the publish/subscribe (pub/sub) messaging domain. When using this messaging domain, the same message can be sent to all subscribers of the topic.

Sending messages to a message topic

The following example illustrates how to send messages to a message topic:

```
package net.ensode.glassfishbook;

import javax.annotation.Resource;
import javax.jms.Connection;
import javax.jms.ConnectionFactory;
import javax.jms.JMSException;
import javax.jms.MessageProducer;
import javax.jms.Session;
import javax.jms.TextMessage;
import javax.jms.Topic;

public class MessageSender
{
  @Resource(mappedName = "jms/GlassFishBookConnectionFactory")
  private static ConnectionFactory connectionFactory;
  @Resource(mappedName = "jms/GlassFishBookTopic")
  private static Topic topic;

  public void produceMessages()
  {
    MessageProducer messageProducer;
    TextMessage textMessage;
    try
    {
      Connection connection = connectionFactory.createConnection();
      Session session = connection.createSession(false,
        Session.AUTO_ACKNOWLEDGE);
      messageProducer = session.createProducer(topic);
      textMessage = session.createTextMessage();
```

```
        textMessage.setText("Testing, 1, 2, 3. Can you hear me?");
        System.out.println("Sending the following message: "
            + textMessage.getText());
        messageProducer.send(textMessage);

        textMessage.setText("Do you copy?");
        System.out.println("Sending the following message: "
            + textMessage.getText());
        messageProducer.send(textMessage);

        textMessage.setText("Good bye!");
        System.out.println("Sending the following message: "
            + textMessage.getText());
        messageProducer.send(textMessage);

        messageProducer.close();
        session.close();
        connection.close();
      }
      catch (JMSException e)
      {
        e.printStackTrace();
      }
    }
    public static void main(String[] args)
    {
      new MessageSender().produceMessages();
    }
  }
```

As we can see, this code is nearly identical to the `MessageSender` class we saw when we discussed point-to-point messaging. As a matter of fact, the only lines of code that are different are the ones that are highlighted. The JMS API was designed this way so that application developers do not have to learn two different APIs for the PTP and pub/sub domains.

As the code is nearly identical to the corresponding example in the *Message queues* section, we will only explain the differences between the two examples. In this example, instead of declaring an instance of a class implementing `javax.jms.Queue`, we declare an instance of a class implementing `javax.jms.Topic`. Just like in the previous examples, we use dependency injection to initialize the `Topic` object. After obtaining a JMS connection and a JMS session, we pass the `Topic` object to the `createProducer()` method in the `Session` object. This method returns an instance of `javax.jms.MessageProducer` that we can use to send messages to the JMS topic.

Receiving messages from a message topic

Just as sending messages to a message topic is nearly identical to sending messages to a message queue, receiving messages from a message topic is nearly identical to receiving messages from a message queue.

```
package net.ensode.glassfishbook;

import javax.annotation.Resource;
import javax.jms.Connection;
import javax.jms.ConnectionFactory;
import javax.jms.JMSException;
import javax.jms.MessageConsumer;
import javax.jms.Session;
import javax.jms.TextMessage;
import javax.jms.Topic;

public class MessageReceiver
{
  @Resource(mappedName = "jms/GlassFishBookConnectionFactory")
  private static ConnectionFactory connectionFactory;
  @Resource(mappedName = "jms/GlassFishBookTopic")
  private static Topic topic;

  public void getMessages()
  {
    Connection connection;
    MessageConsumer messageConsumer;
    TextMessage textMessage;
    boolean goodByeReceived = false;

    try
    {
      connection = connectionFactory.createConnection();
      Session session = connection.createSession(false,
        Session.AUTO_ACKNOWLEDGE);
      messageConsumer = session.createConsumer(topic);
      connection.start();

      while (!goodByeReceived)
      {
        System.out.println("Waiting for messages...");
        textMessage = (TextMessage) messageConsumer.receive();
        if (textMessage != null)
```

```
            {
              System.out.print("Received the following message: ");
              System.out.println(textMessage.getText());
              System.out.println();
            }
            if (textMessage.getText() != null
              && textMessage.getText().equals("Good bye!"))
            {
              goodByeReceived = true;
            }
          }

          messageConsumer.close();
          session.close();
          connection.close();
        }
        catch (JMSException e)
        {
          e.printStackTrace();
        }
      }
      public static void main(String[] args)
      {
        new MessageReceiver().getMessages();
      }
    }
```

Once again, the differences between this code and the corresponding code for PTP are trivial. Instead of declaring an instance of a class implementing `javax.jms.Queue`, we declare a class implementing `javax.jms.Topic`. We use the `@Resource` annotation to inject an instance of this class into our code using the JNDI name we used when creating it in the GlassFish web console. After obtaining a JMS connection and a JMS session, we pass the `Topic` object to the `createConsumer()` method in the `Session` object. This method returns an instance of `javax.jms.MessageConsumer` that we can use to receive messages from the JMS topic.

Using the pub/sub messaging domain as illustrated in this section has the advantage that messages can be sent to several message consumers. This can be easily tested by concurrently executing two instances of the `MessageReceiver` class we developed in this section, then executing the `MessageSender` class we developed in the previous section. We should see console output for each instance, indicating that both instances received all messages.

Just like with message queues, messages can be retrieved asynchronously from a message topic. The procedure to do this is so similar to the message queue version that we will not show an example. To convert the asynchronous example shown earlier in this chapter to use a message topic, simply replace the `javax.jms.Queue` variable with an instance of `javax.jms.Topic` and inject the appropriate instance by using `"jms/GlassFishBookTopic"` as the value of the `mappedName` attribute of the `@Resource` annotation decorating the instance of `javax.jms.Topic`.

Creating durable subscribers

The disadvantage of using the pub/sub messaging domain is that message consumers must be executing when messages are sent to the topic. If the message consumer is not executing at the time, it will not receive the messages, whereas in PTP, messages are kept in a queue until the message consumer executes. Fortunately, the JMS API provides a way to use the pub/sub messaging domain and keep messages in the topic until all subscribed message consumers execute and receive the message. This can be accomplished by creating durable subscribers to a JMS topic.

In order to be able to service durable subscribers, we need to set the `ClientId` property of our JMS connection factory. Each durable subscriber must have a unique client id, therefore a unique connection factory must be declared for each potential durable subscriber.

InvalidClientIdException?

Only one JMS client can connect to a topic for a specific client id. If more than one JMS client attempts to obtain a JMS connection using the same connection factory, a `JMSException` stating that the client id is already in use will be thrown. The solution is to create a connection factory for each potential client that will be receiving messages from the durable topic.

Like we mentioned before, the easiest way to add a connection factory is through the GlassFish web console. Recall that to add a JMS connection factory through the GlassFish web console, we need to expand the **Resources** node on the left hand side, then expand the **JMS Resources** node, click on the **Connection Factories** node, and click on the **New...** button in the main area of the page. Our next example will use the settings displayed in the following screenshot:

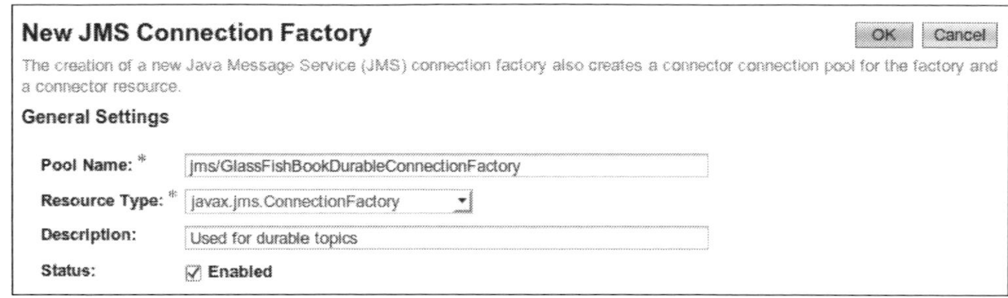

Before clicking on the **OK** button, we need to scroll to the bottom of the page, click on the **Add Property** button, and enter a new property named `ClientId`. Our example will use `ExampleId` as the value for this property.

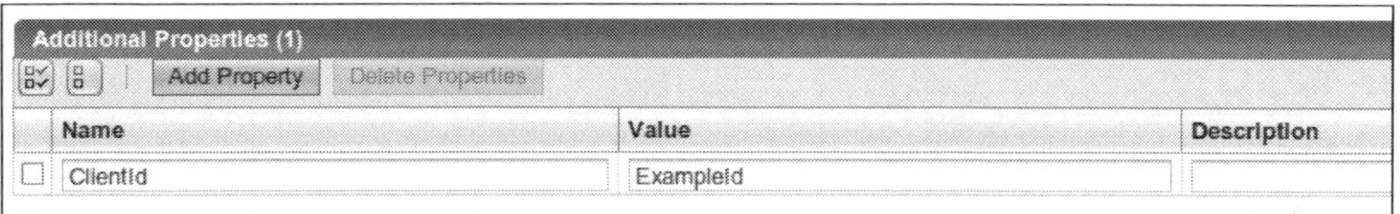

Now that we have set up GlassFish to be able to provide durable subscriptions, we are ready to write some code to take advantage of them:

```
package net.ensode.glassfishbook;

import javax.annotation.Resource;
import javax.jms.Connection;
import javax.jms.ConnectionFactory;
import javax.jms.JMSException;
import javax.jms.MessageConsumer;
import javax.jms.Session;
import javax.jms.TextMessage;
import javax.jms.Topic;

public class MessageReceiver
{
  @Resource(mappedName = "jms/GlassFishBookDurableConnectionFactory")
  private static ConnectionFactory connectionFactory;
  @Resource(mappedName = "jms/GlassFishBookTopic")
  private static Topic topic;
```

```
public void getMessages()
{
  Connection connection;
  MessageConsumer messageConsumer;
  TextMessage textMessage;
  boolean goodByeReceived = false;

  try
  {
    connection = connectionFactory.createConnection();
    Session session = connection.createSession(false,
      Session.AUTO_ACKNOWLEDGE);
    messageConsumer = session.createDurableSubscriber(topic,
      "Subscriber1");
    connection.start();

    while (!goodByeReceived)
    {
      System.out.println("Waiting for messages...");
      textMessage = (TextMessage) messageConsumer.receive();
      if (textMessage != null)
      {
        System.out.print("Received the following message: ");
        System.out.println(textMessage.getText());
        System.out.println();
      }
      if (textMessage.getText() != null
        && textMessage.getText().equals("Good bye!"))
      {
        goodByeReceived = true;
      }
    }

    messageConsumer.close();
    session.close();
    connection.close();
  }
  catch (JMSException e)
  {
    e.printStackTrace();
  }
}
public static void main(String[] args)
{
  new MessageReceiver().getMessages();
}
}
```

As we can see, this code is not much different from the previous examples whose purpose was to retrieve messages. There are only two differences from the previous examples: the instance of `ConnectionFactory` to which we are injecting is the one we set up earlier in this section to handle durable subscriptions, and instead of calling the `createSubscriber()` method on the JMS session object, we are calling `createDurableSubscriber()`. The `createDurableSubscriber()` method takes two arguments: a JMS `Topic` object to retrieve messages from and a string designating a name for this subscription. This second parameter must be unique between all subscribers to the durable topic.

Summary

In this chapter, we covered how to set up JMS connection factories, JMS message queues, and JMS message topics in GlassFish using the GlassFish web console.

We also covered how to send messages to a message queue via the `javax.jms.MessageProducer` interface.

Additionally, we covered how to receive messages from a message queue via the `javax.jms.MessageConsumer` interface. We also covered how to asynchronously receive messages from a message queue by implementing the `javax.jms.MessageListener` interface.

We also saw how to use these interfaces to send and receive messages to and from a JMS message topic.

We covered how to browse messages in a message queue without removing the messages from the queue via the `javax.jms.QueueBrowser` interface.

Finally, we saw how to set up and interact with durable subscriptions to JMS topics.

8
Security

In this chapter, we will cover how to secure Java EE applications by taking advantage of GlassFish's built-in security features.

Java EE security relies on the **Java Authentication and Authorization Service (JAAS)** API. As we shall see, securing Java EE applications requires very little coding. For the most part, securing an application is achieved by setting up users and security groups to a security realm in the application server, then configuring our applications to rely on a specific security realm for authentication and authorization.

Some of the topics we will cover include:

- Admin realm
- File realm
- Certificate realm
- Creating self-signed security certificates
- JDBC realm
- Custom realms

Security realms

Security realms are, in essence, collections of users and related security groups. Users are application users; a user can belong to one or more security groups. The groups that the user belongs to define what actions the system will allow the user to perform. For example, an application can have regular users who can only use the basic application functionality, and it can have administrators that, in addition to being able to use basic application functionality, can add additional users to the system.

Security realms store user information (username, password, and security groups). Applications don't need to implement this functionality; they simply can be configured to obtain this information from a security realm. A security realm can be used by more than one application.

Predefined security realms

GlassFish comes preconfigured with three predefined security realms: **admin-realm**, the **file realm**, and the **certificate realm**. admin-realm is used to manage the user's access to the GlassFish web console and shouldn't be used for other applications. The file realm stores user information in a file. The certificate realm looks for a client-side certificate to authenticate the user.

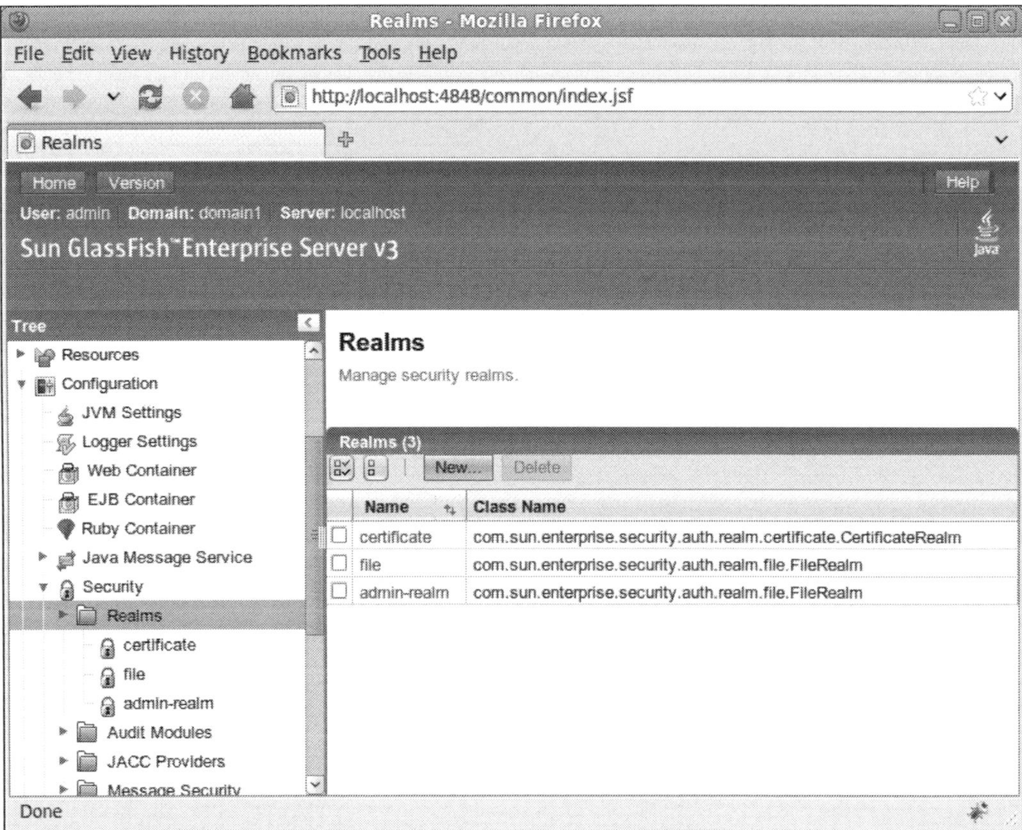

In addition to the predefined security realms, we can add additional realms with very little effort. We will cover how to do this later in this chapter, but first let's discuss GlassFish's predefined security realms.

The admin-realm

To illustrate how to add users to a realm, let's add a new user to the admin-realm. This will allow this additional user to log into the GlassFish web console. In order to add a user to the admin-realm, log into the GlassFish web console, expand the **Configuration** node at the left-hand side, expand the **Security** node, then the **Realms** node, and click on **admin-realm**. The main area of the page should look like the following screenshot:

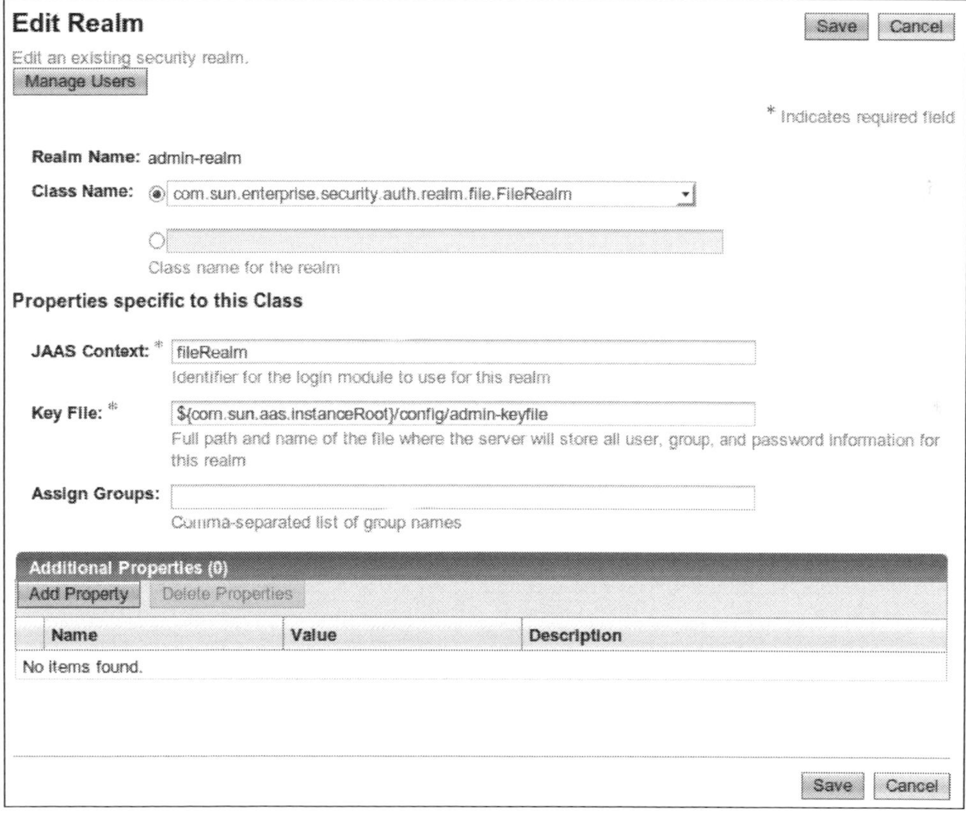

To add a user to the realm, click on the button labeled **Manage Users** at the top left. The main area of the page should now look like this:

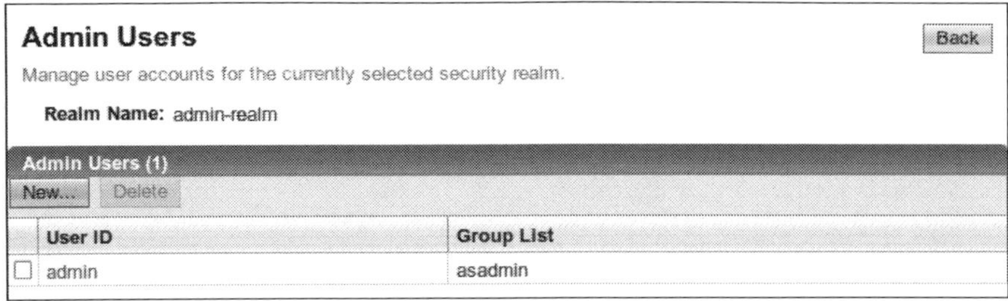

To add a new user to the realm, simply click on the **New...** button at the top left of the screen, then enter the new user information.

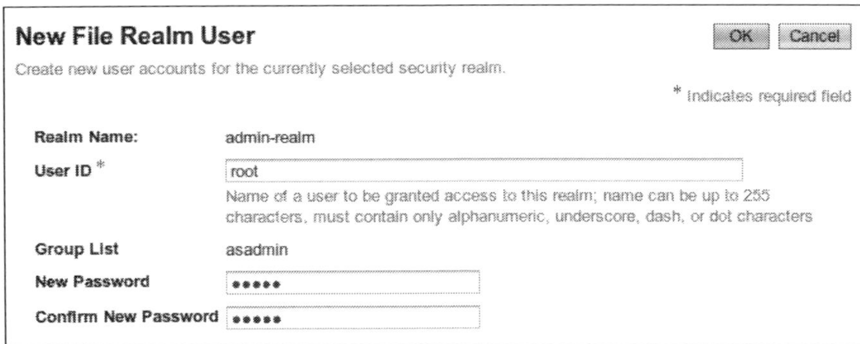

In this screenshot, we added a new user named **root**, added this user to the **asadmin** group, and entered this user's password.

The GlassFish web console will only allow users in the **asadmin** group to log in. Failing to add our user to this security group would prevent him/her from logging into the console.

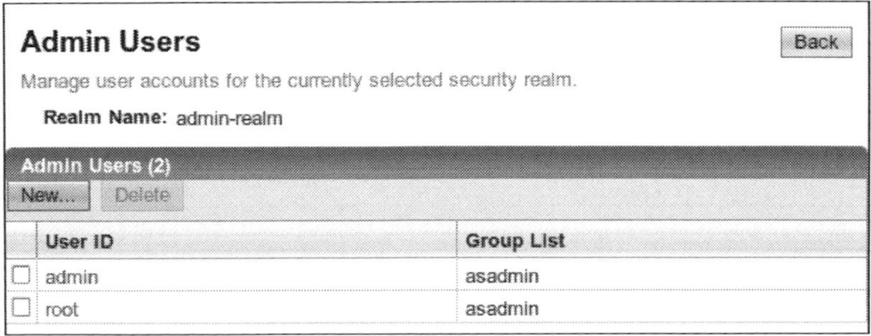

We have now successfully added a new user to the GlassFish web console. We can test this new account by logging into the console with this new user's credentials.

The file realm

The second predefined realm in GlassFish is the file realm. This realm stores user information encrypted in a text file. Adding users to this realm is very similar to adding users to the admin-realm. We can add a user by expanding the **Configuration** node, then expanding the **Security** node, then the **Realms** node, then clicking on **file**, then clicking on the **Manage Users** button, and clicking on the **New...** button.

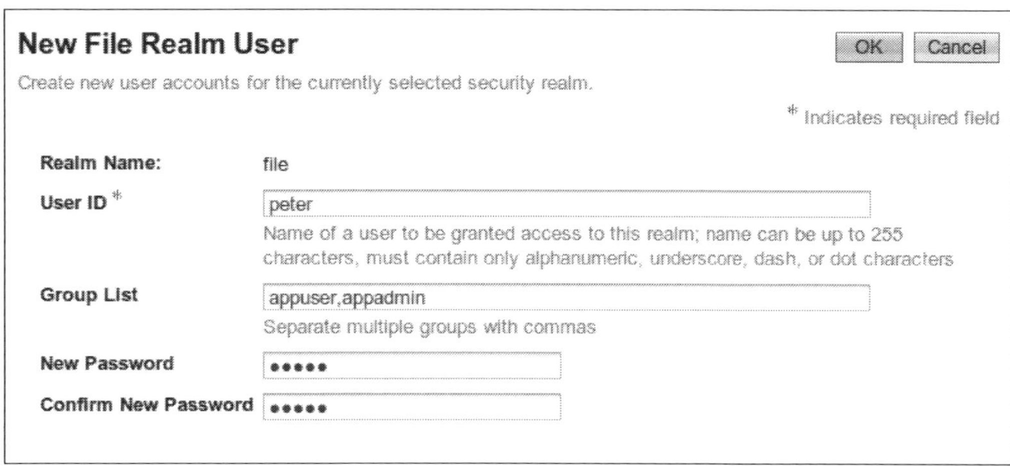

As this realm is meant to be used for our applications, we can come up with our own groups. In this example, we added a user with a **User ID** of **peter** to the groups **appuser** and **appadmin**.

Clicking on the **OK** button should save the new user and take us to the user list for this realm.

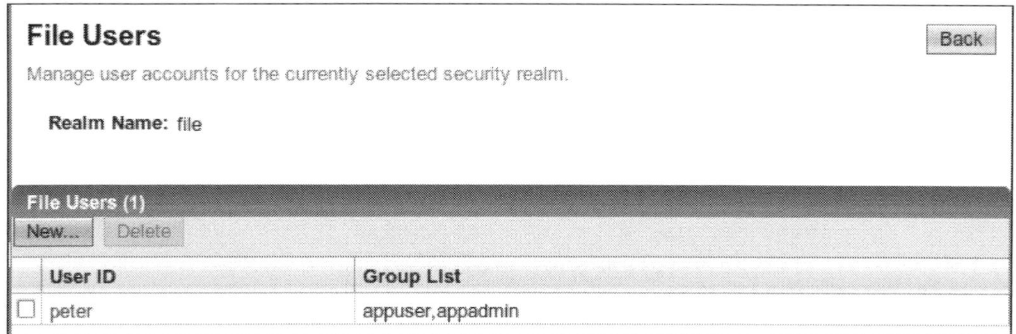

Clicking the **New...** button allows us to add additional users to the realm. Let's add an additional user called **joe** belonging only to the **appuser** group:

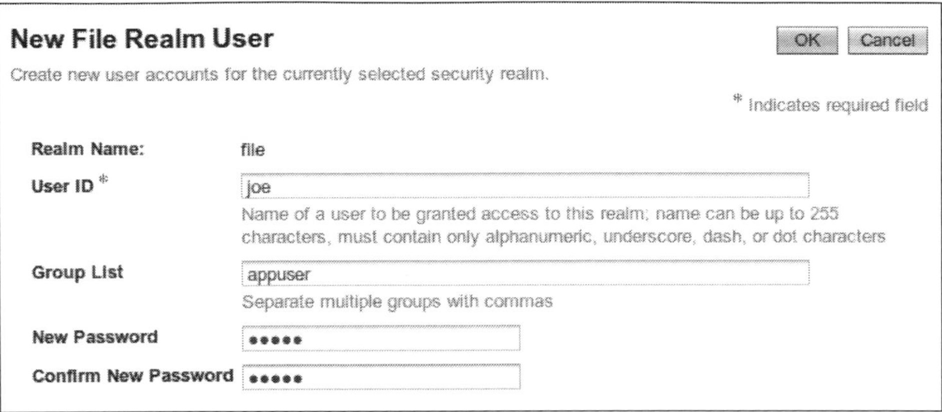

As we have seen in this section, adding users to the file realm is very simple. We will now illustrate how to authenticate and authorize users via the file realm.

File realm basic authentication

In the previous section, we covered how to add users to the file realm and how to assign these users to groups. In this section, we will illustrate how to secure a web application so that only properly authenticated and authorized users can access it. This web application will use the file realm for user access control.

The application will consist of a few very simple JSPs. All authentication logic is taken care of by the application server. Therefore, the only place we need to make modifications in order to secure the application is in its deployment descriptors—`web.xml` and `sun-web.xml`. We will first discuss `web.xml`, which is shown next:

```
<?xml version="1.0" encoding="UTF-8"?>
<web-app xmlns="http://java.sun.com/xml/ns/javaee"
         xmlns:xsi="http://www.w3.org/2001/XMLSchema-instance"
         xsi:schemaLocation="http://java.sun.com/xml/ns/javaee
         http://java.sun.com/xml/ns/javaee/web-app_3_0.xsd"
         version="3.0">
  <security-constraint>
    <web-resource-collection>
      <web-resource-name>Admin Pages</web-resource-name>
      <url-pattern>/admin/*</url-pattern>
    </web-resource-collection>
    <auth-constraint>
```

```
            <role-name>admin</role-name>
          </auth-constraint>
        </security-constraint>
        <security-constraint>
          <web-resource-collection>
            <web-resource-name>AllPages</web-resource-name>
            <url-pattern>/*</url-pattern>
          </web-resource-collection>
          <auth-constraint>
            <role-name>user</role-name>
          </auth-constraint>
        </security-constraint>
        <login-config>
          <auth-method>BASIC</auth-method>
          <realm-name>file</realm-name>
        </login-config>
      </web-app>
```

The `<security-constraint>` element defines who can access pages matching a certain URL pattern. The URL pattern of the pages is defined inside the `<url-pattern>` element, which, as shown in the example, must be nested inside a `<web-resource-collection>` element. Roles allowed to access the pages are defined in the `<role-name>` element, which must be nested inside an `<auth-constraint>` element.

In this example, we define two sets of pages to be protected. The first set of pages is any page whose URL starts with `/admin`. These pages can only be accessed by users with the role of admin. The second set of pages is all pages defined by the URL pattern of `/*`. Only users with the role of user can access these pages. It is worth noting that the second set of pages is a superset of the first set, that is, any page whose URL matches `/admin/*` also matches `/*`. In cases like this, the most specific case "wins". In this particular case, users with a role of user (and without the role of admin) will not be able to access any pages whose URL starts with `/admin`.

The next element we need to add to `web.xml` in order to protect our pages is the `<login-config>` element. This element must contain an `<auth-method>` element that defines the authorization method for the application. Valid values for this element include `BASIC`, `DIGEST`, `FORM`, and `CLIENT-CERT`.

BASIC indicates that basic authentication will be used. This type of authentication will result in a browser-generated pop-up prompting the user for a username and password to be displayed the first time a user tries to access a protected page. Unless using the HTTPS protocol, when using basic authentication, the user's credentials are Base64 encoded, not encrypted. It would be fairly easy for an attacker to decode these credentials, therefore using basic authentication is not recommended.

DIGEST is similar to basic authentication, except it uses an MD5 digest to encrypt the user credentials instead of sending them Base64 encoded.

FORM uses a custom HTML or JSP page containing an HTML form with username and password fields. The values in the form are then checked against the security realm for user authentication and authorization. Unless using HTTPS, user credentials are sent in clear text when using form-based authentication. Therefore, using HTTPS is recommended as it encrypts the data. We will cover setting up GlassFish to use HTTPS later in this chapter.

CLIENT-CERT uses client-side certificates to authenticate and authorize the user.

The <realm-name> element of <login-config> indicates what security realm to use to authenticate and authorize the user. In this particular example, we are using the file realm.

All the web.xml elements we have discussed in this section can be used with any security realm; they are not tied to the file realm. The only thing that ties our application to the file realm is the value of the <realm-name> element. Something else to keep in mind is that not all authentication methods are supported by all realms. The file realm supports only basic and form-based authentication.

Before we successfully authenticate our users, we need to link the user roles defined in web.xml with the groups defined in the realm. We accomplish this in the sun-web.xml deployment descriptor:

```
<?xml version="1.0" encoding="UTF-8" standalone="no"?>
<!DOCTYPE sun-web-app PUBLIC "-//Sun Microsystems, Inc.//DTD
  Application Server 9.0 Servlet 2.5//EN"
  "http://www.sun.com/software/appserver/dtds/sun-web-app_2_5-0.dtd">
<sun-web-app>
  <security-role-mapping>
    <role-name>admin</role-name>
    <group-name>appadmin</group-name>
  </security-role-mapping>
  <security-role-mapping>
    <role-name>user</role-name>
    <group-name>appuser</group-name>
  </security-role-mapping>
</sun-web-app>
```

As can be seen in the example, the `sun-web.xml` deployment descriptor can have one or more `<security-role-mapping>` elements. One of these elements for each role defined in `web.xml` is needed. The `<role-name>` sub-element indicates the role to map. Its value must match the value of the corresponding `<role-name>` element in `web.xml`. The `<group-name>` sub-element must match the value of a security group in the realm used to authenticate users in the application.

In this example, the first `<security-role-mapping>` element maps the `admin` role defined in the application's `web.xml` deployment descriptor to the `appadmin` group we created when adding users to the file realm earlier in the chapter. The second `<security-role-mapping>` maps the `user` role in `web.xml` to the `appuser` group in the file realm.

Like we mentioned earlier, there is nothing we need to do in our code in order to authenticate and authorize users. All we need to do is modify the application's deployment descriptors, as described in this section. As our application is nothing but a few simple JSPs, we will not show the source code for them. The structure of our application is shown in the following screenshot:

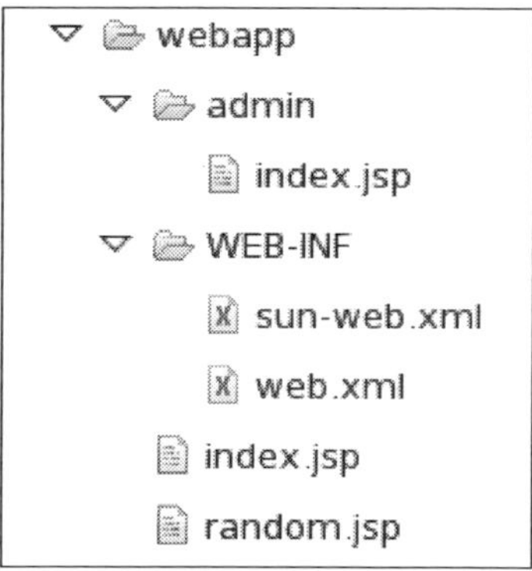

Based on the way we set up our application in the deployment descriptors, users with a role of `user` will be able to access the two JSPs at the root of the application (`index.jsp` and `random.jsp`). Only users with the role of `admin` will be able to access any pages under the `admin` folder, which in this particular case is a single JSP named `index.jsp`.

After packaging and deploying our application, and pointing the browser to the URL of any of its pages, we should see a pop up asking for a username and password.

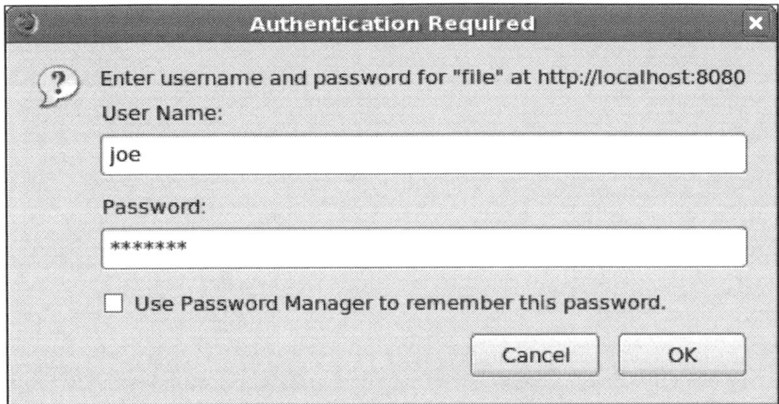

After entering the correct username and password, we are directed to a page we were attempting to see:

At this point, the user can navigate to any page that he is allowed to access in the application, either by following links or by typing the URL in the browser, without having to re-enter his/her username and password.

Notice that we logged in as user **joe**. This user belongs only to the `user` role, therefore he does not have access to any page that starts with `/admin` as the URL. If Joe tries to access one of these pages, he will see the following error message in the browser:

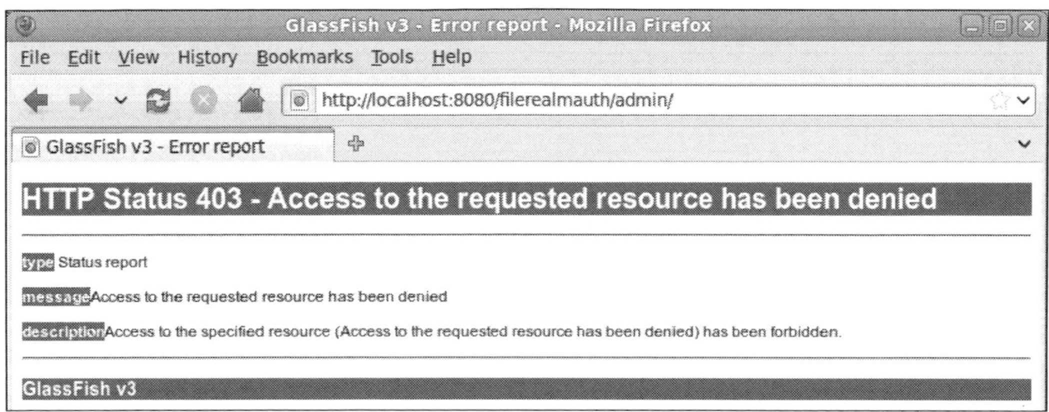

Only users belonging to the `admin` role can see pages that match this URL. When we were adding users to the file realm, we added a user named "peter" that had this role. If we log in as peter, we will be able to see the requested page. For basic authentication, the only way possible to log out of the application is to close the browser. Therefore, to log in as peter, we need to close and reopen the browser.

Like we mentioned before, one disadvantage of the basic authentication method we used in this example is that login information is not encrypted. One way to get around this is to use the HTTPS (HTTP over SSL) protocol. When using this protocol, all information between the browser and the server is encrypted.

The easiest way to use HTTPS is by modifying the application's `web.xml` deployment descriptor.

```
<?xml version="1.0" encoding="UTF-8"?>
<web-app xmlns="http://java.sun.com/xml/ns/javaee"
         xmlns:xsi="http://www.w3.org/2001/XMLSchema-instance"
         xsi:schemaLocation="http://java.sun.com/xml/ns/javaee
           http://java.sun.com/xml/ns/javaee/web-app_3_0.xsd"
         version="3.0">
  <security-constraint>
```

```
        <web-resource-collection>
          <web-resource-name>Admin Pages</web-resource-name>
          <url-pattern>/admin/*</url-pattern>
        </web-resource-collection>
        <auth-constraint>
          <role-name>admin</role-name>
        </auth-constraint>
        <user-data-constraint>
          <transport-guarantee>CONFIDENTIAL</transport-guarantee>
        </user-data-constraint>
      </security-constraint>
      <security-constraint>
        <web-resource-collection>
          <web-resource-name>AllPages</web-resource-name>
          <url-pattern>/*</url-pattern>
        </web-resource-collection>
        <auth-constraint>
          <role-name>user</role-name>
        </auth-constraint>
        <user-data-constraint>
          <transport-guarantee>CONFIDENTIAL</transport-guarantee>
        </user-data-constraint>
      </security-constraint>
      <login-config>
        <auth-method>BASIC</auth-method>
        <realm-name>file</realm-name>
      </login-config>
    </web-app>
```

As we can see, all we need to do to have the application accessed only through HTTPS is to add a `<user-data-constraint>` element containing a nested `<transport-guarantee>` element to each set of pages we want to encrypt. Sets of pages to be protected are declared in the `<security-constraint>` elements in the `web.xml` deployment descriptor.

Now, when we access the application through the (unsecure) HTTP port (by default it is 8080), the request is automatically forwarded to the (secure) HTTPS port (default of 8181).

In this example, we set the value of the `<transport-guarantee>` element to `CONFIDENTIAL`. This has the effect of encrypting all the data between the browser and the server. Also, if a request is made through the unsecured HTTP port, it is automatically forwarded to the secured HTTPS port.

Another valid value for the `<transport-guarantee>` element is `INTEGRAL`. When using this value, the integrity of the data between the browser and the server is guaranteed. In other words, the data cannot be changed in transit. When using this value, a request made over HTTP is not automatically forwarded to HTTPS. If a user attempts to access a secure page via HTTP when this value is used, the browser will deny the request and return a 403 Access Denied error.

The third and last valid value for the `<transport-guarantee>` element is `NONE`. When using this value, no guarantees are made about the integrity or confidentiality of the data. `NONE` is the default value used when the `<transport-guarantee>` element is not present in the application's `web.xml` deployment descriptor.

After making these modifications to the `web.xml` deployment descriptor, redeploying the application and pointing the browser to any of the pages in the application, we should see the following warning page when accessing our application with Firefox:

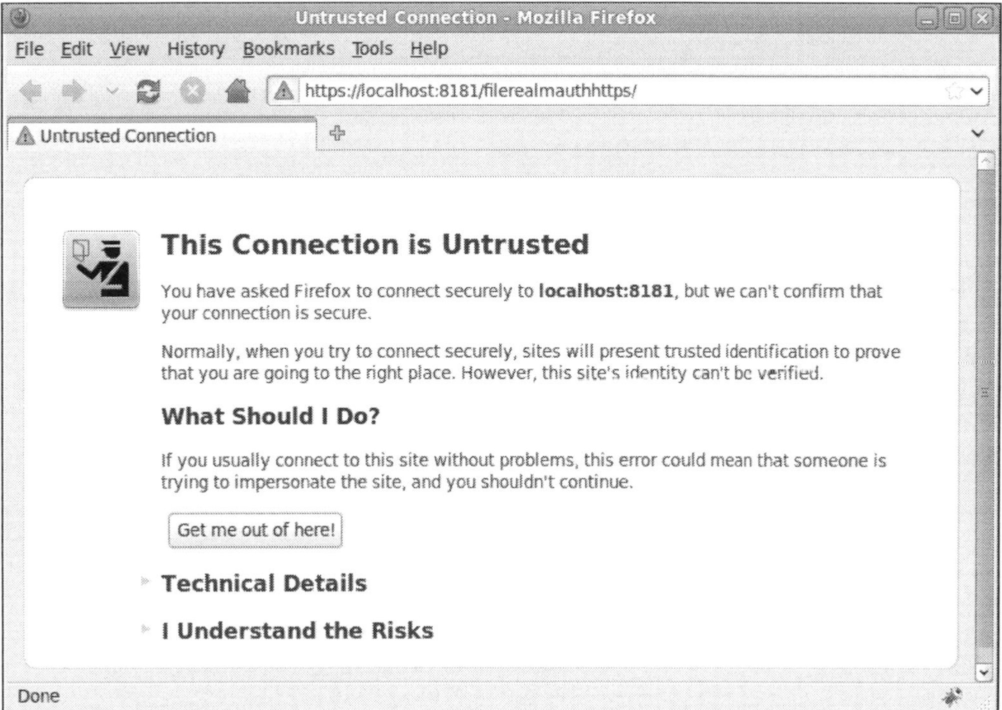

After expanding the **I Understand the Risks** node and clicking on the button labeled **Add Exception...**, we should see a window like the following:

After clicking on the button labeled **Confirm Security Exception**, we are prompted for a username and password. After entering the appropriate credentials, we are allowed access to the requested page.

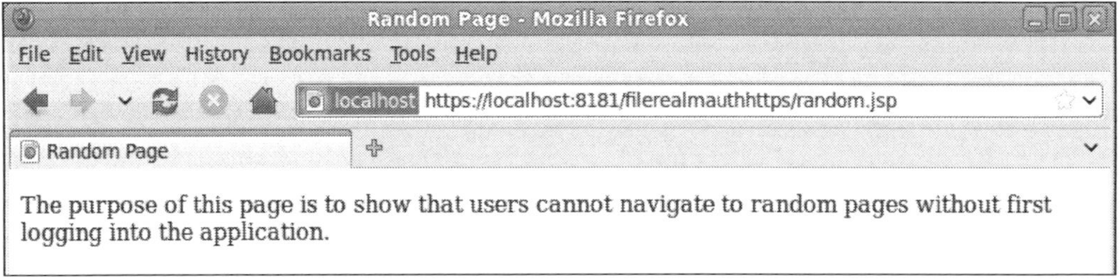

The reason we see this warning is that, in order for a server to use the HTTPS protocol, it must have an SSL certificate. Typically, SSL certificates are issued by certificate authorities such as Verisign or Thawte. These certificate authorities digitally sign the certificate; by doing this, they certify that the server belongs to the entity it claims it belongs to.

A digital certificate from one of these certificate authorities typically costs around $400 USD and expires after a year. As the cost of these certificates may be prohibitive for development or testing purposes, GlassFish comes pre-configured with a self-signed SSL certificate. As this certificate has not been signed by a certificate authority, the browser shows the previous warning window when we try to access a secured page via HTTPS.

Notice the URL in the previous screenshot; the protocol is set to HTTPS and the port is 8181. The URL we pointed the browser to was `http://localhost:8080/filerealmauthhttps/random.jsp`. Because of the modifications we made to the application's `web.xml` deployment descriptor, the request was automatically forwarded to this URL. Of course, users may directly type the secure URL and it will work without a problem.

Any data transferred over HTTPS is encrypted, including the username and password entered in the pop-up window generated by the browser. Using HTTPS allows us to safely use basic authentication. However, basic authentication has another disadvantage: the only way a user can log out from the application is by closing the browser. If we need to allow users to log out of the application without closing the browser, we need to use form-based authentication.

When using form-based authentication, we need to make some modifications to the application's `web.xml` deployment descriptor:

```
<?xml version="1.0" encoding="UTF-8"?>
<web-app xmlns="http://java.sun.com/xml/ns/javaee"
         xmlns:xsi="http://www.w3.org/2001/XMLSchema-instance"
         xsi:schemaLocation="http://java.sun.com/xml/ns/javaee
           http://java.sun.com/xml/ns/javaee/web-app_3_0.xsd"
         version="3.0">
  <security-constraint>
    <web-resource-collection>
      <web-resource-name>Admin Pages</web-resource-name>
      <url-pattern>/admin/*</url-pattern>
    </web-resource-collection>
    <auth-constraint>
      <role-name>admin</role-name>
    </auth-constraint>
  </security-constraint>
  <security-constraint>
    <web-resource-collection>
      <web-resource-name>AllPages</web-resource-name>
      <url-pattern>/*</url-pattern>
    </web-resource-collection>
    <auth-constraint>
      <role-name>user</role-name>
    </auth-constraint>
  </security-constraint>
  <login-config>
```

```
    <auth-method>FORM</auth-method>
    <realm-name>file</realm-name>
    <form-login-config>
      <form-login-page>/login.jsp</form-login-page>
      <form-error-page>/loginerror.jsp</form-error-page>
    </form-login-config>
  </login-config>
  <servlet>
    <servlet-name>LogoutServlet</servlet-name>
    <servlet-class>
      net.ensode.glassfishbook.LogoutServlet
    </servlet-class>
  </servlet>
  <servlet-mapping>
    <servlet-name>LogoutServlet</servlet-name>
    <url-pattern>/logout</url-pattern>
  </servlet-mapping>
</web-app>
```

When using form-based authentication, we simply use FORM as the value of the <auth-method> element in web.xml. When using this authentication method, we need to provide a login page and a login error page. We indicate the URLs for the login page and the login error page as the values of the <form-login-page> and <form-error-page> elements respectively. As can be seen in the example, these elements must be nested inside the <form-login-config> element.

The markup for the login page for our application is shown next:

```
<%@ page language="java" contentType="text/html; charset=UTF-8"
  pageEncoding="UTF-8"%>
<!DOCTYPE html PUBLIC "-//W3C//DTD HTML 4.01 Transitional//EN"
  "http://www.w3.org/TR/html4/loose.dtd">
<html>
  <head>
    <meta http-equiv="Content-Type" content="text/html;
      charset=UTF-8">
    <title>Login</title>
  </head>
  <body>
    <p>Please enter your username and password to access the
       application</p>
    <form method="POST" action="j_security_check">
      <table cellpadding="0" cellspacing="0" border="0">
        <tr>
          <td align="right">Username: </td>
          <td>
            <input type="text" name="j_username">
          </td>
        </tr>
```

```
        <tr>
          <td align="right">Password: </td>
          <td>
            <input type="password" name="j_password">
          </td>
        </tr>
        <tr>
          <td></td>
          <td><input type="submit" value="Login"></td>
        </tr>
      </table>
    </form>
  </body>
</html>
```

The login page for an application using form-based authentication must contain a form whose `method` is `"POST"` and `action` is `"j_security_check"`. We don't need to implement a servlet or anything else to process this form. The code to process it is supplied by the application server.

The form in the login page must contain a text field named `j_username`. This text field is meant to hold the user's username. Additionally, the form must contain a password field named `j_password`, meant for the user's password. Of course, the form must contain a submit button to submit the data to the server.

The only requirement for a login page is for it to have a form whose attributes match those in the previous example, and the `j_username` and `j_password` input fields as described in the preceding paragraph.

There are no special requirements for the error page. Of course, it should show an error message telling the user that login was unsuccessful. However, it can contain anything we wish. The error page for our application simply tells the user that there was an error logging in and links back to the login page to give the user a chance to log back in.

In addition to a login page and a login error page, we added a servlet to our application. This servlet allows us to implement logout functionality, something that wasn't possible when we were using basic authentication.

```
package net.ensode.glassfishbook;

import java.io.IOException;

import javax.servlet.ServletException;
import javax.servlet.annotation.WebServlet;
import javax.servlet.http.HttpServlet;
import javax.servlet.http.HttpServletRequest;
import javax.servlet.http.HttpServletResponse;
```

```
@WebServlet(urlPatterns = {"/logout"})
public class LogoutServlet extends HttpServlet
{
  @Override
  protected void doGet(HttpServletRequest request,
    HttpServletResponse response) throws ServletException,
    IOException
  {
    request.getSession().invalidate();
    response.sendRedirect("index.jsp");
  }
}
```

As we can see, all we need to do to log out the user is invalidate the session. In our servlet, we redirect the response to the `index.jsp` page, as session is invalid at this point, the security mechanism will "kick in" and automatically direct the user to the login page.

We are now ready to test form-based authentication. After building our application, deploying it and pointing the browser to any of its pages, we should see our login page rendered in the browser:

If we submit invalid credentials, we are automatically forwarded to the login error page:

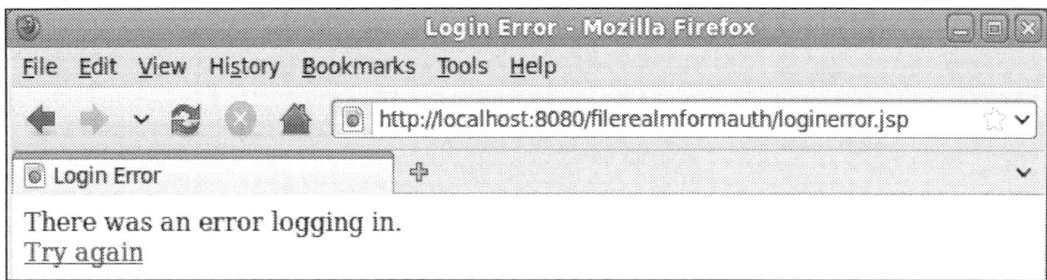

We can click on the **Try again** link to try again. After entering valid credentials, we are allowed into the application:

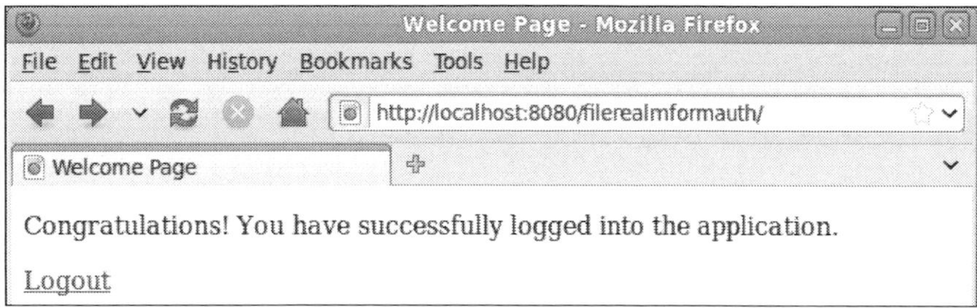

As we can see, we added a **Logout** link to the page. This page directs the user to the logout servlet, which as we mentioned before, simply invalidates the session. From the user's point of view, this link will simply log them out and direct them to the login screen.

The certificate realm

The certificate realm uses client-side certificates for authentication. Just like server-side certificates, client-side certificates are typically obtained from a certificate authority such as Verisign or Thawte. These certificate authorities verify that the certificate really belongs to the entity it says it belongs to.

Obtaining a certificate from a certificate authority costs money and takes some time. It might not be practical to obtain a certificate from one of the certificate authorities when we are developing and/or testing our application. Fortunately, we can create self-signed certificates for testing purposes.

Creating self-signed certificates

We can create self-signed certificates with little effort with the `keytool` utility included with the Java Development Kit.

> We will only briefly cover some of the `keytool` utility functionality. Specifically, we will cover what is necessary to create and import self-signed certificates into GlassFish and into the browser. To learn more about the `keytool` utility, refer to `http://java.sun.com/javase/6/docs/technotes/tools/solaris/keytool.html`.

Generating a self-signed certificate can be accomplished by typing the following command in the command line:

```
keytool -genkey -v -alias selfsignedkey -keyalg RSA -storetype PKCS12
-keystore client_keystore.p12 -storepass wonttellyou -keypass wonttellyou
```

This command assumes that the `keytool` utility is in the system path. This tool can be found under the `bin` directory, under the directory where the Java Development Kit is installed.

Substitute the values for the `-storepass` and `-keypass` parameters with your own password. Both these passwords must be the same in order to successfully use the certificate to authenticate the client. You may choose any value for the `-alias` parameter. You may also choose any value for the `-keystore` parameter. However, the value must end in `.p12`, as this command generates a file that needs to be imported into the web browser, and this file won't be recognized unless it has a `p12` extension.

After entering the previous command in the command line, `keytool` will prompt for some information:

```
What is your first and last name?
  [Unknown]:  David Heffelfinger
What is the name of your organizational unit?
  [Unknown]:  Book Writing Division
What is the name of your organization?
  [Unknown]:  Ensode Technology, LLC
What is the name of your City or Locality?
  [Unknown]:  Fairfax
What is the name of your State or Province?
  [Unknown]:  Virginia
What is the two-letter country code for this unit?
  [Unknown]:  US
Is CN=David Heffelfinger, OU=Book Writing Division, O="Ensode
Technology, LLC", L=Fairfax, ST=Virginia, C=US correct?
  [no]:  y
```

After entering the data for each prompt, `keytool` will generate the certificate, it will be stored in the current directory, and the name of the file will be the value we used for the `-keystore` parameter (in the example, `client_keystore.p12`).

To be able to use this certificate to authenticate ourselves, we need to import it into the browser. The procedure, although similar, varies from browser to browser. In Firefox, this can be accomplished by going to **Edit | Preferences**, then clicking on the **Advanced** icon at the top of the resulting pop-up window, then clicking on the **Encryption** tab:

We then need to click on the **View Certificates** button, click on the **Import** button in the resulting window, then navigate and select our certificate from the directory in which it was created. At this point, Firefox will ask us for the password used to encrypt the certificate. In our example, we used "wonttellyou" as the password. After entering the password, we should see a pop-up window confirming that our certificate was successfully imported. We should then see it in the list of certificates:

We have now added our certificate to Firefox so that it can be used to authenticate ourselves. If you are using another browser, the procedure will be similar. Consult your browser's documentation for details.

The certificate we created in the previous step needs to be exported into a format that GlassFish can understand:

```
keytool -export -alias selfsignedkey -keystore client_keystore.p12
-storetype PKCS12 -storepass wonttellyou -rfc -file selfsigned.cer
```

The value for the `-alias`, `-keystore`, and `-storepass` parameters must match the values used in the previous command. You may choose any value for the `-file` parameter, but it is recommended for the value to end in the `.cer` extension.

As our certificate was not issued by a certificate authority, GlassFish by default will not recognize it as a valid certificate. GlassFish knows which certificates to trust based on the certificate authority that created them. The way this is implemented is that certificates for these various authorities are stored in a keystore named `cacerts.jks`. This keystore can be found in the following location:

```
[glassfish installation
directory]/glassfish/domains/domain1/config/cacerts.jks.
```

In order for GlassFish to accept our certificate, we need to import it into the `cacerts` keystore. This can be accomplished by issuing the following command in the command line:

```
keytool -import -file selfsigned.cer -keystore [glassfish installation
directory]/glassfish/domains/domain1/config/cacerts.jks -keypass
changeit -storepass changeit
```

At this point, `keytool` will display the certificate information in the command line and ask us if we want to trust it.

```
Owner: CN=David Heffelfinger, OU=Book Writing Division, O="Ensode
Technology, LLC", L=Fairfax, ST=Virginia, C=US

Issuer: CN=David Heffelfinger, OU=Book Writing Division, O="Ensode
Technology, LLC", L=Fairfax, ST=Virginia, C=US

Serial number: 4b3bfea1

Valid from: Wed Dec 30 20:30:09 EST 2009 until: Tue Mar 30 21:30:09 EDT
2010

Certificate fingerprints:

   MD5:  CD:77:45:77:5F:30:F1:A2:AE:3F:E3:6F:B5:7F:D1:A2

   SHA1: 8C:2B:53:A7:92:5F:21:17:6F:DD:B2:F0:84:66:DC:83:8F:B7:10:47

   Signature algorithm name: SHA1withRSA
```

```
  Version: 3
Trust this certificate? [no]:  y
Certificate was added to keystore
```

Once we add the certificate to the `cacerts.jks` keystore, we need to restart the domain for the change to take effect.

What we are effectively doing here is adding ourselves as a certificate authority that GlassFish will trust. This, of course, should not be done in a production system.

The value for the `-file` parameter must match the value we used for this same parameter when we exported the certificate.

> `changeit` is the default password for the `-keypass` and `-storepass` parameters for the `cacerts.jks` keystore. This value can be changed by issuing the following command:
>
> ```
> [glassfish installation directory]/glassfish/bin/
> asadmin change-master-password --savemasterpassword
> =true
> ```
>
> This command will prompt for the existing master password and for the new master password. The `-savemasterpassword=true` parameter is optional; it saves the master password into a file called `master-password` in the root directory for the domain. If we don't use this parameter when changing the master password, then we will need to enter the master password every time we want to start the domain.

Now that we have created a self-signed certificate, imported it into our browser, and established ourselves as a certificate authority that GlassFish will trust, we are ready to develop an application that will use client-side certificates for authentication.

Configuring applications to use the certificate realm

As we are taking advantage of Java EE security features, we don't need to modify any code at all in order to use the security realm. All we need to do is modify the application's configuration on its deployment descriptors—`web.xml` and `sun-web.xml`:

```
<?xml version="1.0" encoding="UTF-8"?>
<web-app xmlns="http://java.sun.com/xml/ns/javaee"
         xmlns:xsi="http://www.w3.org/2001/XMLSchema-instance"
         xsi:schemaLocation="http://java.sun.com/xml/ns/javaee
           http://java.sun.com/xml/ns/javaee/web-app_3_0.xsd"
         version="3.0">
  <security-constraint>
```

```
    <web-resource-collection>
      <web-resource-name>AllPages</web-resource-name>
      <url-pattern>/*</url-pattern>
    </web-resource-collection>
    <auth-constraint>
      <role-name>users</role-name>
    </auth-constraint>
    <user-data-constraint>
      <transport-guarantee>CONFIDENTIAL</transport-guarantee>
    </user-data-constraint>
  </security-constraint>
  <login-config>
    <auth-method>CLIENT-CERT</auth-method>
    <realm-name>certificate</realm-name>
  </login-config>
</web-app>
```

The main difference between this web.xml deployment descriptor and the one we saw in the previous section is the contents of the <login-config> element. In this case, we declared CLIENT-CERT as the authorization method and certificate as the realm to use to authenticate. This will have the effect of GlassFish asking the browser for a client certificate before allowing a user into the application.

When using client certificate authentication, the request must always be done via HTTPS. Therefore, it is a good idea to add the <transport-guarantee> element with a value of CONFIDENTIAL to the web.xml deployment descriptor. Recall from the previous section that this has the effect of forwarding any requests through the HTTP port to the HTTPS port. If we don't add this value to the web.xml deployment descriptor, any requests through the HTTP port will fail as client certificate authentication cannot be done through the HTTP protocol.

Notice that we declared that only users in the role of "users" can access any page in the system. We did this by adding the role of users to the <role-name> element nested inside the <auth-constraint> element of the <security-constraint> element in the web.xml deployment descriptor. In order to allow access to authorized users, we need to add them to this role. This is done in the sun-web.xml deployment descriptor:

```
<?xml version="1.0" encoding="UTF-8"?>
<!DOCTYPE sun-web-app PUBLIC "-//Sun Microsystems, Inc.//DTD
  Application Server 9.0 Servlet 2.5//EN"
  "http://www.sun.com/software/appserver/dtds/sun-web-app_2_5-0.dtd">
<sun-web-app error-url="">
  <context-root>/certificaterealm</context-root>
  <security-role-mapping>
    <role-name>users</role-name>
```

```
        <principal-name>CN=David Heffelfinger, OU=Book Writing Division,
          O="Ensode Technology, LLC", L=Fairfax, ST=Virginia, C=US
        </principal-name>
    </security-role-mapping>
</sun-web-app>
```

This assignment is done by mapping the principal (user) to a role in the <security-role-mapping> element in the sun-web.xml deployment descriptor. Its <role-name> sub-element must contain the role name and the <principal-name> sub-element must contain the username. This username is taken from the certificate.

If you are not sure of the name to use, this name can be obtained from the certificate with the keytool utility:

```
keytool -printcert -file selfsigned.cer
Owner: CN=David Heffelfinger, OU=Book Writing Division, O="Ensode
Technology, LLC", L=Fairfax, ST=Virginia, C=US
Issuer: CN=David Heffelfinger, OU=Book Writing Division, O="Ensode
Technology, LLC", L=Fairfax, ST=Virginia, C=US
Serial number: 4b3bfea1
Valid from: Wed Dec 30 20:30:09 EST 2009 until: Tue Mar 30 21:30:09 EDT
2010
Certificate fingerprints:
   MD5:  CD:77:45:77:5F:30:F1:A2:AE:3F:E3:6F:B5:7F:D1:A2
   SHA1: 8C:2B:53:A7:92:5F:21:17:6F:DD:B2:F0:84:66:DC:83:8F:B7:10:47
   Signature algorithm name: SHA1withRSA
   Version: 3
```

The value to use as <principal-name> is the line after Owner. Please note that the value of <principal-name> must be in the same line as its opening and closing elements (<principal-name> and </principal-name>). If there are newline or carriage return characters before or after the value, they are interpreted as being part of the value and validation will fail.

As our application has a single user and a single role, we are ready to deploy it. If we had more users, we would have to add additional <security-role-mapping> elements to our sun-web.xml deployment descriptor; at least one per user. If we had users that belong to more than one role, then we would have to add a <security-role-mapping> element for each role the user belongs, using the <principal-name> value corresponding to the user's certificate for each one of them.

We are now ready to test our application. After we deploy it and point the browser to any page in the application, we should see a screen like the following (assuming the browser hasn't been configured to provide a default certificate any time a server requests one):

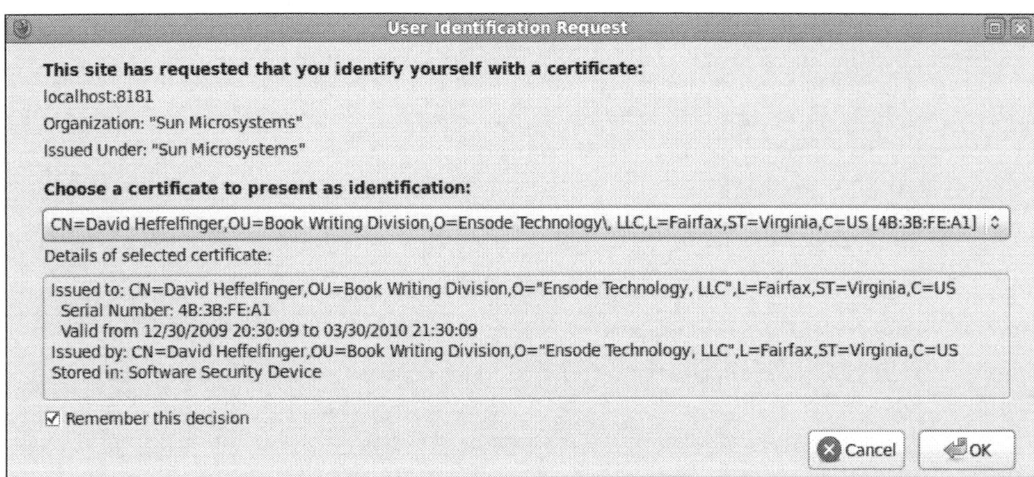

After clicking on the **OK** button, we are allowed to access the application:

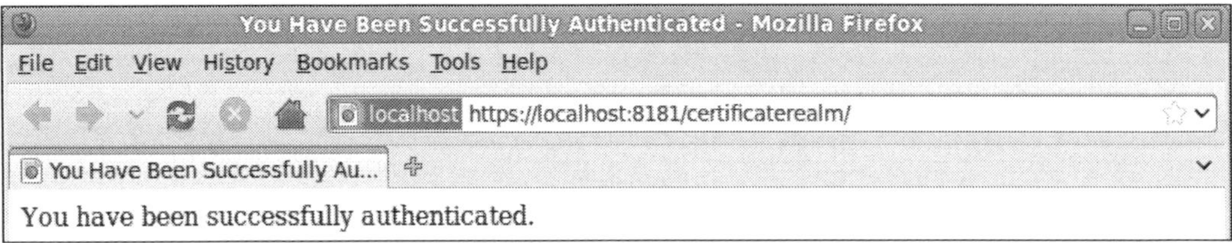

Before allowing access to the application, GlassFish checks the certificate authority that issued the certificate (as we self-signed the certificate, the owner of the certificate and the certificate authority is the same) and checks against a list of trusted certificate authorities. As we added ourselves as a trusted authority by importing our self-signed certificate into the `cacerts.jks` keystore, GlassFish recognizes the certificate authority as a valid one. It then gets the principal name from the certificate and compares it against the entries in the application's `sun-web.xml` deployment descriptor. As we added ourselves to this deployment descriptor and gave ourselves a valid role, we are allowed into the application

Defining additional realms

In addition to the three pre-configured security realms we discussed in the previous section, we can create additional realms for application authentication. We can create realms that behave exactly like the file or admin-realm realms. We can also create realms that behave like the certificate realm. Additionally, we can create realms that use other methods of authentication. We can authenticate users against an LDAP database. We can also authenticate users against a relational database. When GlassFish is installed on a Solaris server, we can use Solaris authentication within GlassFish. Also, if none of these authentication mechanisms fit our needs, we can implement our own.

Defining additional file realms

In the administration console, expand the **Configuration** node, expand the **Security** node, click on the **Realms** node, then click on the **New...** button on the resulting page in the main area of the web console. We should now see a screen like the following:

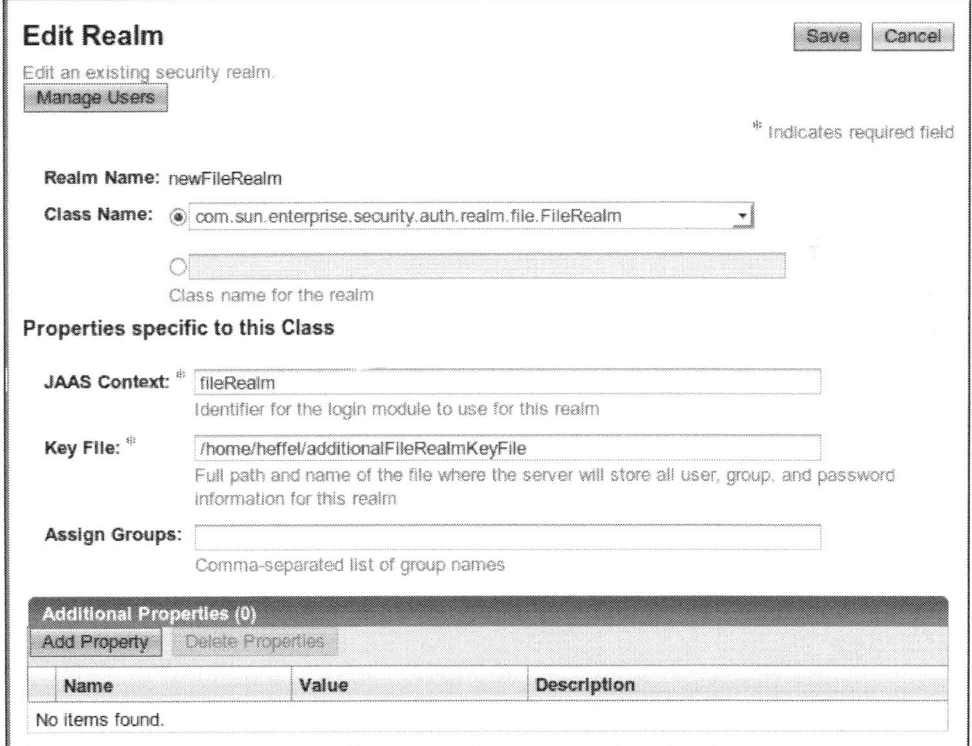

All we need to do to create an additional realm is enter a unique name for it in the **Realm Name** field, pick **com.sun.enterprise.security.auth.realm.file.FileRealm** for the **Class Name** field, and enter a value for the **JAAS context** and **Key File** fields. The value for the **Key File** field must be an absolute path to a file where user information will be stored. For file realms, the value for the **JAAS Context** field must always be **fileRealm**.

After entering all this information, we can click on the **OK** button and our new realm will be created. We can then use it just like the predefined file realm. Applications wishing to authenticate against this new realm must use its name as the value of the `<realm-name>` element in the application's `web.xml` deployment descriptor.

At the time of writing, there is an issue in GlassFish v3 that prevents the custom file realm from being created successfully. A workaround for the issue is to create the key file (as an empty file) in advance, before creating the realm.

Alternatively, a custom file realm can be added from the command line via the `asadmin` utility:

```
asadmin create-auth-realm --classname
com.sun.enterprise.security.auth.realm.file.FileRealm --property
file=/home/heffel/additionalFileRealmKeyFile:jaas-context=fileRealm
newFileRealm
```

The `create-auth-realm` command tells `asadmin` that we want to create a new security realm. The value of the `--classname` parameter corresponds to the security realm class name; notice that it matches the value we selected previously in the web console. The `--property` parameter allows us to pass properties and their values. The value of this parameter must be a colon-separated list of properties and their values. The last argument of this command is the name we wish to give our security realm.

Although it is easier to set up security realms via the web console, doing it through the `asadmin` command line utility has the advantage that it is easily scriptable, allowing us to save this command in a script and easily configure several GlassFish instances.

Defining additional certificate realms

To define an additional certificate realm, we simply need to enter its name in the **Name** field and pick **com.sun.enterprise.security.auth.realm.certificate.CertificateRealm** as the value of the **Class Name** field, then click on the **OK** button to create our new realm.

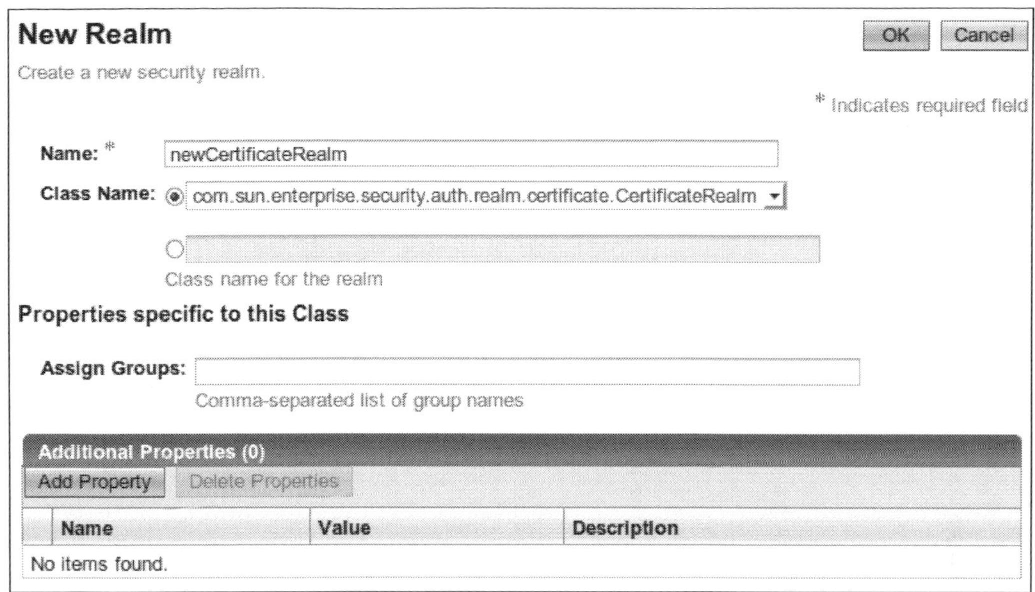

Applications wishing to use this new realm for authentication must use its name as the value of the `<realm-name>` element in the `web.xml` deployment descriptor, and specify `CLIENT-CERT` as the value of its `<auth-method>` element. Of course, client certificates must be present and configured as explained in the *Configuring applications to use the certificate realm* section.

At the time of writing, there is an issue with GlassFish that prevents creating a custom security realm via the web admin console. As a workaround, custom certificate realms can be created via the `asadmin` command line utility.

Alternatively, a custom certificate realm can be created via the command line, via the `asadmin` utility.

```
asadmin create-auth-realm --classname
com.sun.enterprise.security.auth.realm.certificate.CertificateRealm
newCertificateRealm
```

In this case, we don't need to pass any properties like we had to when we created the custom file realm. Therefore, all we need to do is pass the appropriate value to the `--classname` parameter and specify the new security realm name.

Defining an LDAP realm

We can easily set up a realm to authenticate against an LDAP (Lightweight Directory Access Protocol) database. In order to do this, we need to, in addition to the obvious step of entering a name for the realm, select **com.sun.enterprise.security.auth.realm.ldap.LDAPRealm** as the **Class Name** value for a new realm:

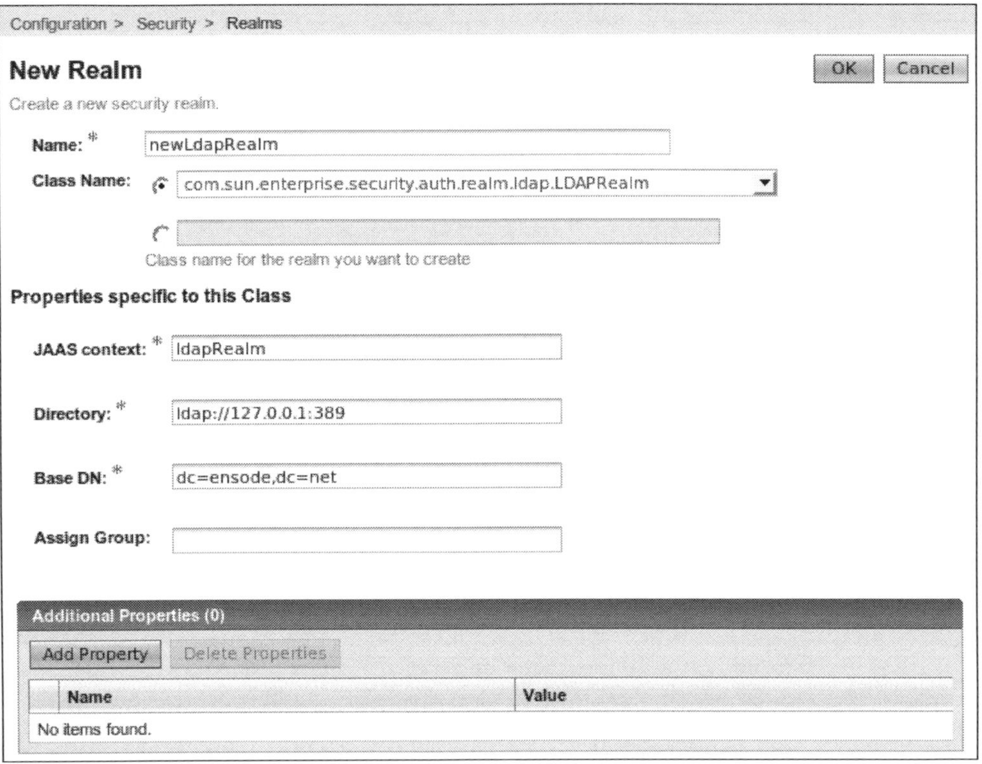

We then need to enter a URL for the directory server in the **Directory** field and the base distinguished name (DN) to be used to search user data as the value in the **Base DN** field.

After creating an LDAP realm, applications can use it to authenticate against the LDAP database. The name of the realm needs to be used as the value of the `<realm-name>` element in the application's `web.xml` deployment descriptor. The value of the `<auth-method>` element must be either `BASIC` or `FORM`. Users and roles in the LDAP database can be mapped to groups in the application's `sun-web.xml` deployment descriptor using the `<principal-name>`, `<role-name>`, and `<group-name>` elements, as discussed earlier in this chapter.

To create an LDAP realm from the command line, we need to use the following syntax:

```
asadmin create-auth-realm --classname
com.sun.enterprise.security.auth.realm.ldap.LDAPRealm --property "jaas-
context=ldapRealm:directory=ldap\://127.0.0.1\:1389:base-
dn=dc\=ensode,dc\=com" newLdapRealm
```

Notice that in this case, the value of the `--property` parameter is between quotes. This is necessary because we need to escape some of the characters in its value, such as all the columns and equal signs. To escape these special characters, we simply prefix it with a backslash (\).

Defining a Solaris realm

When GlassFish is installed in a Solaris server, it can "piggyback" on the operating system authentication mechanism via a Solaris realm. There are no special properties for this type of realm. All we need to do to create one is pick a name for it and select **com.sun.enterprise.security.auth.realm.solaris.SolarisRealm** as the value of the **Class Name** field:

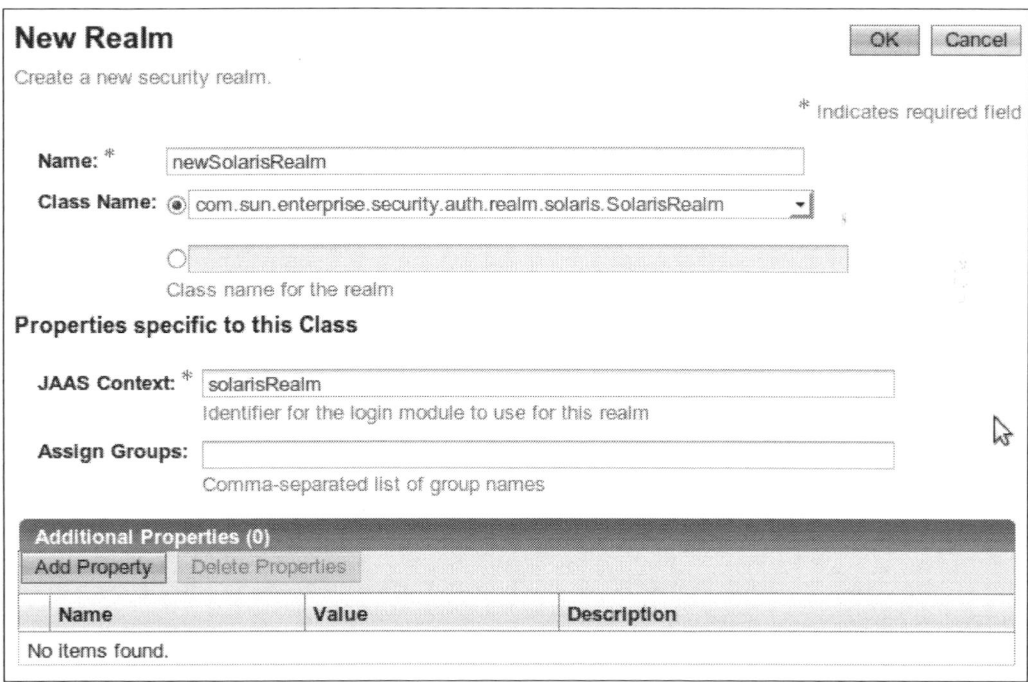

The **JAAS Context** field must be set to `solarisRealm`. After adding the realm, applications can authenticate against it using basic or form-based authentication. Operating system groups and users can be mapped to application roles defined in the application's `web.xml` deployment descriptor via the `<principal-name>`, `<role-name>`, and `<group-name>` elements in its `sun-web.xml` deployment descriptor.

A Solaris realm can be created from the command line as follows:

```
asadmin create-auth-realm --classname
com.sun.enterprise.security.auth.realm.solaris.SolarisRealm --property
jaas-context=solarisRealm newSolarisRealm
```

Defining a JDBC realm

Another type of realm we can create is a JDBC realm. This type of realm uses user information stored in database tables for user authentication.

In order to illustrate how to authenticate against a JDBC realm, we need to create a database to hold user information:

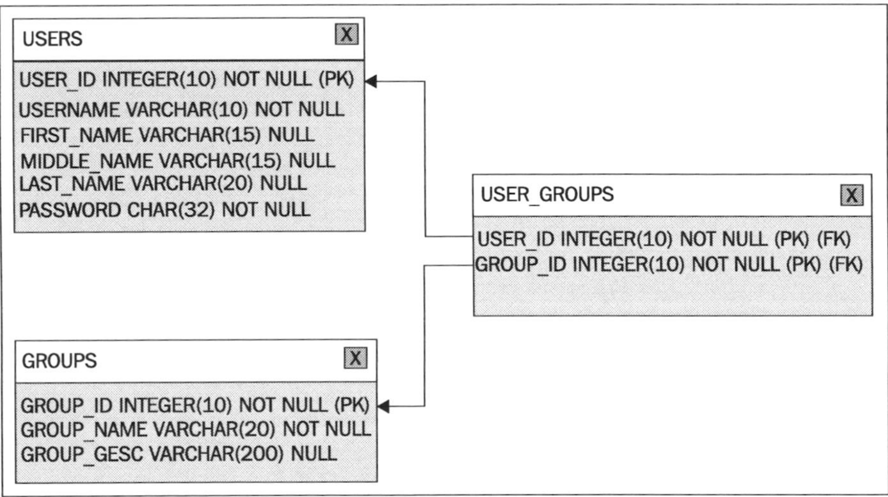

Our database consists of three tables. There is a `USERS` table holding user information, and a `GROUPS` table holding group information. As there is a many-to-many relationship between `USERS` and `GROUPS`, we need to add a join table to preserve data normalization. The name of this table is `USER_GROUPS`.

Notice that the `PASSWORD` column of the `USERS` table is of type `CHAR(32)`. The reason we chose this type instead of `VARCHAR` is that, by default, the JDBC realm expects passwords to be encrypted as an MD5 hash, and these hashes are always 32 characters long.

Passwords can be easily encrypted into a format expected by default by using the `java.security.MessageDigest` class included with the JDK. The following example code will take a clear text password and create an encrypted MD5 hash out of it:

```
package net.ensode.glassfishbook;

import java.security.MessageDigest;
import java.security.NoSuchAlgorithmException;

public class EncryptPassword
{
  public static String encryptPassword(String password)
    throws NoSuchAlgorithmException
  {
    MessageDigest messageDigest = MessageDigest.getInstance("MD5");
    byte[] bs;
    messageDigest.reset();
    bs = messageDigest.digest(password.getBytes());

    StringBuilder stringBuilder = new StringBuilder();

    //hex encode the digest
    for (int i = 0; i < bs.length; i++)
    {
      String hexVal = Integer.toHexString(0xFF & bs[i]);
      if (hexVal.length() == 1)
      {
        stringBuilder.append("0");
      }
      stringBuilder.append(hexVal);
    }
    return stringBuilder.toString();
  }
  public static void main(String[] args)
  {
    String encryptedPassword = null;
    try
    {
      if (args.length == 0)
      {
        System.err.println("Usage: java "
          + "net.ensode.glassfishbook.EncryptPassword "
          + "cleartext");
```

```
            }
            else
            {
                encryptedPassword = encryptPassword(args[0]);
                System.out.println(encryptedPassword);
            }
        }
        catch (NoSuchAlgorithmException e)
        {
            e.printStackTrace();
        }
    }
}
```

The "meat" of this class is its `encryptPassword()` method. It basically takes a clear text string and digests it using the MD5 algorithm by using the `digest()` method of an instance of `java.security.MessageDigest`. It then encodes the digest as a series of hexadecimal numbers. The reason this encoding is necessary is because GlassFish, by default, expects an MD5 digested password to be hex encoded.

When using JDBC realms, the Glassfish users and groups are not added to the realm via the GlassFish console. Instead, they are added by inserting data into the appropriate tables.

Once we have the database that will hold user credentials in place, we are ready to create a new JDBC realm.

We can create a JDBC realm by entering its name in the **Name** field of the **New Realm** form in the GlassFish web console, then selecting **com.sun.enterprise.security.auth.realm.jdbc.JDBCRealm** as the value of the **Class Name** field:

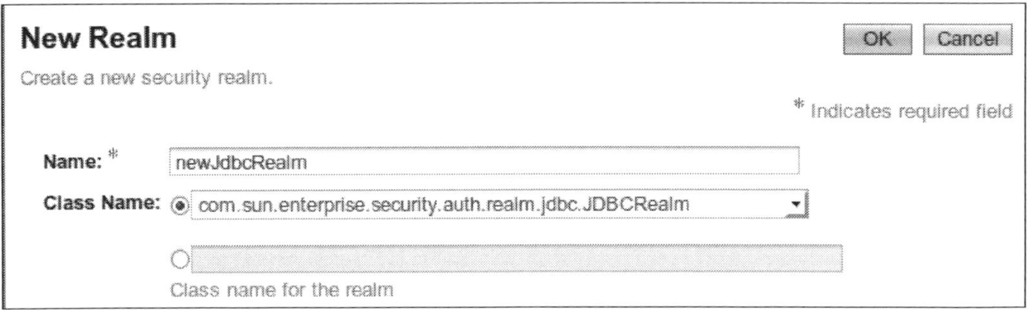

There are a number of other properties we need to set for our new JDBC realm:

Properties specific to this Class

JAAS context: *	jdbcRealm
JNDI: *	jdbc/__UserAuthPool
User Table: *	V_USER_ROLE
User Name: *	USERNAME
Password: *	PASSWORD
Group Table: *	V_USER_ROLE
Group Name: *	GROUP_NAME
Assign Group:	
Database User:	
Database Password:	
Digest:	
Encoding:	
Charset:	

The **JAAS context** field must be set to **jdbcRealm** for JDBC realms. The value of the **JNDI** property must be the JNDI name of the data source corresponding to the database that contains the realm's user and group data. The value of the **User Table** property must be the name of the table that contains the username and password information.

Notice that in the previous screenshot, we used **V_USER_ROLE** as the value for this property. `V_USER_ROLE` is a database view that contains both user and group information. The reason we didn't use the `USERS` table directly is because GlassFish assumes that both the user table and the group table contain a column containing the username. Doing this results in having duplicate data. To avoid this situation, we created a view that we could use as the value of both the **User Table** and **Group Table** properties (to be discussed shortly).

The User Name property must contain a column in the **User Table** that contains the usernames. The Password property value must be the name of a column in the **User Table** that contains the user's password. The value of the **Group Table** property must be the name of the table containing user groups. The Group Name property must contain the name of a column in the **Group Table** containing user group names.

All other properties are optional and, in most cases, left blank. Of special interest is the Digest property. This property allows us to specify the message digest algorithm to use to encrypt the user's password. Valid values for this property include all algorithms supported by the JDK. These algorithms are MD2, MD5, SHA-1, SHA-256, SHA-384, and SHA-512. Additionally, if we wish to store user passwords in clear text, we can do so by using the value "none" for this property.

Once we have defined our JDBC realm, we need to configure our application via its `web.xml` and `sun-web.xml` deployment descriptors. Configuring an application to rely on a JDBC realm for authorization and authentication is done just like when using any other type of realm.

```
<web-app xmlns="http://java.sun.com/xml/ns/javaee"
         xmlns:xsi="http://www.w3.org/2001/XMLSchema-instance"
         xsi:schemaLocation="http://java.sun.com/xml/ns/javaee
           http://java.sun.com/xml/ns/javaee/web-app_3_0.xsd"
         version="3.0">
  <security-constraint>
    <web-resource-collection>
      <web-resource-name>Admin Pages</web-resource-name>
      <url-pattern>/admin/*</url-pattern>
    </web-resource-collection>
    <auth-constraint>
      <role-name>admin</role-name>
    </auth-constraint>
  </security-constraint>
  <security-constraint>
    <web-resource-collection>
      <web-resource-name>AllPages</web-resource-name>
```

```
      <url-pattern>/*</url-pattern>
    </web-resource-collection>
    <auth-constraint>
      <role-name>user</role-name>
    </auth-constraint>
  </security-constraint>
  <login-config>
    <auth-method>FORM</auth-method>
    <realm-name>newJdbcRealm</realm-name>
    <form-login-config>
      <form-login-page>/login.jsp</form-login-page>
      <form-error-page>/loginerror.jsp</form-error-page>
    </form-login-config>
  </login-config>
</web-app>
```

In this example, we set the value of the `<realm-name>` element in the `web.xml` deployment descriptor to `newJdbcRealm`. This is the name we chose to give our realm when we configured it through the GlassFish console.

In this example, we chose to use form-based authentication, but we could have used basic authentication as well.

In addition to declaring that we will rely on the JDBC realm for authentication and authorization, just like with other types of realms, we need to map the roles defined in the `web.xml` deployment descriptor to security group names. This is accomplished in the `sun-web.xml` deployment descriptor:

```
<?xml version="1.0" encoding="UTF-8" standalone="no"?>
<!DOCTYPE sun-web-app PUBLIC "-//Sun Microsystems, Inc.//DTD
  Application Server 9.0 Servlet 2.5//EN"
  "http://www.sun.com/software/appserver/dtds/sun-web-app_2_5-0.dtd">
<sun-web-app>
  <security-role-mapping>
    <role-name>admin</role-name>
    <group-name>Admin</group-name>
  </security-role-mapping>
  <security-role-mapping>
    <role-name>user</role-name>
    <group-name>Users</group-name>
  </security-role-mapping>
</sun-web-app>
```

The value of the `<role-name>` elements must match the corresponding `<role-name>` element in `web.xml`. The value of `<group-name>` must be a value in the column specified by the **Group Name Column** property of the JDBC realm, as specified when it was configured in the GlassFish web console.

A JDBC realm can be created from the command line as follows:

```
asadmin create-auth-realm --classname
com.sun.enterprise.security.auth.realms.jdbc.JDBCRealm
--property jaas-context=jdbcRealm:datasource-
jndi=jdbc/__UserAuthPool:user-table=V_USER_ROLE:user-name-
column=USERNAME:password-column=PASSWORD:group-table=V_USER_ROLE:group-
name-column=GROUP_NAME fooJdbcRealm
```

Defining custom realms

Although the predefined realm types should cover a vast majority of cases, we can create custom realm types if the predefined ones don't meet our needs. Doing so involves coding the custom `Realm` and `LoginModule` classes. Let's first discuss the custom realm class:

```
package net.ensode.glassfishbook;

import java.util.Enumeration;
import java.util.Vector;

import com.sun.enterprise.security.auth.realm.IASRealm;
import com.sun.enterprise.security.auth.realm.
InvalidOperationException;
import com.sun.enterprise.security.auth.realm.NoSuchUserException;

public class SimpleRealm extends IASRealm
{
  @Override
  public Enumeration getGroupNames(String userName)
    throws InvalidOperationException, NoSuchUserException
  {
    Vector vector = new Vector();
    vector.add("Users");
    vector.add("Admin");
    return vector.elements();
  }
  @Override
  public String getAuthType()
  {
```

```
        return "simple";
    }
    @Override
    public String getJAASContext()
    {
        return "simpleRealm";
    }
    public boolean loginUser(String userName, String password)
    {
        boolean loginSuccessful = false;
        if ("glassfish".equals(userName) && "secret".equals(password))
        {
            loginSuccessful = true;
        }
        return loginSuccessful;
    }
}
```

Our custom realm class must extend `com.sun.enterprise.security.auth.realm.IASRealm`. This class can be found inside the `security.jar` file, therefore this JAR file must be added to the CLASSPATH before our realm can be successfully compiled.

The `security.jar` file can be found under `[glassfish installation directory]/glassfish/modules`. When using Maven or Ivy dependency management, this JAR file can be found in the following repository: `http://download.java.net/maven/glassfish`. The group id is `org.glassfish.security` and the artifact id is `security`. At the time of writing, the latest version is `3.0`.

Our class must override a method called `getGroupNames()`. This method takes a single `String` as parameter and returns an `Enumeration`. The `String` parameter is for the username of the user who is attempting to log into the realm. The `Enumeration` must contain a collection of strings indicating which groups the user belongs to. In our simple example, we simply hardcoded the groups. In a real application, these groups would be obtained from some kind of persistent storage (database, file, and so on).

The next method our realm class must override is the `getAuthType()` method. This method must return a `String` containing a description of the type of authentication used by this realm.

These two methods are declared as abstract in the IASRealm (parent) class. Although the getJAASContext() method is not abstract, we should nevertheless override it, as the value it returns is used to determine the type of authentication to use from the application server's login.conf file. The return value of this method is used to map the realm to the corresponding login module.

Finally, our realm class must contain a method to authenticate the user. We are free to call it anything we want. Additionally, we can use as many parameters of any type as we wish. Our simple example simply has the values for a single username and password hardcoded. Again, a real application would obtain valid credentials from some kind of persistent storage. This method is meant to be called from the corresponding login module class:

```
package net.ensode.glassfishbook;

import java.util.Enumeration;

import javax.security.auth.login.LoginException;

import com.sun.appserv.security.AppservPasswordLoginModule;
import com.sun.enterprise.security.auth.realm.
InvalidOperationException;
import com.sun.enterprise.security.auth.realm.NoSuchUserException;

public class SimpleLoginModule extends AppservPasswordLoginModule
{
  @Override
  protected void authenticateUser() throws LoginException
  {
    Enumeration userGroupsEnum = null;
    String[] userGroupsArray = null;
    SimpleRealm simpleRealm;
    if (!(_currentRealm instanceof SimpleRealm))
    {
      throw new LoginException();
    }
    else
    {
      simpleRealm = (SimpleRealm) _currentRealm;
    }
    if (simpleRealm.loginUser(_username, _password))
    {
      try
      {
```

```
            userGroupsEnum = simpleRealm.getGroupNames(_username);
          }
          catch (InvalidOperationException e)
          {
            throw new LoginException(e.getMessage());
          }
          catch (NoSuchUserException e)
          {
            throw new LoginException(e.getMessage());
          }

          userGroupsArray = new String[2];
          int i = 0;
          while (userGroupsEnum.hasMoreElements())
          {
            userGroupsArray[i++] =
              ((String) userGroupsEnum.nextElement());
          }
        }
        else
        {
          throw new LoginException();
        }
        commitUserAuthentication(userGroupsArray);
      }
    }
```

Our login module class must extend the `com.sun.appserv.security.AppservPasswordLoginModule` class. This class is also inside the `security.jar` file; it only needs to override a single method—`authenticateUser()`. This method takes no parameters and must throw a `LoginException` if user authentication is unsuccessful. The `_currentRealm` variable is defined in the parent class; it is of type `com.sun.enterprise.security.auth.realm.Realm`—the parent class of all realm classes. This variable is initialized before the `authenticateUser()` method is executed. The login module class must verify that this class is of the expected type (in our example, `SimpleRealm`). If it is not, a `LoginException` must be thrown.

The other two variables that are defined in the parent class and initialized before the `authenticateUser()` method is executed are `_username` and `_password`. These variables contain the credentials the user entered in the login form (for form-based authentication) or the pop-up window (for basic authentication). Our example simply passes these values to the realm class so that it can verify the user credentials.

The `authenticateUser()` method must call the parent class' `commitUserAuthentication()` method upon a successful authentication. This method takes an array of `String` objects containing the group the user belongs to. Our example simply invokes the `getGroupNames()` method defined in the realm class and adds the elements of the `Enumeration` it returns to an array, then passes that array to the `commitUserAuthentication()` method.

Obviously, GlassFish is unaware of the existence of our custom realm and login module classes. We need to add these classes to GlassFish's `CLASSPATH`. The easiest way to do this is to copy the JAR file containing our custom realm and login module to the following directory:

```
[glassfish installation directory]/glassfish/domains/domain1/lib
```

The last step we need to follow before we can authenticate applications against our custom realm is to add our new custom realm to the domain's `login.conf` file.

```
fileRealm
{
  com.sun.enterprise.security.auth.login.FileLoginModule required;
};
ldapRealm
{
  com.sun.enterprise.security.auth.login.LDAPLoginModule required;
};
solarisRealm
{
  com.sun.enterprise.security.auth.login.SolarisLoginModule required;
};
jdbcRealm
{
  com.sun.enterprise.security.auth.login.JDBCLoginModule required;
};
jdbcDigestRealm
{
  com.sun.enterprise.security.auth.login.JDBCDigestLoginModule
    required;
};
simpleRealm
{
  net.ensode.glassfishbook.SimpleLoginModule required;
};
```

The value before the opening brace must match the return value of the `getJAASContext()` method defined in the realm class. It is in this file that the realm and login module classes are linked to each other. The GlassFish domain needs to be restarted for this change to take effect.

We are now ready to use our custom realm to authenticate the users in our applications. We need to add a new realm of the type we created via GlassFish's admin console:

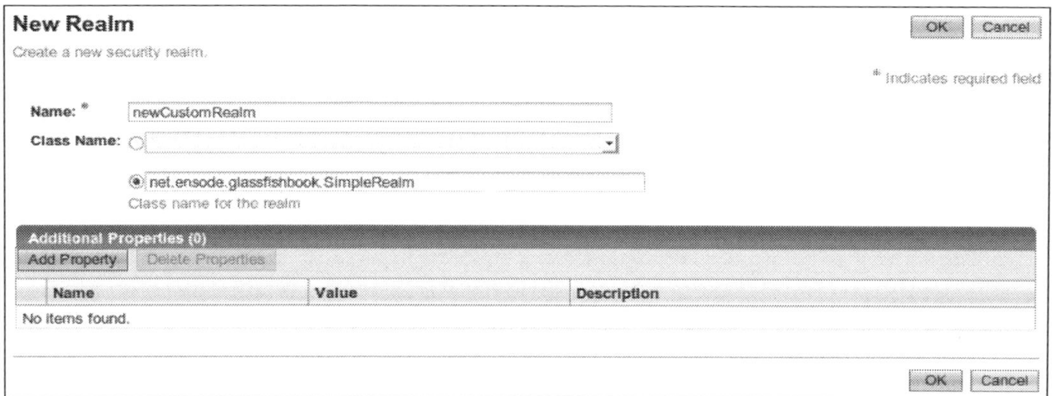

At the time of writing, there is an issue with GlassFish 3 that is preventing the successful creation of custom realms via the web console. As a workaround, custom realms can be created via the `asadmin` command line utility, as described later in this section.

To create our realm name, as usual we need to give it a name. Instead of selecting a class name from the drop-down menu, we need to type it into the text field. Our custom realm didn't have any properties, therefore we don't have to add any in this example. If it did, they would be added by clicking on the **Add Property** button and entering the property name and corresponding value. Our realm would then get the properties by overriding the `init()` method from its parent class. This method has the following signature:

```
protected void init(Properties arg0) throws BadRealmException,
  NoSuchRealmException
```

The instance of `java.util.Properties` it takes as a parameter would be pre-populated with the properties entered in the page shown in the previous screenshot (our custom realm doesn't have any properties, but for those that do, properties are entered in said page).

Once we have added the pertinent information for our new custom realm, we can use it just like we use any of the predefined realms. Applications need to specify its name as the value of the `<realm-name>` element of the application's `web.xml` deployment descriptor. Nothing out of the ordinary needs to be done at the application level.

Just like with standard realms, custom realms can be added via the `asadmin` command line utility:

```
asadmin create-auth-realm --classname
net.ensode.glassfishbook.SimpleRealm newCustomRealm
```

Summary

In this chapter, we covered how to use GlassFish's default realms to authenticate our web applications. We covered the file realm, which stores user information in a flat file, and the certificate realm, which requires client-side certificates for user authentication.

We discussed how to create additional realms that behave just like the default realms by using the realm classes included with GlassFish.

We also covered how to use additional realm classes included in GlassFish to create realms that authenticate against an LDAP database, against a relational database, and how to create realms that "piggyback" into a Solaris server's authentication mechanism.

Finally, we looked at how to create custom realm classes for cases where the included ones don't fit our needs.

9 Enterprise JavaBeans

Enterprise JavaBeans are server-side components that encapsulate the business logic of an application. Enterprise JavaBeans simplify application development by automatically taking care of transaction management and security. There are two types of Enterprise JavaBeans: session beans, which perform business logic, and message-driven beans, which act as a message listener.

Readers familiar with previous versions of J2EE will notice that entity beans were not mentioned in the previous paragraph. In Java EE 5, entity beans were deprecated in favor of the Java Persistence API (JPA). Entity beans are still supported for backwards compatibility. However, the preferred way of doing Object Relational Mapping with Java EE 5 and Java EE 6 is through JPA. Refer to Chapter 5 for a detailed discussion on JPA.

The following topics will be covered in this chapter:

- Session Beans
    - A simple session bean
    - A more realistic example
    - Using a session bean to implement the DAO design pattern
    - Singleton session beans
    - Asynchronous method calls
- Message-driven beans
- Transactions in Enterprise JavaBeans
    - Container-managed transactions
    - Bean-managed transactions

- Enterprise JavaBeans' life cycle
    - Stateful session bean life cycle
    - Stateless session bean life cycle
    - Message-driven bean life cycle
- EJB timer service
- EJB security

Session beans

Like we previously mentioned, session beans typically encapsulate business logic. In Java EE 5, only two artifacts need to be created in order to create a session bean: the bean itself and a business interface. These artifacts need to be decorated with proper annotations to let the EJB container know that they are session beans.

Java EE 6 simplifies session bean development even further. Local interfaces (to be discussed later in the chapter) are now optional. Therefore, to develop a session bean that only requires local access, we only need to develop one artifact—the session bean class.

> Previous versions of J2EE required application developers to create several artifacts in order to create a session bean. These artifacts included the bean itself, a local or remote interface (or both), a local home or a remote home interface (or both), and an XML deployment descriptor. As we shall see in this chapter, EJB development was greatly simplified in Java EE 5, and simplified even further in Java EE 6.

Simple session bean

The following example illustrates a very simple session bean:

```
package net.ensode.glassfishbook;

import javax.ejb.Stateless;

@Stateless
public class SimpleSessionBean
{
  private String message = "If you don't see this, it didn't work!";
  public String getMessage()
  {
    return message;
  }
}
```

The `@Stateless` annotation lets the EJB container know that this class is a **stateless session bean**. There are two types of session beans: stateless and stateful. Before we explain the difference between these two types of session beans, we need to clarify how an instance of an EJB is provided to an EJB client application.

When EJBs (both stateless session beans and message-driven beans) are deployed, the EJB container creates a series of instances of each EJB. This is what is typically referred to as the **EJB pool**. When an EJB client application obtains an instance of an EJB, one of the instances in the pool is provided to this client application.

The difference between stateful and stateless session beans is that stateful session beans maintain **conversational state** with the client, whereas stateless session beans do not. In simple terms, what this means is that when an EJB client application obtains an instance of a stateful session bean, we are guaranteed that the value of any instance variables in the bean will be consistent across method calls. Therefore, it is safe to modify any instance variables on a stateful session bean, as they will retain their value for the next method call. The EJB container saves conversational state by passivating stateful session beans and retrieves said state when the bean is activated. Conversational state is the reason why the life cycle of stateful session beans is a bit more complex than the life cycle of stateless session beans or message-driven beans (EJB life cycle is discussed later in this chapter).

The EJB container may provide any instance of an EJB in the pool when an EJB client application requests an instance of a stateless session bean. For stateless session beans, the value of instance variables is not set to whatever it was in the last method call (this is what passivation/activation does for stateful session beans). As we are not guaranteed the same instance for every method call, values set to any instance variables in a stateless session bean may be "lost" (they are not really lost, the modification is in another instance of the EJB in the pool).

Other than being decorated with the `@Stateless` annotation, there is nothing special about the previous class. Notice that it implements an interface called `SimpleSession`. This interface is the bean's business interface. The `SimpleSession` interface is shown next:

```
package net.ensode.glassfishbook;

import javax.ejb.Remote;

@Remote
public interface SimpleSession
{
  public String getMessage();
}
```

The only peculiar thing about this interface is that it is decorated with the `@Remote` annotation. This annotation indicates that this is a **remote business interface**. What this means is that the interface may be in a different JVM than the client application invoking it. Remote business interfaces may even be invoked across the network.

Business interfaces may also be decorated with the `@Local` interface. This annotation indicates that the business interface is a **local business interface**. Local business interface implementations must be in the same JVM as the client application invoking its methods.

As remote business interfaces can be invoked either from the same JVM or from a different JVM as the client application, at first glance we might be tempted to make all of our business interfaces remote. Before doing so, we must be aware of the fact that the flexibility provided by remote business interfaces comes with a performance penalty, as method invocations are made under the assumption that they will be made across the network. As a matter of fact, most typical Java EE applications consist of web applications acting as client applications for EJBs. In this case, the client application and the EJB are running on the same JVM. Therefore, local interfaces are used a lot more frequently than remote business interfaces.

Once we have compiled the session bean and its corresponding business interface, we need to place them in a JAR file and deploy them. Just like with WAR files, the easiest way to deploy an EJB JAR file is to copy it to `[glassfish installation directory]/glassfish/domains/domain1/autodeploy`.

Now that we have seen the session bean and its corresponding business interface, let's take a look at a client sample application:

```
package net.ensode.glassfishbook;

import javax.ejb.EJB;

public class SessionBeanClient
{
  @EJB
  private static SimpleSession simpleSession;

  private void invokeSessionBeanMethods()
  {
    System.out.println(simpleSession.getMessage());
    System.out.println("\nSimpleSession is of type: "
      + simpleSession.getClass().getName());
  }
  public static void main(String[] args)
  {
```

```
        new SessionBeanClient().invokeSessionBeanMethods();
    }
}
```

This code simply declares an instance variable of type `net.ensode.SimpleSession`, which is the business interface for our session bean. The instance variable is decorated with the `@EJB` annotation. This annotation lets the EJB container know that this variable is a business interface for a session bean. The EJB container then injects an implementation of the business interface for the client code to use.

As our client is a standalone application (as opposed to an EJB artifact such as a WAR file or another EJB JAR file), in order for it to be able to access the code deployed in the server, it must be placed in a JAR file and executed through the `appclient` utility. This utility can be found at `[glassfish installation directory]/glassfish/bin/`. Assuming this path is in the PATH environment variable, and assuming we placed our client code in a JAR file called `simplesessionbeanclient.jar`, we would execute the previous client code by typing the following command in the command line:

```
appclient -client simplesessionbeanclient.jar
```

Executing this command results in the following console output:

```
If you don't see this, it didn't work!
SimpleSession is of type: net.ensode.glassfishbook._SimpleSession_Wrapper
```

We are using Maven 2 to build our code. For this example, we used the Maven Assembly plugin (`http://maven.apache.org/plugins/maven-assembly-plugin/`) to build a client JAR file that includes all dependencies. This frees us from having to specify all the dependent JAR files in the `-classpath` command line option of `appclient`. To build this JAR file, simply invoke `mvn assembly:assembly` from the command line.

This is the output of the `SessionBeanClient` class.

The first line of the output is simply the return value of the `getMessage()` method we implemented in the session bean. The second line of the output displays the fully qualified class name of the class implementing the business interface. Notice that the class name is not the fully qualified name of the session bean we wrote. Instead, what is actually provided is an implementation of the business interface created behind the scenes by the EJB container.

A more realistic example

In the previous section, we saw a very simple, "Hello world" type of example. In this section, we will show a more realistic example. Session beans are frequently used as **Data Access Objects (DAOs)**. They are sometimes used as a wrapper for JDBC calls, other times they are used to wrap calls to obtain or modify JPA entities. In this section, we will take the latter approach.

The following example illustrates how to implement the DAO design pattern in a session bean. Before looking at the bean implementation, let's look at the business interface corresponding to it:

```
package net.ensode.glassfishbook;

import javax.ejb.Remote;

@Remote
public interface CustomerDao
{
  public void saveCustomer(Customer customer);
  public Customer getCustomer(Long customerId);
  public void deleteCustomer(Customer customer);
}
```

As we can see, this code snippet is a remote interface implementing three methods. The `saveCustomer()` method saves customer data to the database, the `getCustomer()` method obtains data for a customer from the database, and the `deleteCustomer()` method deletes customer data from the database. All these methods take an instance of the `Customer` entity we developed in Chapter 4 as a parameter.

Let's now take a look at the session bean implementing the previous business interface. As we are about to see, there are some differences between the way the JPA code is implemented in a session bean versus in a plain old Java object.

```
package net.ensode.glassfishbook;

import javax.ejb.Stateful;
import javax.persistence.EntityManager;
import javax.persistence.PersistenceContext;

@Stateful
public class CustomerDaoBean implements CustomerDao
{
  @PersistenceContext
```

```
    private EntityManager entityManager;

    public void saveCustomer(Customer customer)
    {
      if (customer.getCustomerId() == null)
      {
        saveNewCustomer(customer);
      }
      else
      {
        updateCustomer(customer);
      }
    }
    private void saveNewCustomer(Customer customer)
    {
      entityManager.persist(customer);
    }
    private void updateCustomer(Customer customer)
    {
      entityManager.merge(customer);
    }
    public Customer getCustomer(Long customerId)
    {
      Customer customer;
      customer = entityManager.find(Customer.class, customerId);
      return customer;
    }
    public void deleteCustomer(Customer customer)
    {
      entityManager.remove(customer);
    }
  }
```

The first difference we should notice is that an instance of `javax.persistence.EntityManager` is directly injected into the session bean. In the previous JPA examples, we had to inject an instance of `javax.persistence.EntityManagerFactory`, then use the injected `EntityManagerFactory` instance to obtain an instance of `EntityManager`. The reason we had to do this was that our previous examples were not thread-safe. What this means is that potentially the same code could be executed concurrently by more than one user. As `EntityManager` is not designed to be used concurrently by more than one thread, we used an `EntityManagerFactory` instance to provide each thread with its own instance of `EntityManager`. As the EJB container assigns a session bean to a single client at time, session beans are inherently thread-safe. Therefore, we can inject an instance of `EntityManager` directly into a session bean.

The next difference between this session bean and the previous JPA examples is that in the previous examples, JPA calls were wrapped between calls to `UserTransaction.begin()` and `UserTransaction.commit()`. The reason we had to do this is because JPA calls are required to be in wrapped in a transaction. If they are not in a transaction, most JPA calls will throw a `TransactionRequiredException`. The reason we don't have to explicitly wrap JPA calls in a transaction like in the previous examples is because session bean methods are implicitly transactional. There is nothing we need to do to make them that way. This default behavior is what is known as **container-managed transactions**. Container-managed transactions are discussed in detail later in this chapter.

As mentioned in Chapter 5, when a JPA entity is retrieved in one transaction and updated in a different transaction, the `EntityManager.merge()` method needs to be invoked to update the data in the database. In this case, invoking `EntityManager.persist()` will result in a "Cannot persist detached object" exception.

Invoking session beans from web applications

Frequently, Java EE applications consist of web applications acting as clients for EJBs. Before Java EE 6 was released, the most common way of deploying a Java EE application that consists of both a web application and one or more session beans was to package both the WAR file for the web application and the EJB JAR files into an EAR (Enterprise ARchive) file.

Java EE 6 simplifies the packaging and deployment of applications consisting of both EJBs and web components.

In this section, we will modify the example we saw in the section titled *Integrating JSF and JPA* from Chapter 6 so that the web application acts as a client to the DAO session bean we saw in the previous section.

In order to make this application act as an EJB client, we will modify the `CustomerController` managed bean so that it delegates the logic to save a new customer to the database to the `CustomerDaoBean` session bean we developed in the previous section.

```
package net.ensode.glassfishbook.jsfjpa;

import javax.ejb.EJB;
import javax.faces.bean.ManagedBean;
import javax.faces.bean.ManagedProperty;
```

```
import net.ensode.glassfishbook.Customer;
import net.ensode.glassfishbook.CustomerDaoBean;

@ManagedBean
public class CustomerController
{
  @EJB
  CustomerDaoBean customerDaoBean;
  @ManagedProperty(value = "#{customer}")
  private Customer customer;

  public String saveCustomer()
  {
    String returnValue = "customer_saved";
    try
    {
      customerDaoBean.saveCustomer(customer);
    }
    catch (Exception e)
    {
      e.printStackTrace();
      returnValue = "error_saving_customer";
    }
    return returnValue;
  }
  public Customer getCustomer()
  {
    return customer;
  }
  public void setCustomer(Customer customer)
  {
    this.customer = customer;
  }
}
```

As we can see, all we had to do was declare an instance of the `CustomerDaoBean` session bean, decorate it with the `@EJB` annotation so that an instance of the corresponding EJB is injected, and replace the code to save the data to the database with an invocation to the `saveCustomer()` method defined in the `CustomerDao` business interface.

Notice that we injected an instance of the session bean directly into our client code. The reason we can do this is because of a new Java EE 6 feature. When using Java EE 6, we can do away with local interfaces and use session bean instances directly in our client code.

Now that we have modified our web application to be a client for our session bean, we need to package it in a WAR (web archive) file and deploy it in order to use it.

Singleton session beans

A new type of session bean introduced in Java EE 6 is the **singleton session bean**. A single instance of each singleton session bean exists in the application server.

Singleton session beans are useful to cache database data. Caching frequently used data in a singleton session bean increases performance as it greatly minimizes trips to the database. The common pattern is to have a method in our bean decorated with the `@PostConstruct` annotation. In this method, we retrieve the data we want to cache. We then provide a setter method for the bean's clients to call. The following example illustrates this technique:

```
package net.ensode.glassfishbook.singletonsession;

import java.util.List;
import javax.annotation.PostConstruct;
import javax.ejb.Singleton;
import javax.persistence.EntityManager;
import javax.persistence.PersistenceContext;
import javax.persistence.Query;
import net.ensode.glassfishbook.entity.UsStates;

@Singleton
public class SingletonSessionBean implements
  SingletonSessionBeanRemote
{
  @PersistenceContext
  private EntityManager entityManager;
  private List<UsStates> stateList;

  @PostConstruct
  public void init()
  {
    Query query = entityManager.createQuery("Select us from UsStates
      us");
    stateList = query.getResultList();
```

```
    }

    @Override
    public List<UsStates> getStateList()
    {
      return stateList;
    }
}
```

As our bean is a singleton, all of its clients would access the same instance, avoiding having duplicate data in the database. Additionally, as it is a singleton, it is safe to have an instance variable, as all clients access the same instance of the bean.

Asynchronous method calls

Sometimes, it is useful to have some processing done asynchronously, that is, invoke a method call and return control immediately to the client, without having the client wait for the method to finish.

In earlier versions of Java EE, the only way to invoke EJB methods asynchronously was to use message-driven beans (discussed in the next section). Although message-driven beans are fairly easy to write, they do require some configuration, such as setting up JMS message queues or topics, before they can be used.

EJB 3.1 introduces the `@Asynchronous` annotation that can be used to mark a method in a session bean as asynchronous. When an EJB client invokes an asynchronous method, control immediately goes back to the client, without waiting for the method to finish.

Asynchronous methods can only return `void` or an implementation of the `java.util.concurrent.Future` interface. The following example illustrates both scenarios:

```
package net.ensode.glassfishbook.asynchronousmethods;

import java.util.concurrent.Future;
import java.util.logging.Level;
import java.util.logging.Logger;

import javax.ejb.AsyncResult;
import javax.ejb.Asynchronous;
import javax.ejb.Stateless;

@Stateless
public class AsynchronousSessionBean implements
```

```
    AsynchronousSessionBeanRemote
  {
    private static Logger logger =
      Logger.getLogger(AsynchronousSessionBean.class.getName());

    @Asynchronous
    @Override
    public void slowMethod()
    {
      long startTime = System.currentTimeMillis();
      logger.info("entering " + this.getClass().getCanonicalName()
        + ".slowMethod()");
      try
      {
        Thread.sleep(10000); //simulate processing for 10 seconds
      }
      catch (InterruptedException ex)
      {
        Logger.getLogger(AsynchronousSessionBean.class.getName()).
          log(Level.SEVERE, null, ex);
      }
      logger.info("leaving " + this.getClass().getCanonicalName()
        + ".slowMethod()");
      long endTime = System.currentTimeMillis();
      logger.info("execution took " + (endTime - startTime)
        + " milliseconds");
    }

    @Asynchronous
    @Override
    public Future<Long> slowMethodWithReturnValue()
    {
      try
      {
        Thread.sleep(15000); //simulate processing for 15 seconds
      }
      catch (InterruptedException ex)
      {
        Logger.getLogger(AsynchronousSessionBean.class.getName()).
          log(Level.SEVERE, null, ex);
      }
      return new AsyncResult<Long>(42L);
    }
  }
```

When our asynchronous method returns `void`, the only thing we need to do is decorate the method with the `@Asynchronous` annotation, then call it as usual from the client code.

If we need a return value, this value needs to be wrapped in an implementation of the `java.util.concurrent.Future` interface. The Java EE 6 API provides a convenience implementation in the form of the `javax.ejb.AsyncResult` class. Both the `Future` interface and the `AsyncResult` class use generics. We need to specify our return type as the type parameter of these artifacts.

The `Future` interface has several methods we can use to cancel the execution of an asychronous method: check to see if the method is done, get the return value of the method, or check to see if the method is canceled. The following table lists these methods:

Method	**Description**
`cancel(boolean mayInterruptIfRunning)`	Cancels method execution. If the `boolean` parameter is `true`, then this method will attempt to cancel the method execution even if it is already running.
`get()`	Will return the "unwrapped" return value of the method. The return value will be of the type parameter of the `Future` interface implementation returned by the method.
`get(long timeout, TimeUnit unit)`	Will attempt the "unwrapped" return value of the method. The return value will be of the type parameter of the `Future` interface implementation returned by the method. This method will block for the amount of time specified by the first parameter. The unit of time to wait is determined by the second parameter. The `TimeUnit` enum has constants for NANOSECONDS, MILLISECONDS, SECONDS, MINUTES, and so on. Refer to its JavaDoc documentation for the complete list.
`isCancelled()`	Returns `true` if the method has been cancelled, `false` otherwise.
`isDone()`	Returns `true` if the method has finished executing, `false` otherwise.

As we can see, the `@Asynchronous` annotation makes it very easy to make asynchronous calls without having the overhead of having to set up message queues or topics. Certainly a welcome addition to the EJB 3.1 specification.

Message-driven beans

The purpose of a message-driven bean is to consume messages from a JMS queue or a JMS topic, depending on the messaging domain used (refer to Chapter 7). A message-driven bean must be decorated with the `@MessageDriven` annotation. The `mappedName` attribute of this annotation must contain the JNDI name of the JMS message queue or JMS message topic that the bean will be consuming messages from. The following example illustrates a simple message-driven bean:

```
package net.ensode.glassfishbook;

import javax.ejb.MessageDriven;
import javax.jms.JMSException;
import javax.jms.Message;
import javax.jms.MessageListener;
import javax.jms.TextMessage;

@MessageDriven(mappedName = "jms/GlassFishBookQueue")
public class ExampleMessageDrivenBean implements MessageListener
{
  public void onMessage(Message message)
  {
    TextMessage textMessage = (TextMessage) message;
    try
    {
      System.out.print("Received the following message: ");
      System.out.println(textMessage.getText());
      System.out.println();
    }
    catch (JMSException e)
    {
      e.printStackTrace();
    }
  }
}
```

As we can see, this class is nearly identical to the `ExampleMessageListener` class we saw in Chapter 7. The only differences are the class name and the fact that this example is decorated with the `@MessageDriven` interface. It is recommended, but not required for message-driven beans to implement the `javax.jms.MessageListener` interface. However, message-driven beans must have a method called `onMessage()` whose signature is identical to the previous example.

Client applications never invoke a message-driven bean's methods directly. Instead, they put messages in the message queue or topic, then the bean consumes those messages and acts as appropriate. The previous example simply prints the message to standard output. As message-driven beans execute inside an EJB container, standard output gets redirected to a log. To see the messages in GlassFish's server log, open the `[GlassFish installation directory]/glassfish/domains/domain1/logs/server.log` file.

Transactions in Enterprise JavaBeans

Like we mentioned earlier in this chapter, any EJB methods are automatically wrapped in a transaction by default. This default behavior is known as **container-managed transactions,** as transactions are managed by the EJB container. Application developers may also choose to manage transactions themselves. This can be accomplished by using bean-managed transactions. Both these approaches are discussed in the following sections:

Container-managed transactions

As EJB methods are transactional by default, we run into an interesting dilemma when a session bean is invoked from the client code that is already in a transaction. How should the EJB container behave? Should it suspend the client transaction, execute its method in a new transaction, then resume the client transaction? Should it not create a new transaction and execute its method as part of the client transaction? Should it throw an exception?

By default, if an EJB method is invoked by client code that is already in a transaction, the EJB container will simply execute the session bean method as part of the client transaction. If this is not the behavior we need, we can change it by decorating the method with the `@TransactionAttribute` annotation. This annotation has a `value` attribute that determines how the EJB container will behave when the session bean method is invoked within an existing transaction and when it is invoked outside any transactions. The value of the `value` attribute is typically a constant defined in the `javax.ejb.TransactionAttributeType` enum. The following table lists the possible values for the `@TransactionAttribute` annotation:

@TransactionAttribute value	Description
`TransactionAttributeType.MANDATORY`	Forces the method to be invoked as part of a client transaction. If the method is called outside any transactions, it will throw a `TransactionRequiredException`.
`TransactionAttributeType.NEVER`	The method is never executed in a transaction. If the method is invoked as part of a client transaction, it will throw a `RemoteException`. No transaction is created if the method is not invoked inside a client transaction.
`TransactionAttributeType.NOT_SUPPORTED`	If the method is invoked as part of a client transaction, the client transaction is suspended and the method is executed outside any transaction. After the method completes, the client transaction is resumed. No transaction is created if the method is not invoked inside a client transaction.
`TransactionAttributeType.REQUIRED`	If the method is invoked as part of a client transaction, the method is executed as part of said transaction. If the method is invoked outside any transaction, a new transaction is created for the method. This is the default behavior.
`TransactionAttributeType.REQUIRES_NEW`	If the method is invoked as part of a client transaction, said transaction is suspended and a new transaction is created for the method. Once the method completes, the client transaction is resumed. If the method is called outside any transactions, a new transaction is created for the method.
`TransactionAttributeType.SUPPORTS`	If the method is invoked as part of a client transaction, it is executed as part of said transaction. If the method is invoked outside a transaction, no new transaction is created for the method.

Although the default transaction attribute is reasonable in most cases, it is good to be able to override this default transaction attribute if necessary. For example, transactions have a performance impact, therefore being able to turn off transactions for a method that does not need them is beneficial. For a case like this, we would decorate our method as illustrated in the following code snippet:

```
@TransactionAttribute(value=TransactionAttributeType.NEVER)
public void doitAsFastAsPossible()
{
  //performance critical code goes here.
}
```

Other transaction attribute types can be declared by annotating the methods with the corresponding constant in the `TransactionAttributeType` enum.

If we wish to override the default transaction attribute consistently across all methods in a session bean, we can decorate the session bean class with the `@TransactionAttribute` annotation. The value of its `value` attribute will be applied to every method in the session bean.

Container-managed transactions are automatically rolled back whenever an exception is thrown inside an EJB method. Additionally, we can programmatically roll back a container-managed transaction by invoking the `setRollbackOnly()` method on an instance of `javax.ejb.EJBContext` corresponding to the session bean in question. The following example is a new version of the session bean we saw earlier in this chapter, modified to roll back transactions if necessary:

```
package net.ensode.glassfishbook;

import java.sql.Connection;
import java.sql.PreparedStatement;
import java.sql.ResultSet;
import java.sql.SQLException;

import javax.annotation.Resource;
import javax.ejb.EJBContext;
import javax.ejb.Stateless;
import javax.persistence.EntityManager;
import javax.persistence.PersistenceContext;
import javax.sql.DataSource;

@Stateless
public class CustomerDaoRollbackBean implements CustomerDaoRollback
{
  @Resource
  private EJBContext ejbContext;

  @PersistenceContext
  private EntityManager entityManager;

  @Resource(name = "jdbc/__CustomerDBPool")
```

```
    private DataSource dataSource;

    public void saveNewCustomer(Customer customer)
    {
      if (customer == null || customer.getCustomerId() != null)
      {
        ejbContext.setRollbackOnly();
      }
      else
      {
        customer.setCustomerId(getNewCustomerId());
        entityManager.persist(customer);
      }
    }
    public void updateCustomer(Customer customer)
    {
      if (customer == null || customer.getCustomerId() == null)
      {
        ejbContext.setRollbackOnly();
      }
      else
      {
        entityManager.merge(customer);
      }
    }
    //Additional method omitted for brevity.
  }
```

In this version of the DAO session bean, we deleted the `saveCustomer()` method and made the `saveNewCustomer()` and `updateCustomer()` methods `public`. Each of these methods now checks to see if the `customerId` field is set correctly for the operation we are trying to perform (`null` for inserts and `not null` for updates). It also checks to make sure that the object to be persisted is not null. If any of the checks result in invalid data, the method simply rolls back the transaction by invoking the `setRollBackOnly()` method on the injected instance of `EJBContext` and does not update the database.

Bean-managed transactions

As we have seen, container-managed transactions make it ridiculously easy to write code that is wrapped in a transaction. After all, there is nothing special we need to do to make them that way. As a matter of fact, some developers are sometimes not even aware that they are writing code that will be transactional in nature when they develop session beans. Container-managed transactions cover most of the typical cases that we will encounter. However, they do have a limitation: each method can be wrapped in a single transaction or with no transaction. With container-managed transactions, it is not possible to implement a method that generates more than one transaction. However, this can be accomplished by using **bean-managed transactions**.

```
package net.ensode.glassfishbook;

import java.sql.Connection;
import java.sql.PreparedStatement;
import java.sql.ResultSet;
import java.sql.SQLException;
import java.util.List;

import javax.annotation.Resource;
import javax.ejb.Stateless;
import javax.ejb.TransactionManagement;
import javax.ejb.TransactionManagementType;
import javax.persistence.EntityManager;
import javax.persistence.PersistenceContext;
import javax.sql.DataSource;
import javax.transaction.UserTransaction;

@Stateless
@TransactionManagement(value = TransactionManagementType.BEAN)
public class CustomerDaoBmtBean implements CustomerDaoBmt
{
  @Resource
  private UserTransaction userTransaction;

  @PersistenceContext
  private EntityManager entityManager;

  @Resource(name = "jdbc/__CustomerDBPool")
  private DataSource dataSource;

  public void saveMultipleNewCustomers(List<Customer> customerList)
  {
    for (Customer customer : customerList)
    {
      try
      {
        userTransaction.begin();
        customer.setCustomerId(getNewCustomerId());
        entityManager.persist(customer);
        userTransaction.commit();
```

```
        }
        catch (Exception e)
        {
          e.printStackTrace();
        }
      }
    }
    private Long getNewCustomerId()
    {
      Connection connection;
      Long newCustomerId = null;
      try
      {
        connection = dataSource.getConnection();
        PreparedStatement preparedStatement =
          connection.prepareStatement("select " +
          "max(customer_id)+1 as new_customer_id " +
          "from customers");
        ResultSet resultSet = preparedStatement.executeQuery();
        if (resultSet != null && resultSet.next())
        {
          newCustomerId = resultSet.getLong("new_customer_id");
        }
        connection.close();
      }
      catch (SQLException e)
      {
        e.printStackTrace();
      }
      return newCustomerId;
    }
  }
```

In this example, we implemented a method named `saveMultipleNewCustomers()`. This method takes an `ArrayList` of customers as its sole parameter. The intention of this method is to save as many elements in the `ArrayList` as possible. An exception saving one of the entities should not stop the method from attempting to save the remaining elements. This behavior is not possible using container-managed transactions, as an exception thrown when saving one of the entities would roll back the whole transaction. The only way to achieve this behavior is through bean-managed transactions.

As can be seen in the example, we declare that the session bean uses bean-managed transactions by decorating the class with the `@TransactionManagement` annotation and using `TransactionManagementType.BEAN` as the value for its `value` attribute (the only other valid value for this attribute is `TransactionManagementType.CONTAINER`, but as this is the default value, it is not necessary to specify it).

To be able to programmatically control transactions, we inject an instance of `javax.transaction.UserTransaction`, which is then used in the `for` loop inside the `saveMultipleNewCustomers()` method to begin and commit a transaction in each iteration of the loop.

If we need to roll back a bean-managed transaction, we can do it by simply calling the `rollback()` method on the appropriate instance of `javax.transaction.UserTransaction`.

Before moving on, it is worth noting that even though all the examples in this section were session beans, the concepts explained apply to message-driven beans as well.

Enterprise JavaBeans life cycle

Enterprise JavaBeans go through different states in their life cycle. Each type of EJB has different states. States specific to each type of EJB are discussed in the next sections.

Stateful session bean life cycle

Readers experienced with previous versions of J2EE may remember that in previous versions of the specification, session beans were required to implement the `javax.ejb.SessionBean` interface. This interface provides methods to be executed at certain points in the session bean's life cycle. Methods provided by the `SessionBean` interface include:

- `ejbActivate()`
- `ejbPassivate()`
- `ejbRemove()`
- `setSessionContext(SessionContext ctx)`

The first three methods are meant to be executed at certain points in the bean's life cycle. In most cases, there is nothing to do in the implementation of these methods. This fact resulted in the vast majority of session beans implementing empty versions of these methods. Thankfully, starting with Java EE 5, it is no longer necessary to implement the `SessionBean` interface. However, if necessary, we can still write methods that will get executed at certain points in the bean's life cycle. We can achieve this by decorating the methods with specific annotations.

Before explaining the annotations available to implement the life cycle methods, a brief explanation of the session bean life cycle is in order. The life cycle of a stateful session bean is different from the life cycle of a stateless session bean.

A stateful session bean life cycle contains three states: **Does Not Exist**, **Ready**, and **Passive**.

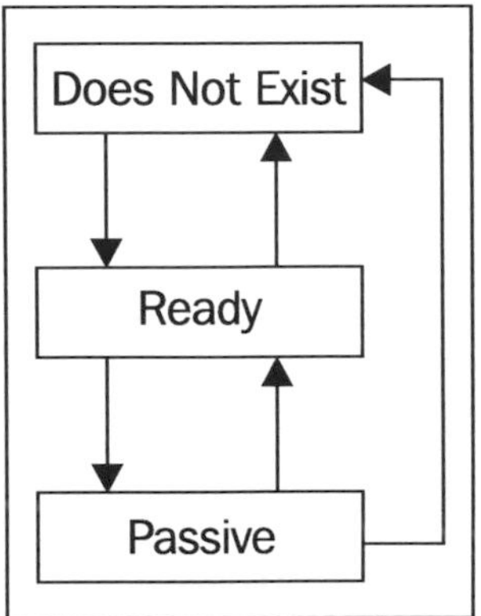

Before a stateful session bean is deployed, it is in the **Does Not Exist** state. Upon successful deployment, the EJB container does any required dependency injection on the bean and it goes into the **Ready** state. At this point, the bean is ready to have its methods called by a client application.

When a stateful session bean is in the **Ready** state, the EJB container may decide to passivate it, that is, to move it from the main memory to the secondary storage. When this happens, the bean goes into the **Passive** state.

If an instance of a stateful session bean hasn't been accessed for a period of time, the EJB container will set the bean to the **Does Not Exist** state. By default, GlassFish will send a stateful session bean to the **Does Not Exist** state after 90 minutes of inactivity. This default value can be changed by going to the GlassFish administration console, expanding the **Configuration** node in the tree at the left-hand side, clicking on the **EJB Container** node, then scrolling down towards the bottom of the page and modifying the value of the **Removal Timeout** text field, then clicking on the **Save** button at the top right of the main page.

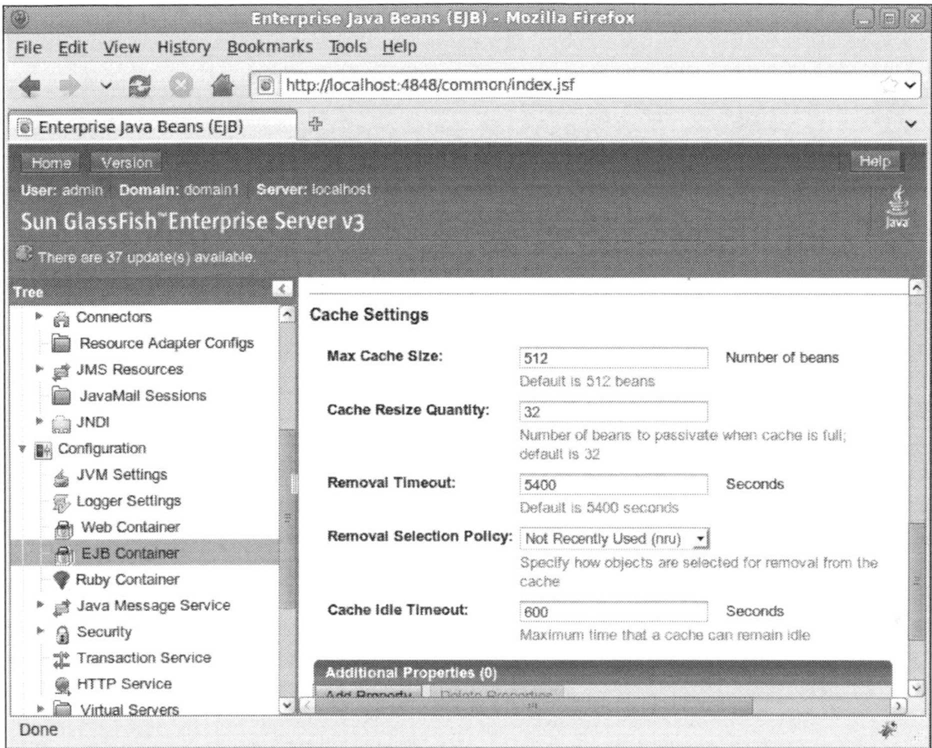

However, this technique sets the timeout value for all stateful session beans. If we need to modify the timeout value for a specific session bean, we need to include a `sun-ejb-jar.xml` deployment descriptor in the JAR file containing the session bean. In this deployment descriptor, we can set the timeout value as the value of the `<removal-timeout-in-seconds>` element:

```
<?xml version="1.0" encoding="UTF-8" standalone="no"?>
<!DOCTYPE sun-ejb-jar PUBLIC "-//Sun Microsystems, Inc.//DTD
  Application Server 9.0 EJB 3.0//EN"
  "http://www.sun.com/software/appserver/dtds/sun-ejb-jar_3_0-0.dtd">
<sun-ejb-jar>
  <enterprise-beans>
    <ejb>
      <ejb-name>MyStatefulSessionBean</ejb-name>
      <bean-cache>
        <removal-timeout-in-seconds>
          600
        </removal-timeout-in-seconds>
      </bean-cache>
    </ejb>
  </enterprise-beans>
</sun-ejb-jar>
```

Even though we are not required to create an `ejb-jar.xml` deployment descriptor for our session beans anymore (this used to be the case in previous versions of the J2EE specification), we can still write one if we wish to do so. The `<ejb-name>` element in the `sun-ejb-jar.xml` deployment descriptor must match the value of the element of the same name in `ejb-jar.xml`. If we choose not to create an `ejb-jar.xml` deployment descriptor, then this value must match the name of the EJB class. The timeout value for a stateful session bean must be the value of the `<removal-timeout-in-seconds>` element. As the name of the element suggests, the unit of time to use is seconds. In the previous example, we set the timeout value to 600 seconds (or 10 minutes).

Any methods in a stateful session bean decorated with the `@PostActivate` annotation will be invoked just after the stateful session bean has been activated. This is equivalent to implementing the `ejbActivate()` method in previous versions of J2EE. Similarly, any method decorated with the `@PrePassivate` annotation will be invoked just before the stateful session bean is passivated. This is equivalent to implementing the `ejbPassivate()` method in previous versions of J2EE.

When a stateful session bean that is in the **Ready** state times out and is sent to the **Does Not Exist** state, any method decorated with the `@PreDestroy` annotation is executed. If the session bean is in the **Passive** state and it times out, methods decorated with the `@PreDestroy` annotation are not executed. Additionally, if a client of the stateful session bean executes any method decorated with the `@Remove` annotation, any methods decorated with the `@PreDestroy` annotation are executed and the bean is marked for garbage collection. Decorating a method with the `@Remove` annotation is equivalent to implementing the `ejbRemove()` method in previous versions of the J2EE specification.

The `@PostActivate`, `@PrePassivate`, and `@Remove` annotations are valid only for stateful session beans. The `@PreDestroy` and `@PostConstruct` annotations are valid for stateful session beans, stateless session beans, and message-driven beans.

Stateless session bean life cycle

A stateless session bean life cycle contains only the **Does Not Exist** and **Ready** states:

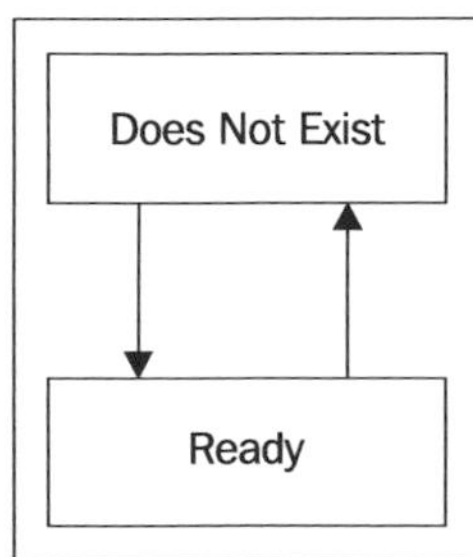

Stateless session beans are never passivated. A stateless session bean's methods can be decorated with the `@PostConstruct` and `@PreDestroy` annotations. Just like in stateful session beans, any methods decorated with the `@PostConstruct` annotation will be executed when the stateless session bean goes from the **Does Not Exist** to the **Ready** state, and any methods decorated with the `@PreDestroy` annotation will be executed when a stateless session bean goes from the **Ready** state to the **Does Not Exist** state. Stateless session beans are never passivated, therefore any `@PrePassivate` and `@PostActivate` annotations in a stateless session bean are simply ignored by the EJB container.

Just like with stateful session beans, we can control how GlassFish manages the life cycle of stateless session beans (and message-driven beans, discussed in the next section) via the administration web console:

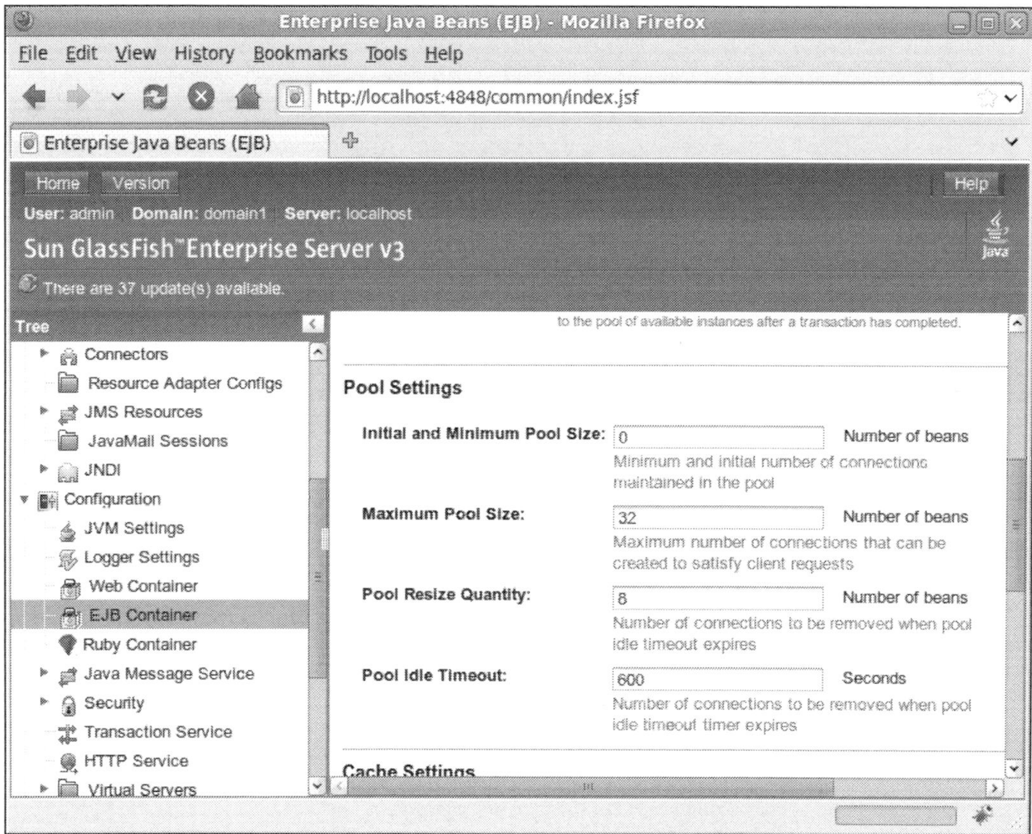

Initial and Minimum Pool Size refers to the minimum number of beans in the pool.

Maximum Pool Size refers to the maximum number of beans in the pool.

Pool Resize Quantity refers to how many beans will be removed from the pool when the pool idle timeout expires.

Pool Idle Timeout refers to the number of seconds or inactivity to wait before removing the beans from the pool.

These settings affect all "poolable" (stateless session beans and message-driven beans) EJBs. Just like with stateful session beans, these settings can be overridden on a case-by-case basis by adding a GlassFish-specific `sun-ejb-jar.xml` deployment descriptor:

```
<?xml version="1.0" encoding="UTF-8"?>
<!DOCTYPE sun-ejb-jar
  PUBLIC "-//Sun Microsystems, Inc.//DTD Application Server 9.0 EJB
    3.0//EN"
  "http://www.sun.com/software/appserver/dtds/sun-ejb-jar_3_0-0.dtd">
<sun-ejb-jar>
  <enterprise-beans>
    <ejb>
      <ejb-name>MyStatelessSessionBean</ejb-name>
      <bean-pool>
        <steady-pool-size>10</steady-pool-size>
        <max-pool-size>60</max-pool-size>
        <resize-quantity>5</resize-quantity>
        <pool-idle-timeout-in-seconds>
          900
        </pool-idle-timeout-in-seconds>
      </bean-pool>
    </ejb>
  </enterprise-beans>
</sun-ejb-jar>
```

`<steady-pool-size>` corresponds to **Initial and Minimum Pool Size** in the GlassFish web console.

`<max-pool-size>` corresponds to **Maximum Pool Size** in the GlassFish web console.

`<resize-quantity>` corresponds to **Pool Resize Quantity** in the GlassFish web console.

`<pool-idle-timeout-in-seconds>` corresponds to **Pool Idle Timeout** in the GlassFish web console.

Message-driven bean life cycle

Just like stateless session beans, message-driven beans contain only the **Does Not Exist** and **Ready** states:

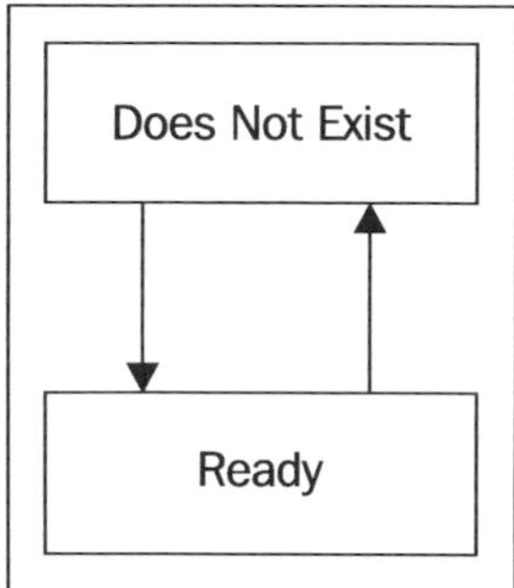

A message-driven bean can have methods decorated with the `@PostConstruct` and `@PreDestroy` annotations. Methods decorated with the `@PostConstruct` annotation are executed just before the bean goes to the **Ready** state. Methods decorated with the `@PreDestroy` annotation are executed just before the bean goes to the **Does Not Exist** state.

EJB timer service

Stateless session beans and message-driven beans can have a method that is executed periodically at regular intervals of time. This can be accomplished by using the **EJB timer service**. The following example illustrates how to take advantage of this service:

```
package net.ensode.glassfishbook;

import java.io.Serializable;
import java.util.Collection;
import java.util.Date;
import java.util.logging.Logger;

import javax.annotation.Resource;
import javax.ejb.EJBContext;
import javax.ejb.Stateless;
import javax.ejb.Timeout;
import javax.ejb.Timer;
import javax.ejb.TimerService;
@Stateless
```

```
public class EjbTimerExampleBean implements EjbTimerExample
{
  private static Logger logger =
    Logger.getLogger(EjbTimerExampleBean.class.getName());
  @Resource
  TimerService timerService;

  public void startTimer(Serializable info)
  {
    Timer timer = timerService.createTimer(new Date(), 5000, info);
  }

  public void stopTimer(Serializable info)
  {
    Timer timer;
    Collection timers = timerService.getTimers();
    for (Object object : timers)
         timer = ((Timer) object);
      if (timer.getInfo().equals(info))
      {
         timer.cancel();
         break;
      }
    }
  }

  @Timeout
  public void logMessage(Timer timer)
  {
    logger.info("This message was triggered by :" + timer.getInfo()
      + " at " + System.currentTimeMillis());
  }
}
```

In this example, we inject an implementation of the `javax.ejb.TimerService` interface by decorating an instance variable of this type with the `@Resource` annotation. We can then create a timer by invoking the `createTimer()` method of this `TimerService` instance.

There are several overloaded versions of the `createTimer()` method. The one we chose to use takes an instance of `java.util.Date` as its first parameter. This parameter is used to indicate the first time the timer should expire (go off). In the example, we chose to use a brand new instance of the `Date` class, which in effect makes the timer expire immediately. The second parameter of the `createTimer()` method is the amount of time to wait, in milliseconds, before the timer expires again. In the previous example, the timer will expire every five seconds. The third parameter of the `createTimer()` method can be an instance of any class implementing the `java.io.Serializable` interface. As a single EJB can have several timers executing concurrently, this third parameter is used to uniquely identify each of the timers. If we don't need to identify the timers, `null` can be passed as a value for this parameter.

> The EJB method invoking `TimerService.createTimer()` must be called from an EJB client. Placing this call in an EJB method decorated with the `@PostConstruct` annotation to start the timer automatically when the bean is placed in the **Ready** state will result in an `IllegalStateException` being thrown.

We can stop a timer by invoking its `cancel()` method. There is no way to directly obtain a single timer associated with an EJB. What we need to do is invoke the `getTimers()` method on the instance of `TimerService` that is linked to the EJB. This method will return a collection containing all the timers associated with the EJB. We can then iterate through the collection and cancel the correct one by invoking its `getInfo()` method. This method will return the `Serializable` object we passed as a parameter to the `createTimer()` method.

Finally, any EJB method decorated with the `@Timeout` annotation will be executed when a timer expires. Methods decorated with this annotation must return `void` and take a single parameter of type `javax.ejb.Timer`. In our example, the method simply writes a message to the server log.

The following class is a standalone client for the previous EJB:

```
package net.ensode.glassfishbook;

import javax.ejb.EJB;

public class Client
{
  @EJB
  private static EjbTimerExample ejbTimerExample;

  public static void main(String[] args)
  {
```

```
        try
        {
          System.out.println("Starting timer 1...");
          ejbTimerExample.startTimer("Timer 1");
          System.out.println("Sleeping for 2 seconds...");
          Thread.sleep(2000);
          System.out.println("Starting timer 2...");
          ejbTimerExample.startTimer("Timer 2");
          System.out.println("Sleeping for 30 seconds...");
          Thread.sleep(30000);
          System.out.println("Stopping timer 1...");
          ejbTimerExample.stopTimer("Timer 1");
          System.out.println("Stopping timer 2...");
          ejbTimerExample.stopTimer("Timer 2");
          System.out.println("Done.");
        }
        catch (InterruptedException e)
        {
          e.printStackTrace();
        }
      }
    }
```

The example simply starts a timer, waits for a couple of seconds, then starts a second timer. It then sleeps for 30 seconds and then stops both the timers. After deploying the EJB and executing the client, we should see some entries like the following in the server log:

```
[#|2007-05-05T20:41:39.518-0400|INFO|sun-
appserver9.1|net.ensode.glassfishbook.EjbTimerExampleBean|_ThreadID=22;_
ThreadName=p: thread-pool-1; w: 16;|This message was triggered by :Timer
1 at 1178412099518|#]

[#|2007-05-05T20:41:41.536-0400|INFO|sun-
appserver9.1|net.ensode.glassfishbook.EjbTimerExampleBean|_ThreadID=22;_
ThreadName=p: thread-pool-1; w: 16;|This message was triggered by :Timer
2 at 1178412101536|#]

[#|2007-05-05T20:41:46.537-0400|INFO|sun-
appserver9.1|net.ensode.glassfishbook.EjbTimerExampleBean|_ThreadID=22;_
ThreadName=p: thread-pool-1; w: 16;|This message was triggered by :Timer
1 at 1178412106537|#]

[#|2007-05-05T20:41:48.556-0400|INFO|sun-
appserver9.1|net.ensode.glassfishbook.EjbTimerExampleBean|_ThreadID=22;_
ThreadName=p: thread-pool-1; w: 16;|This message was triggered by :Timer
2 at 1178412108556|#]
```

These entries are created each time one of the timers expires.

Calendar-based EJB timer expressions

The example in the previous section has one disadvantage: the `startTimer()` method in the session bean must be invoked from a client in order to start the timer. This restriction makes it difficult to have the timer start as soon as the bean is deployed.

Java EE 6 introduced calendar-based EJB timer expressions. Calendar-based expressions allow one or more methods in our session beans to be executed at a certain date and time. For example, we could configure one of our methods to be executed every night at 8:10 pm, which is exactly what our next example does.

```
package com.ensode.glassfishbook.calendarbasedtimer;

import java.util.logging.Logger;
import javax.ejb.Stateless;
import javax.ejb.LocalBean;
import javax.ejb.Schedule;

@Stateless
@LocalBean
public class CalendarBasedTimerEjbExampleBean
{
  private static Logger logger = Logger.getLogger(
    CalendarBasedTimerEjbExampleBean.class.getName());
  @Schedule(hour = "20", minute = "10")
  public void logMessage()
  {
    logger.info("This message was triggered at:"
      + System.currentTimeMillis());
  }
}
```

As we can see in this example, we set the time when the method will be executed via the `javax.ejb.Schedule` annotation. In this particular example, we set our method to be executed at 8:10 pm by setting the `hour` attribute of the `@Schedule` annotation to `"20"` and its `minute` attribute to `"10"` (the value of the `hour` attribute is 24 hour based, setting `hour` to `"20"` is equivalent to 8:00 pm).

The `@Schedule` annotation has several other attributes that allow a lot of flexibility in specifying when the method should be executed. We could, for instance, have a method executed on the third Friday of every month, or on the last day of the month, and so on and so forth.

The following table lists all the attributes in the `@Schedule` annotation that allow us to control when the annotated method will be executed:

Attribute	Description	Example values	Default value
`dayOfMonth`	The day of the month.	"3": the third day of the month "Last": the last day of the month "-2": two days before the end of the month "1st Tue": the first Tuesday of the month	"*"
`dayOfWeek`	The day of the week	"3": every Wednesday "Thu": every Thursday	"*"
`hour`	Hour of the day (24 hour based)	"14": 2:00 pm	"0"
`minute`	Minute of the hour	"10": ten minutes after the hour	"0"
`month`	Month of the year	"2": February "March": March	"*"
`second`	Second of the minute	"5": five seconds after the minute	"0"
`timezone`	Timezone ID	"America/New York"	""
`year`	Four digit year	"2010"	"*"

In addition to single values, most attributes accept the asterisk ("*") as a wild card, meaning that the annotated method will be executed every unit of time (every day, hour, and so on).

Additionally, we can specify more than one value by separating the values with commas. For example, if we needed a method to be executed every Tuesday and Thursday, we could annotate the method as `@Schedule(dayOfWeek="Tue, Thu")`.

We can also specify a range of values; the first value and the last value are separated by a dash (-). To execute a method from Monday through Friday, we could use `@Schedule(dayOfWeek="Mon-Fri")`.

Additionally, we could specify that we need the method to be executed every "n" units of time (for example, every day, every two hours, every ten minutes, and so on). To do something like this, we could use `@Schedule(hour="*/12")`, which would execute the method every 12 hours.

As we can see, the `@Schedule` annotation provides a lot of flexibility as how to specify when we need to get our methods executed. Plus it provides an advantage of not needing a client call to activate the scheduling. It also has the advantage of using cron-like syntax. Therefore, developers familiar with this Unix tool will feel right at home when using this annotation.

EJB security

Enterprise JavaBeans allow us to declaratively decide which users can access their methods. For example, some methods might only be available to users in certain roles. A typical scenario is that only users with a role of administrator can add, delete, or modify other users in the system.

The following example is a slightly modified version of the DAO session bean we saw earlier in this chapter. In this version, some methods that were previously private were made public. Additionally, the session bean was modified to allow only users in certain roles to access its methods.

```
package net.ensode.glassfishbook;

import java.sql.Connection;
import java.sql.PreparedStatement;
import java.sql.ResultSet;
import java.sql.SQLException;

import javax.annotation.Resource;
import javax.annotation.security.RolesAllowed;
import javax.ejb.Stateless;
import javax.persistence.EntityManager;
import javax.persistence.PersistenceContext;
import javax.sql.DataSource;

@Stateless
@RolesAllowed("appadmin")
public class CustomerDaoBean implements CustomerDao
{
  @PersistenceContext
  private EntityManager entityManager;

  @Resource(name = "jdbc/__CustomerDBPool")
  private DataSource dataSource;

  public void saveCustomer(Customer customer)
  {
    if (customer.getCustomerId() == null)
```

```
    {
      saveNewCustomer(customer);
    }
    else
    {
      updateCustomer(customer);
    }
  }

  public Long saveNewCustomer(Customer customer)
  {
    customer.setCustomerId(getNewCustomerId());
    entityManager.persist(customer);
    return customer.getCustomerId();
  }
  public void updateCustomer(Customer customer)
  {
    entityManager.merge(customer);
  }

  @RolesAllowed({ "appuser", "appadmin" })
  public Customer getCustomer(Long customerId)
  {
    Customer customer;
    customer = entityManager.find(Customer.class, customerId);
    return customer;
  }

  public void deleteCustomer(Customer customer)
  {
    entityManager.remove(customer);
  }

  private Long getNewCustomerId()
  {
    Connection connection;
    Long newCustomerId = null;
    try
    {
      connection = dataSource.getConnection();
      PreparedStatement preparedStatement =
        connection.prepareStatement("select max(customer_id)+1 "
        "as new_customer_id from customers");
      ResultSet resultSet = preparedStatement.executeQuery();
      if (resultSet != null && resultSet.next())
      {
        newCustomerId = resultSet.getLong("new_customer_id");
```

```
        }
        connection.close();
      }
      catch (SQLException e)
      {
        e.printStackTrace();
      }
      return newCustomerId;
    }
  }
```

As we can see, we declare what roles have access to the methods by using the `@RolesAllowed` annotation. This annotation can take either a single string or an array of strings as a parameter. When a single string is used as a parameter for this annotation, only users with a role specified by the parameter can access the method. If an array of strings is used as a parameter, users with any of the roles specified by the array's elements can access the method.

The `@RolesAllowed` annotation can be used to decorate an EJB class, in which case its values apply to all the methods in the EJB or to one or more methods. In this second case, its values apply only to the method the annotation is decorating. If, like in our example, both the EJB class and one or more of its methods are decorated with the `@RolesAllowed` annotation, the method-level annotation takes precedence.

Application roles need to be mapped to a security realm's group name. This mapping, along with what realm to use, is set in the `sun-ejb-jar.xml` deployment descriptor:

```
<?xml version="1.0" encoding="UTF-8"?>
<!DOCTYPE sun-ejb-jar PUBLIC "-//Sun Microsystems, Inc.//DTD
  Application Server 9.0 EJB 3.0//EN"
  "http://www.sun.com/software/appserver/dtds/sun-ejb-jar_3_0-0.dtd">
<sun-ejb-jar>
  <security-role-mapping>
    <role-name>appuser</role-name>
    <group-name>appuser</group-name>
  </security-role-mapping>
  <security-role-mapping>
    <role-name>appadmin</role-name>
    <group-name>appadmin</group-name>
  </security-role-mapping>
  <enterprise-beans>
    <ejb>
      <ejb-name>CustomerDaoBean</ejb-name>
      <ior-security-config>
```

```
            <as-context>
              <auth-method>username_password</auth-method>
              <realm>file</realm>
              <required>true</required>
            </as-context>
          </ior-security-config>
        </ejb>
      </enterprise-beans>
    </sun-ejb-jar>
```

The `<security-role-mapping>` element of the `sun-ejb-jar.xml` deployment descriptor does the mapping between application roles and the security realm's group. The value of the `<role-name>` sub-element must contain the application role. This value must match the value used in the `@RolesAllowed` annotation. The value of the `<group-name>` sub-element must contain the name of the security group in the security realm used by the EJB. In the previous example, we map two application roles to the corresponding groups in the security realm. Although in this particular example the name of the application role and the security group match, this does not need to be the case.

> **Automatically matching roles to security groups**
>
> It is possible to automatically match any application roles to identically named security groups in the security realm. This can be accomplished by logging into the GlassFish web console, clicking on the **Configuration** node, clicking on **Security**, then clicking on the checkbox labeled **Default Principal To Role Mapping**, and saving this configuration change.

As can be seen in the example, the security realm to use for authentication is defined in the `<realm>` sub-element of the `<as-context>` element. The value of this sub-element must match the name of a valid security realm in the application server. Other sub-elements of the `<as-context>` element include `<auth-method>`, whose only valid value is `username_password`, and `<required>`, whose only valid values are `true` and `false`.

Client authentication

If the client code accessing a secured EJB is part of a web application whose user has already authenticated, then the user's credentials will be used to determine if the user should be allowed to access the method he/she is trying to execute.

Standalone clients must be executed through the `appclient` utility. The following code illustrates a typical client for the previous secured session bean:

```
package net.ensode.glassfishbook;

import javax.ejb.EJB;

public class Client
{
  @EJB
  private static CustomerDao customerDao;

  public static void main(String[] args)
  {
    Long newCustomerId;

    Customer customer = new Customer();
    customer.setFirstName("Mark");
    customer.setLastName("Butcher");
    customer.setEmail("butcher@phony.org");

    System.out.println("Saving New Customer...");
    newCustomerId = customerDao.saveNewCustomer(customer);

    System.out.println("Retrieving customer...");
    customer = customerDao.getCustomer(newCustomerId);
    System.out.println(customer);
  }
}
```

As we can see, there is nothing the code is doing in order to authenticate the user. The session bean is simply injected into the code via the `@EJB` annotation and it is used as usual. The reason this works is because the `appclient` utility takes care of authenticating the user. Passing the `-user` and `-password` arguments with appropriate values will authenticate the user:

```
appclient -client ejbsecurityclient.jar -user peter -password secret
```

This command will authenticate a user with a username of "peter" and a password of "secret". Assuming the credentials are correct and that the user has the appropriate permissions, the EJB code will execute and we should see the expected output from the previous `Client` class:

```
Saving New Customer...
Retrieving customer...
customerId = 29
firstName = Mark
```

```
lastName = Butcher
email = butcher@phony.org
```

If we don't enter the username and password from the command line, `appclient` will prompt us for a username and password through a graphical window. In our example, entering the following command:

```
appclient -client ejbsecurityclient.jar
```

Will result in a pop-up window like the following to show up:

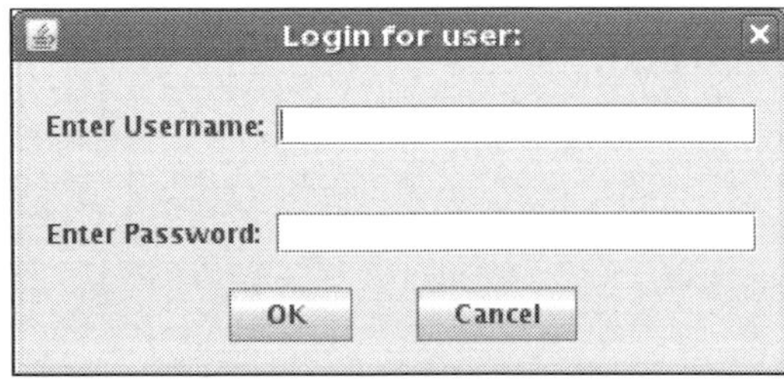

We can simply enter our username and password in the appropriate fields. After validating the credentials, the application will execute as expected.

Summary

In this chapter, we covered how to implement business logic via stateless and stateful session beans. We also explained how to take advantage of the transactional nature of EJBs to simplify implementing the Data Access Object (DAO) pattern.

Additionally, we explained the concept of container-managed transactions and how to control them by using the appropriate annotations. We also explained how to implement bean-managed transactions for cases in which container-managed transactions are not enough to satisfy our requirements.

Life cycles for the different types of Enterprise JavaBeans were covered, including an explanation on how to have EJB methods automatically invoked by the EJB container at certain points in the life cycle.

We also covered how to have EJB methods invoked periodically by the EJB container by taking advantage of the EJB timer service.

Finally, we explained how to make sure that EJB methods are only invoked by authorized users by annotating the EJB classes and/or methods and by adding the appropriate entries to the `sun-ejb-jar.xml` deployment descriptor.

10
Contexts and Dependency Injection

Contexts and Dependency Injection (**CDI**) is a new addition to the Java EE specification as of Java EE 6. It provides several advantages that were previously unavailable to Java EE developers, such as allowing any JavaBean to be used as a JSF managed bean, including stateless and stateful session beans. As its name implies, CDI simplifies dependency injection in Java EE applications.

In this chapter, we will cover the following topics:

- Named beans
- Dependency injection
- Scopes
- Qualifiers

Named beans

CDI provides us with the ability to name our beans via the `@Named` annotation. Named beans allow us to easily inject our beans into other classes that depend on them (see next section), and to easily refer to them from JSF pages via the Unified Expression Language.

The following example shows the @Named annotation in action:

```
package net.ensode.cdidependencyinjection.beans;

import javax.enterprise.context.RequestScoped;
import javax.inject.Named;

@Named
@RequestScoped
public class Customer
{
  private String firstName;
  private String lastName;

  public String getFirstName()
  {
    return firstName;
  }

  public void setFirstName(String firstName)
  {
    this.firstName = firstName;
  }

  public String getLastName()
  {
    return lastName;
  }

  public void setLastName(String lastName)
  {
    this.lastName = lastName;
  }
}
```

As we can see, all we need to do to name our class is to decorate it with the @Named annotation. By default, the name of the bean will be the class name with its first letter switched to lowercase. In our example, the name of the bean would be "customer". If we wish to use a different name, we can do so by setting the value attribute of the @Named annotation. For example, if we wanted to use the name "customerBean" for our previous bean, we could have done so by modifying the @Named annotation as follows:

```
@Named(value="customerBean")
```

Or simply:

```
@Named("customerBean")
```

As the `value` attribute name does not need to be specified, if we don't use an attribute name, then `value` is implied.

This name can be used to access our bean from JSF pages using the Unified Expression Language.

```
<?xml version='1.0' encoding='UTF-8' ?>
<!DOCTYPE html PUBLIC "-//W3C//DTD XHTML 1.0 Transitional//EN"
  "http://www.w3.org/TR/xhtml1/DTD/xhtml1-transitional.dtd">
<html xmlns="http://www.w3.org/1999/xhtml"
      xmlns:h="http://java.sun.com/jsf/html">
  <h:head>
    <title>Enter Customer Information</title>
  </h:head>
  <h:body>
    <h:form>
      <h:panelGrid columns="2">
        <h:outputLabel for="firstName" value="First Name"/>
        <h:inputText id="firstName" value="#{customer.firstName}"/>
        <h:outputLabel for="lastName" value="Last Name"/>
        <h:inputText id="lastName" value="#{customer.lastName}"/>
        <h:panelGroup/>
      </h:panelGrid>
    </h:form>
  </h:body>
</html>
```

As we can see, named beans are accessed from JSF pages exactly like standard JSF managed beans. This allows JSF to access any named bean, decoupling the Java code from the JSF API.

When deployed and executed, our simple application looks like this:

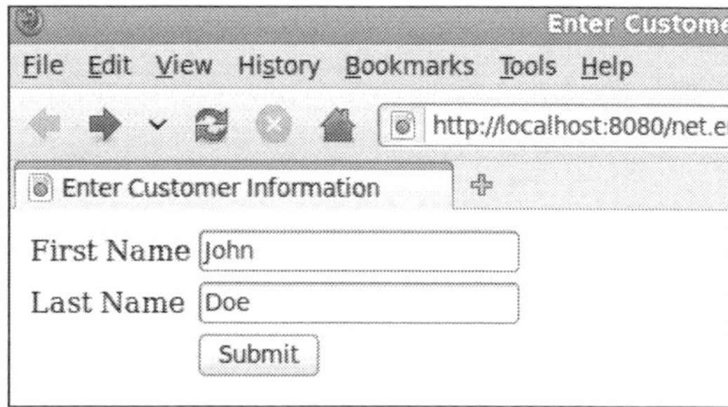

CDI applications must include a `beans.xml` configuration file as the presence of this file tells the application server to activate CDI for the application. The file can be empty, but it must exist. Typically, it would look as follows:

```
<?xml version="1.0" encoding="UTF-8"?>
<beans xmlns="http://java.sun.com/xml/ns/javaee"
       xmlns:xsi="http://www.w3.org/2001/XMLSchema-instance"
       xsi:schemaLocation="http://java.sun.com/xml/ns/javaee
         http://java.sun.com/xml/ns/javaee/beans_1_0.xsd">
</beans>
```

In web applications, this file must be placed under the `WEB-INF` directory in the application's WAR file. In EJB JAR files, this file must be placed in the `META-INF` directory.

Dependency injection

Dependency injection is a technique for supplying external dependencies to a Java class. Java EE 5 introduced dependency injection via the `@Resource` annotation. However, this annotation is limited to injecting resources such as database connections, JMS resources, and so on. Java EE 6 introduces the `@Inject` annotation that can be used to inject instances of Java classes into any dependent objects.

JSF applications typically follow the Model-View-Controller (MVC) design pattern. As such, some JSF managed beans frequently take the role of controllers in the pattern, while others take the role of the model. This approach typically requires the controller managed bean to have access to one or more of the model managed beans.

Because of the pattern described in the previous paragraph, one of the most frequently asked JSF questions is how to access one managed bean from another. There is more than one way to do it, but before CDI, none of the ways were straightforward. Before CDI, the easiest way to do it was to declare a managed property in the controller managed bean, which required modifying the application's `faces-config.xml` file. Another approach was to use code like the following:

```
ELContext elc = FacesContext.getCurrentInstance().getELContext();
SomeBean someBean =
  (SomeBean) FacesContext.getCurrentInstance().getApplication()
    .getELResolver().getValue(elc, null, "someBean");
```

Here, `someBean` is the name of the bean as specified in the application's `faces-config.xml` file. As we can see, neither approach is simple or easy to remember. Fortunately, code like this is not needed anymore in Java EE 6, thanks to CDI's dependency injection capabilities.

```
package net.ensode.cdidependencyinjection.ejb;

import java.util.logging.Logger;
import javax.inject.Inject;
import javax.inject.Named;

@Named
@RequestScoped
public class CustomerController
{
  private static final Logger logger =
    Logger.getLogger(CustomerController.class.getName());
  @Inject
  private Customer customer;

  public String saveCustomer()
  {
    logger.info("Saving the following information \n" +
      customer.toString());
    //If this was a real application, we would have code to save
    //customer data to the database here.
    return "confirmation";
  }
}
```

Notice that all we had to do to initialize our customer instance was to decorate it with the `@Inject` annotation. When the bean is constructed by the application server, an instance of the `Customer` bean is automatically injected into this field. Notice that the injected bean is used in the `saveCustomer()` method. As we can see, CDI makes accessing one bean from another a snap, a far cry from the code we had to use in previous versions of the Java EE specification.

Qualifiers

In some instances, the type of bean we wish to inject into our code may be an interface or a Java superclass, but we may be interested in injecting a subclass or a class implementing the interface. For cases like this, CDI provides qualifiers we can use to indicate the specific type we wish to inject into our code.

A CDI qualifier is an annotation that must be decorated with the `@Qualifier` annotation. This annotation can then be used to decorate the specific subclass or interface implementation we wish to qualify. Additionally, the injected field in the client code needs to be decorated with the qualifier as well.

Suppose our application could have a special kind of customer, wherein frequent customers could be given the status of premium customers. To handle these premium customers, we could extend our `Customer` named bean and decorate it with the following qualifier:

```
package net.ensode.cdidependencyinjection.qualifiers;

import static java.lang.annotation.ElementType.TYPE;
import static java.lang.annotation.ElementType.FIELD;
import static java.lang.annotation.ElementType.PARAMETER;
import static java.lang.annotation.ElementType.METHOD;
import static java.lang.annotation.RetentionPolicy.RUNTIME;
import java.lang.annotation.Retention;
import java.lang.annotation.Target;
import javax.inject.Qualifier;

@Qualifier
@Retention(RUNTIME)
@Target({METHOD, FIELD, PARAMETER, TYPE})
public @interface Premium
{

}
```

Like we mentioned before, qualifiers are standard annotations. They typically have a retention of runtime and can target methods, fields, parameters or types, as illustrated in the previous example. The only difference between a qualifier and a standard annotation is that qualifiers are decorated with the `@Qualifier` annotation.

Once we have our qualifier in place, we need to use it to decorate the specific subclass or interface implementation:

```
package net.ensode.cdidependencyinjection.beans;

import javax.inject.Named;
import net.ensode.cdidependencyinjection.qualifiers.Premium;

@Named
@Premium
public class PremiumCustomer extends Customer
{
  private Integer discountCode;

  public Integer getDiscountCode()
  {
    return discountCode;
  }
```

```
    public void setDiscountCode(Integer discountCode)
    {
      this.discountCode = discountCode;
    }
  }
```

Once we have decorated the specific instance we need to qualify, we can use our qualifiers in the client code to specify the exact type of dependency we need:

```
package net.ensode.cdidependencyinjection.beans;

import java.util.Random;
import java.util.logging.Logger;
import javax.enterprise.context.RequestScoped;
import javax.inject.Inject;
import javax.inject.Named;
import net.ensode.cdidependencyinjection.qualifiers.Premium;

@Named
@RequestScoped
public class CustomerController
{
  private static final Logger logger =
    Logger.getLogger(CustomerController.class.getName());
  @Inject
  @Premium
  private Customer customer;

  public String saveCustomer()
  {
    PremiumCustomer premiumCustomer = (PremiumCustomer) customer;
    premiumCustomer.setDiscountCode(generateDiscountCode());

    logger.info("Saving the following information \n"
      + premiumCustomer.getFirstName() + " "
      + premiumCustomer.getLastName() + ", discount code = "
      + premiumCustomer.getDiscountCode());

    //If this was a real application, we would have code to save
    //customer data to the database here.

    return "confirmation";
  }

  public Integer generateDiscountCode()
  {
    return new Random().nextInt(100000);
  }
}
```

As we used our `@Premium` qualifier to decorate the customer field, an instance of `PremiumCustomer` is injected into that field, as this class is also decorated with the `@Premium` qualifier.

As far as our JSF pages go, we simply access our named bean as usual using its name:

```
<?xml version='1.0' encoding='UTF-8' ?>
<!DOCTYPE html PUBLIC "-//W3C//DTD XHTML 1.0 Transitional//EN"
  "http://www.w3.org/TR/xhtml1/DTD/xhtml1-transitional.dtd">
<html xmlns="http://www.w3.org/1999/xhtml"
      xmlns:h="http://java.sun.com/jsf/html">
  <h:head>
    <title>Enter Customer Information</title>
  </h:head>
  <h:body>
    <h:form>
      <h:panelGrid columns="2">
        <h:outputLabel for="firstName" value="First Name"/>
        <h:inputText id="firstName"
                     value="#{premiumCustomer.firstName}"/>
        <h:outputLabel for="lastName" value="Last Name"/>
        <h:inputText id="lastName"
                     value="#{premiumCustomer.lastName}"/>
        <h:outputLabel for="discountCode" value="Discount Code"/>
        <h:inputText id="discountCode"
                     value="#{premiumCustomer.discountCode}"/>
        <h:panelGroup/>
        <h:commandButton value="Submit"
                         action="#{customerController.saveCustomer}"/>
      </h:panelGrid>
    </h:form>
  </h:body>
</html>
```

In this example, we are using the default name for our bean, which is the class name with the first letter switched to lowercase.

Our simple application renders and acts just like a "plain" JSF application as far as the user is concerned.

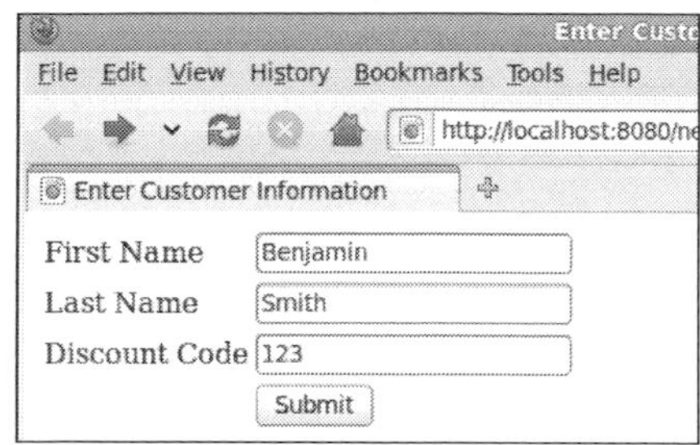

Named bean scopes

Just like JSF managed beans, CDI named beans are scoped. This means that CDI beans are contextual objects. When a named bean is needed, either because of injection or because it is referred from a JSF page, CDI looks for an instance of the bean in the scope it belongs to and injects it to the dependent code. If no instance is found, one is created and stored in the appropriate scope for future use. The different scopes are the context in which the bean exists.

The following table lists the different valid CDI scopes:

Scope	Annotation	Description
Request	`@RequestScoped`	Request-scoped beans are shared through the duration of a single request. A single request could refer to an HTTP request, an invocation to a method in an EJB, a web service invocation, or sending a JMS message to a message-driven bean.
Conversation	`@ConversationScoped`	The conversation scope can span multiple requests, but is typically shorter than the session scope.
Session	`@SessionScoped`	Session-scoped beans across all requests in an HTTP session. Each user of an application gets their own instance of a session-scoped bean.
Application	`@ApplicationScoped`	Application-scoped beans live through the whole application lifetime. Beans in this scope are shared across user sessions.
Dependent	`@Dependent`	Dependent-scoped beans are not shared. Anytime a dependent-scoped bean is injected, a new instance is created.

As we can see, CDI includes all scopes supported by JSF, plus adds a couple of its own. CDI's **request scope** differs from JSF's request scope in which a request does not necessarily refer to an HTTP request. It could simply be an invocation on an EJB method, a web service invocation, or sending a JMS message to a message-driven bean.

The **conversation scope** does not exist in JSF. This scope is longer than the request scope, but shorter than session. It typically spans three or more pages. Classes wishing to access a conversation-scoped bean must have an instance of `javax.enterprise.context.Conversation` injected. At the point where we want to start the conversation, the `begin()` method must be invoked on this object. At the point where we want to end the conversation, the `end()` method must be invoked on it.

CDI's **session scope** behaves just like its JSF counterpart. The life cycle of session-scoped beans is tied to the life of an HTTP session.

CDI's **application scope** also behaves just like the equivalent scope in JSF. Application-scoped beans are tied to the life of an application. A single instance of each application-scoped bean exists per application, which means that the same instance is accessible to all HTTP sessions.

Just like the conversation scope, CDI's **dependent scope** does not exist in JSF. A new dependent-scoped bean is instantiated every time it is needed, usually when it is injected into a class that depends on it.

Suppose we wanted to have a user enter some data that would be stored in a single named bean. However, this bean has several fields, therefore we would like to split the data entry into several pages. This is a fairly common situation and one that is not easy to handle using JSF, or the servlet API for that matter. The reason this situation is not trivial to manage using these technologies is that we can only put a class in the request scope, in which case the class is destroyed after every single request, losing its data in the process; or in session scope, in which the class sticks around in memory long after it is needed. For cases like this, CDI's conversation scope is ideal:

```
package net.ensode.conversationscope.model;

import java.io.Serializable;
import javax.enterprise.context.ConversationScoped;
import javax.inject.Named;
import org.apache.commons.lang.builder.ReflectionToStringBuilder;

@Named
@ConversationScoped
public class Customer implements Serializable
{
```

```
    private String firstName;
    private String middleName;
    private String lastName;
    private String addrLine1;
    private String addrLine2;
    private String addrCity;
    private String state;
    private String zip;
    private String phoneHome;
    private String phoneWork;
    private String phoneMobile;

    public String getAddrCity()
    {
      return addrCity;
    }

    public void setAddrCity(String addrCity)
    {
      this.addrCity = addrCity;
    }

    public String getAddrLine1()
    {
      return addrLine1;
    }

    public void setAddrLine1(String addrLine1)
    {
      this.addrLine1 = addrLine1;
    }

    public String getAddrLine2()
    {
      return addrLine2;
    }

    public void setAddrLine2(String addrLine2)
    {
      this.addrLine2 = addrLine2;
    }

    public String getFirstName()
    {
```

```
    return firstName;
  }

  public void setFirstName(String firstName)
  {
    this.firstName = firstName;
  }

  public String getLastName()
  {
    return lastName;
  }

  public void setLastName(String lastName)
  {
    this.lastName = lastName;
  }

  public String getMiddleName()
  {
    return middleName;
  }

  public void setMiddleName(String middleName)
  {
    this.middleName = middleName;
  }

  public String getPhoneHome()
  {
    return phoneHome;
  }

  public void setPhoneHome(String phoneHome)
  {
    this.phoneHome = phoneHome;
  }

  public String getPhoneMobile()
  {
    return phoneMobile;
  }

  public void setPhoneMobile(String phoneMobile)
```

```
    {
      this.phoneMobile = phoneMobile;
    }

    public String getPhoneWork()
    {
      return phoneWork;
    }

    public void setPhoneWork(String phoneWork)
    {
      this.phoneWork = phoneWork;
    }

    public String getState()
    {
      return state;
    }

    public void setState(String state)
    {
      this.state = state;
    }

    public String getZip()
    {
      return zip;
    }

    public void setZip(String zip)
    {
      this.zip = zip;
    }

    @Override
    public String toString()
    {
      return ReflectionToStringBuilder.reflectionToString(this);
    }
  }
```

We declare that our bean is conversation scoped by decorating it with the `@ConversationScoped` annotation. Conversation-scoped beans also need to implement `java.io.Serializable`. Other than these two requirements, there is nothing special about our code. It is a simple JavaBean with private properties and corresponding getter and setter methods.

> We are using the Apache `commons-lang` library in our code to easily implement a `toString()` method for our bean. `commons-lang` has several utility methods like this that implement frequently needed, tedious to code functionality. `commons-lang` is available in the central Maven repositories and at `http://commons.apache.org/lang`.

In addition to having our conversation-scoped bean injected, our client code must also have an instance of `javax.enterprise.context.Conversation` injected, as illustrated in the following example:

```
package net.ensode.conversationscope.controller;

import java.io.Serializable;
import javax.enterprise.context.Conversation;
import javax.enterprise.context.RequestScoped;
import javax.inject.Inject;
import javax.inject.Named;
import net.ensode.conversationscope.model.Customer;

@Named
@RequestScoped
public class CustomerInfoController implements Serializable
{
  @Inject
  private Conversation conversation;
  @Inject
  private Customer customer;

  public String customerInfoEntry()
  {
    conversation.begin();
    System.out.println(customer);
    return "page1";
  }

  public String navigateToPage1()
  {
    System.out.println(customer);
    return "page1";
```

```
    }

    public String navigateToPage2()
    {
      System.out.println(customer);
      return "page2";
    }

    public String navigateToPage3()
    {
      System.out.println(customer);
      return "page3";
    }

    public String navigateToConfirmationPage()
    {
      System.out.println(customer);
      conversation.end();
      return "confirmation";
    }
  }
```

Conversations can be either **long running** or **transient**. Transient conversations end at the end of a request. Long running conversations span multiple requests. In most cases, we will use long running conversations to hold a reference to a conversation-scoped bean across multiple HTTP requests in a web application.

A long running conversation starts when the `begin()` method is invoked in the injected `Conversation` instance, and it ends when we invoke the `end()` method on this same object.

JSF pages simply access our CDI beans as usual.

```
<?xml version='1.0' encoding='UTF-8' ?>
<!DOCTYPE html PUBLIC "-//W3C//DTD XHTML 1.0 Transitional//EN"
  "http://www.w3.org/TR/xhtml1/DTD/xhtml1-transitional.dtd">
<html xmlns="http://www.w3.org/1999/xhtml"
      xmlns:h="http://java.sun.com/jsf/html">
  <h:head>
    <title>Customer Information</title>
  </h:head>
  <h:body>
    <h3>Enter Customer Information (Page 1 of 3)</h3>
    <h:form>
      <h:panelGrid columns="2">
```

```
            <h:outputLabel for="firstName" value="First Name"/>
            <h:inputText id="firstName" value="#{customer.firstName}"/>
            <h:outputLabel for="middleName" value="Middle Name"/>
            <h:inputText id="middleName" value="#{customer.middleName}"/>
            <h:outputLabel for="lastName" value="Last Name"/>
            <h:inputText id="lastName" value="#{customer.lastName}"/>
            <h:panelGroup/>
            <h:commandButton value="Next"
                     action="#{customerInfoController.navigateToPage2}"/>
          </h:panelGrid>
        </h:form>
      </h:body>
    </html>
```

As we navigate from one page to the next, we keep the same instance of our conversation-scoped bean, therefore all user-entered data remains. When the `end()` method is called on our conversation bean, the conversation ends and our conversation-scoped bean is destroyed.

Keeping our bean in the conversation scope greatly simplifies the task of implementing "wizard-style" user interfaces, where data can be entered across several pages.

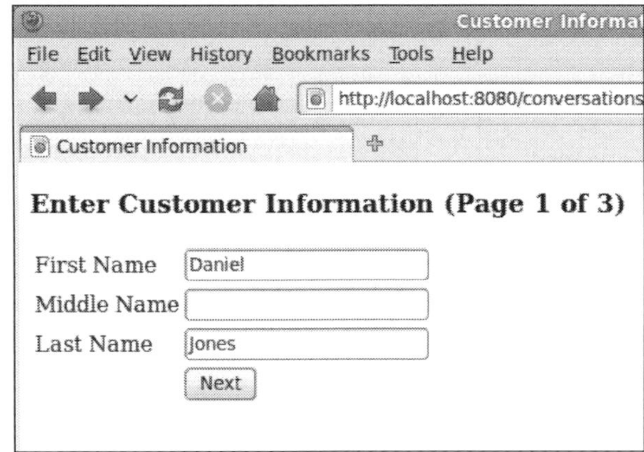

In our example, after clicking on the **Next** button on the first page, we can see our partially populated bean in the GlassFish log:

```
INFO:
net.ensode.conversationscope.model.Customer@6e1c51b4[firstName=Daniel,
middleName=,lastName=Jones,addrLine1=,addrLine2=,addrCity=,state=AL,
zip=<null>,phoneHome=<null>,phoneWork=<null>,phoneMobile=<null>]
```

At this point, the second page in our simple wizard is displayed:

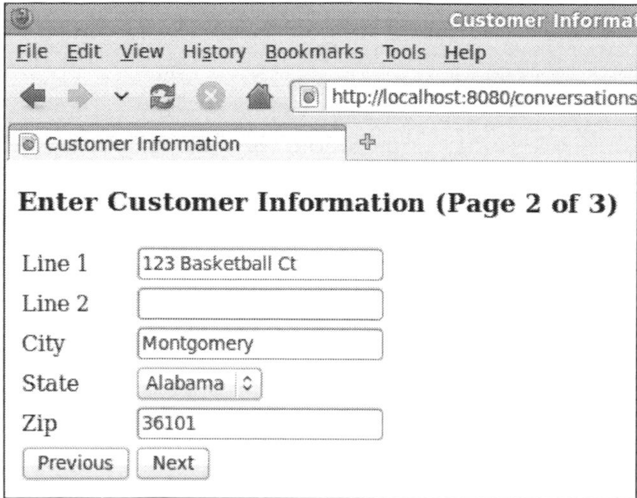

When clicking on **Next**, we can see that additional fields are populated in our conversation-scoped bean:

```
INFO:
net.ensode.conversationscope.model.Customer@6e1c51b4[firstName=Daniel,
middleName=,lastName=Jones,addrLine1=123 Basketball Ct,
addrLine2=,addrCity=Montgomery,state=AL,zip=36101,phoneHome=<null>,
phoneWork=<null>,phoneMobile=<null>]
```

When we submit the third page in our wizard (not shown), additional bean properties corresponding to the fields on that page are populated.

When we are at a point where we don't need to keep the customer information in memory anymore, we need to call the `end()` method on the conversation bean that was injected into our code. This is exactly what we do in our code before displaying the confirmation page:

```
public String navigateToConfirmationPage()
{
  System.out.println(customer);
  conversation.end();
  return "confirmation";
}
```

After the request to show the confirmation page is completed, our conversation-scoped bean is destroyed, as we invoked the `end()` method in our injected `Conversation` class.

We should note that since the conversation scope requires an instance of `javax.enterprise.context.Conversation` to be injected, this scope requires that the action in the command button or link used to navigate between pages be an expression resolving to a managed bean method. Using static navigation with the default behavior introduced in JSF 2.0 (where an action value of "foo" will, by default, navigate to a page named `foo.xml`) won't work, as the `Conversation` instance won't be injected anywhere.

Summary

In this chapter, we provided an introduction to Contexts and Dependency Injection (CDI). We covered how JSF pages can access CDI named beans as if they were JSF managed beans. We also covered how CDI makes it easy to inject dependencies into our code via the `@Inject` annotation. Additionally, we explained how we can use qualifiers to determine what specific implementation of dependency to inject into our code. Finally, we covered all the scopes that a CDI bean can be placed into, which include equivalents to all the JSF scopes, plus an additional two that are not included in JSF, namely the conversation scope and the dependent scope.

11
Web Services with JAX-WS

The Java EE 6 specification includes the JAX-WS API as one of its technologies. JAX-WS is the standard way to develop SOAP (Simple Object Access Protocol) web services in the Java platform. It stands for Java API for XML Web Services. JAX-WS is a high-level API; invoking web services via JAX-WS is done via remote procedure calls. JAX-WS is a very natural API for Java developers.

Web services are application programming interfaces that can be invoked remotely. Web services can be invoked from clients written in any language.

Some of the topics we will cover include:

- Developing web services with the JAX-WS API
- Developing web service clients with the JAX-WS API
- Adding attachments to web service calls
- Exposing EJBs as web services
- Securing web services

Developing web services with JAX-WS

JAX-WS is a high-level API that simplifies development of web services. JAX-WS stands for Java API for XML-Based Web Services. Developing a web service via JAX-WS consists of writing a class with public methods to be exposed as web services. The class needs to be decorated with the `@WebService` annotation. All public methods in the class are automatically exposed as web services; they can optionally be decorated with the `@WebService` annotation. The following example illustrates this process:

```
package net.ensode.glassfishbook;

import javax.jws.WebMethod;
import javax.jws.WebService;
```

```
@WebService
public class Calculator
{
  @WebMethod
  public int add(int first, int second)
  {
    return first + second;
  }

  @WebMethod
  public int subtract(int first, int second)
  {
    return first - second;
  }
}
```

This class exposes its two methods as web services. The `add()` method simply adds the two `int` primitives it receives as parameters and returns the result, the `substract()` method subtracts its two parameters and returns the result.

We indicate that the class implements a web service by decorating it with the `@WebService` annotation. Any methods that we would like exposed as web services can be decorated with the `@WebMethod` annotation, but this isn't necessary; all public methods are automatically exposed as web services.

To deploy our web service, we need to package it in a WAR file. Before Java EE 6, all valid WAR files were required to contain a `web.xml` deployment descriptor in their `WEB-INF` directory. As we have already covered in previous chapters, this deployment descriptor is optional when working with Java EE 6 and is not required to deploy a web service under this environment.

If we choose to add a `web.xml` deployment descriptor, nothing needs to be added to the WAR file's `web.xml` deployment descriptor. In order to successfully deploy our web service, simply having an empty `<web-app>` element in the deployment descriptor will be enough to successfully deploy our WAR file.

```
<?xml version="1.0" encoding="UTF-8"?>
<web-app xmlns="http://java.sun.com/xml/ns/javaee" version="2.5"
         xmlns:xsi="http://www.w3.org/2001/XMLSchema"
         xsi:schemaLocation="http://java.sun.com/xml/ns/javaee
           http://java.sun.com/xml/ns/javaee/web-app_2_5.xsd">
</web-app>
```

After compiling and packaging this code and deployment descriptor in a WAR file and deploying it, we can verify that it was successfully deployed by logging into the GlassFish admin web console and expanding the **Applications** node at the left-hand side. We should see our newly deployed web service listed under this node:

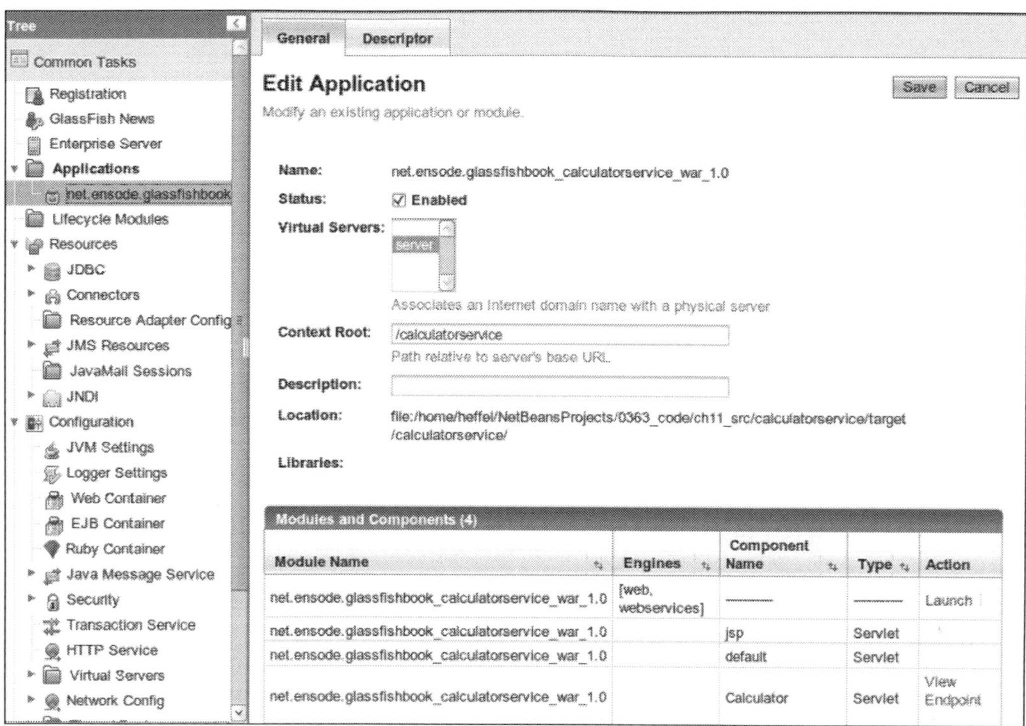
Tree
Common Tasks
Registration
GlassFish News
Enterprise Server
Applications
net.ensode.glassfishbook
Lifecycle Modules
Resources
JDBC
Connectors
Resource Adapter Config
JMS Resources
JavaMail Sessions
JNDI
Configuration
JVM Settings
Logger Settings
Web Container
EJB Container
Ruby Container
Java Message Service
Security
Transaction Service
HTTP Service
Virtual Servers
Network Config
General
Descriptor
Edit Application
Save
Cancel
Modify an existing application or module.
Name:
net.ensode.glassfishbook_calculatorservice_war_1.0
Status:
Enabled
Virtual Servers:
server
Associates an Internet domain name with a physical server
Context Root:
/calculatorservice
Path relative to server's base URL.
Description:
Location:
file:/home/heffel/NetBeansProjects/0363_code/ch11_src/calculatorservice/target/calculatorservice/
Libraries:
Modules and Components (4)
Module Name
Engines
Component Name
Type
Action
net.ensode.glassfishbook_calculatorservice_war_1.0
[web, webservices]
Launch
net.ensode.glassfishbook_calculatorservice_war_1.0
jsp
Servlet
net.ensode.glassfishbook_calculatorservice_war_1.0
default
Servlet
net.ensode.glassfishbook_calculatorservice_war_1.0
Calculator
Servlet
View Endpoint

Notice that there is a **View Endpoint** link at the bottom right of the page. Clicking on this link takes us to the **Web Service Endpoint Information** page, which has some information about our web service.

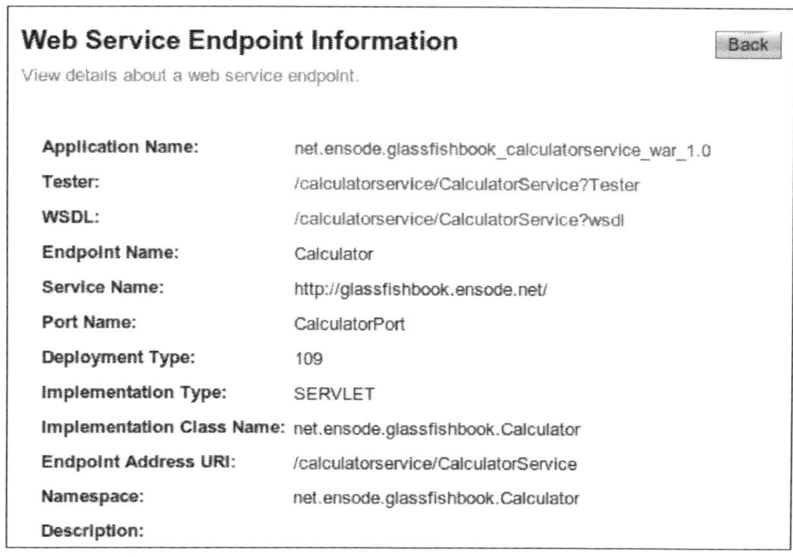
Web Service Endpoint Information
Back
View details about a web service endpoint.
Application Name:
net.ensode.glassfishbook_calculatorservice_war_1.0
Tester:
/calculatorservice/CalculatorService?Tester
WSDL:
/calculatorservice/CalculatorService?wsdl
Endpoint Name:
Calculator
Service Name:
http://glassfishbook.ensode.net/
Port Name:
CalculatorPort
Deployment Type:
109
Implementation Type:
SERVLET
Implementation Class Name:
net.ensode.glassfishbook.Calculator
Endpoint Address URI:
/calculatorservice/CalculatorService
Namespace:
net.ensode.glassfishbook.Calculator
Description:

Notice that there is a link labeled **Tester**; clicking on this link takes us to an automatically generated page that allows us to test our web service:

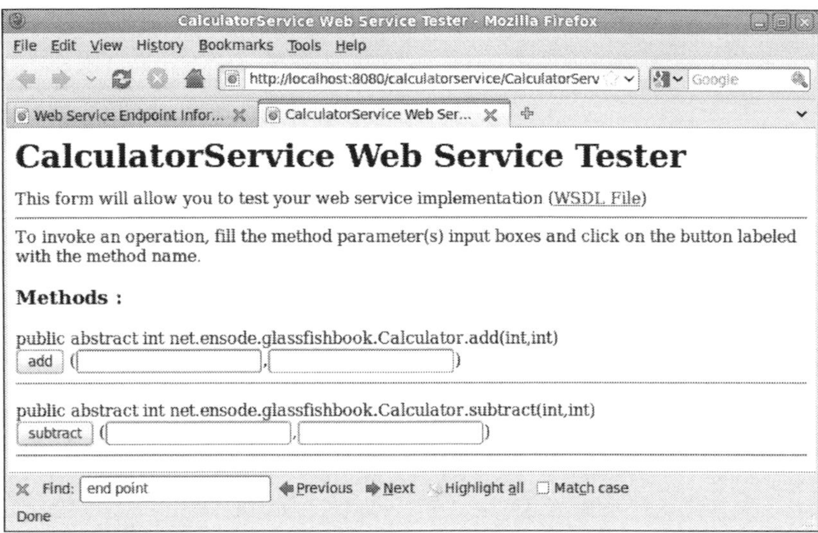

To test the methods, we have to simply enter some parameters in the text fields and click on the appropriate button. For example, entering the values 2 and 3 in the text fields corresponding to the `add` method and clicking on the **add** button would result in the following output:

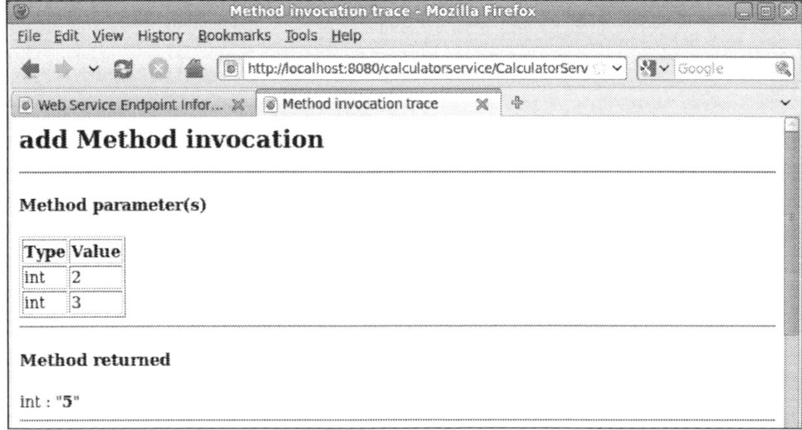

JAX-WS uses the SOAP protocol behind the scenes to exchange information between web services clients and servers. By scrolling down the previous page, we can see the SOAP request and response generated by our test:

SOAP Request

```
<?xml version="1.0" encoding="UTF-8"?>
<S:Envelope xmlns:S="http://schemas.xmlsoap.org/soap/envelope/">
    <S:Header/>
    <S:Body>
        <ns2:add xmlns:ns2="http://glassfishbook.ensode.net/">
            <arg0>2</arg0>
            <arg1>3</arg1>
        </ns2:add>
    </S:Body>
</S:Envelope>
```

SOAP Response

```
<?xml version="1.0" encoding="UTF-8"?>
<S:Envelope xmlns:S="http://schemas.xmlsoap.org/soap/envelope/">
    <S:Body>
        <ns2:addResponse xmlns:ns2="http://glassfishbook.ensode.net/">
            <return>5</return>
        </ns2:addResponse>
    </S:Body>
</S:Envelope>
```

As application developers, we don't need to concern ourselves too much with these SOAP requests, as they are automatically taken care of by the JAX-WS API.

Web service clients need a WSDL (Web Services Definition Language) file in order to generate executable code that they can use to invoke the web service. WSDL files are typically placed in a web server and accessed by the client via its URL. When deploying web services developed using JAX-WS, a WSDL is automatically generated for us. We can see it, along with its URL, by clicking on the **View WSDL** link in the **Web Service Endpoint Information** page.

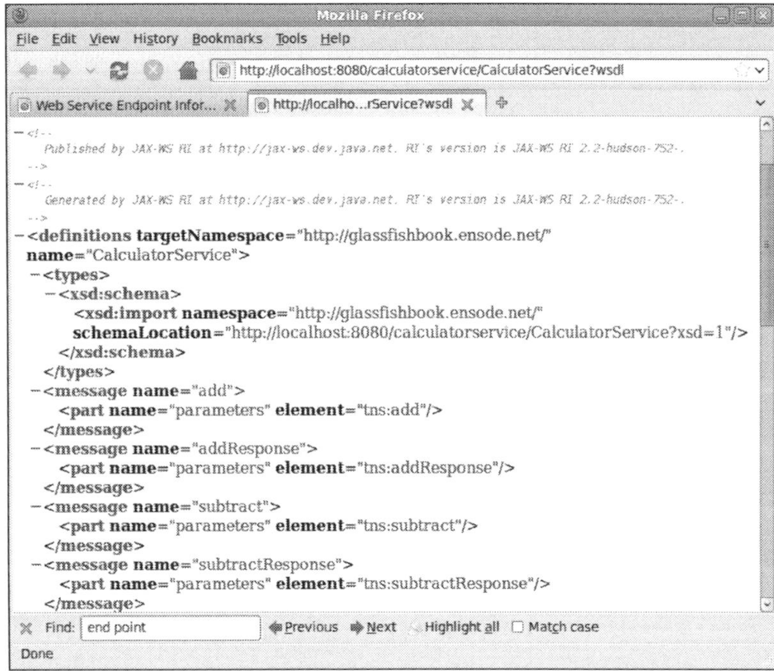

Notice the WSDL's URL in the browser's location text field; we will need this URL when developing a client for our web service.

Developing a web service client

Like we mentioned earlier, executable code needs to be generated from a web service's WSDL. A web service client will then invoke this executable code to access the web service:

GlassFish includes a utility to generate Java code from a WSDL. The name of the utility is `wsimport`. It can be found under `[glassfish installation directory]/glassfish/bin/`. The only required argument for `wsimport` is the URL of the WSDL corresponding to the web service:

```
wsimport http://localhost:8080/calculatorservice/CalculatorService?wsdl
```

This command will generate a number of compiled Java classes that allow client applications to access our web service:

- `Add.class`
- `AddResponse.class`
- `Calculator.class`
- `CalculatorService.class`
- `ObjectFactory.class`
- `package-info.class`
- `Subtract.class`
- `SubtractResponse.class`

Keeping generated source code

By default, the source code for the generated class files is automatically deleted; it can be kept by passing the `-keep` parameter to `wsimport`.

These classes need to be added to the client's CLASSPATH in order for them to be accessible to the client's code.

In addition to the command line tool, Glassfish includes a custom Ant task to generate code from a WSDL. The following Ant build script illustrates its usage:

```
<project name="calculatorserviceclient" default="wsimport"
  basedir=".">
  <target name="wsimport">
    <taskdef name="wsimport"
             classname="com.sun.tools.ws.ant.WsImport">
      <classpath path=
        "/opt/sges-v3/glassfish/modules/webservices-osgi.jar"/>
      <classpath path=
        "/opt/sges-v3/glassfish/modules/jaxb-osgi.jar"/>
      <classpath path="/opt/sges-v3/glassfish/lib/javaee.jar"/>
    </taskdef>
    <wsimport wsdl=
     "http://localhost:8080/calculatorservice/CalculatorService?wsdl"
              xendorsed="true"/>
  </target>
</project>
```

This example is a very minimal Ant build script that only illustrates how to set up the custom `<wsimport>` Ant target. In reality, the Ant build script for the project would have several other targets for compilation, building a WAR file, and so on.

As `<wsimport>` is a custom Ant target and is not standard, we need to add a `<taskdef>` element to our Ant build script. We need to set the `name` and `classname` attributes as illustrated in the example. Additionally, we need to add the following JAR files to the task's CLASSPATH via nested `<classpath>` elements:

- `webservices-osgi.jar`
- `jaxb-osgi.jar`
- `javaee.jar`

`webservices-osgi.jar` and `jaxb-osgi.jar` can be found under the `[glassfish installation directory]/glassfish/modules` directory. `javaee.jar` contains all Java EE 6 APIs and can be found under `[glassfish installation directory]/glassfish/lib`.

Once we set up the custom `<wsimport>` task via the `<taskdef>` element, we are ready to use it. We need to indicate the WSDL location via its `wsdl` attribute. Once this task executes, Java code needed to access the web service defined by the WSDL is generated.

JDK 1.6 comes bundled with JAX-WS 2.1. If we are using this version of JDK, we need to tell Ant to use the JAX-WS 2.2 API included with GlassFish. This can be done easily by setting the `xendorsed` attribute of the custom `wsimport` Ant task to `true`.

Readers using Maven to build their projects can take advantage of Maven's AntRun plugin to execute the `wsimport` Ant target when building their code. This approach is illustrated in the following `pom.xml` file:

```
<?xml version="1.0" encoding="UTF-8"?>
<project xmlns="http://maven.apache.org/POM/4.0.0"
        xmlns:xsi="http://www.w3.org/2001/XMLSchema-instance"
        xsi:schemaLocation="http://maven.apache.org/POM/4.0.0
          http://maven.apache.org/maven-v4_0_0.xsd">
  <modelVersion>4.0.0</modelVersion>
  <groupId>net.ensode.glassfishbook</groupId>
  <artifactId>calculatorserviceclient</artifactId>
  <packaging>jar</packaging>
  <name>Simple Web Service Client</name>
  <version>1.0</version>
  <url>http://maven.apache.org</url>
  <repositories>
    <repository>
```

```
      <id>maven2-repository.dev.java.net</id>
      <name>Java.net Repository for Maven 2</name>
      <url>http://download.java.net/maven/2/</url>
    </repository>
  </repositories>
  <dependencies>
    <dependency>
      <groupId>javax</groupId>
      <artifactId>javaee-api</artifactId>
      <version>6.0</version>
      <scope>provided</scope>
    </dependency>
  </dependencies>
  <build>
    <finalName>calculatorserviceclient</finalName>
    <plugins>
      <plugin>
        <groupId>org.apache.maven.plugins</groupId>
        <artifactId>maven-antrun-plugin</artifactId>
        <executions>
          <execution>
            <phase>generate-sources</phase>
            <configuration>
              <tasks>
                <property name="target.dir" value="target"/>

                <delete
                  dir="${target.dir}/classes/com/testapp/ws/client"/>
                <delete dir=
  "${target.dir}/generated-sources/main/java/com/testapp/ws/client"/>

                <mkdir dir="${target.dir}/classes"/>
                <mkdir dir=
                  "${target.dir}/generated-sources/main/java"/>

                <taskdef name="wsimport"
                         classname="com.sun.tools.ws.ant.WsImport">
                  <classpath path=
      "/home/heffel/sges-v3/glassfish/modules/webservices-osgi.jar"/>
                  <classpath path=
             "/home/heffel/sges-v3/glassfish/modules/jaxb-osgi.jar"/>
                  <classpath path=
                    "/home/heffel/sges-v3/glassfish/lib/javaee.jar"/>
                </taskdef>
                <wsimport
```

```
wsdl="http://localhost:8080/calculatorservice/CalculatorService?wsdl"
                  destdir="${target.dir}/classes"
                  verbose="true"
                  keep="true"
             sourceDestDir="${target.dir}/generated-sources/main/java"
                  xendorsed="true"/>
               </tasks>
               <sourceRoot>
                ${project.build.directory}/generated-sources/main/java
               </sourceRoot>
             </configuration>
             <goals>
               <goal>run</goal>
             </goals>
           </execution>
         </executions>
       </plugin>
       <plugin>
         <groupId>org.apache.maven.plugins</groupId>
         <artifactId>maven-jar-plugin</artifactId>
         <configuration>
           <archive>
             <manifest>
               <mainClass>
                 net.ensode.glassfishbook.CalculatorServiceClient
               </mainClass>
               <addClasspath>true</addClasspath>
             </manifest>
           </archive>
         </configuration>
       </plugin>
       <plugin>
         <groupId>org.apache.maven.plugins</groupId>
         <artifactId>maven-compiler-plugin</artifactId>
         <configuration>
           <source>1.6</source>
           <target>1.6</target>
         </configuration>
       </plugin>
     </plugins>
   </build>
 </project>
```

There is a wsimport Maven plugin, however, at the time of writing, it hasn't been updated to work with JAX-WS 2.2, which is the version included with Java EE 6.

Nested in the `<configuration>` tag corresponding to the AntRun plugin in the `pom.xml` file, we place any Ant tasks we need to execute. Unsurprisingly, the body of this tag in our example looks nearly identical to the Ant build file we just discussed.

Now that we know how to build our code with Ant or Maven, we can develop a simple client to access our web service:

```
package net.ensode.glassfishbook;

import javax.xml.ws.WebServiceRef;

public class CalculatorServiceClient
{
  @WebServiceRef(wsdlLocation =
    "http://localhost:8080/calculatorservice/CalculatorService?wsdl")
  private static CalculatorService calculatorService;

  public void calculate()
  {
    Calculator calculator = calculatorService.getCalculatorPort();
    System.out.println("1 + 2 = " + calculator.add(1, 2));
    System.out.println("1 - 2 = " + calculator.subtract(1, 2));
  }

  public static void main(String[] args)
  {
    new CalculatorServiceClient().calculate();
  }
}
```

The `@WebServiceRef` annotation injects an instance of the web service into our client application. Its `wsdlLocation` attribute contains the URL of the WSDL corresponding to the web service we are invoking.

Notice that the web service class is an instance of a class called `CalculatorService`; this class was created when we invoked the `wsimport` utility. `wsimport` always generates a class whose name is the name of the class we implemented plus the `Service` suffix. We use this service class to obtain an instance of the web service class we developed. In our example, we do this by invoking the `getCalculatorPort()` method on the `CalculatorService` instance. In general, the method to invoke to get an instance of our web service class follows the pattern of `getNamePort()`, where `Name` is the name of the class we wrote to implement the web service. Once we get an instance of our web service class, we can simply invoke its methods like with any regular Java object.

> Strictly speaking, the `getNamePort()` method of the service class returns an instance of a class implementing an interface generated by `wsimport`. This interface is given the name of our web service class and it declares all of the methods we declared to be web services. For all practical purposes, the object returned is equivalent to our web service class.

Recall from Chapter 9 that in order for resource injection to work in a standalone client (that does not get deployed to GlassFish), we need to execute it through the `appclient` utility. Assuming we packaged our client in a JAR file called `calculatorserviceclient.jar`, the command to execute would be:

```
appclient -client calculatorserviceclient.jar
```

After entering this command in the command line, we should see the output of our client on the console:

```
1 + 2 = 3
1 - 2 = -1
```

In this example, we passed primitive types as parameters and return values. Of course, it is also possible to pass objects both as parameters and as return values. Unfortunately, not all standard Java classes or primitive types can be used as method parameters or return values when invoking web services. The reason for this is that behind the scenes, method parameters and return types get mapped to XML definitions, and not all types can be properly mapped.

Valid types that can be used in JAX-WS web service calls are listed as follows:

- `java.awt.Image`
- `java.lang.Object`
- `java.lang.String`
- `java.math.BigDecimal`
- `java.math.BigInteger`
- `java.net.URI`
- `java.util.Calendar`
- `java.util.Date`
- `java.util.UUID`
- `javax.activation.DataHandler`
- `javax.xml.datatype.Duration`
- `javax.xml.datatype.XMLGregorianCalendar`
- `javax.xml.namespace.QName`
- `javax.xml.transform.Source`

Additionally, the following primitive types can be used:

- `boolean`
- `byte`
- `byte[]`
- `double`
- `float`
- `int`
- `long`
- `short`

We can also use our own custom classes as method parameters and/or return values for web service methods, but member variables of our classes must be one of the listed types.

Additionally, it is legal to use arrays both as method parameters or return values. However, when executing `wsimport`, these arrays get converted to lists, generating a mismatch between the method signature in the web service and the method call invoked in the client. For this reason, it is preferred to use lists as method parameters and/or return values, as this is also legal and does not create a mismatch between the client and the server.

JAX-WS internally uses the Java Architecture for XML Binding to create SOAP messages from method calls. The types we are allowed to use for method calls and return values are the ones that JAXB supports. For more information on JAXB, see `https://jaxb.dev.java.net/`.

Sending attachments to web services

In addition to sending and accepting the data types discussed in the previous sections, web service methods can send and accept file attachments. The following example illustrates how to do this:

```
package net.ensode.glassfishbook;

import java.io.FileOutputStream;
import java.io.IOException;

import javax.activation.DataHandler;
import javax.jws.WebMethod;
import javax.jws.WebService;
```

```
@WebService
public class FileAttachment
{
  @WebMethod
  public void attachFile(DataHandler dataHandler)
  {
    FileOutputStream fileOutputStream;
    try
    {
      // substitute "/tmp/attachment.gif" with
      // a valid path, if necessary.
      fileOutputStream = new FileOutputStream("/tmp/attachment.gif");
      dataHandler.writeTo(fileOutputStream);
      fileOutputStream.flush();
      fileOutputStream.close();
    }
    catch (IOException e)
    {
      e.printStackTrace();
    }
  }
}
```

In order to write a web service method that receives one or more attachments, all we need to do is add a parameter of type `javax.activation.DataHandler` for each attachment the method will receive. In the previous example, the `attachFile()` method takes a single parameter of this type and simply writes it to the file system.

Just like with any standard web service, the previous code needs to be packaged in a WAR file and deployed. Once deployed, a WSDL will automatically be generated. We then need to execute the `wsimport` utility to generate code that our web service client can use to access the web service. Like previously discussed, the `wsimport` utility can be invoked directly from the command line or via a custom Ant target. Once we have executed `wsimport` to generate code to access the web service, we can write and compile our client code.

```
package net.ensode.glassfishbook;

import java.io.File;
import java.io.FileInputStream;
import java.io.IOException;
import java.nio.ByteBuffer;
import java.nio.channels.FileChannel;
```

```
import javax.xml.ws.WebServiceRef;

public class FileAttachmentServiceClient
{
  @WebServiceRef(wsdlLocation =
    "http://localhost:8080/fileattachmentservice/"
    + "FileAttachmentService?wsdl")
  private static FileAttachmentService fileAttachmentService;

  public static void main(String[] args)
  {
    FileAttachment fileAttachment =
      fileAttachmentService.getFileAttachmentPort();
    File fileToAttach = new File("src/main/resources/logo.gif");
    byte[] fileBytes = fileToByteArray(fileToAttach);
    fileAttachment.attachFile(fileBytes);
    System.out.println("Successfully sent attachment.");
  }

  static byte[] fileToByteArray(File file)
  {
    byte[] fileBytes = null;

    try
    {
      FileInputStream fileInputStream;
      fileInputStream = new FileInputStream(file);

      FileChannel fileChannel = fileInputStream.getChannel();
      fileBytes = new byte[(int) fileChannel.size()];
      ByteBuffer byteBuffer = ByteBuffer.wrap(fileBytes);
      fileChannel.read(byteBuffer);
    }
    catch (IOException e)
    {
      e.printStackTrace();
    }
    return fileBytes;
  }
}
```

A web service client that needs to send one or more attachments to the web service first obtains an instance of the web service as usual. It then creates an instance of `java.io.File`, passing the location of the file to attach as its constructor's parameter. Once we have an instance of `java.io.File` containing the file we wish to attach, we then need to convert the file into a byte array and pass this byte array to the web service method that expects an attachment.

Notice that, unlike when passing standard parameters, the parameter type used when the client invokes a method expecting an attachment is different from the parameter type of the method in the web server code. The method in the web server code expects an instance of `javax.activation.DataHandler` for each attachment. However, the code generated by `wsimport` expects an array of bytes for each attachment. These arrays of bytes are converted to the right type (`javax.activation.DataHandler`) behind the scenes by the `wsimport` generated code. We as application developers don't need to concern ourselves with the details of why this happens. We just need to keep in mind that when sending attachments to a web service method, the parameter types will be different in the web service code and in the client invocation.

Exposing EJBs as web services

In addition to creating web services, as described in the previous section, public methods of stateless session beans can easily be exposed as web services. The following example illustrates how to do this:

```
package net.ensode.glassfishbook;

import javax.ejb.Stateless;
import javax.jws.WebService;

@Stateless
@WebService
public class DecToHexBean
{
  public String convertDecToHex(int i)
  {
    return Integer.toHexString(i);
  }
}
```

As we can see, the only thing we need to do to expose a stateless session bean's public methods is decorate its class declaration with the `@WebService` annotation. Needless to say, as the class is a session bean, it also needs to be decorated with the `@Stateless` annotation.

Just like regular stateless session beans, the ones whose methods are exposed as web services need to be deployed in a JAR file. Once deployed, we can see the new web service under the **Applications** node in the GlassFish administration web console. Clicking on the application's node, we can see some details in the GlassFish console:

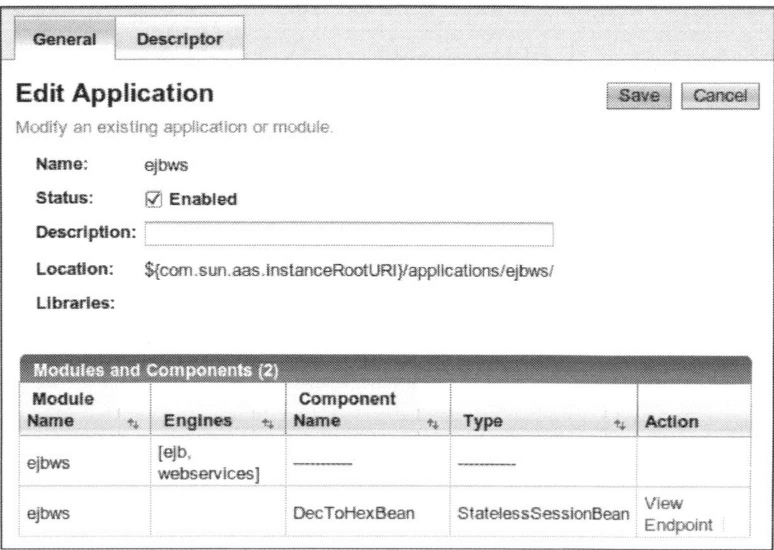

Notice that the value in the **Type** column for our new web service is **StatelessSessionBean**. This allows us to see at a glance that the web service is implemented as an Enterprise JavaBean.

Just like standard web services, EJB web services automatically generate a WSDL for use by its clients. Upon deployment, it can be accessed the same way by clicking on the **View EndPoint** link.

EJB web service clients

The following class illustrates the procedure to be followed to access an EJB web service method from a client application:

```
package net.ensode.glassfishbook;

import javax.xml.ws.WebServiceRef;

public class DecToHexClient
{
  @WebServiceRef(wsdlLocation =
    "http://localhost:8080/DecToHexBeanService/DecToHexBean?wsdl")
  private static DecToHexBeanService decToHexBeanService;
```

```
    public void convert()
    {
      DecToHexBean decToHexBean =
        decToHexBeanService.getDecToHexBeanPort();
      System.out.println("decimal 4013 in hex is: "
        + decToHexBean.convertDecToHex(4013));
    }

    public static void main(String[] args)
    {
      new DecToHexClient().convert();
    }
  }
```

As we can see, nothing special needs to be done when accessing an EJB web service from a client. The procedure is the same as with standard web services.

As the previous example is a standalone application, it needs to be executed via the `appclient` application:

```
appclient -client ejbwsclient.jar
```

This command results in the following output:

```
decimal 4013 in hex is: fad
```

Securing web services

Just like with regular web applications, web services can be secured so that only authorized users can access them. This can be accomplished by modifying the web service's `web.xml` deployment descriptor:

```
<?xml version="1.0" encoding="UTF-8"?>
<web-app xmlns="http://java.sun.com/xml/ns/javaee" version="2.5"
         xmlns:xsi="http://www.w3.org/2001/XMLSchema"
         xsi:schemaLocation="http://java.sun.com/xml/ns/javaee
           http://java.sun.com/xml/ns/javaee/web-app_2_5.xsd">
  <security-constraint>
    <web-resource-collection>
      <web-resource-name>Calculator Web Service</web-resource-name>
      <url-pattern>/CalculatorService/*</url-pattern>
      <http-method>POST</http-method>
    </web-resource-collection>
    <auth-constraint>
      <role-name>user</role-name>
    </auth-constraint>
```

```
    </security-constraint>
    <login-config>
      <auth-method>BASIC</auth-method>
      <realm-name>file</realm-name>
    </login-config>
</web-app>
```

In this example, we modify our calculator service so that only authorized users can access it. Notice that the modifications needed to secure the web service are no different from the modifications needed to secure any regular web application. The URL pattern to use for the `<url-pattern>` element can be obtained by clicking on the **View WSDL** link corresponding to our service. In our example, the URL for the link is `http://localhost:8080/calculatorservice/CalculatorService?wsdl`.

The value to use for `<url-pattern>` is the value right after the context root (in our example, `/CalculatorService`) and before the question mark, followed by a slash and an asterisk.

Notice that the previous `web.xml` deployment descriptor only secures HTTP POST requests. The reason for this is that `wsimport` uses a GET request to obtain the WSDL and to generate the appropriate code. If GET requests are secured, `wsimport` will fail as it will be denied access to the WSDL. Future versions of `wsimport` will allow us to specify a username and password for authentication. In the meantime, the workaround is to secure only POST requests.

The following code illustrates how a standalone client can access a secured web service:

```
package net.ensode.glassfishbook;

import javax.xml.ws.BindingProvider;
import javax.xml.ws.WebServiceRef;

public class CalculatorServiceClient
{
  @WebServiceRef(wsdlLocation =
"http://localhost:8080/securecalculatorservice/
CalculatorService?wsdl")
  private static CalculatorService calculatorService;

  public void calculate()
  {
    //add a user named "joe" with a password of "password"
    //to the file realm to successfuly execute the web service.
    //"joe" must belong to the group "appuser".
```

```
    Calculator calculator = calculatorService.getCalculatorPort();
    ((BindingProvider) calculator).getRequestContext().put(
      BindingProvider.USERNAME_PROPERTY, "joe");
    ((BindingProvider) calculator).getRequestContext().put(
      BindingProvider.PASSWORD_PROPERTY, "password");

    System.out.println("1 + 2 = " + calculator.add(1, 2));
    System.out.println("1 - 2 = " + calculator.subtract(1, 2));
  }

  public static void main(String[] args)
  {
    new CalculatorServiceClient().calculate();
  }
}
```

This code is a modified version of the calculator service standalone client we saw before. This version was modified to access the secure version of the service. As can be seen in the code, all we need to do to access the secured version of the server is put a username and password in the request context. The username and password must be valid for the realm used to authenticate the web service.

We can add the username and password to the request context by casting our web service endpoint class to `javax.xml.ws.BindingProvider` and calling its `getRequestContext()` method. This method returns a `java.util.Map` instance. We can then simply add the username and password by calling the put method in the `Map` and using the constants `USERNAME_PROPERTY` and `PASSWORD_PROPERTY` defined in `BindingProvider` as keys, and the corresponding `String` objects as values.

Securing EJB web services

Just like standard web services, EJBs exposed as web services can be secured so that only authorized clients can access them. This can be accomplished by configuring the EJB via the `sun-ejb-jar.xml` file:

```
<?xml version="1.0" encoding="UTF-8"?>
<!DOCTYPE sun-ejb-jar PUBLIC "-//Sun Microsystems, Inc.//DTD
  Application Server 9.0 EJB 3.0//EN"
  "http://www.sun.com/software/appserver/dtds/sun-ejb-jar_3_0-0.dtd">
<sun-ejb-jar>
  <enterprise-beans>
    <ejb>
      <ejb-name>SecureDecToHexBean</ejb-name>
      <webservice-endpoint>
```

```
            <port-component-name>
              SecureDecToHexBean
            </port-component-name>
            <login-config>
              <auth-method>BASIC</auth-method>
              <realm>file</realm>
            </login-config>
          </webservice-endpoint>
        </ejb>
      </enterprise-beans>
    </sun-ejb-jar>
```

As can be seen in this deployment descriptor, security is set up differently for EJBs exposed as web services than with standard EJBs. For EJBs exposed as web services, security configuration is done inside the `<webservice-endpoint>` element of the `sun-ejb-jar.xml` deployment descriptor.

The `<port-component-name>` element must be set to the name of the EJB we are exposing as a web service. This name is defined in the `<ejb-name>` element for the EJB.

The `<login-config>` element is very similar to the corresponding element in a web application's `web.xml` deployment descriptor. The `<login-config>` element must contain an authorization method defined by its `<auth-method>` sub-element and a realm to use for authentication. The realm is defined by the `<realm>` sub-element.

> Do not use the `@RolesAllowed` annotation for EJBs intended to be exposed as web services. This annotation is intended for when the EJB methods are accessed through its remote or local interface. If an EJB or one or more of its methods are decorated with this annotation, then invoking the method will fail with a security exception.

Once we configure an EJB web service for authentication, package it in a JAR file and deploy it as usual. The EJB web service is now ready to be accessed by clients.

The following code example illustrates how an EJB web service client can access a secure EJB web service:

```
package net.ensode.glassfishbook;

import javax.xml.ws.BindingProvider;
import javax.xml.ws.WebServiceRef;

public class DecToHexClient
{
```

```
  @WebServiceRef(wsdlLocation = "http://localhost:8080/
SecureDecToHexBeanService/SecureDecToHexBean?
  wsdl")
  private static SecureDecToHexBeanService secureDecToHexBeanService;

  public void convert()
  {
    SecureDecToHexBean secureDecToHexBean =
      secureDecToHexBeanService.getSecureDecToHexBeanPort();
    ((BindingProvider) secureDecToHexBean).getRequestContext().put(
      BindingProvider.USERNAME_PROPERTY, "joe");
    ((BindingProvider) secureDecToHexBean).getRequestContext().put(
      BindingProvider.PASSWORD_PROPERTY, "password");

    System.out.println("decimal 4013 in hex is: "
      + secureDecToHexBean.convertDecToHex(4013));
  }

  public static void main(String[] args)
  {
    new DecToHexClient().convert();
  }
}
```

As we can see in this example, the procedure for accessing an EJB exposed as a web service is identical to accessing a standard web service. The implementation of the web service is irrelevant to the client.

Summary

In this chapter, we covered how to develop web services and web service clients via the JAX-WS API. We explained how to incorporate web service code generation for web service clients when using ANT or Maven 2 as a build tool. We also covered the valid types that can be used for remote method calls via JAX-WS. Additionally, we discussed how to send attachments to a web service. We also covered how to expose an EJB's methods as web services. Lastly, we covered how to secure web services so that they are not accessible to unauthorized clients.

12 RESTful Web Services with Jersey and JAX-RS

Representational State Transfer (**REST**) is an architectural style in which web services are viewed as resources and can be identified by Uniform Resource Identifiers (URIs).

Web services developed using the REST style are known as RESTful web services.

Java EE 6 adds support to RESTful web services through the addition of the Java API for RESTful Web Services (JAX-RS). JAX-RS has been available as a standalone API for a while; it became part of Java EE in version 6 of the specification. In this chapter, we will cover how to develop RESTful web services through the JAX-RS API using Jersey—the JAX-RS implementation included by GlassFish.

The following topics will be covered in this chapter:

- Introduction to RESTful web services and JAX-RS
- Developing a simple RESTful web service
- Developing a RESTful web service client
- Path parameters
- Query parameters

Introduction to RESTful web services and JAX-RS

RESTful web services are very flexible. RESTful web services can consume several types of different MIME types, although they are typically written to consume and/or produce XML or JSON (JavaScript Object Notation).

Web services must support one or more of the following four HTTP methods:

- GET - By convention, a GET request is used to retrieve an existing resource
- POST - By convention, a POST request is used to update an existing resource
- PUT - By convention, a PUT request is used to create a new resource
- DELETE - By convention, a DELETE request is used to delete an existing resource

We develop a RESTful web service with JAX-RS by creating a class with annotated methods that are invoked when our web service receives one of these HTTP request methods. Once we have developed and deployed our RESTful web service, we need to develop a client that will send requests to our service. Jersey—the JAX-RS implementation included with GlassFish—includes an API that we can use to easily develop RESTful web service clients. Jersey's client-side API is a value-added feature and is not part of the JAX-RS specification.

Developing a simple RESTful web service

In this section, we will develop a simple web service to illustrate how we can make the methods in our service respond to the different HTTP request methods.

Developing a RESTful web service using JAX-RS is simple and straightforward. Each of our RESTful web services needs to be invoked via its Unique Resource Identifier (URI). This URI is specified by the `@Path` annotation, which we need to use to decorate our RESTful web service resource class.

When developing RESTful web services, we need to develop methods that will be invoked when our web service receives an HTTP request. We need to implement methods to handle one or more of the four types of requests that RESTful web services handle: GET, POST, PUT, and/or DELETE.

The JAX-RS API provides four annotations that we can use to decorate the methods in our web service. The annotations are appropriately named as `@GET`, `@POST`, `@PUT`, and `@DELETE`. Decorating a method in our web service with one of these annotations will make it respond to the corresponding HTTP method.

Additionally, each method in our service must produce and/or consume a specific MIME type. The MIME type to be produced needs to be specified with the `@Produces` annotation. Similarly, the MIME type to be consumed must be specified with the `@Consumes` annotation.

The following example illustrates the concepts we have just explained:

Please note that this example does not "really" do anything. The purpose of the example is to illustrate how to make the different methods in our RESTful web service resource class respond to the different HTTP methods.

```
package com.ensode.jaxrsintro.service;

import javax.ws.rs.Consumes;
import javax.ws.rs.DELETE;
import javax.ws.rs.GET;
import javax.ws.rs.POST;
import javax.ws.rs.PUT;
import javax.ws.rs.Path;
import javax.ws.rs.Produces;

@Path("customer")
public class CustomerResource
{
  @GET
  @Produces("text/xml")
  public String getCustomer()
  {
    //in a "real" RESTful service, we would retrieve data from a
    //database
    //then return an XML representation of the data.

    System.out.println("--- " + this.getClass().getCanonicalName()
      + ".getCustomer() invoked");

    return "<customer>\n"
      + "<id>123</id>\n"
      + "<firstName>Joseph</firstName>\n"
      + "<middleName>William</middleName>\n"
      + "<lastName>Graystone</lastName>\n"
      + "</customer>\n";
  }

  /**
   * Create a new customer
   * @param customer XML representation of the customer to create
   */
```

```
    @PUT
    @Consumes("text/xml")
    public void createCustomer(String customerXML)
    {
      //in a "real" RESTful service, we would parse the XML
      //received in the customer XML parameter, then insert
      //a new row into the database.

      System.out.println("--- " + this.getClass().getCanonicalName()
        + ".createCustomer() invoked");

      System.out.println("customerXML = " + customerXML);
    }

    @POST
    @Consumes("text/xml")
    public void updateCustomer(String customerXML)
    {
      //in a "real" RESTful service, we would parse the XML
      //received in the customer XML parameter, then update
      //a row in the database.

      System.out.println("--- " + this.getClass().getCanonicalName()
        + ".updateCustomer() invoked");

      System.out.println("customerXML = " + customerXML);
    }

    @DELETE
    @Consumes("text/xml")
    public void deleteCustomer(String customerXML)
    {
      //in a "real" RESTful service, we would parse the XML
      //received in the customer XML parameter, then delete
      //a row in the database.

      System.out.println("--- " + this.getClass().getCanonicalName()
        + ".deleteCustomer() invoked");

      System.out.println("customerXML = " + customerXML);
    }
  }
```

Notice that this class is annotated with the `@Path` annotation. This annotation designates the Uniform Resource Identifier (URI) for our RESTful web service. The complete URI for our service will include the protocol, server name, port, context root, the REST resources path (see next sub-section), and the value passed to this annotation.

Assuming our web service was deployed to a server called `example.com`, using the HTTP protocol on port `8080` has a context root of `jaxrsintro`, and a REST resources path of `resources`, then the complete URI for our service would be `http://example.com:8080/jaxrsintro/resources/customer`.

As web browsers generate a GET request when pointed to a URL, we can test the GET method of our service simply by pointing the browser to our service's URI.

Notice that each of the methods in our class is annotated with one of the `@GET`, `@POST`, `@PUT`, or `@DELETE` annotations. These annotations make our methods respond to the corresponding HTTP method.

Additionally, if our method returns data to the client, we declare the MIME type of the data to be returned in the `@Produces` annotation. In our example, only the `getCustomer()` method returns data to the client. We wish to return data in XML format, therefore, we set the value of the `@Produces` annotation to `"text/xml"`. Similarly, if our method needs to consume data from the client, we need to specify the MIME type of the data to be consumed. This is done via the `@Consumes` annotation. All methods except `getCustomer()` in our service consume data. In all cases, we expect the data to be in XML, therefore, we again specify `"text/xml"` as the MIME type to be consumed.

Configuring the REST resources path for our application

As briefly mentioned in the previous section, before successfully deploying a RESTful web service developed using JAX-RS, we need to configure the REST resources path for our application. There are two ways of doing this: we can either use the `web.xml` deployment descriptor or develop a class that extends `javax.ws.rs.core.Application` and decorate it with the `@ApplicationPath` annotation.

Configuring via web.xml

We can configure the REST resources path for our JAX-RS RESTful web services via the `web.xml` deployment descriptor.

Jersey libraries include a servlet that we can configure as usual in our `web.xml` deployment descriptor.

```
<?xml version="1.0" encoding="UTF-8"?>
<web-app xmlns="http://java.sun.com/xml/ns/javaee"
         xmlns:xsi="http://www.w3.org/2001/XMLSchema-instance"
         xsi:schemaLocation="http://java.sun.com/xml/ns/javaee
           http://java.sun.com/xml/ns/javaee/web-app_3_0.xsd"
         version="3.0">
  <servlet>
    <servlet-name>JerseyServlet</servlet-name>
    <servlet-class>
      com.sun.jersey.spi.container.servlet.ServletContainer
    </servlet-class>
    <load-on-startup>1</load-on-startup>
  </servlet>
  <servlet-mapping>
    <servlet-name>JerseyServlet</servlet-name>
    <url-pattern>/resources/*</url-pattern>
  </servlet-mapping>
</web-app>
```

As we can see in this markup, the fully qualified class name of the Jersey servlet is `com.sun.jersey.spi.container.servlet.ServletContainer`, which is the value we add to the `<servlet-class>` element in `web.xml`. We then give this servlet a logical name (we chose `JerseyServlet` in our example), then declare the URL pattern to be handled by the servlet as usual. Any URLs matching the pattern will be directed to the appropriate method in our RESTful web services.

As we can see, configuring the Jersey servlet isn't any different from configuring any other servlet.

Configuring via the @ApplicationPath annotation

As mentioned in previous chapters, Java EE 6 adds several new features to the Java EE specification, so that in many cases, it isn't necessary to write a `web.xml` deployment descriptor. JAX-RS is no different; we can configure the REST resources path in Java code via an annotation.

To configure our REST resources path without having to rely on a `web.xml` deployment descriptor, all we need to do is write a class that extends `javax.ws.ApplicationPath` and decorate it with the `@ApplicationPath` annotation. The value passed to this annotation is the REST resources path for our services.

The following code sample illustrates this process:

```
package com.ensode.jaxrsintro.service.config;

import javax.ws.rs.ApplicationPath;
import javax.ws.rs.core.Application;

@ApplicationPath("resources")
public class JaxRsConfig extends Application
{
}
```

Notice that the class does not have to implement any methods. It simply needs to extend `javax.ws.rs.Application` and get decorated with the `@ApplicationPath` annotation. The class must be public, may have any name, and may be placed in any package.

Testing our web service

Like we mentioned earlier, web browsers send a GET request to any URLs we point them to. Therefore, the easiest way to test GET requests to our service is to simply point the browser to our service's URI.

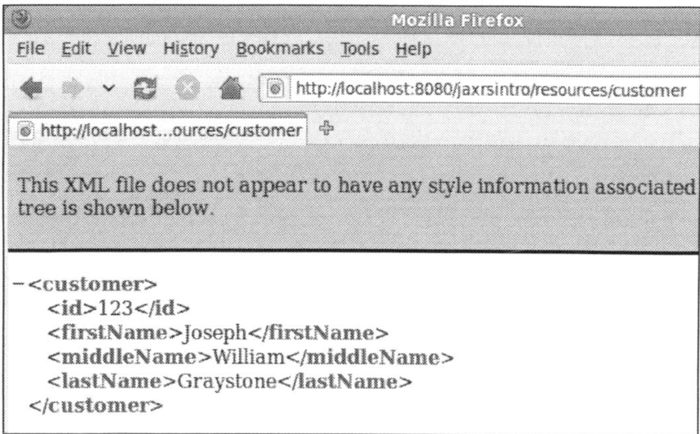

Web browsers only support GET and POST requests. To test a POST request through the browser, we would have to write a web application containing an HTML form having an action attribute value of our service's URI. Although trivial for a single service, it can become cumbersome to do this for every RESTful web service we develop.

Thankfully, there is an open source command line utility called `curl`, which we can use to test our web services. `curl` is included with most Linux distributions and can be easily downloaded for Windows, Mac OS X, and several other platforms. `curl` can be downloaded from `http://curl.haxx.se/`.

`curl` can send all four request method types (GET, POST, PUT, and DELETE) to our service. Our server's response will simply be displayed on the command line console. `curl` takes a `-X` command line option that allows us to specify what request method to send. To send a GET request, we simply need to type the following command into the command line:

```
curl -XGET http://localhost:8080/jaxrsintro/resources/customer
```

This results in the following output:

```
<customer>
<id>123</id>
<firstName>Joseph</firstName>
<middleName>William</middleName>
<lastName>Graystone</lastName>
</customer>
```

This, unsurprisingly, is the same output we saw when we pointed our browser to our service's URI.

The default request method for `curl` is GET. Therefore, the `-X` parameter in our previous example is redundant. We could have achieved the same result by invoking the following command from the command line:

```
curl http://localhost:8080/jaxrsintro/resources/customer
```

After submitting any of the previous two commands and examining the GlassFish log, we should see the output of the `System.out.println()` statements we added to the `getCustomer()` method:

```
INFO: --- com.ensode.jaxrsintro.service.CustomerResource.getCustomer()
invoked
```

For all other request method types, we need to send some data to our service. This can be accomplished by the `--data` command line argument to `curl`:

```
curl -XPUT -HContent-type:text/xml --data
"<customer><id>321</id><firstName>Amanda</firstName><middleName>Zoe
</middleName><lastName>Adams</lastName></customer>"
http://localhost:8080/jaxrsintro/resources/customer
```

As can be seen in this example, we need to specify the MIME type via the `-H` command line argument in `curl` using the format seen in the example.

We can verify that the previous command worked as expected by inspecting the GlassFish log:

```
INFO: ---
com.ensode.jaxrsintro.service.CustomerResource.createCustomer() invoked
INFO: customerXML =
<customer><id>321</id><firstName>Amanda</firstName><middleName>Zoe
</middleName><lastName>Adams</lastName></customer>
```

We can test other request method types just as easily:

```
curl -XPOST -HContent-type:text/xml --data
"<customer><id>321</id><firstName>Amanda</firstName><middleName>Tamara
</middleName><lastName>Adams</lastName></customer>"
http://localhost:8080/jaxrsintro/resources/customer
```

This results in the following output in the GlassFish log:

```
INFO: ---
com.ensode.jaxrsintro.service.CustomerResource.updateCustomer() invoked
INFO: customerXML =
<customer><id>321</id><firstName>Amanda</firstName><middleName>Tamara
</middleName><lastName>Adams</lastName></customer>
```

We can test the delete method by executing the following command:

```
curl -XDELETE -HContent-type:text/xml --data
"<customer><id>321</id><firstName>Amanda</firstName><middleName>Tamara
</middleName><lastName>Adams</lastName></customer>"
http://localhost:8080/jaxrsintro/resources/customer
```

This results in the following output in the GlassFish log:

```
INFO: ---
com.ensode.jaxrsintro.service.CustomerResource.deleteCustomer() invoked
INFO: customerXML =
<customer><id>321</id><firstName>Amanda</firstName><middleName>Tamara
</middleName><lastName>Adams</lastName></customer>
```

Converting data between Java and XML with JAXB

In our previous example, we were processing "raw" XML received as a parameter, as well as returning "raw" XML to our client. In a real application, we would more than likely parse the XML received from the client and use it to populate a Java object. Additionally, any XML that we need to return to the client would have to be constructed from a Java object.

Converting data from Java to XML and back is such a common use case that the Java EE specification provides an API to do it. This API is the Java API for XML Binding (JAXB).

JAXB makes converting data from Java to XML transparent and trivial. All we need to do is decorate the class we wish to convert to XML with the `@XmlRootElement` annotation. The following code example illustrates how to do this:

```
package com.ensode.jaxrstest.entity;

import java.io.Serializable;
import javax.xml.bind.annotation.XmlRootElement;

@XmlRootElement
public class Customer implements Serializable
{
  private Long id;
  private String firstName;
  private String middleName;
  private String lastName;

  public Customer()
  {
  }

  public Customer(Long id, String firstName, String middleInitial,
    String lastName)
  {
    this.id = id;
    this.firstName = firstName;
    this.middleName = middleInitial;
    this.lastName = lastName;
  }

  public String getFirstName()
  {
    return firstName;
```

```
    }

    public void setFirstName(String firstName)
    {
      this.firstName = firstName;
    }

    public Long getId()
    {
      return id;
    }

    public void setId(Long id)
    {
      this.id = id;
    }

    public String getLastName()
    {
      return lastName;
    }

    public void setLastName(String lastName)
    {
      this.lastName = lastName;
    }

    public String getMiddleName()
    {
      return middleName;
    }

    public void setMiddleName(String middleName)
    {
      this.middleName = middleName;
    }

    @Override
    public String toString()
    {
      return "id = " + getId() + "\nfirstName = " + getFirstName()
        + "\nmiddleName = " + getMiddleName() + "\nlastName = "
        + getLastName();
    }
  }
```

As we can see, other than the `@XmlRootElement` annotation at the class level, there is nothing unusual about this Java class.

Once we have a class that we have decorated with the `@XmlRootElement` annotation, we need to change the parameter type of our web service from `String` to our custom class:

```
package com.ensode.jaxbxmlconversion.service;

import com.ensode.jaxbxmlconversion.entity.Customer;
import javax.ws.rs.Consumes;
import javax.ws.rs.DELETE;
import javax.ws.rs.GET;
import javax.ws.rs.POST;
import javax.ws.rs.PUT;
import javax.ws.rs.Path;
import javax.ws.rs.Produces;

@Path("customer")
public class CustomerResource
{
  private Customer customer;

  public CustomerResource()
  {
    //"fake" the data, in a real application the data
    //would come from a database.
    customer = new Customer(1L, "David", "Raymond", "Heffelfinger");
  }

  @GET
  @Produces("text/xml")
  public Customer getCustomer()
  {
    //in a "real" RESTful service, we would retrieve data from a
    //database
    //then return an XML representation of the data.

    System.out.println("--- " + this.getClass().getCanonicalName()
      + ".getCustomer() invoked");

    return customer;
  }

  @POST
```

```
    @Consumes("text/xml")
    public void updateCustomer(Customer customer)
    {
      //in a "real" RESTful service, JAXB would parse the XML
      //received in the customer XML parameter, then update
      //a row in the database.

      System.out.println("--- " + this.getClass().getCanonicalName()
        + ".updateCustomer() invoked");
      System.out.println("---- got the following customer: "
        + customer);
    }

    @PUT
    @Consumes("text/xml")
    public void createCustomer(Customer customer)
    {
      //in a "real" RESTful service, we would insert
      //a new row into the database with the data in th     //customer
  parameter

      System.out.println("--- " + this.getClass().getCanonicalName()
        + ".createCustomer() invoked");
      System.out.println("customer = " + customer);
    }

    @DELETE
    @Consumes("text/xml")
    public void deleteCustomer(Customer customer)
    {
      //in a "real" RESTful service, we would delete a row
      //from the database corresponding to the customer parameter

      System.out.println("--- " + this.getClass().getCanonicalName()
        + ".deleteCustomer() invoked");
      System.out.println("customer = " + customer);
    }
  }
```

As we can see, the difference between this version of our RESTful web service and the previous one is that all parameter types and return values have been changed from `String` to `Customer`. JAXB takes care of converting our parameters and return types to and from XML as appropriate. When using JAXB, an object of our custom class is automatically populated with data from the XML sent from the client. Similarly, return values are transparently converted to XML.

Developing a RESTful web service client

Although `curl` allows us to quickly test our RESTful web services and it is a developer-friendly tool, it is not exactly user friendly. We shouldn't expect to have our user enter `curl` commands in their command line to use our web service. For this reason, we need to develop a client for our services. Jersey—the JAX-RS implementation included with GlassFish—includes a client-side API that we can use to easily develop client applications.

The following example illustrates how to use the Jersey client API:

```
package com.ensode.jaxrsintroclient;

import com.ensode.jaxbxmlconversion.entity.Customer;
import com.sun.jersey.api.client.Client;
import com.sun.jersey.api.client.UniformInterface;
import com.sun.jersey.api.client.WebResource;
import javax.ws.rs.core.MediaType;

public class App
{
  private WebResource baseUriWebResource;
  private WebResource webResource;
  private Client client;
  private static final String BASE_URI =
    "http://localhost:8080/jaxbxmlconversion/resources";

  public static void main(String[] args)
  {
    App app = new App();
    app.initWebResource();
    app.getCustomer();
    app.insertCustomer();
  }

  private void initWebResource()
  {
    com.sun.jersey.api.client.config.ClientConfig config =
      new com.sun.jersey.api.client.config.DefaultClientConfig();
    client = Client.create(config);
    baseUriWebResource = client.resource(BASE_URI);
    webResource = baseUriWebResource.path("customer");
  }

  public void getCustomer()
```

```
    {
      UniformInterface uniformInterface =
        webResource.type(MediaType.TEXT_XML);
      Customer customer = uniformInterface.get(Customer.class);
      System.out.println("customer = " + customer);
    }

    public void insertCustomer()
    {
      Customer customer = new Customer(234L, "Tamara", "A",
        "Graystone");
      UniformInterface uniformInterface =
        webResource.type(MediaType.TEXT_XML);
      uniformInterface.put(customer);
    }
  }
```

The first thing we need to do is create an instance of `com.sun.jersey.api.client.config.DefaultClientConfig`, then pass it to the static `create()` method of the `com.sun.jersey.api.client.Client` class. At this point, we have created an instance of `com.sun.jersey.api.client.Client`. We then need to create an instance of `com.sun.jersey.api.client.WebResource` by invoking the `resource()` method of our newly created `Client` instance, passing the base URI of our web service, as defined in its configuration, as explained earlier in this chapter.

Once we have a `WebResource` instance pointing to the base URI of our web service, we need to create a new instance pointing to the URI of the specific web service we need to target, as defined in its `@Path` annotation. We can do this simply by invoking the `path()` method on `WebResource` and passing a value matching the contents of the `@Path` annotation of our RESTful web service.

The `WebResource` class has a `type()` method that returns an instance of a class implementing `com.sun.jersey.api.client.UniformInterface`. The `type()` method takes a `String` as a parameter that can be used to indicate the MIME type that the web service will handle. The `javax.ws.rs.core.MediaType` class has several `String` constants defined, corresponding to most supported MIME types. In our example, we have been using XML, therefore, we used the corresponding `MediaType.TEXT_XML` constant as the value for this method.

The `UniformInterface` has methods we can invoke to generate the GET, POST, PUT, and DELETE HTTP requests. These methods are appropriately named as `get()`, `post()`, `put()`, and `delete()`.

In the `getCustomer()` method in our example, we invoke the `get()` method that generates a GET request to our web service. Notice that we pass the Java class of the type of data we expect to receive. JAXB automatically populates an instance of this class with the data returned from the web service.

In the `insertCustomer()` method in our example, we invoke the `put()` method on the `UniformInterface` implementation returned by `WebResource.type()`. We pass an instance of our `Customer` class, which JAXB automatically converts to XML before sending it to the server. The same technique can be used when invoking the `post()` and `delete()` methods of `UniformInterface`.

Query and path parameters

In our previous example, we have been working with a RESTful web service to manage a single customer object. In real life, this would obviously not be very helpful. A common case is to develop a RESTful web service to handle a collection of objects (in our example, customers). To determine what specific object in the collection we are working with, we can pass parameters to our RESTful web services. There are two types of parameters we can use: query and path parameters.

Query parameters

We can add parameters to methods that will handle HTTP requests in our web service. Parameters decorated with the `@QueryParam` annotation will be retrieved from the request URL.

The following example illustrates how to use query parameters in our JAX-RS RESTful web services:

```
package com.ensode.queryparams.service;

import com.ensode.queryparams.entity.Customer;
import javax.ws.rs.Consumes;
import javax.ws.rs.DELETE;
import javax.ws.rs.GET;
import javax.ws.rs.POST;
import javax.ws.rs.PUT;
import javax.ws.rs.Path;
import javax.ws.rs.Produces;
import javax.ws.rs.QueryParam;

@Path("customer")
public class CustomerResource
```

```
{
  private Customer customer;

  public CustomerResource()
  {
    customer = new Customer(1L, "Samuel", "Joseph", "Willow");
  }

  @GET
  @Produces("text/xml")
  public Customer getCustomer(@QueryParam("id") Long id)
  {
    //in a "real" RESTful service, we would retrieve data from a
    //database
    //using the supplied id.

    System.out.println("--- " + this.getClass().getCanonicalName()
      + ".getCustomer() invoked, id = " + id);
    return customer;
  }

  /**
   * Create a new customer
   * @param customer XML representation of the customer to create
   */
  @PUT
  @Consumes("text/xml")
  public void createCustomer(Customer customer)
  {
    //in a "real" RESTful service, we would parse the XML
    //received in the customer XML parameter, then insert
    //a new row into the database.

    System.out.println("--- " + this.getClass().getCanonicalName()
      + ".createCustomer() invoked");
    System.out.println("customer = " + customer);
  }

  @POST
  @Consumes("text/xml")
  public void updateCustomer(Customer customer)
  {
    //in a "real" RESTful service, we would parse the XML
    //received in the customer XML parameter, then update
    //a row in the database.
```

```
        System.out.println("--- " + this.getClass().getCanonicalName()
          + ".updateCustomer() invoked");
        System.out.println("customer = " + customer);
        System.out.println("customer= " + customer);
    }

    @DELETE
    @Consumes("text/xml")
    public void deleteCustomer(@QueryParam("id") Long id)
    {
        //in a "real" RESTful service, we would invoke
        //a DAO and delete the row in the database with the
        //primary key passed as the "id" parameter.

        System.out.println("--- " + this.getClass().getCanonicalName()
          + ".deleteCustomer() invoked, id = " + id);
        System.out.println("customer = " + customer);
    }
}
```

Notice that all we had to do was decorate the parameters with the `@QueryParam` annotation. This annotation allows JAX-RS to retrieve any query parameters matching the value of the annotation and assign its value to the parameter variable.

We can add a parameter to the web service's URL, just like we pass parameters to any URL:

```
curl -XGET -HContent-type:text/xml
http://localhost:8080/queryparams/resources/customer?id=1
```

Sending query parameters via the Jersey client API

The Jersey client API provides an easy and straightforward way of sending query parameters to RESTful web services. The following example illustrates how to do this:

```
package com.ensode.queryparamsclient;

import com.ensode.queryparamsclient.entity.Customer;
import com.sun.jersey.api.client.Client;
import com.sun.jersey.api.client.UniformInterface;
import com.sun.jersey.api.client.WebResource;
import javax.ws.rs.core.MediaType;

public class App
{
  private WebResource baseUriWebResource;
```

```
    private WebResource webResource;
    private Client client;
    private static final String BASE_URI =
      "http://localhost:8080/queryparams/resources";

    public static void main(String[] args)
    {
      App app = new App();
      app.initWebResource();
      app.getCustomer();
    }

    private void initWebResource()
    {
      com.sun.jersey.api.client.config.ClientConfig config =
        new com.sun.jersey.api.client.config.DefaultClientConfig();
      client = Client.create(config);
      baseUriWebResource = client.resource(BASE_URI);
      webResource = baseUriWebResource.path("customer");
    }

    public void getCustomer()
    {
      UniformInterface uniformInterface =
        webResource.type(MediaType.TEXT_XML);

      Customer customer =
     (Customer) webResource.queryParam("id", "1").get( Customer.class);
      System.out.println("customer = " + customer);
    }
  }
```

As we can see, all we need to do to pass a parameter is to invoke the `queryParam()` method on `com.sun.jersey.api.client.WebResource`. The first argument to this method is the parameter name and it must match the value of the `@QueryParam` annotation on the web service. The second parameter is the value we need to pass to the web service.

If we need to pass multiple parameters to one of our web service's methods, then we need to use an instance of a class implementing the `javax.ws.rs.core.MultiValuedMap` interface. Jersey provides a default implementation in the form of `com.sun.jersey.core.util.MultiValuedMapImpl` that should suffice for most cases.

The following code fragment illustrates how to pass multiple parameters to a web service method:

```
MultivaluedMap multivaluedMap = new MultivaluedMapImpl();
multivaluedMap.add("paramName1", "value1");
multivaluedMap.add("paramName2", "value2");
String s = webResource.queryParams(multivaluedMap).get(String.class);
```

We need to add all the parameters we need to send to our web service by invoking the `add()` method on our `MultivaluedMap` implementation. This method takes the parameter name as its first argument and the parameter value as its second argument. We need to invoke this method for each parameter we need to send.

As we can see, `com.sun.jersey.api.client.WebResource` has a `queryParams()` method that takes an instance of a class implementing the `MultivaluedMap` interface as a parameter. In order to send multiple parameters to our web service, we simply need to pass an instance of `MultivaluedMap` containing all required parameters to this method.

Path parameters

Another way by which we can pass parameters to our RESTful web services is via path parameters. The following example illustrates how to develop a JAX-RS RESTful web service that accepts path parameters:

```
package com.ensode.pathparams.service;

import com.ensode.pathparams.entity.Customer;
import javax.ws.rs.Consumes;
import javax.ws.rs.DELETE;
import javax.ws.rs.GET;
import javax.ws.rs.POST;
import javax.ws.rs.PUT;
import javax.ws.rs.Path;
import javax.ws.rs.PathParam;
import javax.ws.rs.Produces;

@Path("/customer/")
public class CustomerResource
{
  private Customer customer;

  public CustomerResource()
  {
    customer = new Customer(1L, "William", "Daniel", "Graystone");
```

```
}

@GET
@Produces("text/xml")
@Path("{id}/")
public Customer getCustomer(@PathParam("id") Long id)
{
  //in a "real" RESTful service, we would retrieve data from a
  //database
  //using the supplied id.

  System.out.println("--- " + this.getClass().getCanonicalName()
    + ".getCustomer() invoked, id = " + id);
  return customer;
}

@PUT
@Consumes("text/xml")
public void createCustomer(Customer customer)
{
  //in a "real" RESTful service, we would parse the XML
  //received in the customer XML parameter, then insert
  //a new row into the database.

  System.out.println("--- " + this.getClass().getCanonicalName()
    + ".createCustomer() invoked");
  System.out.println("customer = " + customer);
}

@POST
@Consumes("text/xml")
public void updateCustomer(Customer customer)
{
  //in a "real" RESTful service, we would parse the XML
  //received in the customer XML parameter, then update
  //a row in the database.

  System.out.println("--- " + this.getClass().getCanonicalName()
    + ".updateCustomer() invoked");
  System.out.println("customer = " + customer);
  System.out.println("customer= " + customer);
}

@DELETE
```

```
    @Consumes("text/xml")
    @Path("{id}/")
    public void deleteCustomer(@PathParam("id") Long id)
    {
      //in a "real" RESTful service, we would invoke
      //a DAO and delete the row in the database with the
      //primary key passed as the "id" parameter.

      System.out.println("--- " + this.getClass().getCanonicalName()
        + ".deleteCustomer() invoked, id = " + id);
      System.out.println("customer = " + customer);
    }
  }
```

Any method that accepts a path parameter must be decorated with the `@Path` annotation. The value attribute of this annotation must be formatted as `"{paramName}/"`, where `paramName` is the parameter the method expects to receive. Additionally, method parameters must be decorated with the `@PathParam` annotation. The value of this annotation must match the parameter name declared in the `@Path` annotation for the method.

We can pass path parameters from the command line by adjusting our web service's URI as appropriate. For example, to pass an "id" parameter of 1 to the previous `getCustomer()` method (which handles HTTP GET requests), we could do it from the command line as follows:

```
curl -XGET -HContent-type:text/xml
http://localhost:8080/pathparams/resources/customer/1
```

This returns the expected output of an XML representation of the `Customer` object returned by the `getCustomer()` method:

```
<?xml version="1.0" encoding="UTF-8"
standalone="yes"?><customer><firstName>William</firstName><id>1</id>
<lastName>Graystone</lastName><middleName>Daniel</middleName></customer>
```

Sending path parameters via the Jersey client API

Sending path parameters to a web service via the Jersey client API is easy and straightforward; all we need to do is append any path parameters to the path we use to create our `WebResource` instance. The following example illustrates how to do this:

```
package com.ensode.queryparamsclient;

import com.ensode.queryparamsclient.entity.Customer;
import com.sun.jersey.api.client.Client;
```

```
import com.sun.jersey.api.client.WebResource;

public class App
{
  private WebResource baseUriWebResource;
  private WebResource webResource;
  private Client client;
  private static final String BASE_URI =
    "http://localhost:8080/queryparams/resources";

  public static void main(String[] args)
  {
    App app = new App();
    app.initWebResource();
    app.getCustomer();
  }

  private void initWebResource()
  {
    com.sun.jersey.api.client.config.ClientConfig config =
      new com.sun.jersey.api.client.config.DefaultClientConfig();
    client = Client.create(config);
    baseUriWebResource = client.resource(BASE_URI);
    webResource = baseUriWebResource.path("customer/1");
  }

  public void getCustomer()
  {
    Customer customer =
      (Customer) webResource.get(Customer.class);
    System.out.println("customer = " + customer);
  }
}
```

In this example, we simply appended a value of `1` as the path parameter to the `String` used to build the `WebResource` implementation used to invoke our web service. This parameter is automatically picked up by the JAX-RS API and assigned to the method argument annotated with the corresponding `@PathParam` annotation.

If we need to pass more than one parameter to one of our web services, we simply need to use the following format for the `@Path` parameter at the method level:

```
@Path("/{paramName1}/{paramName2}/")
```

Then, annotate the corresponding method arguments with the `@PathParam` annotation:

```
public String someMethod(@PathParam("paramName1") String param1,
  @PathParam("paramName2") String param2)
```

The web service can then be invoked by modifying the web service's URI to pass the parameters in the order specified in the `@Path` annotation. For example, the following URI would pass the values `1` and `2` for `paramName1` and `paramName2`:

```
http://localhost:8080/contextroot/resources/customer/1/2
```

This URI will work both from the command line or through a web service client we develop with the Jersey client API.

Summary

In this chapter, we discussed how to easily develop RESTful web services using JAX-RS—a new addition to the Java EE specification.

We covered how to develop a RESTful web service by adding a few simple annotations to our code. We also explained how to automatically convert data between Java and XML by taking advantage of the Java API for XML Binding (JAXB).

Finally, we covered how to pass parameters to our RESTful web services via the `@PathParam` and `@QueryParam` annotations.

A
Sending E-mails from Java EE Applications

Applications deployed to GlassFish or any other Java EE-compliant application server frequently need the ability to send e-mails. Thanks to the JavaMail API—part of the Java EE specification—sending e-mails from Java EE applications is fairly simple.

In order to implement the ability to send e-mails from a Java EE application, we need to have access to a mail server, typically one using the **Simple Mail Transfer Protocol (SMTP)**

Configuring GlassFish

Before we can start sending e-mails from our Java EE applications, we need to do some initial GlassFish configuration. A new JavaMail session needs to be added by logging into the GlassFish web console, expanding the **Resources** node in the tree at the left-hand side of the page, then clicking on the **JavaMail Sessions** node.

This can be seen in the following screenshot:

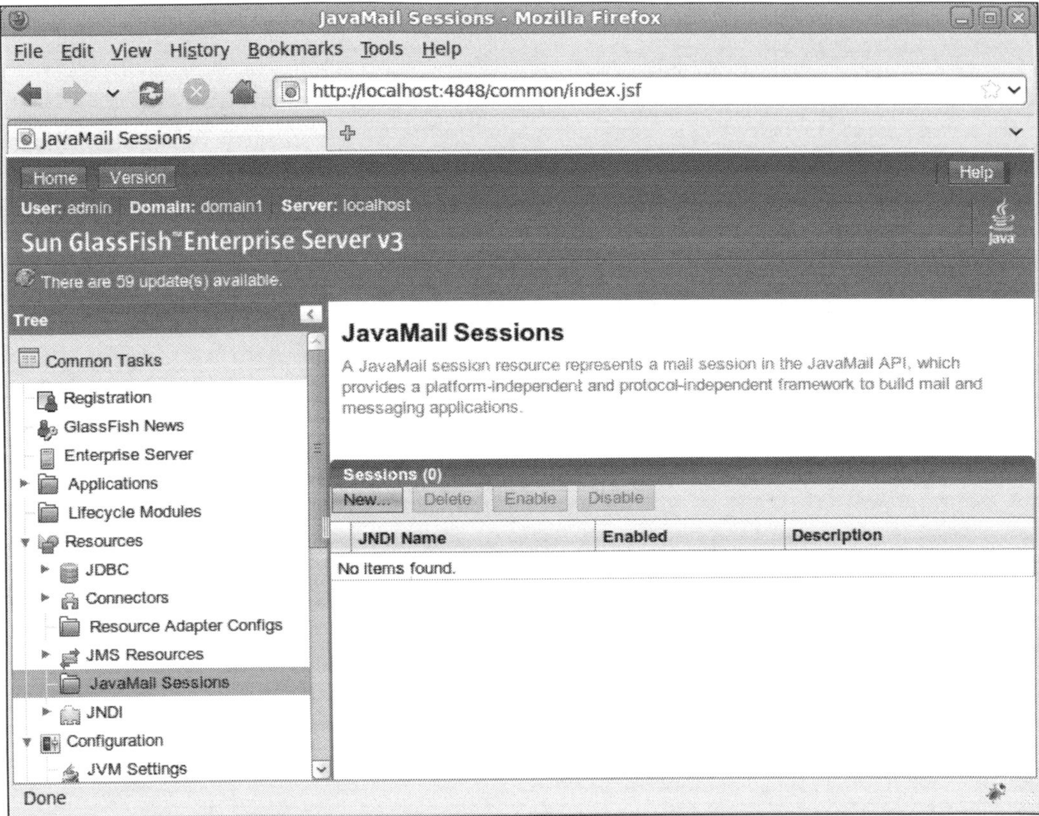

To create a new JavaMail session, we need to click on the **New...** button. The main area of the screen will look as shown in the following screenshot:

New JavaMail Session OK Cancel

A JavaMail session resource represents a mail session in the JavaMail API.

JNDI Name: * mail/myjavamail

Mail Host: * mail.example.com
DNS name of the default mail server

Default User: * mailadmin
User name to provide when connecting to a mail server; must contain only alphanumeric, underscore, dash, or dot characters

Default Return Address: * mailadmin@example.com
E-mail address of the default user

Description:
Makes it easier to find this session later

Status: ☑ **Enabled**

Advanced

Store Protocol: imap
Either IMAP or POP3; default is IMAP

Store Protocol Class: com.sun.mail.imap.IMAPStore
Default is com.sun.mail.imap.IMAPStore

Transport Protocol: smtp
Default is SMTP

Transport Protocol Class: com.sun.mail.smtp.SMTPTransport
Default is com.sun.mail.smtp.SMTPTransport

Debug: ☐ **Enabled**

Additional Properties (0)

Add Property Delete Properties

In the **JNDI Name** field, we need to provide a JNDI name for our JavaMail session. This name must be a valid, unique name of our choosing. Applications will use this name to access the mail session.

In the **Mail Host** field, we need to specify the DNS name of the mail server we will be using to send e-mails.

In the **Default User** field, we need to specify the default username to use to connect to the mail server.

In the **Default Return Address** field, we need to specify the default e-mail address that e-mail recipients can use to reply to messages sent by our applications.

Specifying a fake return address

The default return address does not have to be a real e-mail address; we can specify an invalid e-mail address here. Keep in mind that if we do this, then users will be unable to reply to e-mails sent from our applications. Therefore, it would be a good idea to include a warning in the message body letting the users know that they cannot reply to the message.

We can optionally add a description for the JavaMail session in the **Description** field.

The **Status** checkbox allows us to enable or disable the JavaMail session. Disabled sessions are not accessible by applications.

The **Store Protocol** field is used to specify the value of the storage protocol of the mail server, which is used to allow our applications to retrieve e-mail messages from it. Valid values for this field include **imap**, **imaps**, **pop3**, and **pop3s**. Consult your system administrator for the correct value for your server.

Store protocol ignored if applications only send e-mails

It is a lot more common to have our applications send e-mails than it is to have them receive e-mails. If all applications using our mail session will only be sending e-mails, then the value of the **Store Protocol** field (and the **Store Protocol Class** field, discussed next) will be ignored.

The **Store Protocol Class** field is used to indicate the service provider implementation class corresponding to the specified store protocol. Valid values for this field include:

- **com.sun.mail.imap.IMAPStore** for a store protocol of **imap**
- **com.sun.mail.imap.IMAPSSLStore** for a store protocol of **imaps**
- **com.sun.mail.pop3.POP3Store** for a store protocol of **pop3**
- **com.sun.mail.pop3.POP3SSLStore** for a store protocol of **pop3s**

The **Transport Protocol** field is used to specify the value of the transport protocol of the mail server, which is used to allow our applications to send e-mail messages through it. Valid values for this field include **smtp** and **smtps**. Consult your system administrator for the correct value for your server.

The **Transport Protocol Class** field is used to specify the service provider implementation class corresponding to the specified transport protocol. Valid values for this field include:

- **com.sun.mail.smtp.SMTPTransport** for a transport protocol of **smtp**
- **com.sun.mail.smtp.SMTPSSLTransport** for a transport protocol of **smtps**

The **Debug** checkbox allows us to enable or disable debugging for the JavaMail session.

If we need to add additional properties to the JavaMail session, we can do so by clicking on the **Add Property** button near the bottom of the page, then entering the property name and value in the corresponding fields.

Once we have entered all the required information for our server, we need to click on the **OK** button at the top right of the page to create the JavaMail session. Once it is created, it is ready to be used by deployed applications.

Implementing e-mail delivery functionality

Once we have set up a JavaMail session, as described in the previous section, implementing the e-mail delivery functionality is fairly simple. The process is illustrated in the following code example:

```
package net.ensode.glassfishbook;

import javax.annotation.Resource;
import javax.faces.bean.ManagedBean;
import javax.mail.Message;
import javax.mail.MessagingException;
import javax.mail.Session;
import javax.mail.Transport;
import javax.mail.internet.AddressException;
import javax.mail.internet.InternetAddress;
import javax.mail.internet.MimeMessage;

@ManagedBean
public class FeedbackBean
{
  private String subject;
  private String body;

  @Resource(name = "mymailserver")
  Session session;
```

```
    public String sendEmail()
    {
      try
      {
        Message msg = new MimeMessage(session);
        msg.setRecipient(Message.RecipientType.TO, new
          InternetAddress("customer@customerdomain.com"));
        msg.setSubject(subject);
        msg.setText(body);
        Transport.send(msg);
      }
      catch (AddressException e)
      {
        e.printStackTrace();
        return "failure";
      }
      catch (MessagingException e)
      {
        e.printStackTrace();
        return "failure";
      }
      return "success";
    }

    public String getBody()
    {
      return body;
    }

    public void setBody(String body)
    {
      this.body = body;
    }

    public String getSubject()
    {
      return subject;
    }

    public void setSubject(String subject)
    {
      this.subject = subject;
    }
  }
```

This class is used as a managed bean for a simple JSF application. For brevity, other parts of the application are not shown as they do not deal with e-mail functionality. The full application can be downloaded from this book's website.

The first thing we need to do is inject an instance of the JavaMail session created, as described in the previous section, by adding a class-level variable of type `javax.mail.Session` and decorating it with the `@Resource` annotation. The value of the `name` attribute of this annotation must match the JNDI name we gave our JavaMail session when it was created.

We then need to create an instance of `javax.mail.internet.MimeMessage`, passing the session object as a parameter to its constructor.

Once we create an instance of `javax.mail.internet.MimeMessage`, we need to add a message recipient by invoking its `setRecipient()` method. The first parameter of this method indicates if the recipient is to be sent the message (TO), carbon copied (CC), or blind carbon copied (BCC). We can indicate the type of recipient by using `Message.RecipientType.TO`, `Message.RecipientType.CC`, or `Message.RecipientType.BCC` as appropriate. The second parameter of the `setRecipient()` method indicates the e-mail address of the recipient; this parameter is of type `javax.mail.Address`. This class is an abstract class, therefore we need to use one of its subclasses, specifically `javax.mail.internet.InternetAddress`. The constructor for this class takes a `String` parameter containing the e-mail address of the recipient. The `setRecipient()` method can be invoked multiple times to add recipients to be sent, copied, or carbon copied. Only a single address can be specified for each recipient type.

If we need to send a message to multiple recipients, we can use the `addRecipients()` method of the `javax.mail.Message` class (or one of its subclasses, such as `javax.mail.internet.MimeMessage`). This method takes the recipient type as its first parameter and an array of `javax.mail.Address` as its second parameter. The message will be sent to all recipients in the array. By using this method instead of `setRecipient()`, we are not limited to a single recipient per recipient type.

Once we have specified the recipient or recipients, we need to add the message subject and text by invoking the `setSubject()` and `setText()` methods on the message instance respectively.

At this point, we are ready to send our message. This can be accomplished by invoking the static `send()` method on the `javax.mail.Transport` class. This method takes the message instance as a parameter.

B
IDE Integration

GlassFish provides integration with two of the most popular Java IDE's: NetBeans and Eclipse. NetBeans, being an Oracle (formerly Sun Microsystems) product, just like GlassFish, provides GlassFish integration "out of the box". Oracle provides a GlassFish Eclipse plugin for integration with Eclipse, as well as an Eclipse bundle including the Eclipse Java IDE plus the GlassFish integration plugin.

NetBeans

NetBeans Java and "All" editions contain out of the box support for GlassFish. When installing one of these editions of NetBeans, GlassFish is also installed. NetBeans can be downloaded from `http://www.netbeans.org`.

NetBeans has several project categories; Java EE applications can be created from the Java Web and Java EE categories.

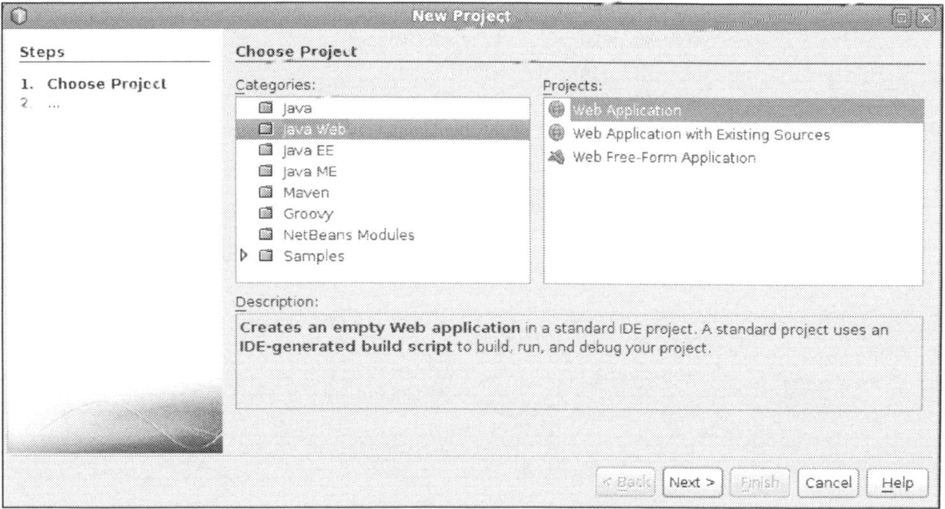

For most project types in the Java EE or Java Web categories, NetBeans requires us to select an application server where the project will be deployed. GlassFish is labeled **GlassFish v3** in the drop-down box used to select a server:

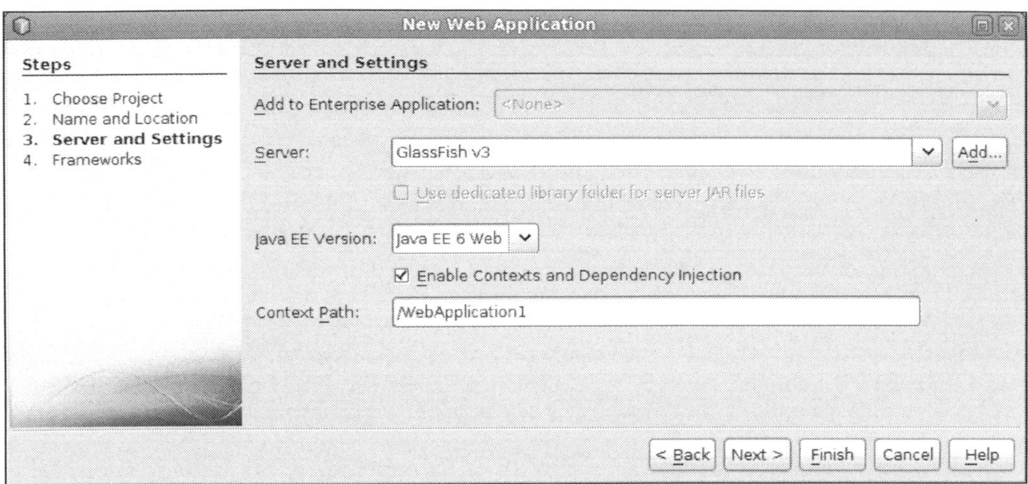

Once we create the project and we are ready to deploy it, we simply need to right-click on the project and select **Deploy** from the resulting pop-up menu:

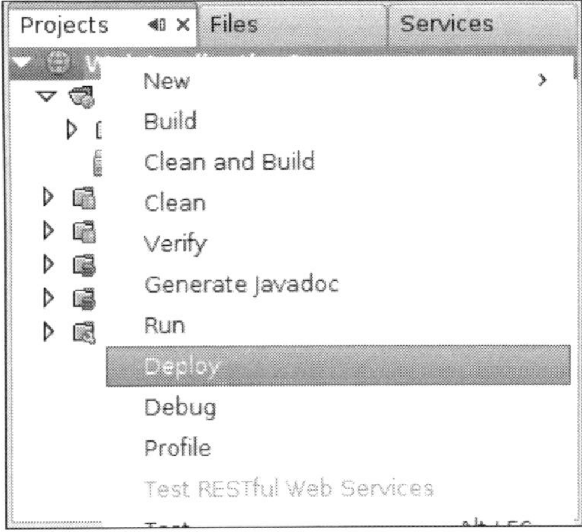

The project will be automatically built, packaged, and deployed. For web applications, we also get the **Run** and **Debug** options. Both of these options, in addition to building, packaging, and deploying the project, automatically open a new browser window and point it to the application's URL. On selecting **Debug**, GlassFish will be started in the debug mode, if necessary, and we can use NetBeans debugger to debug our project.

Additionally, NetBeans features automatic incremental deployment. This means that every time a file is saved (managed bean, EJB, Facelets page, and so on), it is automatically deployed to the server. Our deployed application is updated in real time, as we develop. Testing our changes for the most part is as simple as reloading the current page in the browser, as the user's session is not lost across redeployments. This is a great time-saving feature, a far cry from the build, package, deploy, test cycle we need to go through with most other Java EE application servers.

Eclipse

Unlike NetBeans, Eclipse does not come with GlassFish support out of the box. Fortunately, it is very easy to add GlassFish support. Eclipse can be downloaded from `http://www.eclipse.org`.

In this section, we assume that the Eclipse IDE for Java EE developers is installed. This version of Eclipse includes tools for Java EE (JSF, JPA, EJB, and so on) development.

In order to integrate Eclipse and GlassFish, we need to download the GlassFish server adapter for Eclipse. To do this, we need to right-click on the **Servers** tab at the bottom of the Java EE perspective and select **New** | **Server**:

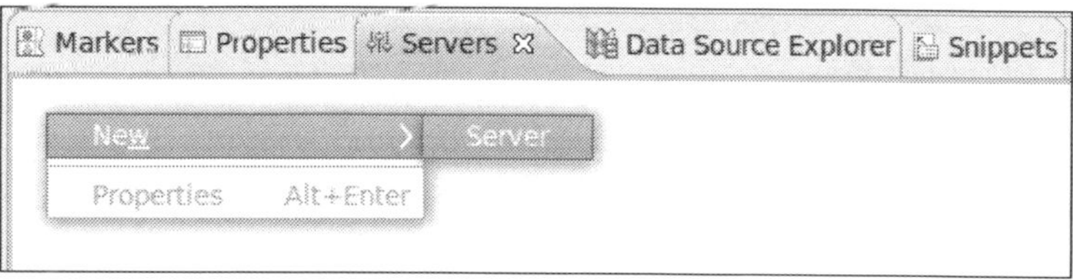

We then need to click on the **Download additional server adapters** link in the window that pops up:

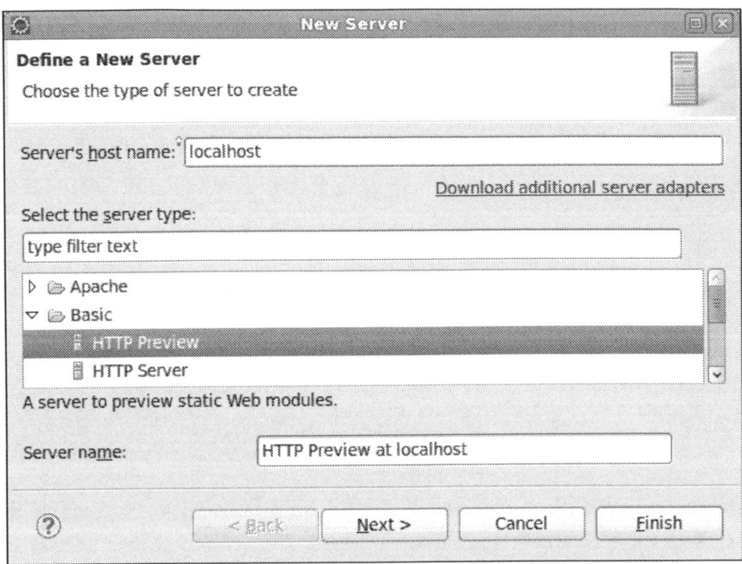

After doing so, a list of all available server adapters will be shown:

We simply need to select GlassFish and click on the **Next >** button.

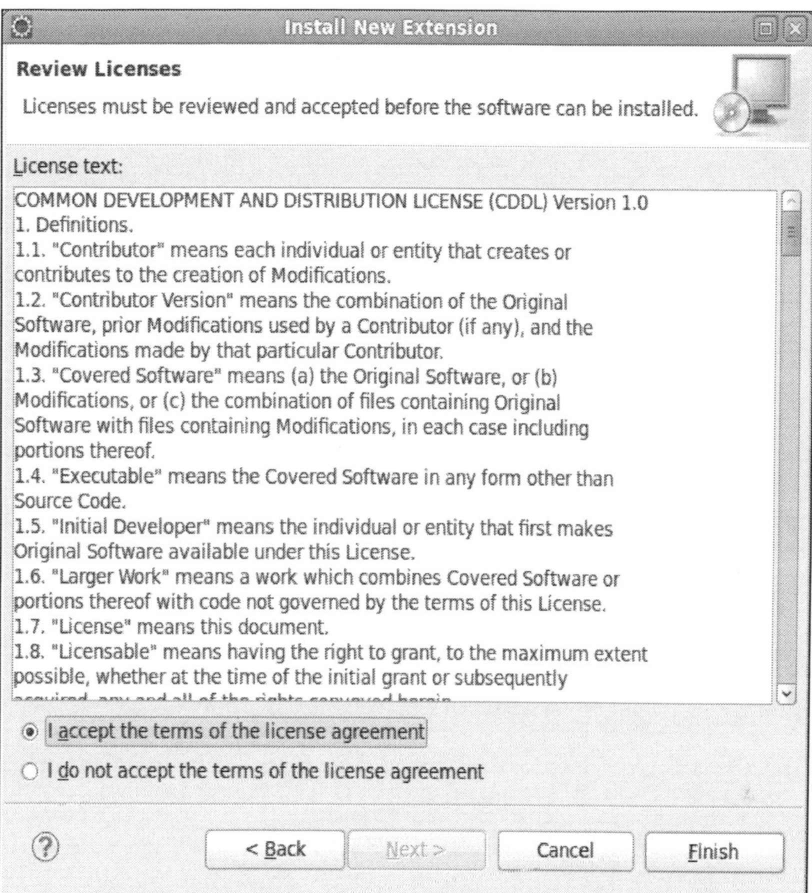

At this point, we need to accept the license agreement and click **Finish**.

After the GlassFish server adapter for Eclipse is downloaded, we are told that it is strongly recommended to restart Eclipse. It is a good idea to do so.

After Eclipse restarts, the GlassFish server adapter is fully installed, and we are ready to deploy our applications to GlassFish straight from Eclipse.

To demonstrate the integration between GlassFish and Eclipse, we will use a project of type Dynamic Web Project, but the procedure is very similar for other Java EE project types.

To create a new Dynamic Web Project, all we need to do is click on **File | New | Dynamic Web Project**.

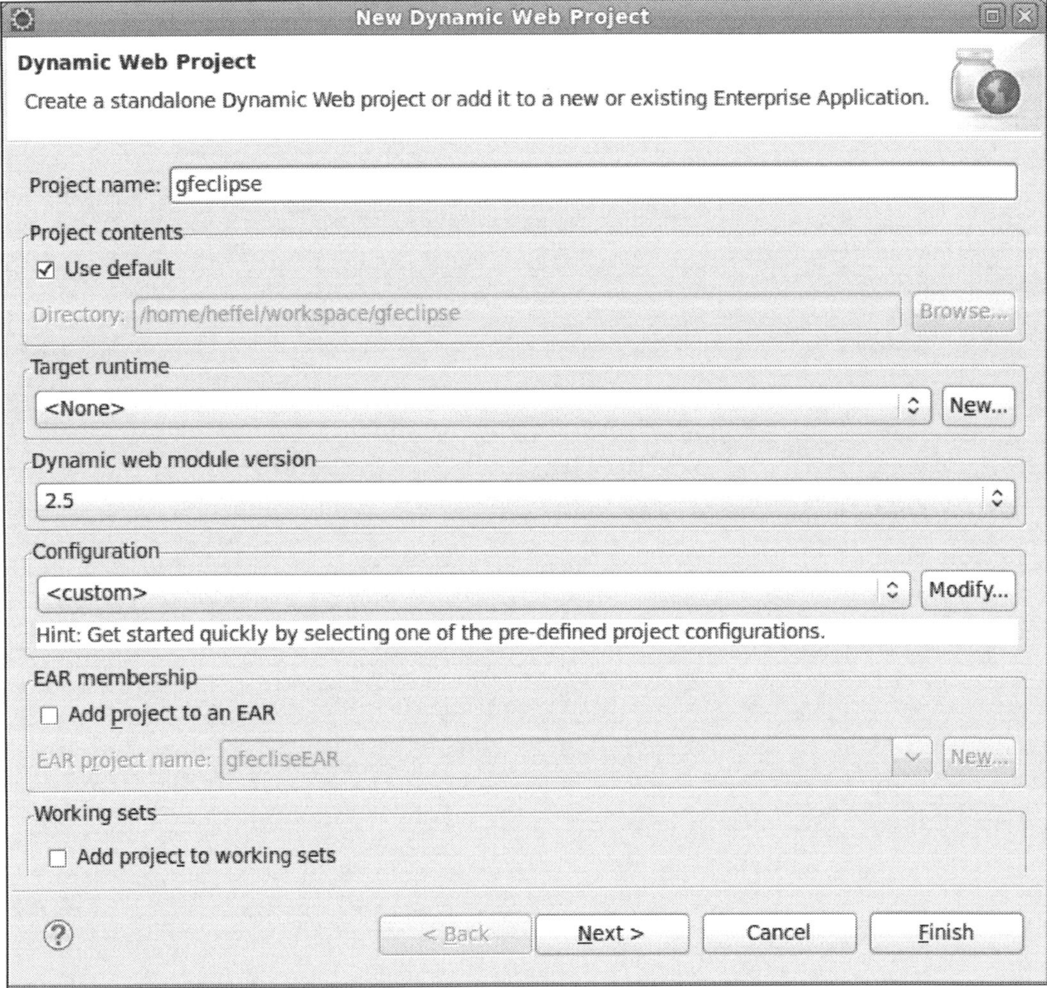

When creating a Dynamic Web Project, Eclipse will ask, among other things, for the **Target runtime** for the project. The target runtime is "Eclipse Speak" for a Java EE application server.

To select GlassFish as our target runtime, we need to click on the **New...** button, then select **GlassFish v3 Java EE 6** from the **GlassFish** folder.

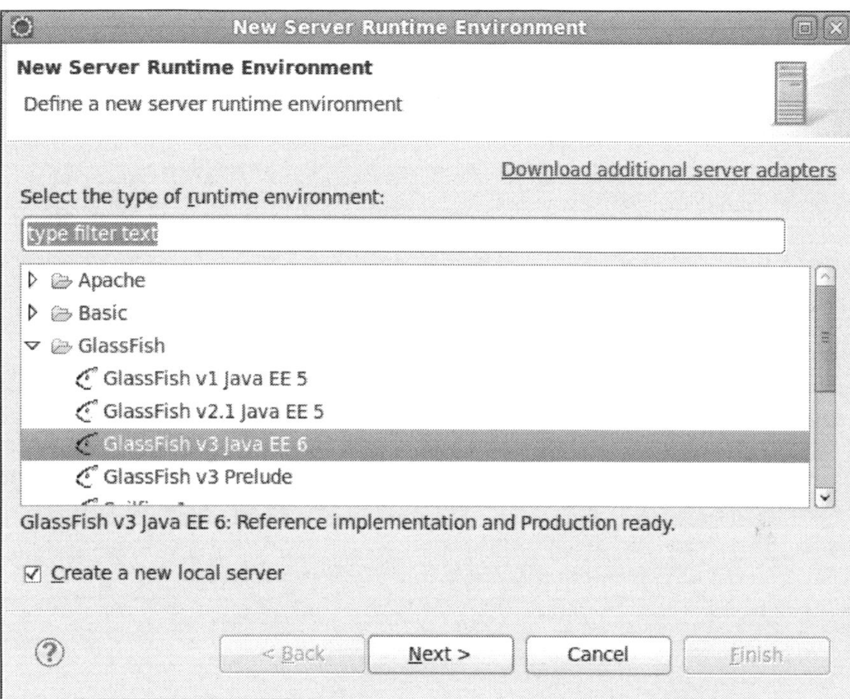

After clicking **Next >**, we need to indicate the directory where GlassFish is installed:

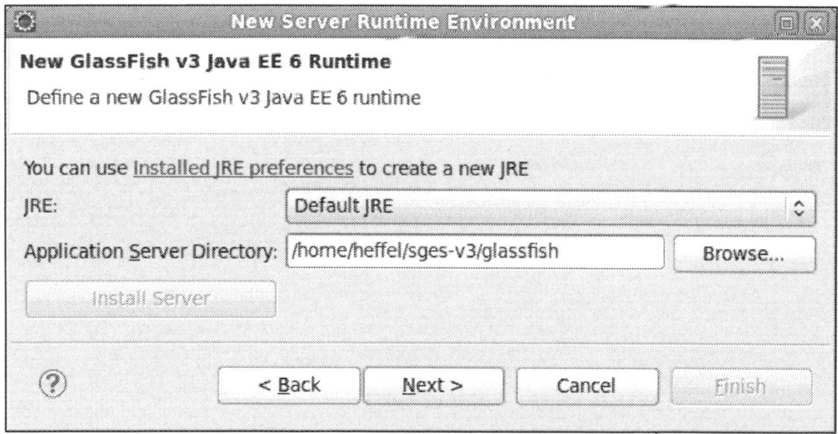

We then need to indicate the domain directory, name, administrator Id, and password for our domain. Most of these fields have sensible defaults. In most cases, the only field we need to enter is the password.

After we finish creating our project, we should see GlassFish in the **Servers** view, which is typically at the bottom of the screen:

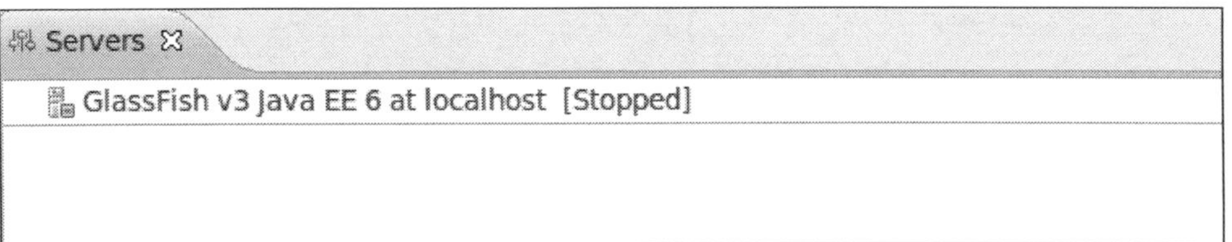

If the **Servers** view is nowhere to be seen, it can be opened by clicking on **Window | Show View | Servers**.

At this point, we are ready to start developing our application. When we are at a point where we need to deploy it, we can do so by clicking on the GlassFish server icon in the **Servers** view and selecting **Publish**:

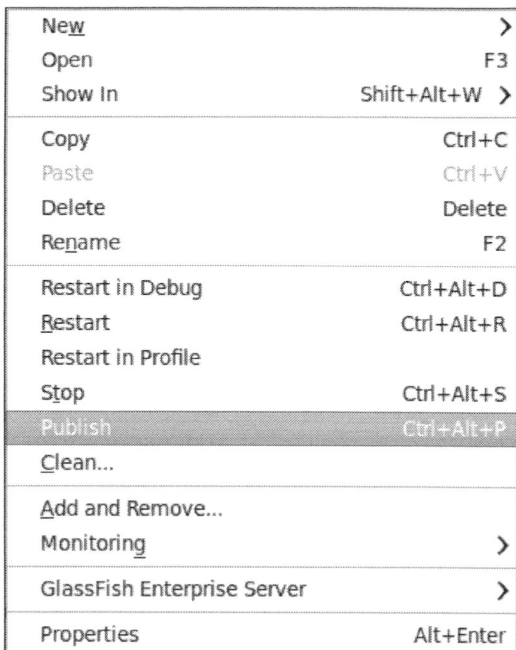

At this point, Eclipse will build, package, and deploy the application.

For web applications, we can execute the application as soon as it is deployed by right-clicking on the project and selecting **Run As | Run on Server**:

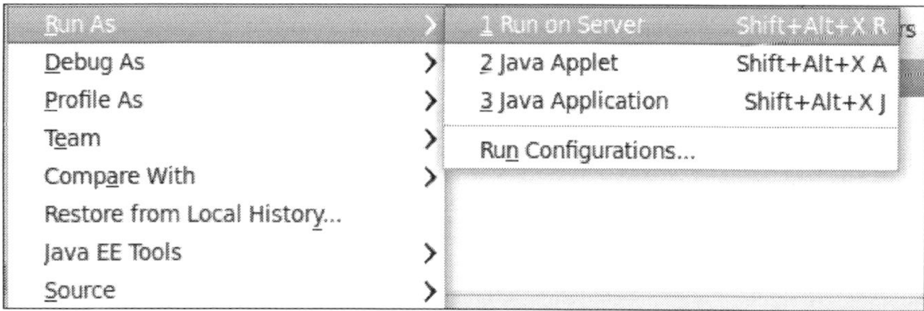

At this point, Eclipse will build, package, deploy the application, and open it in a browser window embedded in Eclipse.

If we wish to debug the application using Eclipse's debugger, we can do so by right-clicking on the project and selecting **Debug As | Debug on Server**. This will cause Eclipse to start or restart GlassFish in debug mode, if necessary, and deploy the application. We can then debug it using Eclipse's built-in debugger.

Index

Symbols

A

B

C

G

H

I

J

K

L

M

N

O

P

Q

R

S

T

U

V

W

X